GOVERNMENT CLOUD PROCUREMENT

In *Government Cloud Procurement*, Kevin McGillivray explores the question of whether governments can adopt cloud computing services and still meet their legal requirements and other obligations to citizens. The book focuses on the interplay between the technical properties of cloud computing services and the complex legal requirements applicable to cloud adoption and use. The legal issues evaluated include data privacy law (GDPR and the US regime), jurisdictional issues, contracts, and transnational private law approaches to addressing legal requirements. McGillivray also addresses the unique position of governments when they outsource core aspects of their information and communications technology to cloud service providers. His analysis is supported by extensive research examining actual cloud contracts obtained through Freedom of Information Act requests. With the demand for cloud computing on the rise, this study fills a gap in legal literature and offers guidance to organizations considering cloud computing.

KEVIN MCGILLIVRAY, PhD has published widely in the areas of law and technology. Kevin also has worked as a researcher on several EU projects including serving as the Data Protection Officer (DPO) on the prestigious Human Brain Project (HBP). Kevin currently serves as DPO for the Norwegian Tax Administration.

Government Cloud Procurement

CONTRACTS, DATA PROTECTION, AND THE QUEST FOR COMPLIANCE

KEVIN MCGILLIVRAY

Shaftesbury Road, Cambridge CB2 8EA, United Kingdom

One Liberty Plaza, 20th Floor, New York, NY 10006, USA

477 Williamstown Road, Port Melbourne, VIC 3207, Australia

314–321, 3rd Floor, Plot 3, Splendor Forum, Jasola District Centre, New Delhi – 110025, India

103 Penang Road, #05–06/07, Visioncrest Commercial, Singapore 238467

Cambridge University Press is part of Cambridge University Press & Assessment, a department of the University of Cambridge.

We share the University's mission to contribute to society through the pursuit of education, learning and research at the highest international levels of excellence.

www.cambridge.org
Information on this title: www.cambridge.org/9781108931519
DOI: 10.1017/9781108942485

© Kevin McGillivray 2022

This publication is in copyright. Subject to statutory exception and to the provisions of relevant collective licensing agreements, no reproduction of any part may take place without the written permission of Cambridge University Press & Assessment.

First published 2022
First paperback edition 2024

A catalogue record for this publication is available from the British Library

ISBN 978-1-108-83767-5 Hardback
ISBN 978-1-108-93151-9 Paperback

Cambridge University Press & Assessment has no responsibility for the persistence or accuracy of URLs for external or third-party internet websites referred to in this publication and does not guarantee that any content on such websites is, or will remain, accurate or appropriate.

To Gro Caroline, Elise, and Leah Saga

Contents

List of Figures		page ix
List of Tables		x
Preface		xi
Acknowledgements		xiii
List of Abbreviations		xv

	PART I SUBJECT MATTER	1
1	Introduction	3
2	Cloud Technology, Organizational Aspects, and Risks	18
	PART II LEGAL REQUIREMENTS AND ADOPTION OF GOVERNMENT CLOUD	29
3	Government Cloud Adoption: Challenges and Obligations	31
4	Location Independence, Jurisdiction, and Law Enforcement Access to Cloud Computing Services	59
5	Data Privacy and Data Protection Issues in Cloud Computing	91
	PART III PRIVATE ORDERING AND CLOUD COMPUTING CONTRACTS	157
6	Contracts Used to Procure Cloud Services I: Study on Contract Structure and Negotiated Terms	159

7	Contracts Used to Procure Cloud Services II: Standard Terms, Impact on Governments, and Lessons Learned	196
8	Conclusion	248
References		253
Index		286

Figures

6.1 US agency FOIA disclosure comparison (USPS and DOE) *page* 162
6.2 FAA SLA 184

Tables

6.1 US government FOIA contracts *page* 161
6.2 UK G-Cloud FOIA contracts 163

Preface

Much of the research in this book is a result of the PhD dissertation I submitted and defended in 2019. When I started work on my dissertation in 2013, one of my first activities was to attend a large-scale cloud computing conference in Brussels. The hotel where it was held was appropriately upmarket and the conference room was packed. The presentations consisted of five-person panels, with each person given ten minutes to present, followed by a brief discussion. Although there was some disagreement over the overall novelty of cloud computing and its global significance, everyone seemed to agree that it was going to be big. The panellists and crowd were excited and more or less everyone seemed to be on the same page.

A recurring assertion made by many of the panellists' presentations was that cloud computing was also going to save the environment. By combining data centres and centralizing computing, cloud computing would shrink the ever-growing carbon footprint being generated by computing and generally reduce the waste produced by redundant data centres. In one panel, the presenters agreed that 'cloud computing' could just as easily have been named 'green computing'. However, at the end of the panel, someone asked whether anyone on the panel actually had any hard numbers or real evidence to show that cloud computing was in fact green.

The former jubilance of the mood in the room was quickly paused. The question posed by that particular conference delegate shifted the discussion from what I had interpreted as primarily promotional to one that was much more analytical. As it later became clear, the question was a good one and the answer is nuanced. Further research on the topic has shown that cloud computing services use vast amounts of energy and in most cases leave large carbon footprints.[1] Since server farms use a great deal of energy, the 'greenness' of the computing depends largely on the source of that energy. If the server farm is located in the United States, as many are, much of that energy likely comes from coal.[2]

---

[1] See generally Jasmine N. Story, 'Cloud Computing and the NSA: The Carbon Footprint of the Secret Servers' (2014) 9 *Pittsburgh Journal of Environmental and Public Health Law* 33–65.

[2] Bryan Walsh, 'Your Data Is Dirty: The Carbon Price of Cloud Computing' (2 April 2014) Time Online. Available at <http://time.com/46777/your-data-is-dirty-the-carbon-price-of-cloud-computing/>. Providing

I was inspired to use my research as a vehicle to help bring forth a more nuanced discussion of cloud computing. In other words, I attempted to avoid 'hype cycles' and circumvent 'conventional wisdom' to take a closer – and longer – look at governments adopting cloud computing services. By obtaining actual contracts using the Freedom of Information Act (FOIA), I was able to move my research past general statements about what could or ought to be included in cloud computing contracts generally to offer a much more detailed discussion. While working with computer scientists and medical professionals on the European Union (EU) projects including Confidential and Compliant Clouds (Coco Cloud) and the Human Brain Project (HBP), I gained a much better understanding of the technical challenges involved in applying legal rules in practice. In some cases, this explained why there might be a compliance gap. In others, it helped me to pinpoint more systemic problems. In short, these steps and experiences put me in a much better position to examine what was actually happening when governments contract for cloud, what controls ought to be in place, and what the stakes are for citizens.

As I am writing this preface, the world is experiencing a global pandemic. Most EU member states are under various levels of lockdown to slow the spread of the COVID-19 virus. Almost my entire public sector organization of over 9,000 employees is now working remotely. This is unprecedented. Many public and private sector employers are now depending on cloud computing services to keep their operations up and running. Not all employers were prepared to deal with remote workers en masse. Responding adequately requires that an organization procure compliant services. To accomplish this, an organization must have an understanding of its legal obligations in order to create coherent polices.

Public administrations that did not have adequate remote infrastructure or a coherent cloud computing strategy are almost certainly taking a hard look at themselves. From video conferencing services to collaboration tools, demand for cloud computing has risen dramatically. My hope is that this book is academically interesting while also useful in addressing the many legal issues that cloud computing raises.

> that 'electricity is produced by fossil fuel sources like coal or natural gas – which together provide nearly three-quarters of U.S. power – our magical cloud may leave a very dirty footprint'.

Acknowledgements

First, thank you to my wife, Gro Caroline Sjølie, for always being supportive of my research, and also for spending many Saturdays and Sundays alone with two young and very active children so I could write. To my daughters Elise and Leah Saga, thank you for making me laugh and always helping me to keep things in perspective. Thank you to my parents, Terry and LaRae McGillivray, for their support. To my parents-in-law Tore and Ragnhild Sjølie, thank you for all of your help while I was writing this book.

Thank you to Lee Bygrave and Knut Kaasen for serving as my PhD dissertation advisors and playing a central role in helping me to complete the research on which this book is based. Thanks to Tobias Mahler and Samson Esayas for sending updates and providing comments on parts of the research that went into it. Thanks to Francis Augusto Medeiros-Logeay for providing helpful comments on earlier drafts and always lending an ear.

The primary research for this book was conducted while I was at the Norwegian Research Center for Computers and Law (NRCCL), University of Oslo (UiO). Thank you to all my NRCCL colleagues for providing a place that was not only academically stimulating but also felt like home. A special thanks to Gro Halvorsen and Karianne Stang for helping me to navigate not only the law faculty but also Norwegian culture and bureaucracy for the past ten years. I would also like to thank Arild Jansen, Dag Wiese Schartum, Olav Torvund, Tommy Tranvik, Darren Read, Luca Tosini, Heidi Beate Bentzen, Peter Davies, Laila Enerstvedt Fimreite, Siri Eriksen, Anne Gunn Berge Bekken, and Worku Urgessa. Also thanks to those at the Department of Private Law including Eli Knotten, Gørill Arnesen, Ørnulf Kristiansen, and Eva Dobos.

I would like to thank my PhD adjudication committee for taking on the difficult and time-consuming task of evaluating my dissertation and also encouraging me to get the work published. Thanks to Emily Weitzenboeck for chairing the committee, Dan Jerker B. Svantesson, and Rolf H. Weber for lending his time and broad expertise to my project.

Thank you to the NRCCL, the University of Oslo, and the Norwegian Research Council for providing generous funding during my time as a PhD researcher. This book would not have been possible without that support.

The views in this book, including any mistakes, are attributable only to me.

Abbreviations

3PAO	third-party assessment organization under the FedRAMP requirements programme
API	application programming interface
AWS	Amazon Web Services
BCRs	Binding Corporate Rules
B2B	business to business
B2C	business to consumer
B2G	business to government
BEA	Battelle Energy Alliance
CASBs	cloud access security brokers
CFPB	Consumer Financial Protection Bureau
CIA	confidentiality, integrity, and availability
CJEU	Court of Justice of the European Union
CLP at QMUL	Cloud Legal Project at Queen Mary University of London
CLOUD Act	Clarifying Lawful Overseas Use of Data Act
CNIL	Commission Nationale de l'Informatique et des Libertés
CSLI	cell-site location information
CSP	cloud service provider
DCFR	Draft Common Frame of Reference
Difi	Norwegian Agency for Public Management and eGovernment
DNS	domain name system
DoC	Department of Commerce
DoE	Department of Energy
DoI	Department of the Interior
DoL	Department of Labor
DoT	Department of Transportation
DPA	data protection authority
DPbD	data protection by design and by default
DPIA	data protection impact assessment

EBA	European Banking Authority
EC	European Commission
EDPB	European Data Protection Board
EDPS	European Data Protection Supervisor
EEA	European Economic Area
EIOPA	European Insurance and Occupational Pensions Authority
ENISA	European Union Agency for Network and Information Security
EPA	Environmental Protection Agency
ESI	electronically stored information
EU	European Union
FAA	Federal Aviation Administration
FAR	Federal Acquisition Regulation
FCA	Financial Conduct Authority (UK)
FCC	Federal Communications Commission
FedRAMP	Federal Risk and Authorization Management Program
FIPs	fair information practices
FIPS	Federal Information Protection Standard
FISA	Foreign Intelligence Surveillance Act
FISMA	Federal Information Security Management Act of 2002
FTC	Federal Trade Commission FTC
GAO	Government Accountability Office
GDPR	General Data Protection Regulation
HIPAA	Health Insurance Portability and Accountability Act
FHFA	Federal Housing Finance Agency
IaaS	infrastructure as a service
ICO	Information Commissioner's Office
ICT	information and communications technology
ISO	International Organization for Standardization
ISPs	internet service providers
IT	information technology
LEA	law enforcement agency
MLATs	mutual legal assistance treaties
MSA	master service agreement
NASA	National Aeronautics and Space Administration
NEH	National Endowment for the Humanities
NIS	Network and Information Security (EU Directive)
NIST	National Institute of Standards and Technology
NSA	National Security Agency
OECD	Organization for Economic Co-operation and Development
OPM	Office of Personnel Management
PaaS	platform as a service
PAs	public administrations

PICSE	Procurement Innovation for Cloud Services in Europe
PII	personally identifiable information
SaaS	software as a service
SCA	Stored Communications Act
SCCs	standard contractual clauses
SCOTUS	Supreme Court of the United States
SLALOM	Service-Level Agreement Legal and Open Model Contracts
SLAs	service-level agreements
SMEs	small- and medium-sized enterprises
SOW	statements of work
ToS	terms of service
ToU	terms of use
USA	United States of America
US Aid	United States Agency for International Development
USDA	United States Department of Agriculture
US DoE	United States Department of Energy
US HHS	US Department of Health and Human Services
USPS	United States Postal Service
VM	virtual machine
VPPA	Videotape Privacy Protection Act
WP29	Article 29 Working Party on the Protection of Individuals with Regard to the Processing of Personal Data

PART I

Subject Matter

1

Introduction

Cloud computing has been promoted as a significant development in information and communications technology (ICT) outsourcing. At its core, cloud computing is a method of providing users with on-demand computing services, generally delivered over the Internet.[1] Cloud computing provides users with data storage, use of software and an array of applications.[2] Combined with improving networks and Internet access, cloud computing makes it possible for users to migrate their data using remote servers and infrastructure owned by third parties.[3] Simply stated, paperwork that in the past was digitalized and moved from the filing cabinet to the personal computer has now moved farther to server parks located around the globe. Worldwide access to documents, innovative services, improved data administration, and advanced security make adopting cloud computing an attractive proposition for many users including governments.

This movement, from local storage to central storage accessed over the Internet, has fundamentally changed the way users interact with their data. With the help of cloud computing, ubiquitous computing has now become a reality.[4] Data is essentially available anywhere at any time and is accessible on multiple devices. Even if the technologies behind it are not new, cloud computing is often billed as the future of computing and has a central place in corporate and governmental ICT strategies.

Providing that cloud computing systems function properly, they have generally not been of interest to the public. However, revelations of access to data by security services and law enforcement agencies(LEAs), data security concerns (including data breaches and data ransom), data loss, and profiling of users by private

---

[1] Christopher S. Yoo, 'The Changing Patterns of Internet Usage' (2010) 63 *Federal Communications Law Journal* 67–90 at 83.
[2] See Peter Mell and Timothy Grance, 'The NIST Definition of Cloud Computing' (2011) *Special Publicaion (NIST SP) 800–145*. https://csrc.nist.gov/publications/detail/sp/800-145/final.
[3] William Jeremy Robison, 'Free at What Cost?: Cloud Computing Privacy under the Stored Communications Act' (2010) 98 *Georgetown Law Journal* 1195–239 at 1198.
[4] Tobias Matzner, 'Why Privacy is Not Enough Privacy in the Context of "Ubiquitous Computing" and "Big Data"' (2014) 12 *Journal of Information, Communication and Ethics in Society* 93–106 at 93. Ubiquitous or 'pervasive' computing refers to computing power that is essentially everywhere.

companies for commercial purposes have all drawn attention to the use of cloud computing.[5] Issues related to cloud computing have been central in cases before both the US Supreme Court and the Court of Justice of the European Union(EU).

The perceived lack of control over data stored on the cloud from either a physical or logical perspective has limited uptake of cloud computing.[6] This is particularly the case in regulated and governmental sectors. In other words, broader adoption of cloud computing by the public sector remains overcast in many areas. The reality of the situation is that the central barriers or bottlenecks to broader cloud adoption are no longer technical problems, but rather legal ones. Therefore, the aim of this book is to analyse the core legal issues that are central to government adoption of cloud computing services.

1.1 GOVERNMENT CLOUD COMPUTING IN CONTEXT

Governments spend substantial amounts of money on their information technology (IT) systems.[7] For instance, in the United States, the president's fiscal year 2019 budget request for IT was more than $90 billion.[8] Although IT systems generally increase government efficiency in delivering services to citizens, when computing systems grow in complexity they demand greater technical competence and become increasingly expensive to operate and maintain.[9] Numerous governments have focused on cloud computing as an important tool for providing state-of-the-art IT at a lower cost. Cloud computing allows governments to obtain computing power on a pay-per-use basis and removes many of the limits that governments have in developing new systems or applications in-house, allowing IT departments to focus on areas critical to their administration. Cloud computing also offers flexibility and a lower cost of ownership than many IT outsourcing services.

Although cloud computing may overcome some challenges and reduce computing expenses, certain aspects of the technology and its deployment raise additional concerns. For example, the cloud service provider's (CSP's) infrastructure is often

---

[5] *American Broadcasting Co., Inc. v. Aereo, Inc.* [2014] 134 S. Ct. 2498. Evaluating the application of copyright laws to new technologies, such as cloud computing. Cheng Lim Saw and Warren B. Chik, 'Whither the Future of Internet Streaming and Time-shifting? Revisiting the Rights of Reproduction and Communication to the Public in Copyright Law after Aereo' (2015) 23 *International Journal of Law and Information Technology* 53–88 at 84.

[6] Rania El-Gazzar, Eli Hustad, and Dag H. Olsen, 'Understanding Cloud Computing Adoption Issues: A Delphi Study Approach' (2016) 118 *Journal of Systems and Software* 64–84 at 73. Finding that global data privacy compliance was among top concerns of cloud clients. W. K. Hon, *Data Localization Laws and Policy: The EU Data Protection International Transfers Restriction through a Cloud Computing Lens* (Cheltenham and Northampton, MA: Edward Elgar 2017), p. 274. Evaluating the differences between logical and physical security.

[7] David A. Powner et al., United States Government Accountability Office (GAO), 'Information Technology: Federal Agencies Need to Address Aging Legacy Systems' (Report 11 June 2019). www.gao.gov/assets/700/699616.pdf.

[8] ibid.

[9] ibid.

opaque, located on a global scale, and spread across many providers. The full extent of the cloud service may not be fully visible to the user. Moving IT services outside of an organization's physical boundaries means lost or reduced control over data and greater reliance on third parties.[10] Rather than the user making key decisions on central information management issues, such as the physical location of the infrastructure, use of subcontractors, and security methods, these aspects are typically determined by the CSP. As a result, users of cloud services (cloud clients) face many difficult questions regarding legal requirements, trust, reliability, and overall security, in addition to technical challenges, such as migration from legacy systems and interoperability.[11]

These factors potentially expose governments to additional security and privacy risks. Further increasing these risks in many cloud models is the delivery of the services over a multi-tenant infrastructure, which involves sharing resources with unknown users. Moreover, controls commonly used or available in traditional IT hosting to meet information security, confidentiality, and privacy requirements – including on-site audits, staff interviews, and individualized non-disclosure agreements – may be unavailable in the cloud computing environment.[12] As a result of the standard structure, users are often required to accept greater – or different – levels of risk than they would under traditional IT outsourcing arrangements. For governments, the level of risk they are required to bear may be too high as the tools they generally employ for mitigating risks are unavailable (e.g. audits of CSPs and subcontractors).

In addition to general security or availability concerns, cloud computing brings with it many compliance challenges affecting data privacy, law enforcement investigations, and even state sovereignty. For example, as cloud users increasingly store important documents and sensitive data on remote servers owned by third parties, questions regarding who has access to that information are becoming more important. From a commercial perspective, theft of critical business information or industrial espionage is a serious threat to the profitability and longevity of commercial enterprises. From the perspective of governments, access by foreign governments to critical state information is a threat to national security.[13] Although much of the discussion on these issues in the media has focused on the US government covertly

---

[10] Wayne Jansen and Timothy Grance, 'Guidelines on Security and Privacy in Public Cloud Computing' (2011) SP 800-144, 12. https://nvlpubs.nist.gov/nistpubs/Legacy/SP/nistspecialpublication800-144.pdf.

[11] David C. Wyld, 'Moving to the Cloud: An Introduction to Cloud Computing in Government' (2009) IBM Center for the Business of Government, 33. www.businessofgovernment.org/sites/default/files/CloudComputingReport.pdf.

[12] See generally Scott Paquette, Paul T. Jaeger, and Susan C. Wilson, 'Identifying the Security Risks Associated with Governmental Use of Cloud Computing' (2010) 27 Government Information Quarterly 245–53 at 248.

[13] Norwegian Ministry of Local Government and Modernisation, 'Cloud Computing Strategy for Norway' (2016) Publication number H-2365 E, 11. www.regjeringen.no/en/dokumenter/cloud-computing-strategy-for-norway/id2484403/.

accessing sensitive information, access concerns extend beyond the US government to include not only other governments but private parties as well.[14]

The aforementioned risks impact many cloud computing users. However, in addition to the reservations held by private businesses or consumers, governments have additional concerns. From a practical perspective, in addition to highly regulated purchasing regimes, government users are often subject to publicly mandated computing security and archive requirements.[15] Unlike the private sector, governments cannot deviate from these requirements. Some of these requirements pose a direct barrier to adopting cloud, while others simply make cloud computing less attractive than more traditional IT outsourcing arrangements.

Governments represent citizens who are the beneficiaries of potential monetary savings from cloud services, but also bear the burden of government oversights in the procurement and operation of those services. Taking into account their position of trust and responsibility to the public, governments are generally required to exercise a higher level of transparency and accountability than private businesses or consumers when contracting for their own computing needs. Similarly, concerns regarding control, sometimes expressed as sovereignty, over data are particularly acute when considering the role of the state. If the state were to lose control over its data, there would be significant consequences for its ability to govern.

An additional concern for governments is that the portfolio or types of data they have are often extremely sensitive. For example, a government may hold census data, tax records, health data, records of criminal offences, and employment and education records, among other data types, on any of its citizens. Furthermore, citizens have little choice but to submit such data to the state in order to obtain services or comply with the law. In other words, although individuals can at least arguably opt out of using services like Google or Facebook, they cannot opt out of paying their taxes. The result is that the data possessed by governments on their citizens is multifaceted, sensitive, and devoid of active or direct consent on the part of the citizen.

In order to offer a standard or an interchangeable service, CSPs tend to provide their contract terms on a standard basis.[16] For governments, the contract terms contained in these offers are often unacceptable as they fail to account for their somewhat unique legal and security requirements. To counter this reality, governments with broader cloud procurement strategies often require CSPs to adhere to specific contract terms or even require that CSPs offer their services based on a contract that is essentially drafted by the government. In theory, central governments have enough negotiating power that they are able to force CSPs to the

---

[14] Fred H. Cate and others, 'Systematic Government Access to Private-sector Data' (2012) 2 *International Data Privacy Law* 195–99 at 196.

[15] See generally the Federal Information Security Management Act of 2002 ('FISMA') 44 USC § 3541 (2002) and the Federal Information Security Management Act of 2002, Pub. L. No. 107–347 (2002).

[16] Kristina Irion, 'Your Digital Home is No Longer Your Castle: How Cloud Computing Transforms the (Legal) Relationship between Individuals and Their Personal Records' (2015) 23 *International Journal of Law and Information Technology* 348–71 at 358–59.

bargaining table and move past the incompatible 'take it or leave it' contract terms faced by consumers and small- and medium-sized enterprises (SMEs).

The question remains: do current approaches to procuring cloud services meet the legal requirements of governments? Do legal requirements amount to traversable roadblocks or dead ends? In other words, are the terms or templates used in cloud procurement programs sufficient to allow governments to meet their legal and security requirements in light of data protection and other applicable laws and regulations? In evaluating these issues, the book focuses on the legal requirements, such as application of the General Data Protection Regulation (GDPR) and specific procurement or contracting requirements, and their application to cloud computing. In the subsequent chapters I assess whether these sources provide legal constraints that limit cloud computing as a viable means of computing for many governments.

1.2 MEETING LEGAL REQUIREMENTS: PROCUREMENT PLANS, CONTRACTS

In the absence of legislation that addresses the challenges of cloud computing, contracts play a central role in filling the gaps. Whether they have accomplished this objective and what legal implications these agreements have for users are ongoing questions. A primary challenge in this regard is that contracts drafted for globally accessible cloud services are still subject to national speed limits in many respects. The current approach to meeting legal requirements for most governments is utilizing contractual means rather than technical ones. That is, rather than building cloud computing systems and becoming CSPs themselves, governments focus on procurement strategies for contracting with private providers.

To provide a better understanding of how these procurement plans work and how they meet data privacy and other legal requirements, I examine the contracting tools of two of the largest and most developed systems currently in use, namely the Government Cloud (G-Cloud) system in the United Kingdom and the Federal Risk and Authorization Management Program (FedRAMP) system in the United States.[17] Much of the contractual analysis is based on an evaluation of the actual content of contracts between US federal agencies and CSPs obtained through the Freedom of Information Act (FOIA) disclosures from the US government.[18] I also evaluate standard agreements offered as part of the United Kingdom's G-Cloud

[17] The United Kingdom was selected for the FOIA study and research generally *prior to* invoking Article 50 of the Treaty on European Union and staring the withdrawal process known as 'Brexit'. The process was not complete by the time this book was finalized. See generally European Commission, 'Negotiating Documents on Article 50 Negotiations with the United Kingdom'. https://ec.europa.eu/commission/brexit-negotiations/negotiating-documents-article-50-negotiations-united-kingdom_en.

[18] The Freedom of Information Act 5 USC § 552, As Amended by Pub. L. No. 104-231, 110 Stat. 3048 (hereinafter 'FOIA'). www.justice.gov/oip/blog/foia-update-freedom-information-act-5-usc-sect-552-amended-public-law-no-104-231-110-stat.

framework in addition to cloud contracts obtained under the UK Freedom of Information Act (UK FOIA) available in the public sphere.

After evaluating legal requirements and governmental plans to meet those requirements, the question then becomes whether there is a compliance gap between what the procurement systems require and what the contracts actually contain. If such a gap exists, what are the potential problems or risks created for citizen and government data? Have government agencies or actors adequately protected the privacy interests of the citizens they represent? If there are gaps between what the FedRAMP system requires and what was procured, are European systems, including the United Kingdom's G-Cloud system, in a better position to prevent these oversights? In other words, if the G-Cloud system had been applied by US agencies, would they have obtained a more compliant or better result? The main objective of this comparison is to determine which requirements led to the best results when applied to the cloud structure.

In addition to specific applicable laws and the contracts designed to act in accordance with those laws, I consider whether governments should be concerned with the centralizing of data that takes place through cloud usage and its potential impact on data sovereignty. In other words, is the creation of centralized storage points, with the massive amounts of critical data stored and managed by private providers, a systemic concern that goes beyond security breaches and other periodic security lapses for governments?[19] If so, how should governments approach these risks?

1.3 IMPACT AND SCOPE

When legal literature on cloud computing first began to be published, there was a considerable focus on whether cloud computing amounted to anything more than a clever marketing term.[20] That debate has now been settled in most circles. Most researchers seem to acknowledge that cloud computing services go one step further, or take a different direction, than those offered or employed in traditional IT hosting or outsourcing arrangements.[21] However, the question remains: how are cloud services best regulated? Should private ordering – including private contracts between parties – retain its primacy in governance or should governments on a top-down basis set more cloud-specific regulations?[22]

[19] David Lametti, 'The Cloud: Boundless Digital Potential or Enclosure 3.0?' (2012) 17 *Virginia Journal of Law & Technology* 192–243 at 214.
[20] Damon C. Andrews and John M. Newman, 'Personal Jurisdiction and Choice of Law in the Cloud' (2013) 73 *Maryland Law Review* 313–84 at 313. Stating that '[t]hough some early detractors criticized the "cloud" as being nothing more than an empty industry buzzword, we contend that by dovetailing communications and calculating processes for the first time in history, cloud computing is – both practically and legally – a shift in prevailing paradigms'.
[21] ibid., 325. Arguing that cloud computing is more than a 'buzzword'.
[22] Anthony Gray, 'Conflict of Laws and the Cloud' (2013) 29 *Computer Law & Security Review* 58–65 at 64. See Chapter 4, evaluating examples of direct legislation in the 'Clarifying Lawful Overseas Use of Data Act (CLOUD Act)'.

As 'cloud clients', governments have great potential to influence the cloud computing market. As noted by Marsden,

> Government, it is often forgotten, does far more to regulate than simply tax and spend, legislate, rule-make and prosecute. It is also the largest procurer of goods and services, the first adopter of many new technologies, and the commissioner of most new basic research, especially in Europe.[23]

For example, as the largest buyer of cloud computing services worldwide, the US government influences how cloud computing develops through both its purchasing power and its legislation.[24] Even if the EU currently lags behind the United States in terms of cloud usage and adoption, the EU has one of the largest potential markets of active Internet users. EU laws and initiatives will shape the future of cloud by either limiting or embracing its adoption in much of the public sector and beyond.[25]

Although this book primarily considers the role of governments as users or adopters of cloud computing, states are also taking on additional roles. Governments also act as contributors to cloud computing research, standards development and as market regulators. For example, by developing model contract terms and playing an active part in the development of certification schemes, governments play an important role in influencing the private ordering that is used to largely regulate cloud computing. If states can effect changes in the way CSPs deliver services, making them more compliant with data privacy laws, then these changes may also trickle down to consumer and business deployments.

1.4 DEFINITIONS, CONCEPTS, AND PARAMETERS

1.4.1 *Article 29 Working Party (WP29) and the European Data Protection Board (EDPB)*

Article 29 of the EU Data Protection Directive specifically established a working party to provide guidance on data protection law in the EU (henceforth WP29). The WP29 had an advisory role and was comprised of one representative from each of the data protection authorities (DPAs) in the EU member states, the European Data Protection Supervisor (EDPS), and the European Commission. At the EU level,

---

[23] Christopher T. Marsden, 'An Empire Entire of Itself? Standards, Domain Names and Government' in Christopher T. Marsden (ed.), *Internet Co-Regulation: European Law, Regulatory Governance and Legitimacy in Cyberspace* (Cambridge: Cambridge University Press 2011), p. 101.

[24] Government Accountability Office (GAO), 'Cloud Computing: Agencies Need to Incorporate Key Practices to Ensure Effective Performance' (2016) GAO-16-325, 3. www.gao.gov/products/GAO-16-325. Estimating that the US federal government spent $2 billion on cloud computing services annually in addition to over $80 billion on IT generally.

[25] European Union Agency for Network and Information Security (ENISA), 'Good Practice Guide for Securely Deploying Governmental Clouds' (2013), 1. www.enisa.europa.eu/publications/good-practice-guide-for-securely-deploying-governmental-clouds.

although non-binding, opinions and guidance by the WP29 have been particularly influential.[26]

With the adoption of the GDPR on 25 May 2018, the WP29 was disbanded. The EDPB has replaced it.[27] This board is an independent European body charged with providing consistent application of the GDPR throughout the EU and facilitating cooperation with national DPAs. The EDPB is similar to the WP29 in make-up; however, the EDPB has the authority to make binding decisions in some instances.[28] After succeeding the WP29, the EDPB adopted GDPR-relevant WP29 guidelines from 2016 until 2018.[29] To avoid confusion, I use WP29 to refer to decisions made under that regime and EDPB to refer to decisions made by the DPA envisioned under the GDPR.

1.4.2 Cloud Computing

Cloud computing is not a new technology, but rather a combination of numerous technologies that have allowed providers to deliver computing power as a service over the Internet.[30] Although this definition is further explored in Chapter 2, I use the terms 'cloud computing service', 'the cloud', and 'cloud' to refer to the delivery of a computing service not a new technology or physical place.[31] Simply stated, cloud computing offers a means of providing users with on-demand computing services over a network. The classification of cloud computing by the National Institute of Standards and Technology (NIST) has been widely accepted in the United States and Europe and is the primary definition used in this book. The NIST definition states:

> Cloud computing is a model for enabling ubiquitous, convenient, on-demand network access to a shared pool of configurable computing resources (e.g. networks, servers, storage, applications, and services) that can be rapidly provisioned and released with minimal management effort or service provider interaction.[32]

---

[26] WP29 was set up under the EU Data Protection Directive 95/46/EC at Art. 29. Lee Bygrave, *Data Privacy Law: An International Perspective* (Oxford: Oxford University Press 2014), p. 19.

[27] GDPR Arts. 63–76 and Recitals 135–40.

[28] EDPB, 'European Data Protection Board Rules of Procedure' (25 May 2018), 6–11. https://edpb.europa.eu/sites/edpb/files/files/file1/edpb_rop_adopted_en.pdf. EDPB is composed of the head of each DPA and the EDPS. The European Commission has participation but no voting rights.

[29] See EDPB, 'Endorsement 1/2018' (25 May 2018). https://edpb.europa.eu/sites/edpb/files/files/news/endorsement_of_wp29_documents_en_0.pdf. Guidelines adopted by the EDPB primarily focus on the GDPR.

[30] Lawrence Lessig, *Code: Version 2.0* (New York: Basic Books 2006), p. 144. There are additional theories on the layers of the Internet. See generally Lawrence B. Solum and Minn Chung, 'The Layers Principle: Internet Architecture and the Law' (2004) 79 *Notre Dame Law Review* 815–948 at 816.

[31] Directive (EU) 2016/1148 of the European Parliament and of the Council of 6 July 2016 concerning measures for a high common level of security of network and information systems across the Union (henceforth 'NIS Directive') Recital 17. Providing that resources that make up cloud computing include 'networks, servers or other infrastructure, storage, applications and services'.

[32] Mell and Grance, 'The NIST Definition of Cloud Computing', 2. Dimitra Liveri and M. A. C. Dekker, 'Security Framework for Governmental Clouds: All Steps from Design to

This definition and the primary actors in cloud are analysed in greater depth in Chapter 2.

1.4.3 Cloud Client

There is a lack of agreement on the terms used to reference the parties to cloud computing services. Because many CSPs use cloud computing services themselves, and one cloud computing service is often layered on top of another, the term 'user' provides an incomplete, and in some cases confusing, reference when describing the final end user of a service.[33] In the United States, the term 'cloud consumer' is often used.[34] However, since legal experts tend to associate 'consumer' with a non-professional living person who is often entitled to additional protections when entering into contracts, the term has the potential to lead to some confusion.[35] This is certainly the case here as this book focuses on governments, and they fall outside the scope of a 'non-professional party' or 'consumer' designation. The final end user of a cloud computing service, whether it is a consumer, government, or business, will be deemed a 'cloud client' throughout this book.

1.4.4 Cloud Service Provider

The CSP is the organization making the cloud computing service available. The CSP manages the services and provides the operational, technical, and legal resources necessary to make the service available to cloud clients accessing it over a network.[36] Depending on the deployment models used (discussed in Chapter 2), the role of the CSP may vary.[37] In many cases, the CSP will also be a cloud client or user of cloud services.

Deployment' (2015) *ENISA*, 3. www.enisa.europa.eu/publications/security-framework-for-governmental-clouds. Providing a standard definition for the term government cloud.

[33] Hon, 'Data Localization Laws and Policy', pp. 3–4. Describing the complex supply chains often found in cloud computing services where CSPs build their individual services using components or infrastructure from other providers.

[34] Fang Liu and others, 'NIST Cloud Computing Reference Architecture' (2011) *Special Publication (NIST SP) 500-292*, 4. www.nist.gov/publications/nist-cloud-computing-reference-architecture. The NIST definition uses the term 'cloud consumer' to define this final end user of a cloud service.

[35] Although there is no uniform definition of 'consumer', this description is in line with the general European approach to defining consumers 'as natural persons acting outside of their trade or profession ... '. Directive 2011/83/EU of the European Parliament and of the Council of 25 October 2011 on Consumer Rights OJ L 304/2011 ('CRD') Art. 2(1).

[36] Lee Badger and others, 'US Government Cloud Computing Technology Roadmap Volume II Release 1.0' (2011) *NIST Technology*, 20.

[37] For example, in the SaaS model, the CSP will provide essentially all aspects of the service to the cloud client on a 'turnkey' basis. Government Accountability Office (GAO), 'Cloud Computing: Additional Opportunities and Savings Need to Be Pursued' (2014) GAO-14-753, 5. www.gao.gov/products/GAO-14-753.

1.4.5 *Information Security or Data Security*

Data security is a concept that is often used in conjunction with data privacy, but it is not equal to data privacy.[38] Stated concisely, data security is a means of ensuring that data are available to authorized users.[39] As defined by one treatise, '[d]ata security consists of a series of layers involving physical security, logical security and security policy'.[40] The extent and necessity of security measures is based on factors such as the nature and size of an organization, the types of data being processed, the security tools available based on resources, and the risks connected to the processing.

1.4.6 *Data Sovereignty*

As it is most often expressed, data sovereignty generally encompasses the ability of an actor to control the physical location where its data resides and/or control access to that data.[41] In many instances definitions focus primarily on physical location and security rather than controls pertaining to logical organization and security. However, the definition varies depending on the field (e.g. legal or computer science).[42]

1.4.7 *Privacy/Data Protection*

The right to privacy is a broad concept without a universal definition that can be applied across legal systems or cultures.[43] In the following pages, I evaluate and use the term 'privacy' through the lens of discourse that has taken place in the EU and the United States.[44] As noted by Bygrave, there are generally four ways of defining privacy, including 'non-interference', 'limited accessibility', 'information control', and the '"intimate or sensitive" aspects of persons' lives'.[45]

The concepts of 'data privacy' and 'data protection' are based on concepts of privacy but are not necessarily equivocal.[46] That is, privacy is often seen as a broader

---

[38] Bygrave, 'Data Privacy Law: An International Perspective', p. 2.
[39] Lauren Henry, 'Information Privacy and Data Security' (2015) 36 *Cardozo Law Review De Novo* 108–18 at 112. Finding that the 'definition of data security understanding is similar in the law literature, the case law, and in industry'.
[40] Megan Costello, 'Data Security Generally' (2017) 1 *Data Security & Privacy Law Westlaw* § 3:2. See Hon, 'Data Localization Laws and Policy', p. 274. Describing logical security as critical.
[41] Kristina Irion, 'Government Cloud Computing and National Data Sovereignty' (2012) 4 *Policy & Internet* 40–71 at 50.
[42] ibid., 356.
[43] Bygrave, 'Data Privacy Law: An International Perspective', p. 27.
[44] As a whole, privacy is a much broader concept than presented in the Anglo-European discussion. See, for example, Graham Greenleaf, *Asian Data Privacy Laws: Singapore – Uncertain Scope, Strong Powers* (Oxford: Oxford University Press 2014).
[45] Bygrave, 'Data Privacy Law: An International Perspective', p. 27. Internal citations and emphasis omitted.
[46] ibid. Providing four distinguishing features separating the concepts.

concept including '[.] ... spatial, bodily, and perhaps psychological dimensions that are usually not directly addressed by data privacy law'.[47] In this book, I use 'data privacy' generally and 'data protection' when referencing European legislation.[48] Privacy requirements are further evaluated in Chapter 5.

1.4.8 Use of the Terms 'State' and 'Government'

Throughout this book, I use the terms 'state' and 'government'. When referring to a government entity adopting a service, I use the term 'government'. When referencing governments, I focus on the political administration of a state, including governments on a national, provincial, regional, or municipal/local level. Thus, I adopt a broad definition of government referring 'collectively to the political organs of a country regardless of their function or level, and regardless of the subject matter they deal with'.[49]

1.4.9 Outsourcing and Offshoring

A concise definition of outsourcing adopted in this book provides 'a long-term collaborative relationship that entrusts business functions or processes to a contractor (the supplier) through a long-term service contract'.[50] Generally, outsourcing refers to an organization transferring work to a third party (domestically or internationally) on a contractual basis. Unlike privatization, where the private actor invests private capital and takes over or obtains an ownership function, outsourcing is essentially temporary and a government does not give up a function by outsourcing to a private actor.[51] Cloud computing is generally categorized as a form of IT outsourcing.[52]

The term 'outsourcing' is often used interchangeably with offshoring. 'Offshoring', which may be included in an outsourcing agreement, involves the provision of a good or service in a foreign country. Creation of the good or service might be on an 'in-house' basis by the company or produced externally by an outside foreign provider. Although the two can be readily combined, for example, where

---

[47] ibid. See Maria Tzanou, *The Fundamental Right to Data Protection: Normative Value in the Context of Counter-terrorism Surveillance* (Oxford: Hart 2017), p. 14.
[48] Bygrave, 'Data Privacy Law: An International Perspective', p. 3.
[49] Bryan A. Garner, 'Government' in Bryan A. Garner (ed.), *Black's Law Dictionary*, 10th ed. (Eagan, MN: Thomson West 2014), pp. 1–2052.
[50] George Kimball, *Outsourcing Agreements: A Practical Guide* (Oxford: Oxford University Press 2010), p. 2.
[51] Steven J. Kelman, 'Federal Contracting in Context: What Drives It, How to Improve It' in Jody Freeman and Martha Minow (eds.), *Government by Contract: Outsourcing and American Democracy* (Cambridge, MA: Harvard University Press 2009), p. 195.
[52] W. K. Hon and Christopher Millard, 'Cloud Technologies and Services' in Christopher Millard (ed.), *Cloud Computing Law* (Oxford: Oxford University Press 2013), p. 31. Providing an overview of the key differences between traditional IT outsourcing and cloud computing.

a third party provides an IT service in a foreign jurisdiction, they are not two sides of the same coin.[53] For example, a CSP may own and control its server infrastructure, even if it is located offshore. Likewise, a CSP may offshore *and* outsource these aspects where the server infrastructure is located abroad and provided by an external partner.[54]

1.5 INPUTS AND APPROACH

Legal analysis is concentrated on the US and UK government cloud computing programs with some additional comparisons to the approaches of various EU/European Economic Area (EEA) member states.[55] A primary source of law in cloud computing comes from the wide range of contracts between CSPs and cloud clients, including Business-to-Consumer (B2C), Business-to-Business (B2B), and Business-to-Government (B2G) agreements.[56] Considering the B2B aspect, terms and conditions used among and between major players to cloud computing services in negotiated contracts are largely unavailable, or at least access to them is substantially limited, for non-parties.[57] For example, one such confidential contract I obtained from a CSP contained the following contract term:

> Neither party will disclose confidential information in violation of the terms and conditions of this Agreement, to any third party, without the prior written consent of the other Party ... *including the terms and conditions* ... [].[58]

Although there were exceptions for disclosure to non-parties in this particular contract, they were limited. Such restrictions on sharing contracts made obtaining a view of the B2B segment of the market difficult. Agreements between CSPs and governments had received comparatively limited focus when compared to B2C

---

[53] Mari Sako, 'Outsourcing and Offshoring: Implications for Productivity of Business Services' (2006) 22 *Oxford Review of Economic Policy* 499–512 at 503.

[54] See generally Margaret M. Blair and others, 'Outsourcing, Modularity, and the Theory of the Firm' (2011) 2011 *Brigham Young University Law Review* 263–314 at 263. https://scholarship.law.vanderbilt.edu/cgi/viewcontent.cgi?article=1025&context=faculty-publications. Defining and explaining outsourcing.

[55] Larry A. DiMatteo, Qi Zhou, and Séverine Saintier, 'Transatlantic Perspectives' in Keith Rowley and others (eds.), *Commercial Contract Law: Transatlantic Perspectives* (Cambridge: Cambridge University Press 2013), p. 2. Noting that even within the common law approach, there are significant differences.

[56] W. Kuan Hon, Christopher Millard, and Ian Walden, 'Negotiating Cloud Contracts: Looking at Clouds From Both Sides Now' (2012) 16 *Stanford Technology Law Review* 79–130 at 79. See also W. Kuan Hon, Christopher Millard, and Ian Walden, 'Negotiated Contracts for Cloud Services' in Christopher Millard (ed.), *Cloud Computing Law* (Oxford: Oxford University Press 2013), p. 73.

[57] Hon, Millard, and Walden, 'Negotiated Contracts for Cloud Services', fn 6. Noting that most interviewees that took part in the seminal study did not wish to be named.

[58] Confidential business-to-business cloud computing contract on file with the Author. Emphasis added.

contracts.[59] Consequently, this book attempts to bridge this gap by evaluating negotiated government cloud contracts.

As governments represent the public, they are often required to provide the public with information regarding their procurement processes, including making copies of contracts available. As a result, 'the law of the parties' in the form of final negotiated contracts is much more widely available in the case of governments than in the case of private parties. Thus, much of the contractual analysis in this book comes from contracts obtained through requests made under the US FOIA in addition to agency audits and reports.

1.6 IDENTIFYING AND LIMITING LEGAL ISSUES

There are many existing laws that directly affect or apply to cloud computing. Although 'core' legal requirements are generally found in the areas of data privacy, consumer protection and jurisdictional requirements, the scope of potentially applicable legal requirements is extensive. The use of cloud computing is also impacted by intellectual property law, antitrust or competition law, criminal law, and even international trade agreements.[60] In the case of governments using cloud computing, procurement and contracting requirements, FOIA requirements and archive requirements add additional layers of regulatory compliance. Additionally, governments often have technical or security standards that are directly applicable to their use of cloud services.

An ongoing struggle in writing this book has been how broadly to draw the scope. Attempting to include all rules applicable to cloud would severely limit the amount of analysis in any area. Conversely, limiting coverage to only data privacy law does not provide an adequately representative picture of the regulatory complexity applicable to cloud computing, particularly from the state or government perspective. While this book does not provide comprehensive coverage of procurement regulations, I consider areas where specific procurement requirements impact cloud adoption by governments. Furthermore, I evaluate the potential impacts of law enforcement and intelligence access on data sovereignty, as these topics are central to the discussion of whether governments should use cloud computing at all.

---

[59] C.f. Wyld, 'Moving to the Cloud', 4. W. Kuan Hon, Christopher Millard, and Ian Walden, 'Public Sector Cloud Contracts' in Christopher Millard (ed.), *Cloud Computing Law* (Oxford: Oxford University Press 2013), p. 108.

[60] Chris Reed and Alan Cunningham, 'Ownership of Information in Clouds' in Christopher Millard (ed.), *Cloud Computing Law* (Oxford: Oxford University Press 2013), pp. 142–63. See also Ian Walden and Laíse Da Correggio Luciano, 'Facilitating Competition in the Clouds' in Christopher Millard (ed.), *Cloud Computing Law* (Oxford: Oxford University Press 2013), pp. 311–29.

1.7 UNDERLYING ISSUES, ASSUMPTIONS, AND IMPORTANCE OF GOVERNMENT CLOUD ADOPTION

When considering the role of governments using cloud computing, I argue they ought to approach the services with a measure of caution. New IT solutions are often enticing, but nonetheless merit careful examination. An awareness campaign by the Free Software Foundation Europe created a poster stating: 'There is no cloud – just other people's computers'.[61] That message resonated with many across the Internet. The idea of placing data on a fluffy cloud gives users a certain feeling of comfort. The data are easily accessible and backup, storage, and consumption all take place effortlessly. However, the reality of the situation is that data stored on cloud computing infrastructures is done outside of the control of the user and requires a great deal of reliance on the CSP in determining how the data are stored and secured. This reality requires a great deal of trust in the CSP. When the cloud user is a government and the data it is storing belongs to or concerns its citizens, the need for careful planning to meet legal requirements is heightened.

In the following chapters, a central theme that emerges is that understanding legal requirements and developing or putting in place a plan to execute those legal requirements have not always received adequate attention when governments procure cloud computing services. Although a significant focus on security and technical measures is an important aspect of cloud computing, governments must also have safeguards in place to manage risks emanating from legal sources, such as compliance with mandatory legislation (e.g. data privacy laws). In particular, governments must include contract terms that sufficiently address the legal challenges posed by cloud computing.

Moreover, when it comes to governments adopting cloud computing, before placing the personal data of their citizens on 'other people's computers', the concern is not only with the typical dichotomies that are often expressed when deploying a new technology. Although the typical 'state *versus* private enterprise' or 'technology *versus* law' contentions are present in cloud computing, they only make up part of the analysis and ultimately only part of the caution expressed in this book. In the case of cloud procurement by public entities, governments and CSPs are acting much more in concert – as partners, even – in the move towards cloud adoption. Governments are seeking – sometimes aggressively – the benefits that cloud offers. While being caught up in the potential of cloud computing, governments may fail to adequately consider and evaluate the risks involved with adoption of the technology, both in the short- and the long-term.

To achieve greater levels of cloud adoption, governments are working closely with CSPs. Based on that reality, governments need to remain objective in their approach to cloud computing and not stand too closely to CSPs on one side of the debate

---

[61] Free Software Foundation Europe (2015). http://download.fsfe.org/advocacy/stickers/thereisnocloud/thereisnocloud-v2-74x74.pdf.

leaving citizens and their right to privacy, along with government accountability and democratic values, on the other. This requires a level of independence from CSPs that includes not becoming overly dependent on or locked in to their providers. Governments have a strong hand to play when negotiating with CSPs. However, without a critical eye, in addition to adequate systems or plans for procurement, governments will ultimately fail to obtain contract terms and cloud services that meet their needs and those of the citizens they represent.

2

Cloud Technology, Organizational Aspects, and Risks

In both the private and public sectors, 'moving to the cloud', or variations of it, has become a common phrase.[1] Commercials created by CSPs often show cluttered files being whisked away to a brighter place where organization and security reign. Although the technical reality of cloud computing is very different, the term 'cloud computing' has proven to be an extremely effective metaphor.[2] In fact, the term has been so effective that it has left some users confused on key issues including where the computing takes place. Despite the clever name, 'the cloud' consists of collections of servers often called 'server farms' or 'server parks' residing in one jurisdiction or dispersed globally.

In addition to worldwide availability, the services are scalable to meet the individual cloud consumer's needs.[3] Furthermore, cloud computing provides users with a simple means to access a range of computing services on an on-demand basis.[4] Cutting-edge computer programs, once reserved for the largest corporations and governments, are now widely available to start-ups and municipalities. In addition to greater choice, for many users, cloud computing also improves security. A final benefit for many users is that they pay only for the computing power they use, limiting the amount of physical infrastructure they need to purchase and potentially reducing wasted processing capacity.[5]

Cloud computing resources are typically delivered over the Internet using a process of server virtualization. With server virtualization, CSPs use a physical server to host

---

[1] David Colarusso, 'Heads in the Cloud, a Coming Storm: The Interplay of Cloud, Encryption, and the Fifth Amendment's Protection against Self-Incrimination' (2011) 17 *Boston University Journal of Science & Technology Law* 69–99 at 80–81.

[2] Mihály J. Ficsor, 'The WIPO "Internet Treaties" and Copyright in the "Cloud"' (2012) ALAI Congress, 1–2.

[3] Joseph A. Nicholson, 'Plus Ultra: Third-Party Preservation in a Cloud Computing Paradigm' (2012) 8 *Hastings Business Law Journal* 191–220 at 199.

[4] W. Kuan Hon and Christopher Millard, 'Cloud Technologies and Services' in Christopher Millard (ed.), *Cloud Computing Law* (Oxford: Oxford University Press 2013), p. 4. Kevin McGillivray, 'Conflicts in the Cloud: Contracts and Compliance with Data Protection Law in the EU' (2014) 17 *Tulane Journal of Technology and Intellectual Property* 217–53.

[5] Daniel J. Gervais and Daniel J. Hyndman, 'Cloud Control: Copyright, Global Memes and Privacy' (2011) 10 *Journal on Telecommunications and High Technology Law* 53–92 at 64.

multiple virtual machines (VMs).[6] Just like physical machines, VMs run their own operating systems and applications. However, unlike traditional computing, many VMs run on the same physical server.[7] By sharing the physical infrastructure or hardware, cloud computing allows providers to utilize a greater proportion of computing resources. That is, if a CSP determines that a physical server has unused capacity, it can utilize that capacity by adding additional VMs. Using VM technology, CSPs can provide everything from data storage to complex data processing.[8]

Depending on whom you ask, either cloud computing does nothing new – represents a logical step in combining existing technologies, or it is a revolution in computing. I tend to agree with those who categorize cloud as a new business or service model rather than a new technology. As aptly provided by Gasser,

> [T]he concept of cloud computing is not necessarily revolutionary, rather it reflects the coalescence of a number of pre-existing technologies that progressed through a natural, evolutionary process to a point where cloud computing became economically and technically feasible. However, the resulting ecosystem – combining different aspects of product, process, and structural innovation mainly at the intersection of technology and economics – produces a value greater than the sum of its parts.[9]

I do not attempt to solve debates around the novelty of cloud computing technology in this book. The remit of this chapter is to analyse cloud computing service and deployment models, and provide a high-level overview on the technology, in order to provide context for applying legal frameworks in a meaningful way.

2.1 DEFINING CLOUD COMPUTING SERVICES

As a point of departure, there is no 'official' definition of cloud computing.[10] Although cloud computing encompasses many different offerings, the term is generally used to describe a method of computing that combines technologies to deliver a variety of services over the Internet.[11] As noted in Section 1.4.2, most governments have adopted the NIST definition in their national plans or strategies.

---

[6] Hon and Millard, 'Cloud Technologies and Services', p. 6. See David Bernstein and others, 'US Government Cloud Computing Technology Roadmap' (2014) *Volume II: High-Priority Requirements to Further USG Agency Cloud Computing Adoption Vol. II*, 10–11. http://dx.doi.org/10.6028/NIST.SP.500-293. Evaluating virtualization in IaaS deployments.

[7] Hon and Millard, 'Cloud Technologies and Services', p. 9.

[8] WP29, 'Opinion on Cloud Computing 05/2012' 196 (2012), 4. https://ec.europa.eu/justice/article-29/documentation/opinion-recommendation/files/2012/wp196_en.pdf.

[9] Urs Gasser, 'Cloud Innovation and the Law: Issues, Approaches, and Interplay' (2014) *Berkman Center Research Publication No. 2014-7*, 1–32 at 5. https://cyber.harvard.edu/node/92450.

[10] Kevin Werbach, 'The Network Utility' (2011) 60 *Duke Law Journal* 1761–840 at 1812–13. Joseph A. Schoorl, 'Clicking the Export Button: Cloud Data Storage and US Dual-Use Export Controls' (2012) 80 *George Washington Law Review* 632–67 at 644.

[11] Jasper P. Sluij and others, 'Cloud Computing in the EU Policy Sphere: Interoperability, Vertical Integration and the Internal Market' (2011) 3 *Journal of Intellectual Property, Information Technology and Electronic Commerce Law* 12–32 at 13.

Where alternative definitions are used, they closely follow the definition set by NIST.[12] Despite criticisms, the NIST definition for cloud computing has become the de facto standard.[13]

However, just because the definition is widely adopted does not mean that it has been easy to apply. In the case of the US government's move to cloud computing, there was substantial confusion in understanding and applying the NIST definition for cloud computing services. For instance, the Department of Energy, with cloud computing contracts valued at over $30 million, failed to apply the NIST (or any) definition to many of the cloud services it procured.[14] As a result, the Department of Energy did not have an overall inventory of the cloud computing services it was using.[15]

This 'misdiagnosis' was not a minor point. In the case of the US government's risk evaluation scheme, defining a service as cloud provides the cornerstone for making certain that security and privacy controls are applied. Therefore, if an agency misinterpreted, mislabelled, or misunderstood that a technology was a cloud computing service, they also likely failed to include crucial contract terms and security measures designed to meet the unique risks of cloud computing. This problem was particularly widespread in US federal agency adoption.[16]

2.2 PARTIES IN CLOUD COMPUTING SERVICES

2.2.1 *Cloud Auditor*

The auditor examines the controls used in a cloud service and determines if the CSP complies with a standard or certification scheme.[17] The auditor typically verifies security or compliance requirements in addition to measuring whether a CSP has met performance levels or privacy requirements.[18] Auditors operate with different

---

[12] Directive 2016/1148 of 6 July 2016 concerning measures for a high common level of security of network and information systems across the Union, OJ 2016 No. L194, of 19 July 2016 (henceforth 'NIS Directive') Art. 4 (19). For instance, the EU NIS Directive defines cloud computing as a 'digital service that enables access to a scalable and elastic pool of shareable computing resources'.

[13] Timothy J. Calloway, 'Cloud Computing, Clickwrap Agreements, and Limitation on Liability Clauses: A Perfect Storm' (2012) 11 *Duke Law & Technology Review* 163–74 at 166. Arguing that the 'federal government's definition of cloud computing is anything but clear'.

[14] Gregory H. Friedman, 'Department of Energy (DoE) Office of Inspector General, Office of Audits and Inspections, Audit Report: The Department of Energy's Management of Cloud Computing Activities' (2014), 1–2. www.energy.gov/sites/prod/files/2014/09/f18/Audit%20Report%20on%20The%20Department%20of%20Energy%27s%20Management%20of%20Cloud%20Computing%20Activities%20-%20DOE%20IG-0918.pdf.

[15] ibid.

[16] Office of Inspector General USDA, 'Audit Report 50501-0005-12: USDA's Implementation of Cloud Computing Services' (2014), 3. www.usda.gov/oig/webdocs/50501-0005-12.pdf. Finding that the USDA also failed to maintain an accurate inventory of its cloud computing systems, listing only seventeen of its thirty-one cloud systems for auditors.

[17] Bernstein and others, 'US Government Cloud Computing Technology Roadmap', 11.

[18] ibid.

levels of independence. On the independent end of the scale, an auditor is employed independently of the CSP. In this case, the auditor is generally a third-party auditing firm with certification or accreditation, to perform the audit. On the other end of the scale, the CSP employs the auditor who is part of the organization. The audit may be conducted on a one-off or a continuous basis.

Although many CSPs are resistant to individual audits, they are a critical point for the adoption of cloud services by governments. Having many independent auditors accessing the CSPs infrastructure brings its own risks. Essentially, if many auditors begin conducting tests on the infrastructure they may impact and even disrupt operations. To avoid this problem, CSPs have one audit conducted against a well-known standard and allow all cloud clients to access the report and, in some circumstances, interview the auditors.

2.2.2 Cloud Brokers or Integrators

The concept of 'cloud integrator' or 'cloud broker' describes an entity that serves as an intermediary or link between the cloud client and the CSP.[19] The broker has several functions. As noted by NIST, '[a]s cloud computing evolves, the integration of cloud services can be too complex for cloud consumers to manage'.[20] Therefore, the function of the broker is generally to assist the cloud client with technical or business aspects of cloud computing adoption.

Although NIST uses the term 'broker', the term 'integrator' is also common, particularly in the EU.[21] The terms or categorizations are generally used interchangeably even if they perhaps suggest different functions. In my view, the term 'integrator' is more correct as it describes a broader range of services than the term 'broker' suggests.[22] However, one could also take the opposite position and argue that the additional factors, including security and liability, are simply part of the brokered package.

The intermediary role integrators provide often takes on properties of technical assistance, negotiation, business, or compliance expertise.[23] On the business side, an integrator may negotiate with CSPs on behalf of the cloud client but does not necessarily have access to cloud client data or involvement in technical processes. Examples of an integrator in this role are those that operate a catalogue of services based on certain business or legal requirements without involvement in the migration or operation of cloud services. Because integrators can offer CSPs volume, they

---

[19] ibid., 11–13.
[20] ibid.
[21] W. Kuan Hon, Christopher Millard, and Ian Walden, 'Negotiating Cloud Contracts: Looking at Clouds from Both Sides Now' (2012) 16 *Stanford Technology Law Review* 79–130 at 90. As evaluated by Hon, Millard, and Walden, integrators are also resellers, CSPs, and outsourcers.
[22] William P. Statsky, 'Broker' in William P. Statsky (ed.), *West's Legal Thesaurus/Dictionary* (Saint Paul, MN: West 1986), p. 105. Defining 'broker' as '[a]n agent who arranges contracts for a fee'.
[23] Bernstein and others, 'US Government Cloud Computing Technology Roadmap', 11–13.

are often in a better position than end users, particularly those seeking lower-value contracts such as municipalities, to negotiate terms with CSPs.[24]

On the technical side, cloud integrators play an important role in customizing services and helping cloud clients move from their legacy or existing systems into cloud services. Furthermore, the integrator may add capabilities such as enhanced security, access or identity management, or audit and reporting capabilities.[25] This can be accomplished by combining a CSP's offering with the integrator's technology or when an integrator contracts with multiple suppliers to provide a service.[26]

To provide a well-publicized example, when exploring cloud adoption for its 30,000 employees, the City of Los Angeles entered into a $7,250,000,00 contract with the integrator Computer Science Corporation (CSC) and an additional contract with Google.[27] As an integrator, CSC would customize certain Google applications while also taking on additional liability. In fact, CSC took on the majority of the risk accepting liability up to $7.7 million instead of Google's standard $1,000 liability cap.[28] In addition to the larger liability cap, CSC also agreed to indemnify the City of Los Angeles for third-party lawsuits, data loss, among other events giving rise to liability. Although the deployment was more limited than originally planned, the contract provides an early example of the role of third parties in bridging the gap between government requirements and CSP offerings.[29]

2.3 CLOUD SERVICE MODELS

The amount of control the cloud client or the CSP has over their data will depend in part on the cloud model being offered. Essentially, service models define the boundary between the CSP and cloud client's network. There are three general service models available:

- Infrastructure as a Service (IaaS) provides the cloud client with computing resources such as processing power and/or storage used by businesses, consumers, and other cloud service providers. Under this model, the user has control over the operating system, applications, and data that is stored on the cloud service. Cloud clients essentially rent the space they need on a virtualized server.

---

[24] W. Kuan Hon, Christopher Millard, and Ian Walden, 'Negotiated Contracts for Cloud Services' in Christopher Millard (ed.), *Cloud Computing Law* (Oxford: Oxford University Press 2013), p. 79.
[25] Bernstein and others, 'US Government Cloud Computing Technology Roadmap', 11.
[26] ibid.
[27] Daniel Carmeli, 'Keep an I on the Sky: E-discovery Risks Forecasted for Apple's iCloud' (2013) *Boston College Intellectual Property and Technology Forum* 1–26 at 12. http://bciptf.org/wp-content/uploads/2013/02/Daniel-Carmeli-Cloud-Computing.pdf.
[28] ibid., 11.
[29] ibid., 12–13. Comparing the City of Los Angeles contract to the terms obtained by the City of Pittsburgh in a similar deployment with Google Applications and finding the City of Los Angeles obtained more favourable terms including much broader indemnities.

- Platform as a Service (PaaS) provides software for constructing (and usually deploying) custom applications.[30] Here the cloud client has control over applications and data but utilizes the CSP's operating system.
- Software as a Service (SaaS)[31] provides the end user with access to software and other computing resources. Under this model, the cloud client has the least amount of control. The cloud client does not control software, applications, or storage used to perform computing functions.

Although I note these are the core services, new variations or business models are being created all the time. The EC has discussed a 'Government as a Service' (GaaS) model, envisioned as a cloud platform for public authorities to 'open their data and services' for government cloud in the EU.[32] However, many of these services are difficult to distinguish from existing models, for example, Communications as a Service (CaaS), Data as a Service (DaaS), Data Protection as a Service (DPaaS), Monitoring as a Service (MaaS), Network as a Service (NaaS), Security as a Service (SECaaS), and the all-inclusive Everything as a Service (XaaS). Many of these variations are more aptly characterized as marketing achievements than technical ones.

The lines between the services are not always clear. Some CSPs provide a mixture of services that incorporate overlapping aspects and result in 'layered' services.[33] CSPs may also be users of other cloud services themselves. For example, a CSP offering SaaS may not have its own server infrastructure. In that case, the SaaS provider will be a cloud client of IaaS. The end user signing up for the SaaS product will essentially be using more than one type of cloud service.[34]

2.4 CLOUD COMPUTING DEPLOYMENT MODELS

In addition to different service models, not all clouds are created with equal accessibility. Currently, there are several primary models of cloud computing, including 'private', 'public', and 'hybrid' clouds.[35]

---

[30] Maury Nichols and others, 'Chasing the Clouds without Getting Drenched: A Call for Fair Practices in Cloud Computing Services' (2011) 16 *Journal of Technology Law & Policy* 193–228 at 198.
[31] ibid. SaaS examples include Google Docs, Salesforce CRM, SAP Business by Design.
[32] European Commission, 'Communication from the Commission to the European Parliament, the Council, the European Economic and Social Committee and the Committee of the Regions European Cloud Initiative – Building a Competitive Data and Knowledge Economy in Europe' (2016) COM (2016) 178 final, 12. https://ec.europa.eu/digital-single-market/en/news/communication-european-cloud-initiative-building-competitive-data-and-knowledge-economy-europe.
[33] Hon and Millard, 'Cloud Technologies and Services', pp. 15–16.
[34] ibid., 13–14. Stating that 'users may not necessarily know how a cloud service has been put together or who supplies, provides, or operates different components'.
[35] See generally Anne C. Datesh, 'Storms Brewing in the Cloud: Why Copyright Law Will Have to Adapt to the Future of Web 2.0' (2012) 40 *American Intellectual Property Law Association Quarterly Journal* 685–726 at 690.

2.4.1 Private Clouds

On the most restrictive (and arguably secure) side of the spectrum, 'private clouds' are cloud computing services dedicated to a single organization or shared by members of the same corporate group.[36] Access to the private cloud is limited and allows the cloud client to exercise stricter boundary controls than other models.[37] If governments are required to store data in one location, private clouds often support jurisdictional and other legal requirements.[38]

2.4.2 Community Clouds

Community clouds are similar to private clouds in that they have controlled access and limit the parties that may use the computing resources. Instead of being limited to a single company, the community can be made up of several actors or organizations with similar security needs. The benefit of such an arrangement is a greater sharing of resources allowing for lower costs than a private cloud while also providing a greater level of security. The downside of a community cloud is that it may not perform either function well.[39] For example, it may be difficult to maintain a high level of security while opening the community resource up to enough actors to gain the benefits of scale including cost savings.

An example of a community cloud aimed at government users is the 'AWS GovCloud (US)' aimed at a community of US government agencies. In addition to only allowing access to a limited community, all cloud infrastructure is located in the United States, and only 'US persons' (a green card holder or citizen as defined by the US Department of State) are allowed to access data or work on GovCloud. The cloud service is restricted in an attempt to help US government users meet their compliance requirements, including meeting certain information security and government computing standards.[40]

2.4.3 Public Clouds

On what is generally considered the less secure side of the spectrum, 'public clouds' provide access to many users, often through the use of large data

---

[36] ibid.
[37] M. Auty and others, 'Inadequacies of Current Risk Controls for the Cloud' (2010) 2010 2nd IEEE International Conference on Cloud Computing Technology and Science 659–66 at 659. www.semanticscholar.org/paper/Inadequacies-of-Current-Risk-Controls-for-the-Cloud-Auty-Creese/eec62251b89662c29e899f0029b3df198dbfae72.
[38] ibid.
[39] Daniele Catteddu, 'Security & Resilience in Governmental Clouds' (17 January 2010), 55–56. www.enisa.europa.eu/publications/security-and-resilience-in-governmental-clouds.
[40] For example, Amazon GovCloud has obtained certification in of the following standards: HIPAA, SOC 1/SSAE 16/ISAE 3402 (formerly SAS70), ISO 27001, FedRAMP, among others. For an overview of Amazon's certifications and compliance, see https://aws.amazon.com/compliance/.

centres.[41] Although public clouds are privately held companies and are not 'public', in the general use of the term or run by governments, they are essentially open to the 'general public' for use.[42] That is, they do not require membership in a specific company or limit users to specific categories. Public clouds are generally the lowest-cost, most accessible, and most widely used cloud option. Many of the benefits of this model result from the large pool of available resources.[43] Moreover, a broad geographical distribution and high levels of security at the sites of the providers bring with them additional resilience and security benefits.[44]

Major concerns for government users with public cloud include the lack of control over the CSP's supply chain, ability to log operations and provide transparency, and inability to cater to regulatory requirements.[45] In many cases a CSP's global infrastructure makes it difficult to comply with individual state regulations requiring that data be stored within a specific jurisdiction.[46] Additional public cloud concerns come from the internal technical complexity of the services, potentially resulting in isolation failure or leakage.[47] Public clouds deal in volume. It is, therefore, generally more difficult for cloud clients to negotiate specific contract terms.

2.4.4 Hybrid Clouds

Organizational forms incorporating aspects of the other structures have also been incorporated. 'Hybrid clouds' combine public and private cloud elements to provide a higher level of security but also allow users to take part in the savings offered by public clouds. Sensitive or core functions are often kept on in-house private networks, while less sensitive functions are sent to public clouds. By combining the services, the cloud client takes advantage of the economy of scale benefits while also receiving the benefits of greater security. However, the cloud client does not obtain the maximum benefits of either security or price.

2.5 CLOUD COMPUTING SECURITY CONCERNS

Although cloud computing may not constitute a new technology, organization of the services creates new security challenges.[48] Concerns surrounding security

---

[41] David Lametti, 'The Cloud: Boundless Digital Potential or Enclosure 3.0?' (2012) 17 *Virginia Journal of Law & Technology* 192–243 at 210–11.
[42] ibid.
[43] Catteddu, 'Security & Resilience in Governmental Clouds', 50.
[44] ibid.
[45] ibid.
[46] ibid.
[47] ibid.
[48] Wayne Jansen and Timothy Grance, 'Guidelines on Security and Privacy in Public Cloud Computing' (2011) SP 800–144, 10–12. https://nvlpubs.nist.gov/nistpubs/Legacy/SP/nistspecialpublication800-144.pdf.

remain one of the primary inhibitors of cloud computing uptake.[49] Cloud security is often evaluated or defined through the lens of Confidentiality, Integrity, and Availability of data (CIA).[50] In addition to data breaches, loss of confidentiality in cloud computing may occur when data is made available to partners, subcontractors, or other parties without permission or a legal basis for access.[51]

Loss of integrity in cloud is generally attributed to problems with retrieval of information, corrupted data, inability to correct data, or other losses.[52] Loss of availability occurs when information is not accessible. Lack of interoperability, 'lock-in', or other limits to data portability can also trigger availability issues.[53] Additionally, a failure or outage at one layer of a service (i.e. the IaaS layer) will affect the SaaS provider and all of their customers.[54] If an outage occurs, the larger the CSP the more likely it is to affect availability of many users or organizations simultaneously.[55]

For example, because of a coding typo, Amazon Web Services (AWS) experienced an outage of its S3 (Simple Storage Solution), a major cloud offering.[56] While trying to diagnose and repair a billing problem on a subset of servers, an incorrect command led to a much wider outage affecting many businesses and providers that rely on AWS infrastructure to provide their services, creating a domino effect.[57] For instance, Apple Inc., which also uses AWS infrastructure to provide some of its iCloud service, also experienced outages.[58] Users with 'smart' lightbulbs were unable to turn on their lights because the cloud-based service managing the technology was also offline.[59] Analysts estimated that the AWS S3 outage cost companies

---

[49] Jared A. Harshbarger, 'Cloud Computing Providers and Data Security Law: Building Trust with United States Companies' (2011) 16 *Journal of Technology Law & Policy* 229–56 at 235–38. See also Roger Clarke, 'Data Risks in the Cloud' (2013) 8 *Journal of Theoretical and Applied Electronic Commerce Research* 59–73 at 59.

[50] W. Kuan Hon, *Data Localization Laws and Policy: The EU Data Protection International Transfers Restriction Through a Cloud Computing Lens* (Cheltenham and Northampton, MA: Edward Elgar 2017), pp. 264–71. Applying the CIA triad to data privacy law. WP29 196, 'Opinion on Cloud Computing 05/2012', 4–6.

[51] WP29 196, 'Opinion on Cloud Computing 05/2012', 5. The WP29 further provides that to 'contribute to confidentiality' encryption should be used when data is 'in transit' and 'at rest' in cloud computing.

[52] ibid., 5.

[53] ibid., 5.

[54] Hon and Millard, 'Cloud Technologies and Services', p. 16. Jansen and Grance, 'NIST Guidelines on Security and Privacy', 18.

[55] ENISA, 'Critical Cloud Computing: A CIIP Perspective on Cloud Computing Services Version 1.0' (2012), 6. www.enisa.europa.eu/publications/critical-cloud-computing.

[56] Samuel Gibbs, 'Typo Blamed for Amazon's Internet-Crippling Outage', *The Guardian Online*, 3 March 2017. www.theguardian.com/technology/2017/mar/03/typo-blamed-amazon-web-services-internet-outage.

[57] ibid.

[58] Rebecca Hersher, 'Amazon and the $150 Million Typo', *National Public Radio Online*, 3 March 2017. www.npr.org/sections/thetwo-way/2017/03/03/518322734/amazon-and-the-150-million-typo.

[59] Gibbs, 'Typo Blamed for Amazon's Internet-Crippling Outage', 1.

in the S&P 500 index $150 million.[60] Although such outages are rare, when they occur, they can be extremely disruptive.

Falling under the broader umbrella of trust, common cloud computing client concerns largely revolve around being able to access their data, unexpected losses of data, and the inability to restrict other parties from accessing information they store on the service.[61] In some cases, cloud clients are able to mitigate security risks by applying proper logical and physical security.[62] Logical protections include encrypting data, reducing access through strict authentication and monitoring networks. Physical security includes protecting infrastructure at the location of the CSP in addition to limiting the network of partners and location of subcontractors. After all, cloud clients face varied levels of risk depending on the data they have and the services they adopt (e.g. IaaS vs. SaaS). In many instances, CSPs will have no intelligible access to data.[63] In others, CSPs will have a great deal.

The lack of transparency of many cloud services, limited ability to audit services, and new or developing industry standards increase the apprehension of cloud clients.[64] For instance, continuous monitoring of security requires a certain level of access to the computing environment, which is under the CSPs control.[65] If CSPs are unwilling to provide information regarding privacy and security measures, the security monitoring will be incomplete.[66] If cloud clients are not able to assess risks, they will also be unable to take the necessary steps to treat or reduce risks to an acceptable level.[67] As a result, the use of public cloud may be essentially 'off-limits' for certain uses or users.[68]

Although this section has focused on problems and security lapses, for the most part, cloud services have been incredibly stable, available, and secure. Generally,

---

[60] Hersher, 'Amazon and the $150 Million Typo', 1.
[61] Jansen and Grance, 'NIST Guidelines on Security and Privacy', 18–22. See also European Data Protection Supervisor, 'Guidelines on the Use of Cloud Computing Services by the European Institutions and Bodies' (2018), 6. https://edps.europa.eu/data-protection/our-work/publications/guidelines/guidelines-use-cloud-computing-services-european_en. Providing that EU institutions cannot lower their level of data protection in order to use cloud computing services.
[62] Hon, 'Localization Laws and Policy', pp. 274–76. Explaining that logical security refers to the software limiting access to data. Physical security regarding the 'metal' where infrastructure resides. Security risks in cloud computing general occur because of breakdowns in logical security rather (e.g. over a network) rather than physical (e.g. access to a server park).
[63] W. K. Hon, Christopher Millard, and Ian Walden, 'What is Regulated as Personal Data in Clouds?' in Christopher Millard (ed.), *Cloud Computing Law* (Oxford: Oxford University Press 2013), p. 175. For instance, if data are managed externally by a cloud client and encrypted before being stored on a CSPs infrastructure, the CSP have no access to their customer data.
[64] Hon, Millard, and Walden, 'Negotiating Cloud Contracts', 112. Gasser, 'Cloud Innovation and the Law: Issues, Approaches, and Interplay', 16.
[65] Jansen and Grance, 'NIST Guidelines on Security and Privacy', 20.
[66] ibid.
[67] ibid.
[68] Christopher S. Yoo, 'Cloud Computing, Contractibility, and Network Architecture' in Christopher S. Yoo and Jean-Francois Blanchette (eds.), *Regulating the Cloud: Policy for Computing Infrastructure* (Cambridge, MA: MIT Press 2015), p. 118.

cloud computing brings with it security and privacy strengths, including stronger platforms, more specialized staff able to commit greater resources to security and privacy issues, stronger platforms resulting from continuous development and testing, greater availability of resources, among others.[69] For SMEs and municipalities, in addition to other government users, the government actor's security will improve substantially when they move their services to cloud. Using a larger provider with a uniform and well-developed platform often results in a more robust secure system that receives constant monitoring and maintenance.[70]

---

[69] Jansen and Grance, 'NIST Guidelines on Security and Privacy', 8.
[70] ibid., 9.

PART II

Legal Requirements and Adoption of Government Cloud

In this part, which contains Chapters 3, 4, and 5, I examine the increasingly common situation in which a government moves from a traditional IT outsourcing solution to cloud computing services. Building on the initial queries and the technical overview presented in Part I, this part evaluates governments' primary legal requirements when using and procuring cloud services. Chapter 3 evaluates the legal obligations that are, to a certain degree, specific to governments adopting cloud computing services. In particular, Chapter 3 focuses on the 'enhanced' or 'special' obligations that governments owe to their citizens. In Chapter 4, this section evaluates conflicts and problem areas associated with access by law enforcement and foreign governments to cloud services. The legal requirements related to data protection and data privacy laws are further evaluated in Chapter 5.

3

Government Cloud Adoption

Challenges and Obligations

Like private industry, governments rely heavily on IT and require increasingly complex systems to deliver their services to citizens. Although often considered among the most cautious to relinquish control over their systems and data, governments have become more willing to outsource their IT needs over the past decades to private providers who carry out a growing list of tasks or functions.[1] As governments have increased their willingness to outsource, changes have also been made in the control and delivery of IT. In addition to a greater willingness to digitize the public sector, the days when states alone owned the most advanced technologies necessary to do so are largely over. Private parties are now in control of the technologies that governments need to run efficiently.[2]

As technological ownership continues to shift away from governments towards control by private actors, governments will either need to build/create the technologies they use in-house or pay private providers to meet those needs.[3] The clear choice for most states has been the latter. In terms of government IT consumption, 'IT-by-contract' is the reality for many states. Governments now outsource everything from email applications to intelligence gathering.[4] The shift away from government in favour of private delivery and control over IT shows no signs of ebbing with cloud

---

[1] Alfred C. Aman and Joseph C. Dugan, 'The Human Side of Public-Private Partnerships: From New Deal Regulation to Administrative Law Management' (2017) 102 *Iowa Law Review* 883–937 at 886. Noting that the kinds of activities governments outsource have also expanded. Michael A. Zuckerman, 'The Offshoring of American Government' (2008) 94 *Cornell Law Review* 165–202 at 168–73.

[2] Kimberly N. Brown, 'Outsourcing, Data Insourcing, and the Irrelevant Constitution' (2015) 49 *Georgia Law Review* 607–91 at 617.

[3] Stan Soloway and Alan Chvotkin, 'Federal Contracting in Context: What Drives It, How to Improve It' in Jody Freeman and Martha Minow (eds.), *Government by Contract: Outsourcing and American Democracy* (Cambridge, MA: Harvard University Press 2009), p. 208. See Nadezhda Purtova, 'Between the GDPR and the Police Directive: Navigating through the Maze of Information Sharing in Public–Private Partnerships' (2018) 8 *International Data Privacy Law* 52–68 at 54.

[4] Simon Chesterman, 'Intelligence Services' in Simon Chesterman and Angelina Fisher (eds.), *Private Security, Public Order: The Outsourcing of Public Services and Its Limits* (Oxford: Oxford University Press 2009), p. 184. Simon Chesterman, '"We Can't Spy ... If We Can't Buy!": The Privatization of Intelligence and the Limits of Outsourcing "Inherently Governmental Functions"' (2008) 19 *European Journal of International Law* 1055–74 at 1056. Arguing that private contractors now ' ...

computing. In the United States, seventeen intelligence agencies entered into a $600 million contract with AWS for the Intelligence Community Information Enterprise (ICITE) cloud deployment for sharing data.[5] In mid 2020 the US government invited bids to build an intelligence agency infrastructure with a contract price of $12.6 billion.[6] Similar high-value procurement contracts are now moving US government defence functions to cloud computing.[7] In short, after dipping their toes in cloud usage, governments have begun jumping in with both feet.

Governmental interest in cloud computing is further evident in cloud computing strategies across the EU and the United States. In adopting cloud computing, most governments have opted to use existing services offered by private CSPs rather than build their own. In other words, 'government clouds', at least in the case of the United States, United Kingdom, and the EU, are procurement, risk assessment, and certification methods rather than plans for developing cloud computing technologies in-house.[8] Thus, governments are pursuing a 'compliance through template' or 'compliance through procurement contract' approach to cloud computing. The goal of these programmes is essentially to require private CSPs to meet the government's requirements, often on the government's contract terms.

Although cloud computing strategies often set lofty goals, outsourcing government IT is a highly debated topic. The debate most often centres on the minimization of traditional barriers between private and public sectors and the potential for conflicts of interest.[9] After all, the result of outsourcing is often that privately held corporations perform functions once thought to be 'inherently governmental'.[10] When private actors begin performing what have traditionally been government functions, questions regarding accountability and transparency become immediately apparent.[11] As noted by Gleeson and Walden, ' ... as "guardians of the public

hold the reins on surveillance technology for the first time in history ... '. Brown, 'Outsourcing, Data Insourcing, and the Irrelevant Constitution', 690.
[5] Louise Amoore, 'Cloud Geographies: Computing, Data, Sovereignty' (2018) 42 *Progress in Human Geography* 4–24 at 5–6.
[6] Frank Konkel, *Nextgov* (8 July 2020) www.nextgov.com/emerging-tech/2020/07/12-billion-intelligence-it-contract-out-bid/166731/.
[7] D. E. Sanger and S. Shane, 'Microsoft Wins Pentagon's $10 Billion JEDI Contract, Thwarting Amazon', *New York Times*, 29 October 2019. www.nytimes.com/2019/10/25/technology/dod-jedi-contract.html.
[8] W. Kuan Hon, Christopher Millard, and Ian Walden, 'Negotiating Cloud Contracts: Looking at Clouds from Both Sides Now' (2012) 16 *Stanford Technology Law Review* 79–130 at 108–10.
[9] Brown, 'Outsourcing, Data Insourcing, and the Irrelevant Constitution', 616. Examples of such outsourcing include military operations on the battlefield, drafting regulations, and management of nuclear weapons sites, among others.
[10] Nina A. Mendelson, 'Six Simple Steps to Increase Contractor Accountability' in Jody Freeman and Martha Minow (eds.), *Government by Contract: Outsourcing and American Democracy* (Cambridge, MA: Harvard University Press 2009), p. 241.
[11] Anne C. L. Davies, *The Public Law of Government Contracts* (Oxford: Oxford University Press 2008), pp. 231–32.

trust" they [governments] have enhanced obligations, whether grounded in law or ethics, to ensure the security of sensitive government data'.[12] This public trust obligation is often reinforced through additional contracting requirements, placed on governments, which focus on transparency, non-discrimination, security, and accountability through independent audits.

Outsourcing is, and will continue to be, a reality in delivering government services. I do not argue that we either can or should reverse the trend. At the same time, as outlined by Soloway and Chvotkin, it is possible to 'recognize the reality of outsourcing but remain concerned about the issues of accountability, transparency, and the protection of the public interest and democratic principles'.[13] Specifically, I am concerned about the ability of states to protect and secure the privacy rights of citizens when governments do their governing using a private provider's infrastructure. Moreover, once private providers gain access to governmental data, what type of impact might this have on citizens? For instance, Google has nearly 100 products aimed at consumers that collect and process data.[14] Citizen-consumers provide a significant amount of data and feed these platforms voluntarily. If Google, which already possesses massive amounts of personal data, then obtains access to government data, ranging from tax information to health and educational records, the potential loss of privacy is enormous.

As a starting point, many of the challenges that governments face in adopting cloud computing services arise from the use of globally sourced services that are often spread across many different providers. However, in addition to the 'bigger' questions surrounding transparency and accountability, many practical barriers to the adoption of cloud are also apparent. Governments are often subject to highly regulated procurement and contracting regimes. Moreover, governments often have strict archival and bookkeeping requirements for audit and other purposes. Additionally, governments are often required to meet FOIA obligations and must have a means of responding to citizen enquiries.[15] The right to request and view governmental documents is an essential element of transparency and in some contexts is considered a fundamental right.[16] Although private providers might have some of the same requirements, such as bookkeeping duties, they are generally more limited in comparison and are not subject to the same types of FOIA disclosure

---

[12] Niamh Gleeson and Ian Walden, 'Placing the State in the Cloud: Issues of Data Governance and Public Procurement' (2016) 32 *Computer Law & Security Review* 683–95 at 684.

[13] Soloway and Chvotkin, 'Federal Contracting in Context', p. 194.

[14] Samson Y. Esayas, 'The Idea of "Emergent Properties" in Data Privacy: Towards a Holistic Approach' (2017) 25 *International Journal of Law and Information Technology* 139–78 at 143–44 and 151–52.

[15] Gleeson and Walden, 'Placing the State in the Cloud', 684.

[16] For example, the Treaty on the Functioning of the European Union Article 15(3) provides that 'Any citizen of the Union, and any natural or legal person residing or having its registered office in a Member State, *shall have a right of access to documents* of the Union's institutions, ... '. Emphasis added. Further, the Charter of Fundamental Rights of the European Union Article 42 provides a similar right to access to documents.

requirements.[17] If private providers are asked to provide information, their obligation to respond is much more limited, as is the scope of their disclosure.

Furthermore, states often hold extremely sensitive data about their citizens, including individual medical records and other data concerning health, income information, employment information, census data, tax records, and in some cases data on criminal convictions. If a government were to lose control over its data, there would be significant political consequences that might even affect a state's ability to govern. Thus, governments have strict obligations to ensure that public information and the IT systems they utilize to store it are secure.[18]

In addition to confidentiality and security obligations, governments need to make certain that the services they choose will be available, accessible, and resilient. For example, if a state outsources its tax assessment systems to a third party and those systems fail or become unavailable, the government may have a difficult time collecting revenue. Furthermore, governments must also keep public data confidential. While private providers may feel comfortable hosting public data abroad or settling disputes regarding their data in a foreign country, this calculation is unusually different for governments as they have more at risk.[19] This is particularly the case when such decisions regard government operations and citizens' data.[20]

Technical difficulties, including interoperability and complications with migration, are also significant concerns for governments. Transitioning away from legacy systems that have been designed, developed, and used exclusively by a government agency for many years often face serious interoperability problems. Organizational and 'cultural' aspects or approaches to government IT may also serve as a barrier. In short, government agencies are often unwilling to cede control over their IT. Furthermore, in addition to more general availability concerns, 'locked-in' and concentration risks emanating from being connected to a single provider are central concerns for governments.[21]

In evaluating governmental barriers to cloud adoption, Section 3.1 provides a general assessment of 'data sovereignty' and concerns surrounding 'contracting out' functions that have traditionally been performed by governments. This chapter further evaluates specific barriers governments face in adopting cloud computing services, and analyses cloud adoption programs or strategies applied by various governments in the EU, United Kingdom, and the United States. Early adopters

---

[17] However, Chapter 3 of the GDPR does provide citizens with certain individual rights to request and obtain personal data from data controllers. See GDPR Art. 15.
[18] Kristina Irion, 'Government Cloud Computing and National Data Sovereignty' (2012) 4 *Policy and Internet* 40–71 at 41.
[19] ibid.
[20] ibid.
[21] Gleeson and Walden, 'Placing the State in the Cloud', 685–86. Additional aspects, such as national security requirements and critical infrastructure obligations, make cloud adoption more complicated for governments.

of government cloud computing, including the United Kingdom's G-Cloud and the United States' FedRAMP, provide examples that are used throughout this book.[22]

3.1 DATA SOVEREIGNTY AS A BARRIER TO GOVERNMENTAL ADOPTION

In addition to the individual value placed on citizen data or information, collectively, this information is extremely important to governments. As provided by Irion, 'public sector information embodies the past, the present, and the future of a - country'.[23] Governments also need to consider the public responsibilities they have to ensure data security and integrity over the long term, among their other custodial roles. In discussing the role of the public sector, the concepts of sovereignty and the protection of public sector data are generally inseparable.[24] Together, they are known as 'data sovereignty'. Given the differences in the existing definitions and conceptions of sovereignty, it is not surprising that competing or even conflicting definitions of data sovereignty have emerged.[25]

In technical publications, the terms 'data sovereignty' and 'data residency' are sometimes used interchangeably. In the cloud context, where information is 'created' and where it is 'stored' are often two separate places. As will be expanded in Chapter 4's examination of jurisdiction, the location of data storage is extremely flexible in cloud computing. Additionally, definitions of sovereignty focused solely on infrastructure location make it difficult to account for copies, backups, and separate concepts like storage location and intelligible access.[26]

Although data sovereignty encompasses many aspects of data control or integrity, it is often more broadly defined than pertaining to security or privacy alone.[27]

---

[22] Analysis in this book is limited to western democracies. Concepts such as public trust, governmental responsibility, and accountability, are likely perceived and evaluated differently on a more global basis.
[23] Irion, 'Government Cloud Computing and National Data Sovereignty', 53.
[24] Kevin Kalinich and others, 'Data Sovereignty and the Cloud: A Board and Executive Officer's Guide' (2013) 1 *Cyberspace Law and Policy Centre, UNSW Faculty of Law* 1–83 at 13. www.cyberlawcentre.org/data_sovereignty/CLOUD_DataSovReport_Full.pdf.
[25] Radim Polčák and Dan Jerker B. Svantesson, *Information Sovereignty: Data Privacy, Sovereign Powers and the Rule of Law* (Northampton, MA: Edward Elgar 2017), p. 60. Kuan Hon, *Data Localization Laws and Policy: The EU Data Protection International Transfers Restriction Through a Cloud Computing Lens* (Cheltenham and Northampton, MA: Edward Elgar 2017), pp. 26–28. See also Kristina Irion, 'Your Digital Home Is No Longer Your Castle: How Cloud Computing Transforms the (Legal) Relationship between Individuals and Their Personal Records' (2015) 23 *International Journal of Law and Information Technology* 348–71 at 356.
[26] Carol M. Celestine, 'Cloudy Skies, Bright Futures? In Defense of a Private Regulatory Scheme for Policing Cloud Computing' (2013) 2013 *University of Illinois Journal of Law Technology and Policy* 142–64 at 148–49. https://heinonline.org/HOL/LandingPage?handle=hein.journals/jltp2013&div=9&id=&page=. Providing 'data sovereignty, or sovereignty in the context of cloud computing, is simply the notion that data should be subject to the laws of the nations in which it is created and stored'.
[27] Ashley Deeks, 'An International Legal Framework for Surveillance' (2015) 55 *Virginia Journal of International Law* 291–368 at 304.

Generally, the concept carries political undertones that go beyond a legal or technical discussion. Moreover, as noted by Hon, 'your country having "sovereignty" over your data is not the same as you having sovereignty over your data'.[28] In that respect, there is also the potential for conflict between data sovereignty and data privacy – at least when the interests of the citizen and the state diverge.

Drawing sovereignty along national lines alone is overly simplistic if the term is to be associated with an actor's ability to maintain *control* over their data. Data might be located within a nation's borders, but if the physical server where the data resides is not secure and can be accessed by those outside the territory, then that data are no longer under the *control* of the sovereign state.[29] After all, having physical control over a server holding data in a specific jurisdiction is not necessarily more secure than data with strong technical/logical protections located abroad.[30]

In the case of states, Irion defined data sovereignty as a '[g]overnment's exclusive authority and control over all virtual public assets, which are not in the public domain, irrespective of whether they are stored on their own or third parties' facilities and premises'.[31] In this book, I generally apply Irion's definition since it recognizes and focuses on control, irrespective of the premises where the data are stored. That is, data may be stored abroad or with a CSP – as long as the government retains adequate control over the data, it may be considered sovereign. Although this concept might benefit from a risk-based approach acknowledging different levels of control, and therefore varied levels of sovereignty, conceptually, the definition is helpful.

The fact that governments are concerned with the requirement to appear in a foreign jurisdiction is unsurprising. Even within a federal sovereign state, actors may be unwilling to accede to the jurisdictions of different levels of government. For example, in guidance on agency cloud adoption by the US Department of Defense (DoD), the US federal government considers its data sovereign, and as such, the jurisdiction of US state courts does not apply.[32] Other states, including the Russian Federation and Singapore, have placed restrictions on the storage of citizen data outside of the country based on apparent sovereignty concerns.[33]

---

[28] Hon, 'Localization Laws and Policy', pp. 27–28.
[29] Christopher Millard, 'Forced Localization of Cloud Services: Is Privacy the Real Driver?' (2015) 2 *IEEE Cloud Computing* 10–14 at 13. Arguing that physical data located in Germany, if poorly protected, could be accessible from anywhere on the planet.
[30] ibid.
[31] Irion, 'Government Cloud Computing and National Data Sovereignty', 41.
[32] Inspector General US Department of Defense (DoD), 'DoD Cloud Computing Strategy Needs Implementation Plan and Detailed Waiver Process' (2014) *Report No DODIG-2015-045*, 23. www.dtic.mil/dtic/tr/fulltext/u2/a613689.pdf. Sasha Segall, 'Jurisdictional Challenges in the United States Government's Move to Cloud Computing Technology' (2013) 23 *Fordham Intellectual Property, Media and Entertainment Law Journal* 1105–53 at 1137.
[33] Hon, 'Localization Laws and Policy', pp. 26–27.

3.2 EXAMPLES OF STATE CLOUD AND IT OUTSOURCING

Before evaluating the limits that governments place on outsourcing to cloud computing or other IT solutions, I evaluate some of the potential risks or harms of such outsourcing. The Section 3.2.1 evaluates three cases that demonstrate the relationship between aspects of outsourcing government IT and their potential risks to citizens and critical infrastructure. The cases include the Norwegian National Health Service, a Norwegian oil company, and a US state government. These cases demonstrate that state outsourcing of IT affects critical infrastructure such as oil platforms, healthcare, and the ability to provide essential services to citizens when the government puts a private actor in charge of a government function. Although not all of the outsourcing deployments are formally defined as cloud services, they outsource and offshore core IT functions to third parties, leaving the government with limited control over those operations, in the same manner as cloud services.

3.2.1 Norwegian and Nordic Outsourcing

Norway, along with other Nordic countries, has been the focus of a raft of media attention related to its IT outsourcing of government functions.[34] In 2017, the Norwegian DPA fined the regional public health service provider Helse Sør-Øst ('Health South-East' or 'HSE') a combined amount of 7.2 million NOK.[35] The fine followed complaints made to the DPA by both patients and employees of HSE concerned about violations of data protection and other laws.[36] Like many other national healthcare services, HSE outsourced certain IT operations to third-party providers.[37] Norwegian authorities allow outsourcing of IT services in the health sector in principle, but outsourcing guidelines require that the provider follow Norwegian law.[38] The HSE outsourcing project is significant because it was the largest IT outsourcing project in which the Norwegian health services moved its IT infrastructure to a provider located outside of the country.[39] The contract was to be

---

[34] L. Tomter and A. C. Remen, 'Datatilsynet Fant Lovbrudd: Millionbøter Etter outsourcing av Sykehus-IT' [The Norwegian Data Protection Authority Found a Violation of the Law: Million NOK Fine for the Outsourcing of Hospital IT], NRK, 27 October 2017. www.nrk.no/norge/million boter-etter-outsourcing-av-sykehus-it-1.13751516.

[35] ibid. The fine was distributed among nine actors in the Norwegian Health Services, requiring a payment of 800,000 NOK (approximately 80,000 EUR) each. Bjørn Erik Thon (Datatilsynet [Norwegian DPA]), *Varsel om vedtak – overtredelsesgebyr – Akershus universitetssykehus HF* [Notification of Decision and Fine – Akershus University Hospital] (2017) 4 (henceforth Norwegian DPA, 'Notification of Decision and Fine').

[36] ibid., 6. An audit conducted by PricewaterhouseCoopers (PwC) found that HSE lacked control over access to their systems. ibid., 8.

[37] ibid., 3.

[38] ibid., 7.

[39] ibid., 3.

performed over a seven-year period with a 6.9 billion NOK (approximately 700 million Euro) price tag.[40]

HSE's outsourcing failed to meet legal requirements on many levels. Specifically, HSE failed to put in place adequate security measures to limit access to patient data.[41] Furthermore, HSE failed to maintain control over patient data by ensuring that those accessing the sensitive health data of 2.8 million Norwegians had the appropriate security clearance.[42] The result was that IT workers in India, Bulgaria, and the United States potentially had access to medical records, including sensitive personal data, without proper controls in place.[43] This violated Norwegian data protection law and the patient medical records law, among other legal acts.[44]

The Norwegian DPA found the overall lack of control over data exercised by HSE to be particularly problematic.[45] Furthermore, the DPA noted that HSE did not conduct risk evaluations on the primary outsourcing provider or its subcontractors, as required under Norwegian law.[46] Overall, the DPA found that HSE had not accounted for, or perhaps did not understand, the legal requirements related to outsourcing hospital functions and sensitive personal data to third parties.

Norway is not alone in facing challenges when outsourcing government IT functions. In neighbouring Sweden, an IT outsourcing scandal essentially forced the resignation of two government ministers.[47] When entering into IT outsourcing/ cloud computing projects, Swedish ministers waived existing security clearance requirements for the foreign IT consultants.[48] As a result, the consultants obtained broad access to not only the Swedish driver's licence database, as planned, but also to information on military and intelligence personnel, individuals in the witness protection programme, and other extremely sensitive personal data. Such broad access violated data protection laws, among others. As in the Norwegian example, the Swedish government failed to maintain adequate levels of control over access to sensitive government data. The Swedish example shows an exceptional disregard for accepted data security practices, such as role-based access.

---

[40] ibid., 7.
[41] ibid., 3–4.
[42] Tomter and Remen, 'The Norwegian Data Protection Authority Found a Violation of the Law'.
[43] Norwegian DPA, 'Notification of Decision and Fine', 11.
[44] ibid., 3–4.
[45] ibid., 10–11.
[46] ibid., 11.
[47] Jon Henley, 'Sweden Scrambles to Tighten Data Security as Scandal Claims Two Ministers', *The Guardian*, 1 August 2017. www.theguardian.com/technology/2017/aug/01/sweden-scrambles-to-tighten-data-security-as-scandal-claims-two-ministers.
[48] S. Shah, 'Director Who Outsourced Swedish Government Database to the Cloud, Where Critical Data Was Compromised, Fined Just £6,500', *Computing*, 24 July 2017. www.computing.co.uk/ctg/news/3014334/director-who-outsourced-swedish-government-database-to-the-cloud-where-critical-data-was-compromised-fined-just-gbp6-500.

3.2.2 Outsourcing Critical Infrastructure

Equinor (previously Statoil) is a formerly Norwegian state-owned oil company where the Norwegian state remains the largest shareholder.[49] To reduce IT expenses, Equinor outsourced many of its core IT functions. Working remotely from India, IT consultants had access and control over offshore oil platforms in the North Sea in addition to onshore production facilities.[50] Although the IT consultants would be performing maintenance and other functions, control over production was designed to take place locally. However, the logical protections in the system broke down, posing serious risks to employees and others.[51]

At an Equinor refinery in Norway, employees were preparing to load 50,000 cubic meters of fuel into a tanker ship.[52] An Indian IT consultant gave an incorrect command to the system, thereby shutting down production at the Norwegian facility. In attempting to correct the mistake, twenty-two additional unauthorized logins were made to the 'secure' system from India.[53] Based on the outsourcing plan, none of the actors should have been able to access the critical systems they shut down.[54] When asked about the risks, an Equinor employee adroitly noted: 'we are not exactly making chocolate here'.[55] The employee went on to explain that such mistakes are extremely dangerous and put the lives of those on the platforms at risk, among others.[56] Allowing remote access and control over core aspects of oil production raises many safety and security questions. Moreover, accidents are extremely costly and environmentally hazardous.

An additional issue with the outsourcing was that Equinor had little oversight or ability to conduct background checks on the credentials of the Indian IT consultants. It was further determined that many of the Indian IT consultants did not understand that they were supporting oil production and were under the assumption that Equinor was just another office building.[57] Based on media reports, it was clear that Equinor lacked oversight and ultimately control over the scope of its outsourcing.[58] Indian IT consultants had much greater access to its essential

---

[49] The Norwegian state owns approximately 70 per cent of Equinor shares. See www.equinor.com/en/about-us/corporate-governance/the-norwegian-state-as-shareholder.html.

[50] A. C. Remen and L. Tomter, 'Tastefeilen Som Stoppet Statoil' [The Typo That Stopped Statoil], NRK, 28 October 2016. www.nrk.no/norge/xl/tastefeilen-som-stoppet-statoil-1.13174013.

[51] H. Hills, 'Key Error in India Halted Production at Mongstad', Norway Today Online, 28 October 2016. http://norwaytoday.info/finance/key-error-india-halted-production-mongstad/. Providing ' ... 29 incidents where Indian IT workers have broken down barriers to platforms, onshore and central Statoil – but several sources have stated to NRK that the scale is much larger'.

[52] Remen and Tomter, 'The Typo That Stopped Statoil'.

[53] ibid.

[54] ibid.

[55] ibid.

[56] ibid.

[57] ibid.

[58] ibid. C.f. Petroleumstilsynet [Petroleum Safety Authority], 'Uriktige påstander om IKT-tilsyn i NRK' [Incorrect Claims on ICT Supervision at NRK] www.ptil.no/nyheter/uriktige-pastander-om-ikt-tilsyn

facilities, and Equinor had much less ability to limit access, than was prudent given the scope and seriousness of oil production. For instance, certain authorizations were intended to give a small number of 'super users' access to a greater number of facilities. However, the passwords were shared and spread among the IT outsourcing provider's employees. Eventually, over 100 users possessed the ability to stop oil production in Norway from abroad. This represented a sharp departure from acceptable security practices. Following the incident at the Norwegian facility, Equinor decided to move its 'critical tasks on IT infrastructure' back to Norway to be conducted internally.[59]

3.2.3 Outsourcing Government Obligations: State of Indiana v. IBM

The previous examples have primarily focused on data protection and data security. The following case shows how IT outsourcing of government functions can affect the delivery of essential government services and the importance of the contracts underlying the services. In the early 2000s, the US state of Indiana sought to improve how it delivered welfare services.[60] To provide citizens with everything from medical care to emergency food benefits, the state entered into a ten-year, $1.3 billion outsourcing contract with IBM to modernize its services. Indiana anticipated that IBM would streamline the way it provided welfare services to some of its most vulnerable populations employing remote eligibility, centralization, and the delivery of web-based services, including access to medical care, food, housing, and other life-sustaining benefits.

The outsourcing did not go as planned, and the project collapsed.[61] Citizens were unable to schedule medical appointments; they randomly lost their eligibility for services. Wait times for processing applications went up, and people were unable to contact officials.[62] In some cases, patients suffered complications as a result of delays.[63] Moreover, benefits were revoked without giving the legally required notice or adhering to other due process/procedural protections, including the right to appeal denials.[64] The US federal government became involved and voiced its

-i-nrk-article12392-702.html. The Petroleum Safety Authority's webpage maintains that NRK overstated aspects of its reporting on Equinor's outsourcing. This page has been removed and the Petroleum Safety Authority (PSA) has been admonished for failing to adequately address the incident. See also The Office of the Auditor General, 'Investigation of the PSA's Follow-up of Health, Safety and Environment in the Petroleum Industry' (2019) Document 3:6, 9–10. www.riksrevisjonen.no/globalassets/reports/en-2018-2019/psafollowup.pdf.

[59] Reuters Staff, 'Statoil Moves Key IT Tasks from India Back to Norway', *Reuters*, 30 June 2017. www.reuters.com/article/statoil-norway-cyber-idUSL8N1JR41E.

[60] *State of Indiana v. IBM*, 51 NE 3d 150 at 153 (Ind. 2016). See Wendy Netter Epstein, 'Contract Theory and the Failures of Public-Private Contracting' (2013) 34 *Cardozo Law Review* 2211–60 at 2222–23.

[61] Aman and Dugan, 'The Human Side of Public-Private Partnerships', 909.

[62] *State of Indiana v. IBM*, 51 NE 3d 150 at 1537 (Ind. 2016).

[63] Epstein, 'Failures of Public-Private Contracting', 2224.

[64] *State of Indiana v. IBM*, 51 NE 3d 150 at 156–57 (Ind. 2016).

concerns over the delivery of Medicare services and other federally funded programs.[65] Although IBM increased its staff and adjusted the outsourcing/centralization plans in an attempt to address the issues, delivery of services did not substantially improve.

Consequently, Indiana terminated its contract with IBM 'for cause' on a breach of contract theory.[66] At issue before the court was whether IBM materially breached the contract. Essentially, the question before the court was whether many 'smaller' failures added up to a material breach of the contract. The master service agreement (MSA) provided that a breach is material considering the agreement as a whole.[67] Therefore, the court evaluated whether IBM's performance failures, taken together, constituted a material breach. In making its determination, the court placed a great deal of emphasis on certain 'policy objectives' enumerated in the contract. The policy objectives focused on providing 'accurate', 'timely', and 'efficient' services to citizens.[68] The various levels of the Indiana court system had different opinions on the impact or status of the policy objectives in contract interpretation.[69] The Indiana Supreme Court found the policy objectives relevant.

An additional issue raised by the Indiana Supreme Court was the standard applicable in analysing the breach of contract. Both the trial and appellate court applied the common law standard for breach in Indiana, which follows the Restatement (Second) of Contracts § 241 (1981).[70] Because the contract terms were unambiguous in this matter, the Indiana Supreme Court held that 'the default common law Restatement factors do not apply in this case because the plain language of the MSA provides for evaluating the materiality of a breach'.[71] In other words, when a contract clearly provides the standard for addressing the breach, that standard governs.[72]

Although not necessarily a ground-breaking case for contract theory, the case is important for governments adopting cloud computing for two main reasons. First, it raises the preliminary question of what types of services (or data) are appropriate for cloud computing. If a government moves services that provide a gateway to medical care and food for its neediest citizens, and those systems fail, the fallout is likely to be serious. This is especially true for vulnerable populations as they are often in the most precarious positions and have the least capacity to assert their rights and inform the government of its failures.[73] Second, when protecting the interests of citizens,

---

[65] ibid., 156.
[66] ibid., 157.
[67] ibid., 159.
[68] ibid., 161.
[69] State of Indiana v. IBM, 51 NE 3d 150 at 162 (Ind. 2016). Finding that the policy objects were at the 'heart of the contract'.
[70] ibid., 160. The Restatement (Second) of Contracts § 241.
[71] ibid., 160.
[72] ibid., 169.
[73] Aman and Dugan, 'The Human Side of Public-Private Partnerships', 897.

contract terms are extremely important. Without the clear policy objectives placing citizens at the forefront of the contract, Indiana might have faced a much different situation. Although the citizens were not directly named as beneficiaries in the contract, their rights were included when providing the standard for breach as the policy interests were designed around protecting citizen beneficiaries. Including the interests of citizens in the contract terms was an extremely important factor in maintaining governmental accountability when outsourcing a government function.

3.3 GOVERNMENT AS A CLOUD CLIENT: PUBLIC ACTORS USING PRIVATE TOOLS

When governments access the private market to obtain IT services, they rely heavily on contracts.[74] Although states may be treated like other private parties when contracting, there are significant differences in the responsibilities states have towards citizens and the tools they have available to them to manage and mitigate such risks. In addition to the data sovereignty concerns outlined earlier, states have obligations to their citizens that differ greatly from the responsibilities corporations have towards their customers. Therefore, the contracts states enter into should reflect these priorities. As provided by Davies, 'the government does not cease to be the government simply because it is placing a contract'.[75] As such, unlike private actors, governments are often required to provide a greater level of transparency in their procurement and operating processes. These requirements may align poorly with aspects of the opaque cloud computing structure.

For example, a corporate cloud client might be able to accept contract terms that reduce or even exclude warranties or liability on behalf of the CSP, agree to litigate disputes in a foreign jurisdiction or submit disagreements to alternative dispute resolution. When accepting a CSP's contract terms, the corporate cloud client may obtain insurance for risks that they cannot manage through security or limit through other organizational or contractual measures. The types of risks governments face do not always lend themselves to the same degree of flexibility in accepting, externalizing, or mitigating risk. Although situations exist where a state can simply write a check – or perhaps have an insurer do so – not all damages incurred by governments can be recompensed monetarily. Moreover, if a private company experiences a massive data breach, they can declare bankruptcy, change their company name, or even cease operations. For governments, these types of extreme measures are rarely viable options.

In addition to the responsibilities governments have as stewards of their citizens' data, governments are also charged with using public funds responsibly and

---

[74] ibid., 916.
[75] Davies, 'The Public Law of Government Contracts', p. 88.

effectively. As such, procurement requirements generally require a means to evaluate and view the transactions that governments have entered into with private parties. Governments often have specific frameworks or contracting requirements for procuring goods or services of any type.[76] Primarily, procurement rules focus on ensuring fair competition and non-discrimination, while also promoting other goals.[77] In the following sections, I evaluate how these goals are approached through the principles of transparency and accountability.

3.3.1 Transparency

In a general sense, transparency refers to clarity and openness.[78] In EU public procurement, transparency serves two primary functions.[79] The first is to create a system of openness and to limit discrimination on a national basis.[80] The second is to encourage best practices and competition on both the supply and demand sides of the market.[81] However, as provided by Georgieva, there is a lack of 'theoretical consensus on what transparency in procurement actually means in practice'.[82]

In cloud computing, the term 'transparency' is widely used in the context of standard contracts and service-level agreements (SLAs), auditability, security, and other standards.[83] In that context, transparency is often used as a synonym for promoting openness in contrast to opaque systems and proprietary technologies. In the procurement context, transparency generally refers to the amount of information provided surrounding the process of selecting a contractor.[84] The life cycle of transparency requirements starts with a public announcement of an opportunity to provide services, an open bidding process with defined time frames and rules for placing a bid, public announcement of bid winners, and the ability to challenge a decision following an award.[85]

[76] Gleeson and Walden, 'Placing the State in the Cloud', 685. See Davies, 'The Public Law of Government Contracts', p. 42. In addition to the general rules of contract, public law or procurement rules create an overlay that deals with contractual issues specific to governments.
[77] Rick Canavan, 'Public Procurement and Frameworks' in Christopher H. Bovis (ed.), *Research Handbook on EU Public Procurement Law* (Cheltenham: Edward Elgar 2016), p. 122.
[78] William P. Statsky, 'Transparency' in William P. Statsky (ed.), *West's Legal Thesaurus/Dictionary*, special deluxe ed. (Eagan, MN: West 1986), p. 755. Defined as 'clear', 'definable', or 'comprehensible'.
[79] Christopher Bovis, 'The Principles of Public Procurement Regulation' in C. H. Bovis (ed.), *Research Handbook on EU Public Procurement Law* (Cheltenham and Northampton, MA: Edward Elgar 2016), p. 35.
[80] ibid.
[81] ibid.
[82] Irena Georgieva, 'The EU Principles in Public Procurement. Transparency – Origin and Main Characteristics' in Irena Georgieva (ed.), *Using Transparency against Corruption in Public Procurement: A Comparative Analysis of the Transparency Rules and Their Failure to Combat Corruption* (Cham: Springer 2017), p. 8.
[83] Umar Ismail and others, 'A Framework for Security Transparency in Cloud Computing' (2016) 8 *Future Internet* 1–22 at 5–7.
[84] Georgieva, 'The EU Principles in Public Procurement', p. 7.
[85] Gleeson and Walden, 'Placing the State in the Cloud', 689.

In addition to transparency throughout the bidding process, many states allow competitors to protest bids and/or disqualify improperly obtained contract awards.[86] At least one of these protections' goals is to make the state a neutral party. This neutrality ought to lead to the best offer winning, in turn providing citizens with the best value for their taxes. Another goal is that the process will allow either government oversight officers or competing bidders to uncover irregularities, fraud, and other abuses.[87] How formally these requirements are put in place varies among governments. Nevertheless, the general goal of setting certain objective criteria is to avoid unfair competition and distorted markets, corruption, or 'backroom' deals.[88]

Although states have some discretion when awarding contracts (for example, they can throw out abnormally low offers), their flexibility is limited when the bidding parties meet objective criteria.[89] Unlike private industry, non-discrimination principles prescribed by legislation or trade agreement often limit the discretion of a state to choose a specific CSP on a subjective basis. For example, a Norwegian municipality cannot generally prohibit a CSP located in Germany from competing for a procurement contract.[90] Similarly, if the government's 'preferred' vendor does not provide the most advantageous bid on an objective basis, the government's ability to choose that vendor over others (e.g. Microsoft instead of Google) is limited.

3.3.2 Accountability

When it comes to states procuring goods or services, the term 'accountability' is often centred on making government agency 'answerable' based on some objective measure. For instance, under EU procurement regulations, accountability incorporates objectivity, consistent processes, contractual compliance, and judicial redress.[91] In procurement requirements, accountability is built-in on two levels. On the first level, the background rules (e.g. legislation, agency regulations, etc.) for contracting must contain appropriate representation and safeguards.[92] On the second level, the

---

[86] Soloway and Chvotkin, 'Federal Contracting in Context', pp. 227–28. In the US, the Government Accountability Office (GAO) adjudicates such protests. US federal courts have jurisdiction to hear challenges. See generally *Amazon Web Services, Incorporated* v. *United States*, 113 Fed. Cl. 102 (2014). Evaluating a bid protest by IBM for a $600 million USD cloud computing contract between the Central Intelligence Agency (CIA) and AWS.
[87] ibid.
[88] Bovis, 'The Principles of Public Procurement Regulation', pp. 47–49.
[89] ibid., 36–37 and 50.
[90] The Law Firm of Føyen Torkildsen AS, 'Utredning av Juridiske Forhold ved Bruk av Nettsky i Kommunal Sektor – En Mulighetsstudie' [Report on the Legal Aspects of Cloud Computing in the Municipal Sector: A Feasibility Study], (2015) *Norwegian Association of Local and Regional Authorities R&D Project No. 144008*, 17. www.ks.no/globalassets/endelig-rapport-om-bruk-av-skytjenester-i-kommunal-sektor.pdf.
[91] ibid., 46. Judicial redress focuses on available remedies. ibid., 57–58.
[92] Soloway and Chvotkin, 'Federal Contracting in Context', p. 199.

terms of the contract provide an additional avenue with which to enforce accountability through the specific terms.[93]

If the background rules do not 'guide' principles of accountability into the contracts, they are unlikely to find their way into the agreements. An effective accountability regime requires both *ex ante* evaluations of contracting powers and *ex post* evaluations of contracting performance. With the increase in government outsourcing, a number of authors have raised concerns regarding accountability measures in private–public contracts.[94]

3.3.3 Legitimacy

Legitimacy is often used in concert with accountability and transparency in gauging the acceptability of a process. The term 'legitimacy' is frequently applied either positively (legitimate) or negatively (illegitimate) to describe a process or result. Defined generally, legitimacy means 'lawfulness'.[95] Even if governments may legitimately procure cloud computing services, they must also ensure that the systems follow applicable legal frameworks (e.g. data privacy laws) if they also intend to maintain the legitimacy they have obtained through the democratic process. There is not a 'transitory property' wherein the private provider obtains the government's legitimacy even if the private provider is effectively filling the shoes of the government actor. Therefore, the legitimacy that governments gain through democratic means cannot be passed intact onto CSPs without first ensuring that the proper legal and potentially technical controls are in place. If legal requirements and democratic principles are completely abandoned, legitimacy will also disappear.

3.3.4 Availability and Accessibility

If government systems become unavailable as the result of a technical or security problem, citizens run the risk of being denied government services. Loss of services may be relatively inconsequential, such as a minor delay experienced in registering a vehicle. However, it is not difficult to imagine the consequences if core services were to become unavailable. For instance, the inaccessibility of a medical journal could have a catastrophic impact on some users. Disappearing from a citizen registry has the potential to deprive an individual of access to effectively all government services that rely on such a system. Even with minor glitches, governments risk losing citizen confidence.

---

[93] ibid.
[94] Aman and Dugan, 'The Human Side of Public-Private Partnerships', 887–88.
[95] Bryan A. Garner and Henry Campbell Black, 'Legitimacy' in Bryan A. Garner and Henry Campbell Black (eds.), *Black's Law Dictionary*, 10th ed. (Saint Paul, MN: Thomson Reuters 2014), p. 454.

By putting third-party CSPs in charge of these services, particularly for 'mission critical' applications, the government becomes extremely dependent on CSPs when data outages or losses occur.[96] When a government moves to the cloud, whether a municipality's officers can answer their emails, applications can be processed, or bills can be sent to citizens may depend almost entirely on their CSP's response time instead of the government's IT department. In some cases, this is often an improvement.[97] Generally, cloud services have proven to be extremely resilient. Nonetheless, the reality of the situation is that the public sector relies heavily on third parties to carry out its mandate.

3.3.5 Loss of Competence over IT Systems

In addition to accountability and transparency concerns, there is also apprehension over the diminished capacity or loss of expertise over resources that have been outsourced.[98] Failing to maintain a certain level of competence over IT functions arguably amounts to a failure to manage strategic resources. As noted by one author, although organizations often outsource certain aspects of their IT services, they ' ... take care to retain a strong nucleus of their own highly qualified employees to orchestrate and monitor that network'.[99]

Although third-party auditors fill the oversight role to some extent, without a core level of competence, it is difficult for governments to monitor the IT services they use.[100] For instance, even if a government receives a copy of a third-party audit, the report might not contain information that specifically addresses the government's systems or vulnerabilities. It may also be difficult to address further questions or customize audit requests. If the government has lost its internal competence, it will be unable to assess services on its own and must rely on additional third parties. This only compounds the reliance on third parties (i.e. the audit provider). Furthermore, if a government uses one CSP and becomes completely dependent on that CSP and its proprietary technology, then the government risks paying whatever the CSP decides to charge.

---

[96] Scott Paquette, Paul T. Jaeger, and Susan C. Wilson, 'Identifying the Security Risks Associated with Governmental Use of Cloud Computing' (2010) 27 *Government Information Quarterly* 245–53 at 251.
[97] NASA Office of Inspector General, 'NASA's Progress in Adopting Cloud-Computing Technologies' (29 July 2013), 4–5. https://oig.nasa.gov/docs/IG-13-021.pdf.
[98] Jody Freeman and Martha Minow, 'Introduction: Reframing the Outsourcing Debates' in Jody Freeman and Martha Minow (eds.), *Government by Contract: Outsourcing and American Democracy* (Cambridge, MA: Harvard University Press 2009), p. 5.
[99] John D. Donahue, 'The Transformation of Government Work: Causes, Consequences, and Distortions' in Jody Freeman and Martha Minow (eds.), *Government by Contract: Outsourcing and American Democracy* (Cambridge, MA: Harvard University Press 2009), p. 57.
[100] ibid.

3.4 PROCUREMENT REQUIREMENTS AND CLOUD BARRIERS

In evaluating the sluggish adoption of cloud computing by governments in the EU, the EC has conducted several studies and financed research projects to identify potential barriers.[101] Essentially, the EC studies found that in addition to concerns over privacy and security that most cloud clients shared, governments encountered additional barriers, including difficulty in comparing costs in the bidding process, restrictions on external storage, and cultural barriers to using external providers.[102] In some cases, there were specific barriers that limited or discouraged cloud computing, such as requirements that archives remain within national boundaries.[103] In other cases, the barriers were not direct, but had a similar impact. In the following subsections, these barriers are further evaluated.

3.4.1 Price Comparisons

Government demands for fixed prices or total costs upfront have proven difficult for CSPs that often apply 'pay-for-use' or 'pay-as-you-go' arrangements.[104] Although EU procurement law often requires that a total cost for the contract be set in order to advertise the tender and obtain bids, estimating costs and setting budgets for tenders is less straightforward for cloud computing than traditional outsourcing.[105] Although cloud services may be less expensive for states, without a total or final price quote, mandatory boxes in the procurement application will go unchecked, thereby making cloud service providers either ineligible or uncompetitive. Moreover, in areas where cloud computing is stronger on price, procurement systems may not be equipped to recognize this advantage or to handle comparisons.

For example, if the government considers the total cost of ownership (TCO) in providing a similar IT service on its own by including the cost of purchasing servers and absorbing maintenance costs, energy bills, and employee compensation and pensions, cloud computing becomes much more competitive.[106] Add to that the

---

[101] Procurement Innovation for Cloud Services in Europe (PICSE), 'Procuring Cloud Services Today: Experiences and Lessons Learned from the Public Sector' (2016), 18. www.picse.eu/sites/default/files/Procuring%20cloud%20services%20today_22072015.pdf.
[102] ibid.
[103] Procurement Innovation for Cloud Services in Europe (PICSE), 'PICSE: Procurement Innovation for Cloud Services in Europe: D3.1 Procurement Barriers Report' (2015), 26–28. Finding that specific public procurement barriers include language requirements, national security, archiving and other legislative obligations. See Føyen Torkildsen AS, 'Report on the Legal Aspects of Cloud Computing in the Municipal Sector', 18.
[104] PICSE, 'Procuring Cloud Services Today', 1.
[105] Gleeson and Walden, 'Placing the State in the Cloud', 692.
[106] Jan Tore Sanner, 'Cloud Computing Strategy for Norway Report' (2016), 17–18. www.regjeringen.no/en/dokumenter/cloud-computing-strategy-for-norway/id2484403/. Providing the total cost calculation should also include energy consumption, employee costs (including pensions etc.), networks, building costs, licences, and hardware.

flexibility of not owning the infrastructure and being able to change services when a superior one becomes available, and cloud becomes increasingly attractive.

3.4.2 Contracting for Cloud Using an IT Outsourcing Template

Governmental procurement requirements often apply the same contracting standards whether the item being acquired is a building, software, or a server. If a government is only purchasing one of these items, the distinction works. However, cloud computing services include aspects of both hardware and software and therefore do not always fit into the narrowly drawn categories of such contracting structures. As a result, the contract required may be unclear or a poor fit for procurement purposes.[107]

Although this binary distinction has been a challenge for cloud adoption, government approaches are changing to more cloud-friendly contracts. For example, in Norway, standard government procurement contracts traditionally made a clear distinction between contracting for software and contracting for operational services.[108] The Norwegian Digitalisation Agency has modified and created new contracts to aid government agencies in adopting cloud computing services.[109] The contracts account for services such as SaaS and allow the CSP's standard terms to be included, as long as the contract accounts for other legal requirements (e.g. data privacy).

However, even where governments take a more nuanced approach to procuring IT, cloud computing services are often at a disadvantage. Taking again the example of Norway, the government's cloud strategy provides that cloud services 'shall be assessed on the same basis as other solutions'.[110] The UK Financial Conduct Authority (FCA) takes a similar approach, providing that cloud computing 'is considered outsourcing and firms need to consider the relevant regulatory obligations and how they comply with them'.[111] However, given the differences in cloud models (e.g. pricing, delivery, standardization, etc.), cloud often does not compete

---

[107] ibid., 18.
[108] ibid. See Direktoratet for forvaltning og ikt (Difi) [The Norwegian Agency for Public Management and eGovernment], '*Kjøpsavtalen* (SSA-K)' [IT Sales and Purchase Agreement]. This agreement applies to procurements of IT equipment and/or software. Difi, '*Driftsavtalen* (SSA-D)' [Operational Services Contract]. This agreement covers a wide range of operational services, focusing on standard services. Standard contracts www.anskaffelser.no/verktoy/kontrakter-og-avtaler/kjopsavtalen-ssa-k.
[109] Difi, 'Avtale om løpende tjenestekjøp (SSA-L)' [Agreement Concerning Ongoing Purchases of Services via the Internet]. www.anskaffelser.no/verktoy/avtale-om-lopende-tjenestekjop-ssa-l. This 'ongoing services purchase' contract can be used by government agencies to procure standard services, such as SaaS, where the ability to change standard CSP terms is limited.
[110] Sanner, 'Cloud Computing Strategy for Norway', 5.
[111] Financial Conduct Authority (FCA), 'FG16/5: Guidance for Firms Outsourcing to the "Cloud" and Other Third Party IT Services' (2016), 3. www.fca.org.uk/publications/finalised-guidance/fg16-5-guidance-firms-outsourcing-cloud-and-other-third-party-it.

well when compared to traditional IT outsourcing when it is based on terms or templates designed for IT outsourcing.[112]

3.4.3 Data Location Barriers

For governments, additional legal barriers to adopting cloud computing arise from requirements that data be stored in a specific location. Such requirements are often referred to as data localization laws.[113] As described by Selby, there are generally two types of data localization laws. The first is a policy by national governments to require CSPs (and others) to store data 'about Internet users in their country on servers located within the jurisdiction of that national government (localized data hosting)'.[114] The second focuses on requiring ISPs 'to route data packets sent between Internet users located in their jurisdictions across networks located only within their jurisdiction (localized data routing)'.[115] In this section, I focus on the former.

Generally, data localization requirements mandate that data remain within national borders or within a specified region. These barriers may be direct (i.e. specifically requiring that data be stored in-country) or indirect in that they have the effect of limiting data flows.[116] For example, a requirement that data must be accessible for audit at all times does not directly require that the data be stored in a jurisdiction. However, such a guarantee may be very difficult to provide if the data are stored on a global infrastructure. Data localization requirements are often justified on data security grounds or as necessary to retain control over data in the long term for historical and archival purposes and public registries, among other custodial roles.[117] As noted earlier, collectively, the value of citizen data is extremely important for governments and is at the core of the concept of 'data sovereignty'.[118] As such, governments are often sceptical of solutions that separate them from their territorial control over such data.

In a Norwegian study commissioned to analyse the rules and regulations that pose the greatest barriers to cloud computing, the working group found several such laws, providing prohibitions on data storage outside of the country. The Norwegian Public Archives Act explicitly provides that archival material may not be stored out of the

---

[112] Sanner, 'Cloud Computing Strategy for Norway', 27–28. Noting that the Norwegian requirements for standard government contract terms and conditions do not align with the standard contracts offered by CSPs.
[113] John Selby, 'Data Localization Laws: Trade Barriers or Legitimate Responses to Cybersecurity Risks, or Both?' (2017) 25 *International Journal of Law and Information Technology* 213–32 at 214.
[114] ibid.
[115] ibid.
[116] European Commission, 'Facilitating Cross-Border Data Flow in the Digital Single Market: Study on Data Location Restrictions' (SMART 2015/0054, 2017), 18. Finding regulatory barriers, both direct and indirect, to the location of data were most prevalent in areas such as health, financial, citizen, judicial, and tax or accounting data.
[117] Lov om Arkiv 4 desember 1992 nr 24 §§ 9(b). Available only in Norwegian.
[118] Irion, Your Digital Home Is No Longer Your Castle', 23.

country. Similarly, the Norwegian Bookkeeping Act also places some requirements on data location and restricts storage of digital accounting material to EEA countries.[119] In practice, only Nordic countries have been able to meet this requirement.[120] An EC rapport has also identified similar provisions in Portugal and Slovenia as creating localization barriers that limit realization of a digital single market.[121]Additional 'indirect' requirements inhibiting cloud computing include certain national technical requirements that are difficult to meet on a mass scale.[122]

3.4.4 Summarizing Procurement Barriers

Although the previously-mentioned barriers provide some challenges, they do not generally amount to an outright ban on EU member states adopting cloud services.[123] Outside of the few countries with strict data localization laws, most EU states are free to adopt cloud. However, the 'indirect barriers' requiring local audits or very specific local technical or privacy measures remain a significant roadblock for many. These de facto barriers simply make it safer, and perhaps easier, to choose traditional IT outsourcing solutions instead.

3.5 EUROPEAN INITIATIVES TO ADOPT CLOUD AT THE GOVERNMENT LEVEL

Although EU member states are drafting cloud computing strategies and making plans for adopting it, crossing the line from cloud planning to cloud deployment has been difficult.[124] When that jump is made, it is often limited to 'non-critical' government services on a small scale.[125] In the Nordic countries, municipalities were early adopters, attempting to move services to the cloud in Norway, Sweden, and Denmark with varied results.[126] However, results across the continent are

---

[119] Sanner, 'Cloud Computing Strategy for Norway', 20. Føyen Torkildsen AS, Report on the Legal Aspects of Cloud Computing in the Municipal Sector', 20–22.
[120] ibid., 20.
[121] European Commission, 'Facilitating Cross-Border Data Flow in the Digital Single Market', 21.
[122] ibid., 61–63.
[123] Gleeson and Walden, 'Placing the State in the Cloud', 694. Finding the most significant barriers include (1) misconceptions about the secrecy of government data, and (2) incompatibilities between cloud and the pay-as-you-go approach to procurement in EU law.
[124] European Union Agency for Network and Information Security (ENISA), 'Good Practice Guide for Securely Deploying Governmental Clouds' (2013), 7. www.enisa.europa.eu/publications/good-practice-guide-for-securely-deploying-governmental-clouds. Finding very few 'operational government Cloud infrastructures' in the EU. See Dimitra Liveri and M. Dekker, 'Framework for Governmental Clouds: All Steps from Design to Deployment' (2015) *European Union Agency for Cybersecurity (ENISA)*, 1. The exceptions being the UK, Spain, Demark, and, to some extent, Estonia.
[125] ENISA, 'Good Practice Guide for Securely Deploying Governmental Clouds', p. 8.
[126] Marius Jørgenrud, 'Her er brevet som forbyr Google Apps' [Here is the Letter Prohibiting Google Apps], *Digi*, 24 January 2012. www.digi.no/887985/her-er-brevet-som-forbyr-google-apps.

relatively mixed. In the following sections, I evaluate government plans at the EU level before considering individual national plans.

At the national level, numerous EU member states have developed plans for adopting cloud computing. These plans generally focus on either procuring existing applications from external providers or moving aspects of current solutions, such as storage/backup, to the cloud. EU governmental strategies utilize various deployment models (e.g. SaaS, PaaS, and IaaS) and include public, private, and hybrid cloud configurations. In other words, the strategies are relatively open and cover the spectrum of cloud technology. Broadly speaking, some trends have emerged that depend on the size of the governmental unit, type of data, and budget.[127]

Although many EU national strategies have been created, the majority of the EU cloud procurement plans have been slow to get off the ground, with many occupying either a non-operational or an abandoned status.[128] With few exceptions, most European countries seem to remain in perpetual planning phases.[129] As noted in an European Union Agency for Network and Information Security (ENISA) study, outside of a few individual applications, most of the planned government cloud adoption is 'far from being implemented'.[130] When operational, the EU public sector cloud has generally followed the following procurement approaches or models: (1) the 'marketplace and procurement' model; (2) the 'resource pooling' model; and (3) the 'standalone applications' model.[131]

3.5.1 Marketplace and Procurement Model

The marketplace and procurement model focuses primarily on creating a procurement framework or process that allows states to adopt or purchase solutions from external providers in a defined marketplace.[132] With its top-down approach, the model simplifies the process of adopting cloud computing by providing CSPs with a central procurement point (i.e. 'a cloud store') to offer their services. Furthermore, this approach provides public sector agencies with a clear path for purchasing services. The road to adoption is generally paved by creating standard contracts,

---

[127] ENISA, 'Good Practice Guide for Securely Deploying Governmental Clouds', p. 7. Study finding that implemented or planned government cloud services were IaaS 70 per cent, PaaS 46 per cent, and SaaS 85 per cent, while only 28 per cent of agencies were willing to adopt a 'public cloud model' as opposed to 'private' or 'community cloud' models.
[128] European Commission Directorate-General for Communications Networks European Commission, Content and Technology, 'Analysis of Cloud Best Practices and Pilots for the Public Sector – Final' (2012), 13. https://ec.europa.eu/digital-single-market/en/news/analysis-cloud-best-practices-and-pilots-public-sector.
[129] Daniele Catteddu, 'Security & Resilience in Governmental Clouds – Making an Informed Decision' (2011) *ENISA*, 5. Certain exceptions include the UK, Spain and Denmark, among others.
[130] European Commission, 'Analysis of Cloud Best Practices and Pilots for the Public Sector', 16.
[131] ibid., 20–27.
[132] ibid., 20.

guidelines, and other governance requirements that both CSPs and agencies must adopt.

The model focuses primarily on cost savings and offerings. The marketplace model also incorporates the public cloud deployment model to a much greater extent than the other two EU public procurement models. Although this model may be restrictive and limits the use of cloud for sensitive data, it covers a wide variety of applications and cloud deployment types, from SaaS to IaaS. It also gives agencies the opportunity to adopt new applications rather than going through the expense of transferring legacy applications or 'cloudifying' existing apps.[133]

The primary advantages of the marketplace model are access and ease of adoption for public entities. As the only model that has led to significant adoption of cloud services by public entities in the EU, the model's deployment or utility is also a primary advantage.[134] Examples of this model include the United Kingdom's G-Cloud and the United States' FedRAMP model, both evaluated further in the text.[135] In the case of G-Cloud, both SMEs and global providers have the opportunity to create applications and sell services to the public sector. The model effectively allows governments to dip their toes into the cloud computing pool without fully committing significant financial resources or sensitive agency data to cloud.

3.5.2 The Resource Pooling Model

The second deployment category is called the 'resource pooling' model, which has the goal of developing a common infrastructure or platform accessible by many governmental entities.[136] The model is designed to give individual agencies the flexibility to purchase or develop their own applications while utilizing a central or shared 'pool' of computing power.[137] Consequently, a central aspect of this model is creating central governmental cloud infrastructure that many levels of government can access.[138] This model primarily uses IaaS infrastructure, allowing individual agencies to develop more personalized or specific applications that will operate on the shared infrastructure.[139]

---

[133] ibid., 21. 'Cloudifying' or 'cloudification' is converting existing application programs in order to make use of cloud computing services. See Juncal Alonso, Marisa Escalante, and Leire Orue-Echevarria, 'Transformational Cloud Government (TCG): Transforming Public Administrations with a Cloud of Public Services' (2016) 97 *Procedia Computer Science* 43–52 at 49. Evaluating the process of cloudification.

[134] European Commission, 'Analysis of Cloud Best Practices and Pilots for the Public Sector', 20. This model is in many ways favoured. Currently, this approach is used in Portugal, the UK, and, to some extent, in the Netherlands.

[135] ibid., 21. See also Cabinet Office and The Rt. Hon Lord Maude of Horsham, 'Government Adopts "Cloud First" Policy for Public Sector IT', *Press Release*, 5 May 2013. www.gov.uk/government/news/government-adopts-cloud-first-policy-for-public-sector-it.

[136] European Commission, 'Analysis of Cloud Best Practices and Pilots for the Public Sector', 25.

[137] ibid.

[138] ibid.

[139] ibid., 23.

By creating a common infrastructure, by either consolidating data centres or using private cloud solutions, the model has the potential for broad application with a strong central direction from the national government.[140] This model allows for greater control over data placed in the cloud, including a greater focus on privacy and general security.[141] On a long-term basis, this model has the potential to allow wider uses across agencies and even the storing of more sensitive data types.[142]

The main barriers to this model are therefore technical and financial. On the technical side, transferring and integrating legacy systems is extremely difficult and costly. In some cases, it may be essentially impossible to move some systems to the cloud, and the system must be redeveloped. Additionally, involving CSPs on such a central or high level in public IT has the potential to lock the government into one provider's solution. Obtaining acceptable contract and SLA terms may also prove challenging.[143] As a result of the significant start-up expenses associated with resource pooling, the model has not been widely adopted.

3.5.3 Stand-alone Applications

This model of cloud deployment simply involves ministries creating their own applications, or cloudifying existing applications, for use by the individual agency.[144] By taking applications that are currently in existence, development costs may be less. In areas where savings are obtainable through cloud computing, such as storage costs, these advantages can be incorporated into the existing applications. However, the model is primarily 'decentralized' and focuses chiefly on cost savings rather than enhancing security or creating new applications.[145] Given the pragmatic approach taken in reusing existing applications, this model is generally the most widely deployed across the EU member states.[146] As a long-term plan, the stand-alone applications model has limited utility.

3.6 THE UK CLOUD COMPUTING STRATEGY

The United Kingdom has been a significant market for CSPs and was one of the 'early adopters' of cloud computing in the EU.[147] In 2013, the UK government

---

[140] ibid., 24–25.
[141] ibid.
[142] ibid., 23.
[143] ibid.
[144] ibid., 2.
[145] ibid., 27.
[146] ibid.
[147] European Commission, 'Facilitating Cross-Border Data Flow in the Digital Single Market', 84. Citing studies from 2013 finding that the 'UK dominated the European data centre market' with around 60 per cent of market share. See also Alison Pritchard, 'Cloud Guide for the Public Sector', *Government Digital Service*, 31 March 2020. www.gov.uk/government/publications/cloud-guide-for-the-public-sector/cloud-guide-for-the-public-sector.

introduced its 'cloud first' policy mandate.[148] The policy requires that when public sector organizations are procuring new services, they consider and fully evaluate cloud computing solutions before considering another option.[149] The cloud-first policy is 'mandatory for central government and strongly recommended to the wider public sector'.[150] If central governments choose an option outside of cloud, they must show that the solution offers better value than a comparable cloud offering.[151] The United Kingdom also has a 'public cloud first' requirement and encourages adoption of SaaS models, 'particularly for enterprise IT and back office functions'.[152]

The primary method for procuring cloud services for UK public agencies is using the G-Cloud programme. Despite its name, G-Cloud is not a cloud technology but rather a procurement method. The G-Cloud initiative provides UK public sector bodies with a 'compliant' means for procuring and adopting cloud computing services.[153] Eligible cloud services are made available as part of the 'Digital Marketplace', which allows the public sector to purchase cloud services directly from CSPs.[154] The Digital Marketplace contains technical information, prices, and CSP terms and conditions.[155] Cloud services are divided into three lots, including 'cloud hosting', 'cloud software', and 'cloud support'.[156] The programme is often cited as an example of a successful European cloud initiative and a potential model for other EU member states.[157]

Although the G-Cloud framework is intended to be flexible, underlying public procurement requirements limit some of this flexibility. Government buyers must therefore evaluate the information provided by CSPs (e.g. services, prices, and terms) and directly award contracts on that basis. By following the G-Cloud process, government buyers avoid having to comply with many of the procedural public procurement requirements for each individual procurement. However, if the

---

[148] ibid. The policy was reassessed in 2019 and remains a flagship technology policy.
[149] UK Government Digital Service, 'Government Cloud First Policy' (2017), 1. www.gov.uk/guidance/government-cloud-first-policy#consider-cloud-solutions-before-alternatives.
[150] ibid.
[151] ibid. This requires showing that the agency has secured ' . . . the best mix of quality and effectiveness for the least outlay over the period of the use of the goods or services bought'. HM Treasury, 'Managing Public Money' (2015), Annex 4.6. www.gov.uk/government/uploads/system/uploads/attachment_data/file/454191/Managing_Public_Money_AA_v2_-jan15.pdf.
[152] UK Government Digital Service, 'Government Cloud First Policy', 1.
[153] UK Crown Commercial Service, 'G-Cloud 9 Framework: Overview and Buyers Guide' (2017), 5. www.gov.uk/guidance/g-cloud-buyers-guide.
[154] ibid., 5–6. Digital marketplace catalogue. www.gov.uk/digital-marketplace. Previously 'CloudStore'. For an overview of initial G-Cloud deployment, see W. Kuan Hon, Christopher Millard, and Ian Walden, 'Public Sector Cloud Contracts in Cloud Computing Law' in Christopher Millard (ed.), *Cloud Computing Law* (Oxford: Oxford University Press 2013), pp. 109–12.
[155] UK Crown Commercial Service, 'G-Cloud 9 Framework: Overview and Buyers Guide', 5.
[156] ibid., 7–9.
[157] Francesca Spagnoli, Francesco Bellini, and Alessandra Ghi, 'A Methodology for the Impact Assessment of a G-Cloud Strategy for the Italian Ministry of the Economic Development' in Cecilia Rossignoli, Mauro Gatti, and Rocco Agrifoglio (eds.), *Organizational Innovation and Change: Managing Information and Technology* (Cham: Springer International 2016), pp. 11–25.

government buyer deviates from the G-Cloud structure and requires additional information or bid processes, the purchaser risks breaching the terms of the G-Cloud framework, and purchases will be considered non-compliant.[158] In other words, the Digital Marketplace is intended to put CSPs on equal footing, which means that running additional processes might affect the fairness and transparency of the framework process. The impact and contractual requirements of the programme are evaluated further in Chapters 6 and 7.

3.7 THE US CLOUD COMPUTING STRATEGY

The US federal government is also pursuing a 'cloud-first' strategy as it is particularly keen to move away from its current legacy systems. The US strategy is reasonably straightforward. If a secure and cost-effective cloud option exists, federal agencies are required to consider its implementation.[159] If an agency has a current strategy that does not include cloud computing, it must re-evaluate its policy to include cloud computing. For the US government, a cloud-first strategy is a relatively natural progression because privatization and outsourcing in many areas have long been a central strategy for delivering government services.[160]

From the contracting phase to the operational stage of data centres, the US federal government spends significant amounts of money on a per agency basis to store and manage its data. In 2009, it began planning a shift in data storage from agency-owned data centres to cloud-based services.[161] The goal of this shift was to reduce the federal government's investment in IT services and to reverse the trend of increasing data centre expenditures.[162] Outside of peak usage times, much of the computing power purchased remains unused for substantial periods of the year.[163] Estimates on the savings created by using cloud computing are on average 50 per cent, but they vary widely by agency.[164]

Currently, the US federal government spends a majority of its IT funds on maintaining outdated legacy systems.[165] These outdated legacy systems include

---

[158] UK Crown Commercial Service, 'G-Cloud 9 Framework: Overview and Buyers Guide', 14–15. Specifically, if buyers require '... mini competition RFP, RFQ, RFI, negotiation or issuing an ITT'.
[159] ibid.
[160] Soloway and Chvotkin, 'Federal Contracting in Context', p. 205. In the US, contrary to popular belief, the 'size' of government and expenditures have not shrunk but has been contracted out to private providers.
[161] Patricia Moloney Figliola, 'Cloud Computing: Background, Status of Adoption by Federal Agencies, and Congressional Action', *Congressional Research Service (CRS)*, 25 March 2020, 1–14 at 1. www.fas.org/sgp/crs/misc/R42887.pdf.
[162] ibid., 5. To address this problem, the data Center Optimization Initiative (DCOI) was created.
[163] ibid.
[164] Patricia Moloney Figliola and Eric A. Fischer, 'Overview and Issues for Implementation of the Federal Cloud Computing Initiative: Implications for Federal Information Technology Reform Management', *Congressional Research Service (CRS)*, 20 January 2015, 7. www.fas.org/sgp/crs/misc/R42887.pdf. Projected agency savings range from 10 per cent to 250 per cent.
[165] David A. Powner, 'Federal Agencies Need to Address Aging Legacy Systems' (2016) *Report: GAO-16-696T*, 6–7. www.gao.gov/products/GAO-16-696T.

those that rely on obsolete programming languages developed in the 1950s and systems that continue to use eight-inch floppy drives, among others.[166] To put this into perspective, in 2015, US federal agencies spent US $61 billion of their US $80 billion budget on maintaining legacy systems.[167] An updated report from 2019 cites little improvement. Because the legacy systems become more expensive to maintain every year, less of the IT budget is available for developing new systems as time goes on. If this trend continues, eventually the cost of maintaining legacy systems could consume the entire IT budget. This pattern is unsustainable.

In its cloud computing strategy, the US government maintains that, like other governments that purchase cloud computing in bulk, it will be able to effectively negotiate contract terms with CSPs and obtain the necessary concessions to meet federal security and privacy requirements. This apparent government advantage exists for several reasons. For example, unlike consumers or SMEs, governments purchase services in large quantities and on a payment-for-use rather than a data-for-use basis.[168] Governments use their bargaining position in an attempt to obtain services that satisfy their complex requirements in areas such as the following: security and privacy requirements, liability of CSPs and their suppliers, warranties, and service levels.[169]

The US 'cloud-first' strategy has its critics.[170] Like users in the private sector, chief information officers in federal agencies have raised concerns about cloud security levels, the cost (and feasibility) of migrating current legacy systems to cloud services and the loss of control that is part and parcel of cloud computing.[171] Particularly salient concerns shared by information officers are the overall reliability, availability, privacy, and portability of federal data stored on the cloud. Like their EU counterparts, US federal agencies using cloud computing will still need to meet complex regulatory requirements. Although the regulatory approach is different, US federal agencies are also required to maintain a high level of control and oversight over citizen data.

A key component of the US cloud strategy is FedRAMP. FedRAMP is aimed at addressing the risks present in cloud computing while also streamlining the procurement process.[172] The FedRAMP programme is mandatory and must be

---

[166] ibid., 15. Providing that several federal agencies continue to use programming languages developed in the late 1950s and early 1960s and 8-inch floppy disks.
[167] ibid., 6–7.
[168] Wayne Jansen and Timothy Grance, 'Guidelines on Security and Privacy in Public Cloud Computing' (2011) SP 800–144, 6. https://nvlpubs.nist.gov/nistpubs/Legacy/SP/nistspecialpublication800-144.pdf. NIST has categorized classes of 'public clouds' based on whether the service is paid for or supported by advertising.
[169] W. Kuan Hon, Christopher Millard, and Ian Walden, 'Negotiated Contracts for Cloud Services' in Christopher Millard (ed.), *Cloud Computing Law* (Oxford: Oxford University Press 2013), p. 89.
[170] Segall, 'Jurisdictional Challenges in the United States Government's Move to Cloud Computing Technology', 1108.
[171] Figliola, 'Cloud Computing: Background, Status of Adoption by Federal Agencies', 6.
[172] Matthew Metheny, *Federal Cloud Computing: The Definitive Guide for Cloud Service Providers* (Rockland, MA: Elsevier Science 2012), p. 217. For further explanation of FedRAMP procurement requirements, see Kevin McGillivray, 'FedRAMP, Contracts, and the U.S. Federal Government's

implemented by federal agencies using cloud computing.[173] FedRAMP is designed to provide a standardized approach to the security assessment, authorization, and monitoring of cloud computing. The aim of the FedRAMP evaluation is to create a 'do once, use many times' system to maximize efficiency in cloud adoption.[174] The FedRAMP programme provides a means for agencies to verify that certain controls are in place before adopting cloud computing.[175] By creating a government-wide standard, FedRAMP intends to provide federal agencies with the means to rapidly adopt cloud computing and mitigate risk while also reducing many of the risk-evaluation and procurement expenses common in IT hosting. As of 2019, use of the FedRAMP program has increased significantly as a means of government cloud procurement.[176]

3.8 CONCLUSION

This chapter evaluated how a government's considerations when deciding to move services from an in-house or traditional IT outsourcing solution to cloud computing differ from those of other types of users, such as private corporations. In addition to meeting technical challenges, governments have additional legal obligations and responsibilities towards citizens. The most 'visible' or tangible legal obstacles include public contracting, archive requirements, and FOIA obligations. Although they may create some hurdles for governments adopting cloud computing, they do not generally result in a prohibition.

In addition to the more concrete barriers, less tangible obligations include transparency, accountability, and ultimately legitimacy concerns. For example, enlisting SaaS providers for the purposes of aiding citizens in filing taxes, operating healthcare journals, or applying for housing assistance are all tasks for which cloud computing is technically well suited. However, it will also put private parties in charge of – and in some cases give them access to – sensitive citizen data. If the services are not performed adequately, governments may fail in upholding some of their core responsibilities. Furthermore, if private providers were able to combine or

Move to Cloud Computing: If an 800-pound Gorilla Can't Tame the Cloud, Who Can?' (2016) 17 *Columbia Science and Technology Law Review* 336–401 at 354 and fn 64.
[173] Defense Information Systems Agency (DISA), 'Department of Defense (DoD) Cloud Computing Security Requirements Guide Version 1 Release 1 Report' (2015). https://info.publicintelligence.net/DoD-CloudSecurity.pdf.
[174] FedRAMP, 'Program Overview' (7 May 2020). www.fedramp.gov/how-agencies-can-reuse-a-fedramp-authorization/.
[175] McGillivray, FedRAMP, Contracts, and the U.S. Federal Government's Move to Cloud Computing', 354 and fn 67.
[176] Ann W. Moessbauer and others, 'Cloud Computing Security: Agencies Increased their Use of the Federal Authorization Program, but Improved Oversight and Implementation Are Needed', *Governmental Accountability Office GAO*, December 2019, 2. www.gao.gov/assets/710/703193.pdf. Finding 'the number of authorizations granted through FedRAMP by the 24 agencies increased from 390 to 926, a 137 per cent increase'.

enrich data they collect commercially with data that are traditionally controlled by the state (e.g. tax data, employment data, educational records, criminal records, etc.), it would have serious negative consequences for citizens and their privacy. In short, there would truly be few secrets left.

In many cases, cloud computing allows governments to acquire cost-effective, secure, and state-of-the-art IT. It also seems clear that cloud computing will continue to play an important role in delivering government IT. However, when adopting cloud computing services, governments must carefully assess their means and methods of accounting for and implementing both transparency and accountability requirements. On the transparency side, this requires applying objective criteria, such as oversight, in the contracting process and maintaining the means to audit services and agreements. In many cases, governments already have processes in place that (with some retrofitting) will allow them to meet these obligations. For example, updating procurement contracting precedents to account for cloud computing services.

Accountability requires that governments adopting cloud computing incorporate mandatory rules and requirements and that such requirements can be verified and enforced throughout the cloud computing infrastructure. If this cannot be done as planned, governments should be flexible. This might require reconsidering the types of services they will outsource, the types of data stored with private providers; and making adjustments to the overall scope of usage. In addition to their obligations to individual citizens, governments must also consider such accountability obligations in the greater context of data sovereignty and the collective value of such information. Therefore, governments must take a broad view in determining their cloud strategy.

4

Location Independence, Jurisdiction, and Law Enforcement Access to Cloud Computing Services

Much of the challenge that governments face when adopting cloud computing services stems from the perceived loss of control over the information they store with a CSP. Control over data is multifaceted. On the one hand, control implies the active management or steering of data, and on the other, it implies limiting or reducing access by others on a physical or logical basis. One element of the control problem in cloud computing results from too many untrusted 'cooks' in the supplier 'kitchen'. Another central aspect of the problem is the lack of control over where things happen in cloud computing services, including determining (and limiting) the locations of providers, the location of infrastructure, and uncontrolled (or uncontrollable) access to data. For many governments, overcoming the control obstacle remains a barrier to cloud adoption.

This chapter focuses primarily on the legal basis for asserting jurisdiction over cloud computing services and why this matters for governments. Although the chapter is framed around governmental concerns, it has broader application. At the outset, I note that the topic of jurisdiction and the Internet is vast, complex, and in many respects unsettled.[1] Simply put, a single or universal standard that can be applied globally does not yet exist. With the existing standards for finding jurisdiction, there is also disagreement regarding their scope and effect.

Rather than creating fictitious fact patterns or relying on hypotheticals, much of the analysis of cloud access is done through the lens of *Re Warrant to Search a Certain Email Account Controlled & Maintained by Microsoft Corporation*.[2] In this case, the US government sought access to the content of a cloud-based email account stored on a server located in Ireland. Throughout this text, I refer to the case generically as the 'Microsoft warrant' case. Although the Microsoft warrant case does

---

[1] Cristos Velasco, Julia Hörnle, and Anna-Maria Osula, 'Global Views on Internet Jurisdiction and Trans-border Access' in Serge Gutwirth, Ronald Leenes, and Paul De Hert (eds.), *Data Protection on the Move* (Dordrecht: Springer 2016), pp. 465–76.

[2] *Re Warrant to Search a Certain Email Account Controlled & Maintained by Microsoft Corp*, F Supp. 3d (2014). *Microsoft Corp v. United States*, 829 F 3d 197 (2d Cir. 2016). *Microsoft Corp v. United States*, 855 F 3d 53 (2d Cir. 2017). *On Writ of Certiorari to the United States Court of Appeals for the Second Circuit*, 584 US (2018).

not involve access to government data specifically, it shows the complexity of applying jurisdictional frameworks to location-independent cloud computing services. In particular, it reveals the conflict between territorial and extraterritorial access to such services and the legal status or protection of data stored in the cloud more generally. The case also concerns a CSP that is widely used by governments.

In the legal context, jurisdiction determines the power of a court to hear and decide a dispute.[3] The scope of the court's power is generally limited to an area with physical or political boundaries.[4] Within such a physical or political area, the government or sovereign has the ability to regulate the conduct occurring therein.[5] When referring to jurisdiction in this chapter, I am referring to the ability of a court to hear a dispute over events occurring within an area based on political boundaries.[6] As will be expanded on further throughout this chapter, jurisdiction is a broad and complex concept.[7]

4.1 LOCATION OF CLOUD COMPUTING SERVICES

Although jurisdictional conflicts predate cloud computing, existing jurisdictional problems have been exacerbated by such technology. Depending on the configuration of the cloud computing service, data are often stored in numerous physical locations.[8] This has many positive aspects, including making services resilient, accessible, and much more insulated against natural disasters or other similar events that were once catastrophic to a government's data.[9] However, the global flexibility associated with cloud computing comes with a measure of vulnerability. Because data are stored outside of the government or organization, the potential for access by third parties is also present. As discussed further in Chapter 5, the Court of Justice of the European Union (CJEU) has also acknowledged the existence of surveillance by the US government. Specifically, the US National Security Agency (NSA) widely

---

[3] Radim Polčák and Dan Jerker B. Svantesson, *Information Sovereignty: Data Privacy, Sovereign Powers and the Rule of Law* (Northampton, MA: Elgar 2017), p. 43.

[4] Anna-Maria Osula, 'Transborder Access and Territorial Sovereignty' (2015) 31 *Computer Law and Security Review* 719–35 at 721.

[5] Cedric Ryngaert, *Jurisdiction in International Law* (Oxford: Oxford University Press 2008), pp. 9–11. Noting that 'the lines between prescriptive jurisdiction, conflict of laws, and personal jurisdiction, which all stem from the transnational character of private litigation, have become blurred'.

[6] Dan Jerker B. Svantesson, 'Jurisdictional Issues and the Internet – A Brief Overview 2.0' (2018) 34 *Computer Law and Security Review* 715–22 at fn 1.

[7] Ryngaert, 'Jurisdiction in International Law', pp. 1–4.

[8] Sasha Segall, 'Jurisdictional Challenges in the United States Government's Move to Cloud Computing Technology' (2013) 23 *Fordham Intellectual Property, Media and Entertainment Law Journal* 1105–53 at 1119. WP29, 'Update of Opinion 8/2010 on Applicable Law in Light of the CJEU Judgement in Google Spain - WP179 Update' (2015), 22. https://ec.europa.eu/newsroom/article29/items/640614 .

[9] M. Dekker and Dimitra Liveri, 'Cloud Security Guide for SMEs: Cloud Computing Security Risks and Opportunities for SMEs' (2015), 6. www.enisa.europa.eu/activities/Resilience-and-CIIP/cloud-computing/security-for-smes/cloud-security-guide-for-smes.

and indiscriminately accessed data stored with CSPs. Similar programs have been in place in the United Kingdom.[10] For states, this has raised serious questions regarding the physical (and logical) control of data entrusted to CSPs.[11]

Although cloud services are 'available everywhere', or at least anywhere there is an internet connection, they also have physical components with ascertainable locations. To be precise, cloud services are hosted on computer servers with physical locations.[12] However, determining where that location is can be a difficult and technical question with varied answers. Depending on the CSP's technical and organizational makeup, some cloud services will be unable to pinpoint the exact jurisdictional location of their users' data.[13] Within the same service, data are often divided into different pieces or fragments that may all be stored in different jurisdictions.[14] Even if the records are not fragmented, exact copies of records or files can be located in multiple jurisdictions simultaneously in server parks and on PCs and mobile devices.[15] The reality is that pointing to one place where data are located is becoming not only increasingly difficult, but the distinction is far from the most important or relevant factor.

Although it is of consequence that data have a location in cloud services, the relevance of this location is different than when applied in the offline world.[16] For instance, tangible items sought in a police investigation have traditionally existed in the sovereign territory of one state at a time.[17] Whether a firearm stored in a basement safe or stolen documents stored in a safety deposit box, law enforcement agents can point to a tangible item and tie it to one location. Law enforcement agencies (LEAs) also have specific legal tools granting them permission to obtain such physical evidence.

---

[10] *Big Brother Watch and Others v. the United Kingdom* (applications nos. 58170/13, 62322/14 and 24960/15) (ECHR, 13 September 2018). Finding that the UK bulk interception and surveillance by GCHQ under the UK Regulation of Investigatory Powers (RIPA) Act violated Article 8 of the European Convention on Human Rights because it contained insufficient oversight in its means of interception and safeguards.

[11] François LeSieur, 'Regulating Cross-Border Data Flows and Privacy in the Networked Digital Environment and Global Knowledge Economy' (2012) 2 *International Data Privacy Law* 93–104 at 98.

[12] John D. Vandenberg and others, 'Brief for 51 Computer Scientists as Amici Curiae in Support of the Respondent', *Amici Curie Brief filed in Amici Curie Brief filed in US v. Microsoft Corporation*, 8. www .scotusblog.com/case-files/cases/united-states-v-microsoft-corp/. Providing that data stored on a cloud service is ' . . . always stored in at least one specific location . . . '.

[13] Dan Jerker B. Svantesson, *Solving the Internet Jurisdiction Puzzle* (Oxford: Oxford University Press 2017), pp. 72–73. Citing the example of Google cloud computing services.

[14] ibid., 17–18.

[15] ibid.

[16] Dan Jerker B. Svantesson, 'Against "Against Data Exceptionalism"' (2016) 10 *Masaryk University Journal of Law and Technology* 200–11 at 210–11. https://doi.org/10.5817/MUJLT2016-2-4.

[17] Vivek Krishnamurthy and Mason Kortzus, 'Brief Amicus Curiae of UN Special Rapporteur on the Right to Privacy Joseph Cannataci in Support of Neither Party', *Amici Curie Brief filed in US v. Microsoft Corporation*, 17. www.supremecourt.gov/DocketPDF/17/17-2/24918/20171222120327043_35632%20pdf% 20Krishnamurthy.pdf.

Because cloud computing services often separate the user, provider, infrastructure, and access points, finding a specific and consistent approach to determining jurisdiction is an unsolved problem. Traditionally, a great deal of emphasis has been placed on the physical location (rather than the virtual location) of the data. As a starting point, in most cloud computing arrangements, a territorial claim for jurisdiction – either *in personam* or *in rem* – could be made in at least the following situations:

(1) The state where the CSP is physically located. This could be based on the place of incorporation or principal place of operations, among others.
(2) If the CSP stores data and has infrastructure in a state, an *in rem* territorial claim can be made based on the location of the servers or other physical infrastructure or property.
(3) The state from which the CSP has access to or controls the cloud service. This would likely include multiple states.
(4) The state from which the cloud client accesses the cloud service.
(5) If data are collected, the location of the individual whom the data concerns.
(6) If data are processed in a jurisdiction, the location where such processing takes place.

There are many examples of worldwide data transfers that are regularly taking place in the cloud computing context. For example, when a European-based user uploads data to a cloud service located in the United States, is the storage of that data now subject to US jurisdiction since it is physically located in the United States, or is the EU the more logical forum as the data are accessed and consumed there? How should remote access for support be treated? What about the nations through which the data transits when it is copied or backed up along the way?[18] Is the evaluation of jurisdiction based on the physical location of data too tenuous or feeble, even if it has traditionally formed an important basis for determining jurisdiction?

In addition to concerns around every state being able to find some sort of jurisdictional nexus and claim of jurisdiction over CSPs, it is also worth considering that the opposite problem could also emerge. That is, it may become difficult to find *any* connection. In addition to their global distribution, by design, CSPs often try to control jurisdiction over their services contractually or through corporate arrangements. Although CSP marketing departments produce advertisements that focus on the cloud being 'available everywhere', CSP legal departments often focus on availability in much narrower terms – at least for the purposes of establishing jurisdiction. As noted in a Council of Europe (CoE) report on cloud computing:

> Service providers may set up complex business arrangements through which a third party may become the trustee of their data so as to insulate themselves from legal

[18] Jennifer Daskal, 'The Un-Territoriality of Data' (2015) 125 *Yale Law Journal* 326–98 at 336. Discussing the mobility, and often unusual path of data between or among jurisdictions.

process. Or service providers may organise themselves so that they appear to have no headquarters or physical presence and *thereby evade any jurisdiction*.[19]

Swinging the pendulum in the other direction, if jurisdictional lines are drawn too broadly, CSPs would also find themselves subject to the jurisdictions of essentially wherever they – or their subcontractors – have infrastructure. In addition to using server location as a nexus, other infrastructure, the location of people, sales offices, IT support, or corporate operations might also be targeted or used to form a jurisdictional basis. For instance, if courts are more willing to find even rather tenuous connections, such as the point of access, as sufficient for determining jurisdiction, CSPs could go from being 'available everywhere' to 'available to be sued everywhere'.

In addition to drawing jurisdictional boundaries too narrowly or too broadly, problems may also arise if more than one state (or court) has a legitimate claim to jurisdiction over a matter. That is, if the legal issue raised by the use of cloud computing results in a legal issue that affects more than one country, there is potential for conflict over which court is most appropriate to adjudicate the matter. If such claims cannot be reconciled, it has the potential to create conflicts between or among states.[20] In this chapter, I focus primarily on problems in determining jurisdiction and law enforcement access to cloud data. However, once a jurisdictional determination is made, courts must then decide which law to apply and address legal questions related to enforcement of the judgment.

In the case of a cloud computing service, the state in which the CSP's servers are physically located may have a valid claim for jurisdiction. Additionally, the jurisdiction from which the services are accessed or consumed may also have a valid jurisdictional claim over aspects of the service. If these claims do not conflict, they can generally coexist. In some situations, including comity or an inconvenient forum, courts will decline to enforce their jurisdiction in favour of a more suitable one.[21] However, in cloud computing services there is a great deal of potential for conflict and there may not always be a clear or even suitable jurisdiction.

Control over data is increasingly being considered as intertwined with state sovereignty. Maintaining control is often equated with keeping data stored within one physical location or jurisdiction where the government has physical access. If

---

[19] Council of Europe (CoE), 'Criminal Justice Access to Electronic Evidence in the Cloud: Recommendations for Consideration by the T-CY' (2016) *Final Report of the Cybercrime Convention Committee (T-CY) Cloud Evidence Group*, 8. Emphasis added. www.coe.int/en/web/cybercrime/ceg. Paul M. Schwartz, 'Legal Access to the Global Cloud' (2018) 118 *Columbia Law Review* 1681–762 at 1697–98. Describing the 'data trust model' used by Microsoft wherein a separate trusted third party from the CSP is given access to the data, adding a level of managerial or organizational control.

[20] Ryngaert, 'Jurisdiction in International Law', p. 127.

[21] Francis Augusto Medeiros, 'Is ".com" International? The .com gTLD: An Analysis of its Global Nature through the Prism of Jurisdiction' (2013) 21 *International Journal of Law and Information Technology* 269–312 at 288.

states follow an approach where maintaining sovereignty requires physically storing data in a specific location, the jurisdictional aspect also becomes increasingly important for states entrusting their data to CSPs.[22] In my opinion, such an extreme focus on location is largely misplaced. More important than physical access to servers is intelligible access to data. That is, having physical control over the 'metal' or a server only containing encrypted shards of data will not yield much information. However, having remote access through which files can be accessed and viewed interferes with sovereignty to a much greater extent, even if the access takes place from around the globe.[23] Therefore, although location has some significance, focusing too intently on location or a specific jurisdiction is a diversion when it comes to protecting sovereignty.

4.2 ASSERTING JURISDICTION ON THE INTERNET

The rationale or justification for asserting jurisdiction generally includes at least two elements: (1) the sovereignty of the state over its territory and (2) the ability of national courts to apply national laws within their competence.[24] Along those lines, two aspects of jurisdiction are relatively constant, regardless of the originating jurisdiction or legal system. These include its ties to state sovereignty and the ability of a state to make certain judicial determinations over acts occurring domestically.[25] Jurisdiction is thus an essential element of state sovereignty.[26] In addition to finding or asserting jurisdiction over a matter, person, or property, specific jurisdictional theories are also carved out to provide specific rules or doctrines covering everything from 'antitrust jurisdiction' to 'universal jurisdiction'. There are also different approaches taken to determining jurisdiction based on legal tradition.[27]

When referring to 'jurisdiction' over the Internet, the concepts of 'applicable law' and 'jurisdiction' are often conflated as having the same meaning. Although they may blur together in some instances, they can generally be distinguished as follows. Jurisdiction refers to the state or entity with the regulatory power to hear or regulate a dispute.[28] Applicable law refers to the substantive (rather than the procedural) law that is applicable to the particular dispute.[29] In cases involving foreign actors or

---

[22] Segall, 'Jurisdictional Challenges in the United States Government's Move to Cloud Computing Technology', 1137–40.
[23] Christopher Millard, 'Forced Localization of Cloud Services: Is Privacy the Real Driver?' (2015) 2 *IEEE Cloud Computing* 10–14 at 13.
[24] Velasco, Hörnle, and Osula, 'Global Views on Internet Jurisdiction and Trans-border Access', p. 465.
[25] Malcolm N. Shaw, *International Law* (Cambridge: Cambridge University Press 2003), p. 572. See also Ryngaert, 'Jurisdiction in International Law', p. 5.
[26] Shaw, 'International Law', p. 572. Describing jurisdiction as 'a vital and indeed central feature' of state sovereignty.
[27] Velasco, Hörnle, and Osula, 'Global Views on Internet Jurisdiction and Trans-border Access', p. 465.
[28] Christopher Kuner, 'Data Protection Law and International Jurisdiction on the Internet (Part I)' (2010) 18 *International Journal of Law and Information Technology* 176–93 at 178.
[29] Svantesson, 'Jurisdictional Issues and the Internet', 717. Noting that even when applying a foreign law, states apply their own procedure.

actions, a determination of whether a court has jurisdiction is often 'the first thing a court has to decide'.[30] Although applicable law and jurisdiction overlap, this chapter primarily considers a national court's jurisdiction. In particular, when the 'metal', or servers, making up a CSP's infrastructure are located in one state and the courts of another assert jurisdiction over data that is accessible globally.

The basis for a court to find jurisdiction over a matter will depend on the claims brought forth or the legal theory asserted. Absent a contractual choice defining the place of jurisdiction – considered further in the text – the location of where an event occurred or where the parties are located is often the most relevant factor in a jurisdictional claim.[31] For instance, in the case of taxation law, the focus is often on international headquarters. In intellectual property rights litigation, jurisdictional rules often focus on the location of the business. The location where an injury occurred is a central factor in determining jurisdiction under tort law. The status of the parties to the action is often of consequence as consumers are given special protection in areas such as online contracting. Even if there is no single rule that fits all of these cases, location tends to weigh heavily. However, many of the factors that have been used to make a finding of jurisdiction, such as the location of a party to a contract, are often difficult to discern or relatively meaningless in the Internet context.[32]

Building on the role of state sovereignty in jurisdiction, Kuner defines the jurisdictional justifications that are most widely applied to asserting jurisdiction in the data protection context as 'effects', 'territoriality', 'personality', and 'protective' principles.[33] The effects principle refers to a state's ability to 'prescribe law with respect to conduct that has a substantial effect within its territory'.[34] Applying jurisdiction based on effects has been primarily used in the areas of competition or antitrust law.[35] In many circumstances, the effects principle is redundant, as states would generally have other legitimate jurisdictional interests, such as the protective principle or another basis for asserting jurisdiction.[36] However, as noted by

[30] J. J. Fawcett, J. Harris, and M. G. Bridge, *International Sale of Goods in the Conflict of Laws* (Oxford: Oxford University Press 2005), s. 2.01.
[31] Svantesson, 'Jurisdictional Issues and the Internet', 718.
[32] ibid. Criticizing the application of the location of contract formation as a basis for jurisdiction as 'arbitrary and a legal fiction' when applied online.
[33] Kuner, 'Data Protection Law and International Jurisdiction on the Internet (Part I)', 188–91. See also Simon Bradshaw, Christopher Millard, and Ian Walden, 'Standard Contracts for Cloud Services' in Christopher Millard (ed.), *Cloud Computing Law* (Oxford: Oxford University Press 2013), pp. 47–48. Contract studies found that almost all CSPs had a contract clause specifying jurisdiction.
[34] Restatement (Fourth) of Foreign Relations Law (2016): Jurisdiction § 213 Jurisdiction Based on Effects. See also Kuner, 'Data Protection Law and International Jurisdiction on the Internet (Part I)', 190–91.
[35] Restatement (Fourth) of Foreign Relations Law (2016): Jurisdiction § 213 Jurisdiction Based on Effects, note 2. See also Restatement (Third) of Foreign Relations Law § 402 Bases of Jurisdiction to Prescribe (1987). See also Svantesson, 'Solving the Internet Jurisdiction Puzzle', pp. 30–33.
[36] ibid., 32.

Svantesson, the effects doctrine is useful for providing a base when other justifications are not applicable.[37] For instance, Svantesson uses the example of a company's foreign cloud service being hacked.[38] If the crime of hacking does not take place in the nation state where the company or the CSP is located, but clearly affects the business in that state, the effects principle may be the most appropriate grounds for the affected state to assert jurisdiction.[39]

The *territoriality principle*, as applied to jurisdiction, provides states with jurisdiction over acts that occur within their sovereign territory.[40] This principle is primarily concerned with location and is based on the premise that 'sovereignty and jurisdiction can only be comprehended in relation to territory'.[41] At first blush, this approach may seem unproblematic. As applied generally, territorial jurisdiction gives a state the authority to 'prescribe law with respect to persons, property, and conduct within its territory'.[42] However, as noted by Kuner, ' ... the Internet greatly complicates application of the territoriality principle, since it can be nearly impossible to localize an online action as occurring in a particular State'.[43] In the cloud computing context, an open question remains regarding how significant the connection must be to give rise to jurisdiction. Network cables? A server park? Entire files stored on a server? Fragments of files, or even metadata? Assertions for a finding of jurisdiction could be made for any of these elements.

As a basis for jurisdiction, the territorial principle and the Internet are a poor fit.[44] As Daskal explains, data moves from place to place, 'generally without the conscious choice – or even knowledge – of the data "user"'.[45] Because clear lines are often difficult to draw, the location of the server where the data is being stored often becomes the focal point.[46] In many instances, the location of the server and its connection to the parties is tenuous at best. Additionally, the focus provides the jurisdiction where the CSP is located with excessive influence. For instance, in the United States, where many CSPs happen to be located, server location is central for determining jurisdiction.[47]

[37] ibid.
[38] ibid.
[39] ibid., 32–33.
[40] Ryngaert, 'Jurisdiction in International Law', p. 42. Kuner, 'Data Protection Law and International Jurisdiction on the Internet (Part I)', 188.
[41] Osula, 'Transborder Access and Territorial Sovereignty', 722.
[42] Restatement (Fourth) of Foreign Relations Law (2016): Jurisdiction § 212 Jurisdiction Based on Territory, comment (a).
[43] Kuner, 'Data Protection Law and International Jurisdiction on the Internet (Part I)', 188.
[44] Burke T. Ward and Janice C. Sipior, 'The Internet Jurisdiction Risk of Cloud Computing' (2010) 27 *Information Systems Management* 334–39 at 335. The focus on physical presence as a basis for jurisdiction has become less relevant in cloud.
[45] Daskal, 'The Un-Territoriality of Data', 329.
[46] Svantesson, 'Solving the Internet Jurisdiction Puzzle', p. 63.
[47] Segall, 'Jurisdictional Challenges in the United States Government's Move to Cloud Computing Technology', 1122. Citing several cases where server location was determined to be a relevant connecting factor, even in cases where the defendant was not located in the state. *Aitken*

The *personality principle* allows a state to prescribe law to its nationals located outside of its territory, including natural persons and corporations.[48] The *protective principle* aims to protect a state from an act committed abroad that impacts its sovereignty.[49] A primary example would be serious violations that compromise the security of a state, such as a cyberattack. This principle focuses on protecting the state rather than the individual.[50]

4.3 JURISDICTION IN PUBLIC AND PRIVATE INTERNATIONAL LAW

In this section, I provide a limited overview of the current jurisdictional framework for asserting jurisdiction in public international law and its impact on cloud computing.[51] In the area of jurisdiction, public and private international law approaches have traditionally been assigned distinct spheres.[52] However, they often apply similar concepts and justifications in their jurisdictional frameworks.[53] As noted by Polčák and Svantesson, there is a clear link between the concepts, and in some instances, the principles falling under public international law have been imported or applied in the realm of private international law.[54] As in the view of Ryngaert:

> [I]t is not surprising that the lines between prescriptive jurisdiction, conflict of laws, and personal jurisdiction, which all stem from the transnational character of private litigation, have become blurred. A conceptual reconstruction of the exercise of jurisdiction over extraterritorial and transnational situations by courts is not an easy undertaking then. In such situations, jurisdiction becomes a multi-layered legal concept involving both public and private international law elements.[55]

Although I agree that the distinction between private and public law creates confusion when evaluating jurisdiction, a distinction nevertheless exists in legal doctrine. Private international law (or conflicts of law) focuses on when a state, within its jurisdiction, may exercise or decline jurisdiction, determine applicable law, and recognize or enforce a foreign judgment.[56] While states often enter into international agreements that function on a much broader basis than domestic

---

v. *Commc'ns Workers of Am.*, 496 F Supp. 2d 653, 659 (E.D. Va. 2007). Holding that the location of a company's server, along with some if its employees, was enough to find jurisdiction in that state.

[48] Kuner, 'Data Protection Law and International Jurisdiction on the Internet (Part I)', 188–89.
[49] ibid., 190.
[50] ibid.
[51] Polčák and Svantesson, 'Information Sovereignty', p. 41. Noting 'public international law is an enormously diverse discipline'.
[52] Dan Jerker B. Svantesson, 'A New Jurisprudential Framework for Jurisdiction: Beyond the Harvard Draft' (2015) 109 *American Journal of International Law Unbound* 69–74 at 72–73.
[53] ibid.
[54] Polčák and Svantesson, 'Information Sovereignty', pp. 159–61.
[55] ibid.
[56] ibid., 41.

legislation, private international law is effectively domestic law and determined by each individual state.[57]

In private international law, parties are generally free to make certain choices regarding jurisdiction and applicable law. These choices in contractual matters on a B2B or B2G basis are generally effective, falling under the freedom of parties to contract. Although choosing a form and law to be applied in the case of a dispute may provide a level of certainty or predictability in some instances, it will not always control the jurisdiction or applicable law. If a choice of forum (or law) has not been agreed to by the parties, or is not applicable as a result of the legal issue before the court (e.g. intellectual property rights or tort), the court must sort out conflict of laws and personal or adjudicative jurisdiction, among other issues.[58] The treatment of a forum selection clause will also vary depending on the legal issue, the status of the parties (e.g. consumer), and the legal tradition where the contract is interpreted.[59]

In public international law, there are three primary or generally accepted types of jurisdiction, including: (1) prescriptive jurisdiction, (2) judicial jurisdiction, and (3) enforcement jurisdiction. A possible fourth type, investigative jurisdiction, is also evaluated later in the text. In addition to discussions over the category under which the principles should fall (i.e. private or public law), the number of principles, what is included as part of those principles, and even the names of the principles escape consensus.[60]

As argued by Svantesson, there is a 'serious lack of agreement' among commentators and experts in this area.[61] Furthermore, ' ... the complexity in distinguishing between the noted three types of jurisdiction has led commentators into errors and lacking conceptual sharpness'.[62] Therefore, I proceed with a note of caution and the following caveat. Given the controversy and confusion in this area, the framework and discussion I provide later make up *a* picture rather than *the* picture of jurisdictional principles applicable to cloud computing services.

4.3.1 Prescriptive Jurisdiction

Prescriptive jurisdiction refers to the state's ability to make and apply laws regarding persons or things within its territory (i.e. land, internal waters, territorial sea,

---

[57] Svantesson, 'Jurisdictional Issues and the Internet', 717. See also Faye Fangfei Wang, *Internet Jurisdiction and Choice of Law: Legal Practices in the EU, US and China* (Cambridge: Cambridge University Press 2010), pp. 8–14.
[58] Ryngaert, 'Jurisdiction in International Law', p. 11. See Wang, 'Internet Jurisdiction and Choice of Law', pp. 91–130. Examining the private international law rules for choice of law in the EU, United States, and China.
[59] Kevin McGillivray, 'A Right Too Far? Requiring Cloud Service Providers to Deliver Adequate Data Security to Consumers' (2017) 25 *International Journal of Law and Information Technology* 1–25 at 6–7. https://doi.org/10.1093/ijlit/eaw011.
[60] Svantesson, 'Solving the Internet Jurisdiction Puzzle', p. 161.
[61] ibid.
[62] ibid., 162.

and airspace).[63] Specifically, prescriptive jurisdiction focuses on the authority of a state to apply its laws to ' ... persons, property, or conduct'.[64] Pursuant to the Restatement Fourth on jurisdiction, prescriptive jurisdiction may generally be exercised where 'there is a genuine connection between the subject of the regulation and the state seeking to regulate'.[65] This connection relies primarily on territoriality, effects in a territory, active or passive personality, or protection.[66] This type of jurisdiction is generally associated with a state's legislative rather than judicial branch.[67] As a result, it is sometimes referred to as 'legislative jurisdiction'.[68]

Prescriptive jurisdiction also allows a state to 'apply its laws to cases involving a foreign element' in addition to domestic acts.[69] Prescriptive jurisdiction is not exclusive, and in the online context it will often be concurrent.[70] In the case of data protection law, this would include applying the GDPR to a state located outside of the EU, based on targeting.[71] Although this authority is applied broadly, in most areas, states limit its application to substantial contacts.[72] Even if prescriptive jurisdiction allows states to prescribe or acquire jurisdiction beyond their borders, enforcing such jurisdictional determinations is difficult.

4.3.2 Judicial Jurisdiction

Judicial (or adjudicative) jurisdiction, or *in personam* jurisdiction, as it is often referred to in the United States, is the power of courts to claim jurisdiction over individuals and make decisions that bind them.[73] This individual person (or in some cases, thing) is subject to the judicial process of the courts in that state.[74] This type of jurisdiction is largely concerned with the interests of an individual or party brought before a court in a dispute.[75] In the United States, determining whether a court may

---

[63] Shaw, 'International Law', p. 572. Henry H. Perritt Jr, Jonathan Taylor, and John Morgan, 'Achieving Legal and Business Order in Cyberspace: A Report on Global Jurisdiction Issues Created by the Internet' (2000) 55 *Business Lawyer* 1801–946 at 1873.
[64] Restatement (Fourth) of Foreign Relations Law: Jurisdiction § 211 TD No 2 (2016), § 211 Customary International Law Governing Jurisdiction to Prescribe. Comment (a).
[65] ibid.
[66] ibid.
[67] Anthony J. Colangelo, 'What is Extraterritorial Jurisdiction' (2014) 99 *Cornell Law Review* 1303–52 at 1310–11.
[68] ibid.
[69] Kuner, 'Data Protection Law and International Jurisdiction on the Internet (Part I)', 184.
[70] ibid. See also Svantesson, 'Solving the Internet Jurisdiction Puzzle', p. 20. Providing that international law allows for concurrent jurisdiction.
[71] Kuner, 'Data Protection Law and International Jurisdiction on the Internet (Part I)', 184.
[72] Perritt Jr, Taylor, and Morgan, 'Achieving Legal and Business Order in Cyberspace', 73.
[73] Ryngaert, 'Jurisdiction in International Law', p. 11.
[74] Colangelo, 'What is Extraterritorial Jurisdiction', 1311.
[75] Ryngaert, 'Jurisdiction in International Law', p. 12.

exercise jurisdiction *in personam* focuses on minimum contacts.[76] In the EU, courts generally focus on the place of domicile or residence of the defendant.[77]

4.3.3 Enforcement Jurisdiction

Enforcement jurisdiction refers to a state's ability to require compliance (or punish noncompliance) with a law.[78] Enforcement jurisdiction is often based on the principle of territoriality, focusing heavily on the enforcement of actions based on location.[79] The seminal case in this regard is the *Lotus* case, which considers the limits of application of jurisdiction under international law involving ships colliding in international waters.[80] As succinctly summarized by Kuner, the *Lotus* takeaway is that '... a State may not directly enforce its law beyond its borders, but that applying its law to the conduct taking place beyond its borders is largely permissible, as long as there are recognized legal grounds for doing so'.[81]

4.3.4 Investigative Jurisdiction

Investigative jurisdiction relates to a state's power to investigate a matter outside of its adjudicative jurisdiction.[82] Unlike the other categories listed earlier, investigative jurisdiction is a suggested or emerging approach principally derived from a branch or element of enforcement jurisdiction.[83] However, investigative jurisdiction focuses more closely on a test for obtaining evidence rather than jurisdiction over the offence itself. That is, a state is not required to have enforcement jurisdiction over a matter for investigatory purposes and can seek evidence even when it is not actively adjudicating or prosecuting the offence. In other words, the state is seeking evidence of a crime rather than jurisdiction over the criminal act. This is an important distinction to make in the cloud computing context as the two are very often located in separate and distinct jurisdictions.[84]

---

[76] ibid., 12–14. Discussing its broad application in the United States and limits.
[77] ibid.
[78] Restatement (Third) of Foreign Relations Law §§ 401 et seq. I. '(c) jurisdiction to enforce, i.e., to induce or compel compliance or to punish noncompliance with its laws or regulations, whether through the courts or by use of executive, administrative, police, or other nonjudicial action'.
[79] Dan Jerker B. Svantesson and Lodewijk van Zwieten, 'Law Enforcement Access to Evidence Via Direct Contact with Cloud Providers – Identifying the Contours of a Solution' (2016) 32 *Computer Law & Security Review* 671–82 at 678.
[80] Kuner, 'Data Protection Law and International Jurisdiction on the Internet (Part I)', 184–87. Citing *SS Lotus (France v. Turkey)*, 1927 PCIJ (ser. A) No. 10 (7 September 1927), 19. For further analysis of the case, including dissents, see Svantesson, 'Solving the Internet Jurisdiction Puzzle', pp. 15–24.
[81] Kuner, 'Data Protection Law and International Jurisdiction on the Internet (Part I)', 185.
[82] Polčák and Svantesson, 'Information Sovereignty', p. 45.
[83] Svantesson, 'Solving the Internet Jurisdiction Puzzle', p. 166.
[84] ibid., 168. The activity being investigated and the evidence sought for that investigation are not the same thing.

The primary argument for keeping investigative jurisdiction distinct from its moorings in enforcement jurisdiction is that a state may have a range of interests in investigating activities without ever moving to assert jurisdiction over the matter.[85] For instance, as part of its investigation, the state may determine that it does not have a legitimate interest in applying enforcement jurisdiction over the matter or that the matter should be handled by another state.[86] Therefore, in addition to the three primary or conventional types of jurisdiction, Svantesson suggests that 'investigative jurisdiction' has the potential to offer added nuance to the application of jurisdiction over the Internet.[87]

The point of departure in the approach is to move from a fixed application to a more principle-based/totality of the circumstances-type assessment. The advantage of this approach is its flexibility. Courts applying such a test would likely develop diverging interpretations. However, they would be working off the same template or model.

4.4 TERRITORIAL VERSUS EXTRATERRITORIAL APPLICATION

Regardless of the Internet technology, a reoccurring theme and complicating factor is whether an act is territorial or extraterritorial. Conceptually, it seems logical that the two can be separated and compartmentalized. Regulation occurring within a state's borders is territorial. Regulation that is applied or effected beyond a state's borders is extraterritorial. Results of the dualistic formula include the following: if a state goes beyond domestic control and legislates on matters that have an impact outside of its borders, the application of the legislation is extraterritorial and likely raises issues of international law.[88] States justify the extraterritorial application of their laws by using several theories anchored in territoriality and sovereignty.[89]

In a pre-globalized world, questions of extraterritoriality had a more limited audience. Extraterritoriality was mostly a concern for multinational corporations and other global actors dealing with complex transborder antitrust or environmental issues.[90] The Internet has significantly expanded the actors affected by issues of extraterritoriality and the number of laws with extraterritorial application.[91] These changes have some potential consequences. For example, Reed argues that the

---

[85] Dan Svantesson and Felicity Gerry, 'Access to Extraterritorial Evidence: The Microsoft Cloud Case and Beyond' (2015) 31 *Computer Law & Security Review* 478–89 at 480.
[86] ibid.
[87] Svantesson, 'Solving the Internet Jurisdiction Puzzle', p. 165.
[88] Ryngaert, 'Jurisdiction in International Law', p. 6. Noting that the term 'extraterritoriality' itself is confusing.
[89] Osula, 'Transborder Access and Territorial Sovereignty', 723. Colangelo, 'What is Extraterritorial Jurisdiction', 1312–13. See also Chris Reed, *Making Laws for Cyberspace* (Oxford: Oxford University Press 2012), p. 39. Describing the effects doctrine as a 'very blunt instrument' because '[i]t will always be unclear which effects in the jurisdiction will trigger the application of the law'.
[90] Reed, 'Making Laws for Cyberspace', pp. 31–32.
[91] ibid.

expansion of extraterritoriality has the potential for greater conflict and the 'unintended and inappropriate application of national laws ... '.[92] Reed also points out that broad extraterritorial application of laws carries the risk of lowering respect for laws more generally.[93] In many cases, extraterritorial application in drafting legislation is unintentional.

Confusion in this area is unfortunate because the distinction is central to answering legal questions falling under both private and public international law.[94] As asserted by Svantesson ' ... extraterritoriality is the key ingredient in every controversial claim of jurisdiction in relation to the Internet'.[95] If such regulation could be kept to a binary 'inside' or 'outside' designation, the distinction might be workable. However, this is not the case.[96]

The crux of much of Svantesson's criticism of the territorial/extraterritorial distinction and the principle of territoriality is not the rise of new technologies eroding a tried and true principle.[97] Rather, much of his argument is that the distinction itself is oversimplified and has become unworkable.[98] In short, the disproportionate focus on location or territory is no longer a meaningful (or meaningful enough) distinction in many areas.[99] However, when this bright-line or dualistic distinction is applied to the Internet or cloud computing, it simply does not function.[100] The dualistic status quo distinction lacks the flexibility needed and does not provide the means to create bright-line rules.

This point was aptly demonstrated by Amoore, citing the testimony of Foreign Secretary Philip Hammond before the UK Intelligence and Security Committee (ISC) of Parliament.[101] The testimony took place after the revelation of the US PRISM program by Edward Snowden.[102] As supplied by Amoore, Foreign Secretary Hammond, ' ... manifestly fails to understand the complex spatial form of data stored, transferred or analysed in the cloud'.[103] Hammond testified as follows:

Q: The distinction between internal and external to the UK is important because there are tighter restrictions on analysing internal data ... But if the sender and

---

[92] ibid., 32.
[93] ibid., 33–35. C.f. Svantesson, 'Solving the Internet Jurisdiction Puzzle', pp. 133–35. Arguing that regulatory overreaching, by making jurisdictional claims with no real chance of success, is not a problem *per se*.
[94] Svantesson, 'Solving the Internet Jurisdiction Puzzle', p. 40.
[95] ibid.
[96] Kuner, 'Data Protection Law and International Jurisdiction on the Internet (Part I)', 188.
[97] Svantesson, 'Solving the Internet Jurisdiction Puzzle', pp. 40–44.
[98] ibid.
[99] ibid., 44.
[100] ibid., 45.
[101] Louise Amoore, 'Cloud Geographies: Computing, Data, Sovereignty' (2016) 42 *Progress in Human Geography* 4–24 at 8–9.
[102] ibid.
[103] ibid., 8.

4.4 Territorial versus Extraterritorial Application 73

recipient of an email are both in the UK, will it be treated as internal even if the data is routed overseas on its journey?

A: So, I think ... er ... and I invite my colleagues to step in if I get this technically wrong ... But I think ... er ... it's an internal communication. [At this point the civil servants flanking the Minister lean in: 'I don't think that can be right'.]

A: Let me finish my train of thought ... my understanding is, er, because of the technical nature of the internet ... it is possible it could be routed to servers outside the UK ... Please correct me if I misinterpreted that ... I'm sorry, I have misled you in my use of terms ... I'm trying to be helpful.

Q: Well you will be relieved to know that was the easy one. Now, the case of social media ... if all of my restricted group of Facebook friends are in the UK ... and I post something to Facebook, surely that should be internal?

A: [following whispers from civil servants] 'erm ... no actually, if you put something on Facebook and the server is outside of the UK it will be treated as an external communication.

Q: What about cloud storage, where no other person is involved at all. It may be my decision to upload photographs to Dropbox. Would these communications be regarded as external because they are on US servers?

A: Aaah ... er ... My colleagues will ... oh ... well .... Yes, I am advised if the server is overseas they will be regarded as external.[104]

As argued by Amoore, this testimony shows the difficulty that even a minister in charge of authorizing and signing warrants for intercepting communications has significant difficulty understanding and explaining how those rules apply to cloud technology.[105]

From a practical perspective, the difficulty in determining jurisdiction under the existing regime is a primary concern for not only cloud clients and CSPs but also courts. When evaluating and applying the territorial/extraterritorial distinction to a typical cloud computing scenario, many equally correct answers can be given regarding a finding of jurisdiction. Although this is interesting and challenging academically, it is extremely problematic for those that must adhere to these rules. When applied to cloud computing, it does not take long for cracks to emerge. Simply put, the framework breaks down when confronted with reality.[106] Continuing on a path with an extreme focus on borders, when location is of little consequence to the technology being regulated, conflicts and legal rules that are both confusing and difficult to apply are bound to be the result.

---

[104] ibid., 8–9.
[105] ibid.
[106] ibid., 43. See further, Dan Jerker B. Svantesson, 'Extraterritoriality and Targeting in EU Data Privacy Law: The Weak Spot Undermining the Regulation' (2015) 5 *International Data Privacy Law* 226–34 at 226.

4.5 LAW ENFORCEMENT AGENCY ACCESS

Applying jurisdictional rules to law enforcement access (LEA) to data stored on the cloud brings with it an additional set of challenges.[107] As a starting point, it is often unclear which law applies or where a search should occur, raising issues of both domestic and international law.[108] In criminal law, a further distinction is often made regarding jurisdiction over the offence and jurisdiction over the evidence.[109] Thereby, with minimal exertion of effort, the same fact pattern can result in a search that is entirely domestic (territorial) or international (extraterritorial). Generally, there are three primary approaches to evaluating LEA access, including:

(1) The search occurs in the jurisdiction where the law enforcement agents examine the data.[110] For example, if an email message is viewed on a computer in the LEA's jurisdiction, the search is not extraterritorial. For the purposes of determining jurisdiction, under this theory, everything of consequence took place under the LEA's jurisdiction. A search under this theory falls under domestic law.
(2) The search takes place both where the target computer or server is located and where the LEA is located.[111] This search has both territorial and extraterritorial application and concerns both domestic and international law.
(3) The search takes place where the computer is located, regardless of where the information is viewed or the location of the LEA. Under this theory, the search is extraterritorial, if the server is located in a different jurisdiction than the LEA and requires the application of mutual legal assistance treaties (MLATs).[112] MLATs provide a treaty-based means for LEAs to cooperate and provide assistance with judicial and executive oversight.

There are competing theories on the permissibility of foreign LEA access outside of the MLAT system, including both the permissiveness of and impact on international law.[113] On a practical level, regardless of their position on the location of a search, most states provide domestic LEA access to private-sector data. Although access to data by US law enforcement and security services is likely the most often discussed,

---

[107] CoE, 'Criminal Justice Access to Electronic Evidence in the Cloud', 8.
[108] ibid. Polčák and Svantesson, 'Information Sovereignty', p. 193.
[109] ibid., 194.
[110] Osula, 'Transborder Access and Territorial Sovereignty', 723–24. See also Schwartz, 'Legal Access to the Global Cloud', 1712. A Fourth Amendment search occurs at the point of human observation, including appearing on a computer screen. See also Orin S. Kerr, 'Searches and Seizures in a Digital World' (2005) 119 Harvard Law Review 531–85 at 551.
[111] Osula, 'Transborder Access and Territorial Sovereignty', 724.
[112] US Department of State, 7 Foreign Affairs Manual (FAM) § 962.1 (2013). https://fam.state.gov/fam/07fam/07fam0960.html.
[113] Osula, 'Transborder Access and Territorial Sovereignty', 725.

government access in the criminal context is not exceptional.[114] In a global study of government access to data, researchers concluded that

> ... in every country we studied, even those nations with otherwise comprehensive data protection laws, access for regulatory, law enforcement, and national security purposes is often excluded from such laws; alternatively, they are treated as accepted purposes for which access is authorized under separate laws that may or may not provide adequate safeguards against possible abuses.[115]

Although EU member states arguably have more stringent data protection requirements than places like the United States, law enforcement and national security authorities are also granted exceptions (or exemptions) from the requirements of data protection law. Under the laws of most Western democratic countries, national security authorities are usually given greater latitude in obtaining access to privately held data than LEAs.[116]

Because of these grants of authority, CSPs are often required to assist law enforcement or security agencies in accessing data stored on their systems.[117] Currently, there are many different approaches that LEAs take to gaining access from CSPs.[118] CSPs also take different approaches to how and when they provide access. If governments have broad access to data stored with CSPs in their territories, or via infrastructure occupying their territories, a CSP's location is significant.[119] Given the number of providers and the volume of communications passing through its territory, the US government has many opportunities to gain such access. In the following sections, I examine this access through the lens of a specific case.

4.6 ACCESS IN ACTION: THE MICROSOFT WARRANT CASE

The Microsoft warrant case provides a useful backdrop for examining issues related to transborder access to cloud services. The factual background is relatively straightforward. After finding probable cause for a search, a federal magistrate judge issued a warrant authorizing federal agents to obtain the contents of an email account operated by Microsoft. US federal law enforcement agents then served Microsoft

---

[114] Andrew Kirschenbaum, 'Beyond Microsoft: A Legislative Solution to the SCA's Extraterritoriality Problem' (2018) 86 *Fordham Law Review* 1923–62 at 1946–48.
[115] Ira S. Rubinstein, Gregory T. Nojeim, and Ronald D. Lee, 'Systematic Government Access to Private-Sector Data' in Fred H. Cate and James X. Dempsey (eds.), *Bulk Collection: Systematic Government Access to Private-Sector Data* (Oxford: Oxford University Press 2017), pp. 6–7.
[116] ibid., 7. Although some EU member states, notably Germany, have scaled back or limited investigative powers, such rules have generally remained in place. ibid., 99.
[117] ibid., 100. Noting that certain laws in the United States and the United Kingdom even require that technologies be designed with this access in mind.
[118] Svantesson and van Zwieten, 'Law Enforcement Access to Evidence Via Direct Contact with Cloud Providers', 672.
[119] Judith Rauhofer and Caspar Bowden, 'Protecting Their Own: Fundamental Rights Implications for EU Data Sovereignty in the Cloud' (2013) *No 2013/28 Edinburgh School of Law Research Paper* 1–31 at 11–12.

with a warrant to produce all data related to the email account.[120] In responding to law enforcement, Microsoft determined that some of the information regarding the account was stored in the United States, while the rest was stored in its data centre in Ireland.

Microsoft turned over data about the account located in the United States.[121] This included account-related information such as when emails were sent, recipients of the emails, and other limited communications. However, Microsoft did not supply the actual content of the email messages. The data were stored as part of the Microsoft account information held in Dublin. Microsoft argued that because the information was stored on a server in Ireland, the data did not reside in the United States, and any disclosure thereof was subject to Irish law.[122] As a result, Microsoft maintained that the US government would have to access the data via traditional international channels for obtaining records stored abroad, including the use of MLATs.[123]

The central legal issue in the case was the location of the data and jurisdiction of the search warrant in the US state of Washington (territorial) or the data centre in Ireland (extraterritorial).[124] Both parties agreed that the data were stored in Ireland.[125] However, the ability, ease, and means of accessing the data were disputed.[126] Furthermore, as evaluated later, the parties disagreed over *where* the access took place. That is, would the US LEA be accessing data in the United States when it viewed the records, or would this happen in Ireland where the data were stored?

The Microsoft case has a relatively complex procedural history winding through the US federal court system and resulting in several lengthy judicial decisions.[127] The case was ultimately appealed to the Supreme Court of the United States (SCOTUS), which agreed to hear the case. After the oral arguments, but before a decision in the case was reached, the president signed into law the Clarifying Lawful Overseas Use of Data (CLOUD) Act, therefore amending the 1986 Stored Communications Act (SCA).[128] The CLOUD Act effectively settled the dispute at

---

[120] ibid., 203. The warrant was written using boilerplate text, commanding Microsoft to search "[t]he PREMISES known and described as the email account [redacted]@MSN.COM, which is controlled by Microsoft Corporation'.

[121] ibid., 204.

[122] *Microsoft Corp v. United States*, 202–09.

[123] See generally, Yonatan L. Moskowitz, 'MLATS and the Trusted Nation Club: The Proper Cost of Membership' (2016) 41 *Yale Journal of International Law Online* 1–14.

[124] *Microsoft Corp v. United States*, 202–09. There were additional questions regarding the categorization of order as a warrant.

[125] ibid.

[126] ibid.

[127] *Re Warrant to Search a Certain Email Account Controlled & Maintained by Microsoft Corp.*, 15 F Supp 3d 466 (SDNY 2014). The district court affirmed the magistrate's decision *Re Warrant to Search a Certain E-Mail Account Controlled and Maintained by Microsoft Corp.*, 829 F. 3d 197, 204–05 (CA2 2016). *Microsoft Corp v. United States* [2d Cir 2017] 855 F 3d 53. Henceforth '*Microsoft v. US En Banc*'.

[128] The CLOUD Act was included as part of the Consolidated Appropriations Act, 2018, Pub L. 115–41, amending the Stored Communications Act, 18 USC § 2701.

issue between the United States and Microsoft, and the Court thereafter vacated the judgment.[129] Although the Microsoft warrant case has been resolved, the case remains useful for evaluating how courts evaluate cloud computing technology and apply existing legal frameworks to cloud computing.[130]

4.6.1 The Microsoft Service

If the case had featured a purely domestic provider, rendering a judgment would have been relatively straightforward. However, because of the organization of Microsoft's email/cloud services, complying with the warrant became complicated. The Microsoft email service at issue uses a network of global data centres for storing its user content. Microsoft's cloud infrastructure was described by the Second Circuit Court of Appeals as follows:

> Microsoft currently makes 'enterprise cloud service offerings' available to customers in over 100 countries through Microsoft's 'public cloud.' ... Microsoft 'manage[d] over one million server computers in [its] data centers worldwide, in over 100 discrete leased and owned data center facilities, *spread over 40 countries.*' These facilities, it avers, 'host more than 200 online services, used by over 1 billion customers and over 20 million businesses worldwide'.[131]

To increase the speed of access and reduce delay, or 'data latency', Microsoft's customer data were segmented into several global regions and stored in the region that is physically closest to the user.[132] The user, who self-reports their physical address or location, effectively determined where the data are stored. Based on this self-reported region, all 'content data', such as email, calendar entries, and documents, were stored in a designated global zone.[133] Some non-content data, including information about the account, was stored in the United States regardless of the user's self-reported location.[134] However, the bulk of the information, including the information generally sought after by law enforcement, was often stored outside of the United States.

Among other locations, Microsoft has a data centre in Dublin, Ireland.[135] In the case, the user of the account at issue designated an Irish address to be associated with the account. As a result, the related 'content data' were stored at Microsoft's Dublin centre. Once such 'content data' are moved to Ireland, it was removed from US-based servers. Although Microsoft emphasizes that there is a significant legal and

---

[129] On Writ of Certiorari to the United States Court of Appeals for the Second Circuit, 584 US (2018).
[130] Schwartz, 'Legal Access to the Global Cloud', 1690. Also finding that the Microsoft warrant case and a Google case with a similar fact pattern '... remain highly useful as a pedagogical matter' even after the CLOUD Act.
[131] *Microsoft Corp v. United States*, 202–03. Internal citations omitted and emphasis added.
[132] ibid., 202.
[133] ibid., 203.
[134] ibid. Once data is transferred to the Dublin centre, the bulk of data in the United States are deleted.
[135] ibid.

geographical separation of its US headquarters and its Irish subsidiary, this separation is not complete. Microsoft is able to access the data stored in Ireland – or in any of its global data centres – and return that information to the United States.[136]

However, obtaining data in this manner requires complicated processes outside of normal operating routines. As argued by fifty-one computer scientists acting as *amici curiae*, it '... is impossible to retrieve data from a high security data centre in Ireland without complex physical actions occurring in Ireland'.[137] Microsoft and others argued emphatically that the search would be conducted abroad, even if that did not mean sending agents from Redmond, Washington, on a plane to Ireland to retrieve the files. However, the reviewing US courts seemed sceptical of this argument. For example, a dissent in the Second Circuit Court of Appeals' decision to deny an *en banc* hearing provided the following:

> Extraterritoriality need not be fussed over when the information sought is already within the grasp of a domestic entity served with a warrant. The warrant in this case can reach what it seeks because the warrant was served on Microsoft, and Microsoft has access to the information sought. It need only touch some keys in Redmond, Washington. If I can access my emails from my phone, then in an important sense my emails are in my pocket, notwithstanding where my provider keeps its servers.[138]

In its opinion, the Second Circuit Court of Appeals found that 'Microsoft acknowledges that, by using a database management program that can be accessed at some of its offices in the United States, it can "collect" account data that are stored on any of its servers globally and bring that data into the United States'.[139] However, the Court acknowledged that even if the data were subject to almost instantaneous transfer, the data were located on Irish soil.[140]

How easily or readily Microsoft US is able to access data located in Ireland was a point of contention by legal and technical experts. In cases pertaining to LEA warrants to access Google Cloud computing services, courts have reached different results based largely on the technical organization of the services.[141] Essentially, with Google cloud, the only individuals able to reconstruct data that have been split and encrypted globally are located in the United States. Foreign data centres do not have the same control as they did in the Microsoft deployment.[142]

---

[136] ibid.
[137] Vandenberg and others, 'Brief for 51 Computer Scientists as Amici Curiae', 16–24.
[138] *Microsoft v. US En Banc*, 61.
[139] ibid., 203.
[140] *Microsoft v. US En Banc*, 59.
[141] Kirschenbaum, 'Beyond Microsoft', 1923–62 at 1946–48. Discussing cases applying warrants to Google cloud services. See also Schwartz, 'Legal Access to the Global Cloud', 1692–95. Finding the technical difference was that Google used a 'data shard' cloud deployment storing components of data both globally and domestically. Microsoft, on the other hand, used a 'data location cloud', storing data extraterritorially.
[142] ibid. See *Re Search Warrant to Google* [2017] 232 F.Supp.3d at 708, 709.

On appeal, the Second Circuit Courts' majority opinion was almost solely concerned with territoriality. That is, the Court focused on the place of storage rather than the place where the data were to be viewed, and it followed established rules for interpreting the applicable legislation and the effects of warrants.[143] However, the decision did not account for the reality of data flows in cloud computing services or the Internet more generally. In many ways, instead of evaluating how a law from 1986 should apply to technology in 2016, the Court did the opposite. That is, the Court did not acknowledge the monumental changes in technology that had taken place over the previous thirty years and instead applied the 1986 SCA to 2016 technology as if it still had 1986 capabilities. By taking that approach, it became much easier to apply the SCA to cloud computing. However, its accuracy, utility, and overall longevity were, in my opinion, significantly limited. The case also shows that Courts, at least in this instance, continue to equate a digital file stored in a server with a piece of paper stored in a filing cabinet, regardless of its properties – including (in)accessibility.

In a concurring opinion, Circuit Judge Gerard E. Lynch found the case to be much closer and this line between national and international to be much less clear.[144] Judge Lynch pointed out that this case was not about an expansion of privacy rights, stating ' ... I concur in the result, but without any illusion that the result should even be regarded as a rational policy outcome, let alone celebrated as a milestone in protecting privacy'.[145] Judge Lynch was critical of Microsoft's ability to avoid compliance with a valid search warrant by ' ... choosing – in its own discretion – to store them on a server in another country'.[146] In particular, Judge Lynch highlighted the arbitrariness of making the level of privacy a cloud computing user receives is dependent on a CSP's data management practices and contractual agreements rather than traditional protections like constitutional rights.[147]

However, Microsoft was able to give Americans a much greater level of protection than they are provided under the US Constitution – as long as they provide a foreign address when self-reporting their location.[148] Judge Lynch further noted, ' ... the very idea of online data being located in a particular physical "place" is becoming rapidly outdated, because computer files can be fragmented and dispersed across many servers'.[149] Further, in the Second Circuit Court of Appeals' opinion denying an *en banc* rehearing, the majority provided the following opinion:

---

[143] ibid., 209.
[144] *Matter of Warrant to Search Email Account* [2016] 829 F.3d 222.
[145] ibid., 233.
[146] ibid., 224.
[147] ibid.
[148] ibid.
[149] ibid. Quoting Orin S. Kerr, 'The Next Generation Communications Privacy Act' (2014) 162 *University of Pennsylvania Law Review* 373–419 at 408.

With a less anachronistic statute or with a more flexible armature for interpreting questions of a statute's extraterritoriality, we might well reach a result that better reconciles the interests of law enforcement, privacy, and international comity.

In an analytic regime, for example, that invited a *review of the totality of the relevant circumstances* when assessing a statute's potential extraterritorial impact, we might be entitled to consider the residency or citizenship of the client whose data is sought, the nationality and operations of the service provider, the storage practices and conditions on disclosure adopted by the provider, and other related factors.[150]

It is clear that the court recognized that the application of the SCA to cloud computing services presents a difficult situation. It is important to challenge the assumption that the Microsoft Warrant represents a victory for privacy, at least in terms of sustainability. After all, an LEA search can – and often must – take into account privacy interests. In most cases, digital files should be afforded an equal level of protection to the equivalent document stored on paper; they should necessarily not be entitled to more.

As a final note, the Microsoft warrant case was not simply a dualistic choice between privacy on the one side and the US government on the other. In my view, it demonstrates a range of issues and interests at stake. Although the privacy implications are important, the cost of denying LEAs access to cloud services must also be recognized. For instance, prolonged, more expansive and in some cases, limiting or making prosecution of serious criminal offences impossible.

4.7 THE CLARIFYING LAWFUL OVERSEAS USE OF DATA ACT

The CLOUD Act amended the SCA by addressing (1) the reach of US warrant authority, and (2) foreign governments' access to data stored in the United States.[151] In the Microsoft warrant litigation, the CLOUD Act makes it clear that it has extraterritorial application.[152] Specifically, the CLOUD Act provides that

> A [service provider] shall comply with the obligations of this chapter to preserve, backup, or disclose the contents of a wire or electronic communication and any record or other information pertaining to a customer or subscriber within such provider's possession, custody, or control, *regardless of whether such communication, record, or other information is located within or outside of the United States*.[153]

---

[150] *Microsoft v. US En Banc*, 60. Emphasis added.
[151] The Cloud Act was passed as part of the Consolidated Appropriations Act, 2018, Pub. L. 115–41. Codified as amended at 18 USC §§ 2701–12. See Jennifer Daskal, 'Microsoft Ireland, the CLOUD Act, and International Lawmaking 2.0' (2018) 71 *Stanford Law Review Online* 9–16 at 11.
[152] See 18 USC § 2713 (2018). Emphasis added.
[153] *On Writ of Certiorari to the United States Court of Appeals for the Second Circuit*, 584 US, 3 (2018). Citing the CLOUD Act § 103(a)(1). Emphasis added.

4.7 The Clarifying Lawful Overseas Use of Data Act

With aforementioned amendment, SCOTUS mooted the Microsoft warrant case discussed earlier.[154] The US government obtained its requested warrant, and it resolved the dispute over extraterritorial application of the SCA.[155] Although the Act settled the Microsoft warrant case, it naturally has much broader application and will now require CSPs to disclose personal data to US LEA if the CSP is under US jurisdiction.[156]

From its beginnings, the CLOUD Act was subject to criticism based on its content and transparency around the legislative process.[157] There has also been a great deal of confusion surround application of the law. The CLOUD Act does not alter (or 'fix') the existing MLAT process.[158] The Act allows a 'qualifying foreign government' to issue warrants to US-based CSPs.[159] To become a qualified foreign government, the state must enter into an executive data sharing agreement with the United States.[160] This executive agreement essentially qualifies the foreign government to make direct requests to CSPs outside of the existing MLAT framework creating an expedited process for the United States (and likely other western countries) to obtain data stored with CSPs that fall under US jurisdiction.[161] The first such agreement is between the United States and the United Kingdom.[162]

Although the Act provides significant expansion of the SCA by allowing extraterritorial access, it also addresses some of the pressing practical problems that were present in the Microsoft warrant case. Specifically, the Act provides CSPs with a clear means to object to the disclosure of data and dispute a warrant. When a CSP objects to disclosure and files a motion to quash within the fourteen-day

---

[154] ibid.
[155] ibid.
[156] EDPB and EDPS, 'ANNEX. Initial Legal Assessment of the Impact of the US CLOUD Act on the EU Legal Framework for the Protection of Personal Data and the Negotiations of an EU-US Agreement on Cross-Border Access to Electronic Evidence' (10 July 2019), 1–2. https://edpb.europa.eu/sites/edpb/files/files/file2/edpb_edps_joint_response_us_cloudact_annex.pdf.
[157] Sarah Aitchison, 'Privacy in the Cloud: The Fourth Amendment Fog' (2018) 93 *Washington Law Review* 1019–55 at 1049. Arguing that 'the CLOUD Act is ultimately a move backward' and more comprehensive data protection reform is needed. C.f. Chris Cook, 'Cross-Border Data Access and Active Cyber Defense: Assessing Legislative Options for a New International Cybersecurity Rulebook' (2018) 29 *Stanford Law & Policy Review* 205–36 at 228. Arguing that the CLOUD Act is a substantial improvement and addresses many of the privacy concerns raised by civil liberties advocates.
[158] Secil Bilgic, 'Something Old, Something New, and Something Moot: The Privacy Crisis under the Cloud Act' (2018) 32 *Harvard Journal of Law & Technology* 321–55 at 334–35.
[159] SCA § 2703(h)(1).
[160] SCA § 2703(h)(1)(A)(i–ii). See also Daskal, 'Microsoft Ireland, the CLOUD Act, and International Lawmaking 2.0', 13.
[161] Bilgic, 'The Privacy Crisis under the Cloud Act', 351.
[162] 'Agreement between the Government of the United Kingdom of Great Britain and Northern Ireland and the Government of the United States of America on Access to Electronic Data for the Purpose of Countering Serious Crime Cite US and UK Agreement' (Washington, DC 3 October 2019). https://assets.publishing.service.gov.uk/government/uploads/system/uploads/attachment_data/file/836969/CS_USA_6.2019_Agreement_between_the_United_Kingdom_and_the_USA_on_Access_to_Electronic_Data_for_the_Purpose_of_Countering_Serious_Crime.pdf.

requirement, the data-seeking LEA is provided with an opportunity to respond. In determining if an order to disclose should be modified, the reviewing court may only modify or quash the disclosure requirement if it finds that

(i) the required disclosure would cause the provider to violate the laws of a qualifying foreign government;
(ii) based on the totality of the circumstances, the interests of justice dictate that the legal process should be modified or quashed; and
(iii) the customer or subscriber is not a US person and does not reside in the United States.[163]

Such an option did not exist for Microsoft. In the Microsoft warrant case, the company was held in civil contempt for failing to comply with the orders of the lower court. In addition to facing significant penalties for not complying with the warrant, Microsoft also spent significant sums on legal fees. Although companies like Microsoft, Google, and Amazon can afford these legal fights – at least on a limited scale – start-ups and smaller companies cannot. Therefore, a clear means to object and a summary process for doing so has the potential to increase privacy protections for users of start-ups or smaller companies while also making such CSPs more competitive.

The CLOUD Act recognizes that CSPs have legal obligations in other countries and provides a formal process or mechanism to object to disclosure based on those obligations. For instance, in determining whether 'the interests of justice dictate that the legal processes should be modified', the reviewing court has multiple factors to consider in its comity analysis, including aspects such as national legal obligations, importance of evidence, among others.[164] The non-dispositive totality of the circumstantial factors also offers flexibility. In particular, allowing courts to consider the importance to the investigation of the information required to be disclosed is an important addition.

In the prosecutions of certain particularly serious crimes, such as images of child sexual exploitation, data stored with a CSP may be the only evidence available. Although privacy and data protection are important, any legal framework governing access to cloud computing and similar services must include allowances or exceptions for criminal prosecution. In other criminal prosecutions, such as the narcotics trafficking in the Microsoft warrant case, there is generally physical evidence accessible by prosecutors in addition to the digital evidence. In those cases, granting access to data stored on the cloud may be less justifiable since charges can still be pursued by using evidence other than the data stored on a cloud service.

The CLOUD Act also provides some allowance for comity (i.e. allowing CSPs to file a motion to annul or modify warrants issued under the Act).[165] However, it is also

---

[163] 18 USC § 2703(h). Emphasis added.
[164] 18 USC § 2703(h)(2)(A–B).
[165] EDPB and EDPS, 'Initial Legal Assessment of the Impact of the US CLOUD Act', 1–2.

a formalized expansion of SCA extraterritoriality that will likely be difficult to align with European data protection law. The CLOUD Act does little to build trust or cooperation on a multilateral basis and is likely setting up CSPs operating globally for conflicts of laws challenges.[166] For example, the CLOUD Act will most likely conflict with the prohibitions on international data transfers under the GDPR and the obligations to have a legal basis for data processing under GDPR Article 6 (lawfulness of processing) or the transfer requirements under GDPR Chapter V. As it stands, the Cloud Act does not clearly meet either of these requirements.[167]

The GDPR generally prohibits transfers of personal data to third countries.[168] This general prohibition has a number of exceptions. For instance, under GDPR Article 48, transfers based on an international agreement, such as MLATs, are allowed.[169] Unlike the previous MLAT agreements, an order under the Cloud Act will not be allowed under GDPR Article 48 as it is not based on an international agreement.[170] The EDPB and the EDPS have provided that unless a CLOUD Act warrant is recognized or made enforceable on the basis of an international agreement, the conditions for transfer under the GDPR will be very difficult to meet.[171] Therefore, transfers under the CLOUD Act do not qualify for recognized derogations under Article 49 (i.e. 'transfer necessary for important reasons of public interest').

The EDPB and the EDPS also opine that data transfers to LEAs under the CLOUD Act would violate Article 47 of the EU Charter because right to an effective remedy could not be exercised in practice.[172] The level of privacy protection afforded by the CLOUD Act for non-US citizens is more limited, a great deal of power is vested in the US Attorney general with limited basis for review, and the act arguably contains fewer procedural and substantive safeguards when compared to the MLAT system.[173] Guidance from the EDPB and the EDPS suggests that CSPs subject to the GDPR, ' ... should generally refuse direct requests and refer the requesting third country authority to an existing mutual legal assistance treaty or agreement'.[174]

As a final important point of clarification, the CLOUD Act focuses on aiding investigations of US law enforcement authorities by ordering electronic communications. Determinations made under the act are subject to the same level of scrutiny as other investigations. As noted in the EDPB and the EDPS guidance, 'the

---

[166] Bilgic, 'The Privacy Crisis under the Cloud Act', 351.
[167] EDPB and EDPS, 'Initial Legal Assessment of the Impact of the US CLOUD Act', 6–7. In particular, there are no clear grounds for lawful processing under Article 6.
[168] For further evaluation of this limitation, see Chapter 5.
[169] GDPR Art. 48.
[170] EDPB and EDPS, 'Initial Legal Assessment of the Impact of the US CLOUD Act', 3.
[171] ibid., 8.
[172] ibid., 5.
[173] Bilgic, 'The Privacy Crisis under the Cloud Act', 337–38.
[174] EDPB and EDPS, 'Initial Legal Assessment of the Impact of the US CLOUD Act', 3.

CLOUD Act does not authorise any systematic, large scale and/or indiscriminate collection of personal data, but rather governs targeted requests, subject to procedural safeguards, concerning specific law enforcement investigations'.[175] US legislative instruments that allow for mass collection of data for national security purposes are evaluated further in the next section.

4.8 ACCESS BY INTELLIGENCE AGENCIES

In addition to LEAs, access to data by foreign intelligence agencies is also a principal concern for governments adopting cloud computing. Globally, most states provide a legal basis for intelligence agencies to obtain data from internet service providers (ISPs), CSPs, and other private providers offering electronic communications services.[176] As provided in Chapter 3, most global CSPs are located in the United States and are under American jurisdiction. Therefore, much of the concern surrounding government access to cloud storage and applications is centred on US intelligence programs and the legal regime that provides a legal basis for such access. The broad powers granted to US agencies have resulted in programs allowing the NSA, CIA, and the FBI to conduct wide-ranging real-time surveillance, including the PRISIM and UPSTREAM programs, as discussed further in the text.[177] The US legal framework that supports intelligence gathering and requires CSPs to provide access and information to US intelligence agencies are therefore of global relevance.

The information available surrounding surveillance programs – and in some cases their legal authority – is limited. However, oversight boards, journalists, activists, and courts have contributed to the available knowledge surrounding mass surveillance by the US government.[178] The following section frames the problem that surveillance enabling intelligence legislation causes for governments – particularly European ones – adopting cloud computing services. The legislative picture is complex, opaque, and incomplete.[179] There is also disagreement on the scope and scale of the surveillance programs. However, two pieces of US legislation are particularly problematic from the point of view of EU data protection law and thereby have the potential to limit adoption of US CSPs by European governments.

---

[175] ibid., 2.
[176] Ira S. Rubinstein, Gregory T. Nojeim, and Ronald D. Lee, 'Systematic Government Access to Personal Data: A Comparative Analysis' (2014) 4 *International Data Privacy Law* 96–119 at 98–99.
[177] ibid., 101. Outlining the 'bulk collection by the NSA of metadata on a large percentage of telephone calls to, from, and within the USA'.
[178] Privacy and Civil Liberties Oversight Board, 'Report on the Surveillance Program Operated Pursuant to Section 702 of the Foreign Intelligence Surveillance Act' (2 July 2014), 1–191. https://fas.org/irp/offdocs/pclob-702.pdf. Glenn Greenwald, 'NSA Collecting Phone Records of Millions of Verizon Customers Daily', *The Guardian*, 6 June 2013 11.05 BST. www.theguardian.com/world/2013/jun/06/nsa-phone-records-verizon-court-order.
[179] ibid., 20.

These include Section 702 of the Foreign Intelligence Surveillance Act (FISA) and Executive Order (EO) 12333.[180]

4.8.1 FISA Section 702 and Executive Order 12333

FISA was enacted in 1978 with the aim of creating specific procedures to limit abuses connected to surveillance surrounding foreign intelligence.[181] There are two types of FISA orders. The conventional or traditional FISA order authorizes surveillance when there is probable cause to believe that the target of the surveillance is a foreign power and that foreign power (or its agent) is using the facilities where surveillance is being directed.[182] There are two specific courts with the power to authorize surveillance for intelligence purposes after a finding of probable cause. These include the Foreign Intelligence Surveillance Court of Review (FISCR) and Foreign Intelligence Surveillance Court (FISC).[183] Once Section 702 procedures are approved, the FISC court may issue annual certification.[184]

The contemporary FISA Section 702, as adopted by the FISA Amendments Act of 2008, provides a legal basis to compel electronic communication services providers to provide data for intelligence purposes.[185] As succinctly stated by the Privacy and Civil Liberties Oversight Board:

> The Statutory scope of Section 702 can be defined as follows: Section 702 of FISA permits the Attorney General and the Director of National Intelligence to jointly authorize the (1) targeting of persons who are not United States persons, (2) who are reasonably believed to be located outside the United States, (3) with the compelled assistance of an electronic communication service provider, (4) in order to acquire foreign intelligence information.[186]

The target or focus of Section 702 orders cannot intentionally include US persons and must be approved by the FISC designed to evaluate orders issued under

---

[180] Foreign Intelligence Surveillance Act (FISA) Amendments Act of 2008, Pub. L. No. 110–261, 122 Stat. 2436 (2008) (codified as amended at 50 U.S.C. §1881a (2012)). See also Presidential Policy Directive – 28 does not authorize any surveillance activities but establishes principles how authorized activities are to be conducted.

[181] Rachel G. Miller, 'FISA Section 702: Does Querying Incidentally Collected Information Constitute a Search under the Fourth Amendment?' (2020) 95 *Notre Dame Law Review Reflection* 142. Citing Foreign Intelligence Surveillance Act of 1978, 50 U.S.C. §§1801–85 (2012).

[182] Miller, 'FISA Section 702', 139–57 at 142–45. Providing a background of the traditional FISA and the Section 702 legislation following amendment.

[183] ibid., 142. Citing 50 U.S.C. § §1803(a).

[184] ibid., 144. See Privacy and Civil Liberties Oversight Board, 'Report on the Surveillance Program', 26–31. Describing and evaluating the FISC Section 702 review process.

[185] *Data Protection Commissioner and Facebook Ireland Limited* v. *Maximillian Schrems*, Irish High Court Commercial [2016 No. 4809]. www.dataprotection.ie/sites/default/files/uploads/2018-12/High%20Court%20Judgment_03_10_2017.pdf (Henceforth 'Irish High Court'), para. 167. Rubinstein, Nojeim, and Lee, 'Systematic Government Access to Personal Data', 102.

[186] Privacy and Civil Liberties Oversight Board, 'Report on the Surveillance Program', 20.

FISA.[187] Service providers, including CSPs located in the United States, are required by law to provide information under such orders.[188] Section 702 allows for the collection of emails, phone calls, text messages, and other electronic communications on a large scale.

The agency seeking a surveillance order under Section 702 does not have to show that the target is the agent of a foreign state.[189] Section 702 also contains obligations to reduce data collected on US persons including 'targeting and minimization procedures' designed to ensure the surveillance target is outside of the United States and 'querying procedures' designed to limit data collection to that which is reasonably likely to return intelligence information.[190] However, as a result of the type of collection that Section 702 authorizes, incidental collection of data on US persons is inevitable. Researchers believe that Section 702 FISA surveillance has resulted in the 'incidental' collection of data of millions of US persons.[191] The legislation applies broadly to 'electronic communications service providers' which includes everything from telecommunications carriers to CSPs.

An additional basis for intelligence gathering under US law is EO 12333. Provisions of EO 12333 provide the primary basis for the NSA to obtain foreign intelligence.[192] Unlike FISA Section 702, orders issued under EO 12333 are not governed by statute or subject to judicial review.[193] The orders allow for open and expansive collection of data for foreign intelligence purposes. The definition of 'foreign intelligence' provides few limits on the scope of data collection by US agencies. Although EO 12333 does not allow for collection of data inside the United States, it does allow for the collection of data in transit to the United States.[194] This includes underwater transatlantic cables that transfer data from the EU to the United States for storage and processing in cloud computing services.[195]

4.8.2 PRISM and UPSTREAM Collection

In data collection under the PRISM program, the US government sends an identifying attribute such as an email address to a US-based provider, and the provider (e.g.

---

[187] Miller, 'FISA Section 702', 144. Noting that intelligence agencies do not have to seek FISC orders for each acquisition.
[188] Irish High Court, para. 186.
[189] ibid., para. 168.
[190] Miller, 'FISA Section 702', 144–46.
[191] ibid., 148. See also Elizabeth Goitein and Faiza Patel, 'What Went Wrong with the FISA Court' (2015) *Brennan Center for Justice at New York University School of Law*, 51. www.brennancenter.org/sites/default/files/analysis/What_Went_%20Wrong_With_The_FISA_Court.pdf.
[192] Irish High Court, para. 175.
[193] ibid.
[194] ibid., para. 176.
[195] ibid., para. 176.

4.8 Access by Intelligence Agencies

a US-based CSP) is compelled to provide the communication sent from that provider to the US government agency.[196] A typical example or fact pattern looks something like this:

> The NSA learns that John Target, a non-U.S. person located outside the United States, uses the email address 'johntarget@usa-ISP.com' to communicate with associates about his efforts to engage in international terrorism. The NSA applies its targeting procedures (described below) and "tasks"johntarget@usa-ISP.com to Section 702 acquisition for the purpose of acquiring information about John Target's involvement in international terrorism.
>
> The FBI would then contact USA-ISP Company (a company that has previously been sent a Section 702 directive) and instruct USA-ISP Company to provide to the governmental communications to or from email address johntarget@usa-ISP.com. The acquisition continues until the government"detasks"johntarget@usa-ISP.com.[197]

The collection that takes place using the PRISM program is 'downstream' and communications are obtained directly from US service providers. The data obtained through the PRISM program includes metadata, email logs, IP addresses, and web searches. The NSA uses the PRISM program to obtain data stored and processed with CSP platforms, including major providers like Microsoft and Google, following FISA Court approval.[198] The vast majority of NSA interceptions of Internet communications occur through PRISM.[199] The CIA and FBI also obtain certain information through the PRISM collection.[200] The legal basis for the data collection that takes place under PRISM is largely based on FISA Section 702 and the legislation is a vital component of the PRISM program.[201] PRISIM accounts for approximately 90 per cent of the surveillance conducted under Section 702.[202]

A second surveillance program, UPSTREAM compels assistance from providers that control the telecommunications backbone over which Internet and telecommunications traffic is transmitted.[203] Expert testimony before the Irish High Court provided that 'the NSA copies and searches streams of Internet traffic as data flows across the internet backbone'.[204] Rather than the compelled assistance of CSPs and other similar providers, UPSTREAM surveillance focuses on obtaining information directly from wiretaps on telecommunications cables.[205] Information obtained

[196] Privacy and Civil Liberties Oversight Board, 'Report on the Surveillance Program', 7.
[197] ibid., 34.
[198] Rubinstein, Nojeim, and Lee, 'Systematic Government Access to Personal Data', 101. Citing reports that PRISM allowed the NSA to directly access the servers of leading CSPs.
[199] Privacy and Civil Liberties Oversight Board, 'Report on the Surveillance Program', 33–34.
[200] ibid., 34–35.
[201] Rubinstein, Nojeim, and Lee, 'Systematic Government Access to Personal Data', 116.
[202] Irish High Court, para. 186.
[203] Privacy and Civil Liberties Oversight Board, 'Report on the Surveillance Program', 35. Shrems II, para. 62.
[204] Irish High Court, para. 180.
[205] Privacy and Civil Liberties Oversight Board, 'Report on the Surveillance Program', 7.

through UPSTREAM is provided to the NSA.[206] Unlike PRISM, neither the CIA nor the FBI has access to the data collected.[207]

Initially, the legal authority for collecting UPSTREAM information came largely from Section 215 of the US Patriot Act in addition to FISA Section 702.[208] After filtering data on US persons, the UPSTREAM program collects over 26 million internet transactions per year.[209] The US government argues that targeting under UPSTREAM is not mass or indiscriminate, pointing to filtering mechanisms that sort through billions for transactions. However, European Courts do not generally agree with this position.[210] By its very nature, the program sifts through vast numbers of non-relevant communications in order to acquire those the NSA deems relevant for intelligence purposes.[211]

4.8.3 Remedies and Protections

As provided in the earlier text, both FISA Section702 and EO 12333 have some – albeit limited – provisions that limit the access US intelligence agencies have to data. Collection is subject to oversight by executive branch through the Department of Justice, the Office of the Director of National Intelligence, and the FISA Court.[212] Minimization procedures require that searches under PRISM are 'reasonably likely to return foreign intelligence information'.[213] NSA procedures also include limits on the storage and retention of data in addition to outlining routines for deletion or purging.[214] These procedures are designed to balance national security and privacy interests. However, the reality is that apart from data acquired by mistake, data are rarely deleted or purged until required under general retention limits.

As aptly characterized provided by the Irish High Court, 'the basic principle is that surveillance is legal unless forbidden and there is no requirement ever to give notice in relation to surveillance'.[215] In particular, European Courts have been concerned with protection of the privacy rights of non-US persons. Data subjects located in the EU do not have a cause of action under Section 702 to challenge surveillance orders

---

[206] ibid., 35.
[207] ibid.
[208] Section 215 of the Patriot Act amended 50 U.S.C. § 1861. Section 215 allowed for bulk collection of telephony metadata maintained by telephone companies. The USA FREEDOM Act, enacted on the 2nd in 2015, placed some limits on the collections that took place Section 215 of the US-PATRIOT Act. On 15 March 2020, Section 215 of the PATRIOT Act expired.
[209] Irish High Court, para. 181.
[210] ibid., para. 190. Finding that 'it is clear that there is mass indiscriminate processing of data by the United States government agencies, whether this is described as mass or targeted surveillance'.
[211] ibid., paras. 186–87.
[212] Privacy and Civil Liberties Oversight Board, 'Report on the Surveillance Program', 8.
[213] ibid., 50–51. Describing minimization as 'one of the most confusing terms in FISA'.
[214] ibid., 48–50.
[215] Irish High Court, para. 192.

and are not provided with the same protections or remedies as US citizens.[216] This is essentially a result of the limited application of the Fourth Amendment to the US constitution on the US government's ability to intercept data to non-US persons.[217] In addition to falling outside of the protections of the US Constitution, minimization procedures, use, and data retention limits do not apply to non-US persons.[218] From a data protection perspective, EU courts and regulatory authorities have been critical on the lack of protections and redress afforded to persons residing in the EU. These issues are evaluated further in Chapter 5.

4.9 CONCLUSION

I am of the opinion that data are 'different' that in many ways pose unique legal challenges.[219] Unlike boxes of paper documents, digital records flow globally and effectively instantaneously. In contrast to bank notes, data are not fungible or interchangeable. Unlike commercial paper or loan documents, personal data have a much less clear standard than property that can be bought or sold. In some countries, data protection is a fundamental right. In others, it is not. The differences between a digital file and a paper one have legal implications that the current approach to jurisdiction simply does not address very well. If meaningful reform is to take place, it must acknowledge and better account for the properties of the subject matter being regulated. I therefore agree with many of the criticisms made by Svantesson, Polčák, and Kuner regarding doctrinal confusion relating to jurisdiction and the public law–private law framework used to address those issues.

The tenor of the arguments for keeping the current jurisdictional framework read often as an 'appeal to tradition'. As that line of logic goes, even if there is substantial evidence of stress on the systems, we have applied them for so long that the same practices ought to be continued. To be clear, I am not suggesting that we replace the current jurisdictional framework just because it is dated or because the Internet has come along. For instance, as I find in Chapters 6 and 7, the long-standing doctrine of contract has been extremely resilient and flexible when applied to cloud computing. The central problem with much of the current jurisdictional framework, as both my research experience and the Microsoft warrant case can attest, is that it is no longer operable.

---

[216] Schrems II, para. 65.
[217] Irish High Court, para. 168. Miller, 'FISA Section 702', 150–51.
[218] Schrems II, para.192. Finding that neither Section702 of the FISA nor E.O.12333 grants data subjects located in the EU with a cause of action against US authorities or any other effective remedy.
[219] Daskal, 'The Un-Territoriality of Data', 326. Arguing that data poses new challenges. Andrew Keane Woods, 'Against Data Exceptionalism' (2016) 68 *Stanford Law Review* 729–89 at 752. Arguing that data does not pose new challenges. Svantesson, 'Against "Against Data Exceptionalism"', 210–11. Arguing that Woods has misunderstood much of the problem. Schwartz, 'Legal Access to the Global Cloud', 1703. In responding to whether cloud computing raises new legal issues – 'it depends'.

Despite its flaws, the CLOUD Act modernizes the existing SCA and will perhaps provide CSPs with clearer answers as to when disclosure is required. However, implementing the CLOUD Act on a global basis will require a great deal of negotiation between the United States and EU member states, among others. Although the United Kingdom has been willing to sign on, given the CLOUD Act's clash with the GDPR, it is unclear how broadly it can actually be employed by EU member states.[220] If the result of the CLOUD Act is a race to create many regional agreements, it is possible that we might simply exchange the balkanization of cloud computing services for a balkanization of legislation. However, given what is at stake – particularly given the fundamental rights approach taken to data protection in the EU – reaching an agreement will be difficult. For governments considering the broader adoption of cloud, how this balance will be addressed is a crucial question. At present, it is one that has not been satisfactorily answered – or at least not sufficiently answered – to encourage governments to adopt cloud services.

Access to cloud computing services for intelligence purposes by the US government will continue to cause problems for European governments that wish to use US-based CSPs. Legal data transfers from the EEA to the United States become much more difficult as a result of US intelligence activities. As will be evaluated further in Chapter 5, these practices put both users and CSPs in difficult positions.

---

[220] At the time of writing, the UK is on the verge of leaving the EU.

5

Data Privacy and Data Protection Issues in Cloud Computing

The challenge of using cloud computing while also meeting EU data protection requirements is a well-documented problem.[1] In an early position paper on the subject, the EDPS argued that compliance with EU data protection law for data controllers is 'very difficult or even impossible' in a cloud computing environment.[2] Data protection risks in cloud computing primarily emanate from lack of control, an absence of clear lines of accountability and responsibility, and complex and somewhat diffuse legal requirements. Primary inhibitors are the scope and scale of data processing, the physical location where data processing takes place, apprehensions over data access by subcontractors including support, and contractual relationships that often provide insufficient guarantees that are necessary to meet EU data protection requirements.[3]

When governments adopt cloud computing, they are effectively subject to EU data protection law on the same basis as private providers.[4] However, given their obligations prescribed under national law and responsibility to the public, governments face unique challenges. In the context of the EU GDPR, the law applies broadly to the processing of personal data across sectors.[5] Application of the GDPR creates novel issues when applied to cloud computing that governments must address. For that

---

[1] European Commission, 'Commission Staff Working Document Accompanying the Commission Communication "Unleashing the Potential of Cloud Computing in Europe"' (2012), 1, 8. Providing that '[d]ata protection emerged from the consultation and the studies launched by the Commission as a key area of concern that could impede the adoption of cloud computing'. European Commission, 'Measuring the Economic Impact of Cloud Computing in Europe' (2016), 4–5. Finding data protection remains a central concern.

[2] Peter Hustinx, 'Opinion of the European Data Protection Supervisor on the Commission's Communication on "Unleashing the Potential of Cloud Computing in Europe"' (2012) *European Data Protection Supervisor*, 1–30 at 6. https://edps.europa.eu/sites/edp/files/publication/12-11-16_cloud_computing_en.pdf.

[3] WP29 196, 'Opinion on Cloud Computing 05/2012' (2012), 1–27, 4–6. Citing also cites the loss of CIA, isolation, intervenability, and portability.

[4] Niamh Gleeson and Ian Walden, 'Placing the State in the Cloud: Issues of Data Governance and Public Procurement' (2016) 32 *Computer Law & Security Review* 683–95 at 685 and fn 11.

[5] Regulation (EU) 2016/679 of the European Parliament and of the Council of 27 April 2016 on the protection of natural persons with regard to the processing of personal data and on the free movement

reason, this book focuses on evaluating data protection issues that pose particular barriers for governments attempting to adopt cloud computing, although the analysis in this chapter is by no means an issue limited to governmental cloud adoption.

In addition to EU data protection law and application of the GDPR, this chapter also analyses limited aspects of US data privacy law and its impact on cloud computing adoption. Along with an overview of the constitutional and statutory privacy picture, the US section focuses on privacy laws applicable to data processing by the US federal government. This evaluation is largely focused on the US cloud computing program FedRAMP introduced in Chapter 3.[6] Finally, the chapter considers the relationship between data privacy and data security and the impact that this has on cloud adoption.

5.1 DATA PRIVACY AND DATA PROTECTION LAW

Although the history of data privacy law is outside of the scope of this book, in the EU, data protection and privacy are granted high legal standing.[7] For instance, the right to a private and family life and the right to the protection of personal data are fundamental rights enshrined in Articles 7 and 8 of the Charter of Fundamental Rights of the EU.[8] In Article 8, the Charter provides that '[e]veryone has the right to the protection of personal data concerning him or her'.[9] In the European Convention on Human Rights, the right to respect for a 'private and family life' is also recognized in Article 8.[10] Further, the EU is also home to ' ... the oldest, most comprehensive, and most bureaucratically cumbersome data privacy laws at both national and sub-national levels'.[11] Although the right to privacy is qualified and must be balanced against other rights and interests, including those of national security and public safety, it is nevertheless weighted heavily.[12]

---

of such data, and repealing Directive 95/46/EC (General Data Protection Regulation) (Text with EEA relevance) [2016] OJ L 119, 1.

[6] Primarily in 'The US Cloud Computing Strategy' Chapter 3.

[7] For an analysis of that history, see Lee A. Bygrave, *Data Protection Law: Approaching its Rationale, Logic, and Limits* (Alphen aan den Rijn: Kluwer Law International 2002). For examples of privacy laws 'elsewhere', see generally Graham Greenleaf, *Asian Data Privacy Laws: Trade & Human Rights Perspectives* (Oxford: Oxford University Press 2014).

[8] Charter of Fundamental Rights of the European Union, [2012] OJ C 326 391–407 (henceforth 'the Charter'). Lee Bygrave, *Data Privacy Law: An International Perspective* (Oxford: Oxford University Press 2014), pp. 58–61. See also Juliane Kokott and Christoph Sobotta, 'The Distinction between Privacy and Data Protection in the Jurisprudence of the CJEU and the ECtHR' (2013) 3 *International Data Privacy Law* 222–28, 222–23. Providing that ' ... there are two distinct but related systems to ensure the protection of fundamental and human rights in Europe'.

[9] The Charter Art. 8(1).

[10] Council of Europe, Convention for the Protection of Human Rights and Fundamental Freedoms (European Convention on Human Rights, as Amended) (ECHR) Art. 8, 1950 (henceforth 'the Convention').

[11] Bygrave, 'Data Privacy Law: An International Perspective', p. 100.

[12] GDPR Art. 2(2)(d). See also GDPR Recital 4.

The concepts of 'data privacy' and 'data protection' are based on the aims or notion of privacy, but are not necessarily equivalent.[13] As a whole, privacy is an amorphous concept that is notoriously difficult to define.[14] Data protection generally incorporates aspects of the broader right to privacy, although they are not equivalent. However, in the European legal context ' ... there is conclusive evidence in favour of treating data protection interests as an integral part of a more general right to privacy'.[15]

Data protection is a field in motion. The long-standing Data Protection Directive[16] was replaced by the GDPR, which entered into force in 2016 and began being applied from 25 May 2018.[17] The GDPR is designed to harmonize EU data protection law with direct legal effect in all EU member states.[18] Compared to the situation under the Directive, the GDPR provides a much more consistent legal framework and a CSP that is compliant in one member state is much more likely to be compliant across the EU.[19] However, even as a regulation with direct legal effect, the GDPR allows for derogations, which result in variations among the EU member states.[20] Like the Directive that preceded it, the GDPR remains a principle-based legislative instrument with room for interpretation. Guidelines, opinions, and national interpretations of the GDPR remain under development. Supervisory authorities, courts, and the many actors subject to the GDPR are still deciphering the law.

In addition to the GDPR, the ePrivacy Directive 2002/58/EC (as revised by Directive 2009/136/EC) ('ePrivacy Directive') has some application to cloud computing.[21] The

[13] Bygrave, 'Data Privacy Law: An International Perspective', pp. 3–4. Providing four distinguishing features separating the concepts. See Maria Tzanou, *The Fundamental Right to Data Protection: Normative Value in the Context of Counter-terrorism Surveillance* (Oxford: Hart 2017), pp. 21–22. Discussing the 'vivid academic debate' on whether data protection is a 'separate or autonomous fundamental right distinct from the right to privacy'. Internal references omitted.
[14] Bygrave, 'Data Protection Law: Approaching its Rationale, Logic, and Limits', p. 4.
[15] ibid., 181. See Kokott and Sobotta, 'The Distinction between Privacy and Data Protection', 228. Finding that ' ... privacy and the protection of personal data are closely linked in the jurisprudence of the European Court of Human Rights and the Court of Justice of the European Union, but they should not be considered to be identical'.
[16] Directive 95/46/EC of the European Parliament and of the Council of 24 October 1995 on the protection of individuals with regard to the processing of personal data and on the free movement of such data, OJ L 281, 31–50 (henceforth '95/46/EC' or 'the Directive').
[17] GDPR Art. 99(2). Additionally, several groundbreaking data protection cases, examined later, were also decided.
[18] GDPR Art. 99. Providing that '[t]his Regulation shall be binding in its entirety and directly applicable to all member states'.
[19] Kevin McGillivray, 'Conflicts in the Cloud: Contracts and Compliance with Data Protection Law in the EU' (2014) 17 *Tulane Journal of Technology and Intellectual Property* 217 at 238–53. Evaluating application of the Directive to cloud computing.
[20] Certain activities fall outside of the scope of the GDPR. See GDPR Art. 2(d). Furthermore, member states have the ability to introduce derogations to the GDPR in areas such as national security, defence, and public security, among others. See GDPR Art. 23. See also GDPR Articles 85–91 for specific data processing situations allowing for derogations.
[21] WP29 196, 'Opinion on Cloud Computing 05/2012', 6 and fn 5.

ePrivacy directive is currently under revision.[22] Depending on the outcome of that process, it may also apply to 'Over-the-Top' service providers that operate over the internet impacting CSPs.[23] An additional legislative source is the EU Directive on the security of networks and information systems ('NIS Directive'), which aims at increasing cyber security in the EU overall by focusing on critical and digital infrastructure.[24] In particular, CSPs, along with other digital service providers, will be required to comply with certain aspects of NIS, such as security notifications.[25]

It is also important to note that while the move from the Directive to the GDPR is important for cloud computing users and providers, the GDPR does not completely break from the moorings set out in the Directive. Judicial decisions and secondary sources based on the Directive remain instructive when evaluating the GDPR. However, it is also important to keep in mind that the GDPR is a much more expansive instrument. Under the GDPR, entities processing personal data have increased accountability, data breach notification, and data governance obligations.[26] These obligations include, among others, a heightened duty of care, and the responsibility to demonstrate compliance and accountability on many levels.[27]

As a final introductory note, the EDPB has replaced the WP29. The EDPB is charged with providing guidance on the application of the GDPR throughout the EU. Although the EDPB has endorsed the GDPR-related WP29 guidelines, it has not endorsed all earlier WP29 opinions or those based on the earlier EU data protection directive.[28] However, WP29 opinions that have not been endorsed remain instructive. In this chapter, I reference opinions from both the WP29 and the EDPB noting whether guidance has been endorsed.

[22] European Data Protection Board, 'Statement of the EDPB on the Revision of the ePrivacy Regulation and its Impact on the Protection of Individuals with Regard to the Privacy and Confidentiality of their Communications' (25 May 2018), 1, 2. https://edpb.europa.eu/our-work-tools/our-documents/other/edpb-statement-eprivacy-25052018_en.
[23] ibid., 2.
[24] Directive (EU) 2016/1148 of the European Parliament and of the Council of 6 July 2016 concerning measures for a high common level of security of network and information systems across the Union. http://data.europa.eu/eli/dir/2016/1148/oj. Henceforth ('NIS Directive').
[25] ibid., NIS Art. 16(1). The NIS Directive defines cloud computing at Art. 4(19) as ' . . . a digital service that enables access to a scalable and elastic pool of shareable computing resources'. The NIS directive leaves open the opportunity for EU Member States to public-sector bodies to ' . . . ensure specific security requirements when they contract cloud computing services'. ibid., Recital 56. See also P. T. J. Wolters, 'The Security of Personal Data under the GDPR: A Harmonized Duty or a Shared Responsibility?' (2017) 7 *International Data Privacy Law* 165–78 at 169.
[26] GDPR provisions include the 'accountability principle' at Art 5(2), data protection by design and by default Art. 25, records of processing activities Art. 30, security of processing Art. 32, data breach notification requirements Articles 33–34, data protection impact assessments (DPIA) Articles 35–36, and data protection officer (DPO) requirements Articles 37–39, among other obligations.
[27] GDPR Art. 24. As the cloud user is generally the party making decisions regarding the 'purposes and means of the processing', they will be considered the data controller. GDPR Art. 4(7). See also GDPR Art. 28(1) ' . . . the controller shall use only processors providing . . . appropriate technical and organizational measures . . . '. GDPR Art. 28 and Art. 4(8). For liability and compensation see GDPR Art. 82.
[28] A list of WP29 opinions endorsed by the EDPB. https://edpb.europa.eu/news/news/2018/endorsement-gdpr-wp29-guidelines-edpb_en.

5.2 MATERIAL SCOPE AND APPLICATION OF EUROPEAN DATA PROTECTION LAW

Data stored with CSPs are generally grouped into two distinct categories. The first is data stored and processed by the cloud client on the CSP's infrastructure ('cloud-processed data'). The second is data provided to the CSP when a user enters into a contract or registers for a service, which includes their user name, billing address, credit card information, and other data necessary for subscribing to the service ('user-related data'). As a starting point, the GDPR applies to 'the processing of personal data', which may include both types of data.

In determining whether activities fall within the material scope of the GDPR, two elements must be evaluated. First, the data must be 'processed'.[29] The processing of personal data includes ' ... any operation or set of operations which is performed on personal data ... '.[30] Further, the GDPR applies to processing data 'wholly or partly by automatic means'.[31] As noted by the EDPB, following the broad definition of 'processing' in the GDPR, 'in practice ... all imaginable handling of personal data constitutes processing'.[32] From turnkey SaaS webmail solutions to IaaS storage, cloud computing provides users with many data processing options.[33] Based on the functionality of cloud services, effectively all service models meet the definition of 'processing' for GDPR purposes.[34]

The second necessary element for the GDPR to be applicable is that the data must be 'personal'. The focus on personal data intends to protect the rights of the 'data subject', that is, the 'identified or identifiable natural person' to which the data being processed and collected refers.[35] This protection is limited to 'natural' living persons and thus does not apply to legal or deceased persons.[36] Because EU data protection law takes a relatively rigid approach in its application, determining whether data are personal is the crucial element.[37] Either the law applies completely if the data are

---

[29] ibid., Case C-230/14, *Weltimmo s.r.o. v. Nemzeti Adatvédelmi és Információszabadság Hatóság* [2015], [37].

[30] GDPR Art. 4(2). *Google Spain SL, Google Inc v. Agencia Espannola de Proteccion de Datos (AEPD), Mario Costeja Gonzalez* [2014], [28]. Examples of data processing in the search engine context.

[31] W. K. Hon, *Data Localization Laws and Policy: The EU Data Protection International Transfers Restriction through a Cloud Computing Lens* (Camberley and Northampton, MA: Edward Elgar 2017), p. 11. As argued by Hon, data protection law includes essentially ' ... everything that can be done to or with personal data ... '.

[32] EDPB, 'Guidelines 07/2020 on the Concepts of Controller and Processor in the GDPR' version 1.0 (Adopted on 2 September 2020), 24 (para. 77). Citing GDPR Art. 4(2).

[33] WP29 196, 'Opinion on Cloud Computing 05/2012', 4. Discussing a variety of processing applications including ' ... agendas and calendars, filing systems for online document storage and outsourced email solutions'.

[34] GDPR Art. 2(1).

[35] GDPR Art. 4(1). See also WP29, 'Opinion 4/2007 on the Concept of Personal Data WP 136' (20 June 2007), 6.

[36] GDPR Art. 1(1). GDPR Recital 27.

[37] W. K. Hon, Christopher Millard, and Ian Walden, 'What is Regulated as Personal Data in Clouds?' in Christopher Millard (ed.), *Cloud Computing Law* (Oxford: Oxford University Press 2013), pp. 189–90. Evaluating the all or nothing approach to data protection law.

determined to be personal or it falls outside of the scope of the GDPR when it is not.[38] Pursuant to the GDPR, personal data includes

> *any information* relating to an identified or identifiable natural person ('data subject'); an identifiable natural person is one who can be *identified, directly or indirectly*, in particular by reference to an identifier such as a name, an identification number, location data, an online identifier or to one or more factors specific to the physical, physiological, genetic, mental, economic, cultural or social identity of that natural person.[39]

In determining whether data are personal, EU data protection law takes an expansive view.[40] For instance, in the case *Nowak* v. *Data Protection Commissioner*, the CJEU determined that written exam answers provided by a candidate could be considered personal data.[41] In its analysis, the CJEU focused on the expansive construction of the 'any information' standard in the Directive.[42] The *Nowak* case signals that like the broad approach to 'processing', many data types can be considered 'personal'.

Although expansive, the inclusion of 'any information' does not mean that all data stored on cloud services are personal data.[43] For example, certain commercial data or trade secrets, although sensitive and possibly subject to other laws, are not personal data and are thus beyond the purview or scope of the GDPR.[44] The ability to identify the data subject, directly or indirectly, in addition to the key aspect of linkability, is central in determining application.[45] Thus, even commercial or tax data are personal when it can be linked to an individual.

To determine whether an individual is 'identified or identifiable', the GDPR sets the boundary at applying 'all the means reasonably likely to be used' to identify the individual.[46] The GDPR definition clarifies that specific identifiers, including those

---

[38] GDPR Art. 4(5). Pseudonymized data provides a possible third category. However such data is still considered personal.
[39] GDPR Art. 4(1). Emphasis added.
[40] WP 29, 'Opinion 4/2007 on the Concept of Personal Data WP 136', 4.
[41] *Peter Nowak* v. *Data Protection Commissioner* (C-434/16) CJEU [2017], [62].
[42] ibid., [34].
[43] Hon, 'Data Localization Laws and Policy', p. 11. Arguing that the definition of personal data was broad under the Directive and has become even broader under the GDPR.
[44] Furthermore, even if the data being processed is personal it may still fall outside of GDPR application if it is for the purposes of preventing crime or public security. GDPR Art. 2(2).
[45] *Peter Nowak* v. *Data Protection Commissioner* (C-434/16) CJEU [2017], [61]–[63]. See Oskar Josef Gstrein and Gerard Jan Ritsema van Eck, 'Mobile Devices as Stigmatizing Security Sensors: The GDPR and a Future of Crowdsourced "Broken Windows"' (2018) 8 *International Data Privacy Law* 69, 80. Evaluating the 'objective' or 'relative' criteria for a finding of personal data.
[46] GDPR Recital 26. Indirect sources, such as IP addresses, passwords and user IDs, metadata, and insufficiently anonymized data are considered personal as the data subject can still be identified, even if some additional effort is required. WP29, 'Opinion 136 4/2007 on the Concept of Personal Data', 1–26 at 6. See Bygrave, 'Data Privacy Law: An International Perspective', p. 131. Arguing that the term 'likely' can be equated to an assessment of 'probability', while 'reasonably' establishes the 'difficulty' in making such a connection.

5.2 Material Scope and Application of European Data Protection Law

commonly used in digital technologies, may be considered personal or capable of identifying the data subject.[47] Moreover, by focusing on 'online identifiers' in its definition, the GDPR spells out explicitly that many of the tools used by CSPs can be considered personal data when they provide the requisite linkability.[48]

In the CJEU case *Breyer* v. *Germany*, the court considered whether a dynamic IP address constitutes personal data.[49] The CJEU determined that a dynamic IP address can be deemed personal data if the IP address, combined with additional information, constitutes 'a means likely reasonably to be used to identify the data subject'.[50] Given the ruling in *Breyer* v. *Germany* and the text of the GDPR, the ability of CSPs (and others) to categorize these identifiers as non-personal data is limited.[51] For CSPs, the result is conceivably very significant as the current practice of using IP addresses and other similar identifiers has the potential to increase overall liability. That is, if the identifiers are considered as personal data, the GDPR will apply and CSPs will be responsible for processing that data in a compliant manner.

The CJEU ruling in *Breyer* v. *Germany* focused on the *possibility* of identification rather than the *likelihood*.[52] Depending on the solution, organization, and security measures, governments may potentially shield data subjects from having their data accessed and tracked by CSPs. In a typical government deployment, the government enters into a contract with a CSP leaving no account-related personal data and no direct link to an individual citizen, as would be the case in a consumer contract (C2B). However, if governments apply a solution where a CSP has access to identifiers that are linkable or can identify data subjects, the data will be considered personal. For example, if a solution provides data subjects with direct access to a government service and the CSP manges innlogging or other athentification procedures.

While the GDPR applies broadly, it does not apply in all instances. Areas where data protection is reduced or not applicable generally include national security or the prosecution of criminal offences and 'purely personal or household activity'.[53] An additional category falling outside of the scope of GDPR application is anonymized data – if data are anonymized, it is no longer considered personal.[54] As such,

---

[47] GDPR Art. 4(1).
[48] GDPR Recital 30. Including 'online identifiers provided by their devices, applications, tools and protocols, such as internet protocol addresses, cookie identifiers or other identifiers such as radio frequency identification tags'. Bygrave, 'Data Privacy Law: An International Perspective', p. 137. Prior to the GDPR, IP addresses were widely considered to be personal data in the EU member states.
[49] *Breyer* v. *Germany* (C-582/14) CJEU [2016], [30].
[50] ibid., [44]–[49].
[51] 'Identifiers' or technologies (e.g. internet protocol addresses and cookie identifiers) are used for means of explanation rather than limitation. Even if the GDPR provides specific examples, they are by no means exhaustive.
[52] *Breyer* v. *Germany* (C-582/14) CJEU [2016], [48].
[53] GDPR Art. 2(2–4). However, even these categories have limits. For example, providing personal data to a foreign law enforcement agency requires a legal basis. The household exception under GDPR Art. 2(2)(c) will have little utility for government users.
[54] GDPR Recital 26. See also WP29, 'Opinion 216 05/2014 on Anonymisation Techniques' (2014), 5 ('WP29 216').

anonymized data have the potential to pave a much less burdensome path to compliance for cloud clients and CSPs. For example, if a cloud client renders their data anonymous before storing it with an IaaS provider, the GDPR requirements in this chapter are inapplicable.[55] However, given the difficulty in creating truly anonymous datasets, the bar for anonymization has been set extremely high in the EU and applying this exception in practice is difficult.[56]

Although there is no prescriptive standard for data anonymization in the GDPR, the WP29 provides that anonymized data requires 'irreversibility preventing identification of the data subject', taking into account all the means 'reasonably likely to be used' for identification.[57] In determining whether the process of anonymization is sufficiently robust, the WP29 considers 'whether identification has become "reasonably" impossible'.[58] Further, the WP29 opinion prescribes that the process preventing re-identification must be 'irreversible' for the data to be considered fully anonymized.[59] Advancements in technology, such as Big Data, complicate this assessment.[60] The reality is that data that are truly anonymous in 2021 may be identifiable in 2031 given the likelihood of increased computing power and/or the ability to combine multiple datasets.[61] In other words, the status of anonymous data is not static.[62]

In the cloud computing context, the Cloud Legal Research Project (CLP) at Queen Mary University of London (QMUL) made a compelling argument that strongly encrypted data should not be considered personal data.[63] That is, if data are

[55] ibid., 11.
[56] ibid., 6. Further, the subjective intentions of the controller and processor regarding anonymization are irrelevant to the application of data protection law. ibid., 10.
[57] WP29 216 (2014), 56. However, the WP29 does not provide a methodology for meeting full anonymization. Khaled El Emam and Cecilia Álvarez, 'A Critical Appraisal of the Article 29 Working Party Opinion 05/2014 on Data Anonymization Techniques' (2015) 5 *International Data Privacy Law* 73–87 at 74.
[58] WP29 216 (2014), 8.
[59] ibid., 5. El Emam and Álvarez, 'A Critical Appraisal of the Article 29 Working Party on Data Anonymization Techniques', 75. Arguing that the 'zero risk' approach taken by the WP29 effectively means no existing technique will allow for anonymization, particularly in the Big Data setting. See also Luca Bolognini and Camilla Bistolfi, 'Pseudonymization and Impacts of Big (Personal/Anonymous) Data Processing in the Transition from the Directive 95/46/EC to the New EU General Data Protection Regulation' (2017) 33 *Computer Law & Security Review* 171–81 at 180.
[60] WP29 216 (2014), 9.
[61] Paul Voigt and Axel von dem Bussche, 'Practical Implementation of the Requirements under the GDPR' in *The EU General Data Protection Regulation (GDPR)* (Cham: Springer 2017), pp. 14–15. https://link.springer.com/book/10.1007%2F978-3-319-57959-7. Providing that anonymization carries with it inherent risk factors and requires monitoring.
[62] Samson Esayas, 'The Role of Anonymisation and Pseudonymisation under the EU Data Privacy Rules: Beyond the "All or Nothing" Approach' (2015) 6 *European Journal of Law and Technology* 6–7. https://ejlt.org/index.php/ejlt/article/view/378. Providing that '... effectively anonymized data should be supported by the following follow-up measures: (1) Identify new risks and re-evaluate the residual risk(s) regularly, (2) assess whether the controls for identified risks suffice and adjust accordingly, and (3) monitor and control the risks'.
[63] Hon, Millard, and Walden, 'What is Regulated as Personal Data in Clouds?', p.182.

5.2 Material Scope and Application of European Data Protection Law

properly or 'strongly' encrypted following best practices before being sent to a CSP, it should not be treated as personal data as the data are not intelligible or accessible to the CSP or anyone else lacking the means for decryption.[64] Although the CLP at QMUL did not argue that encryption is always a sufficient condition for cloud data to be considered anonymous, project papers argued that a more nuanced approach to the application of data protection law is needed.[65]

Although encryption is an important aspect of security for cloud clients, re-identification is possible using a key. Therefore, the process fails to meet the 'irreversibility' standard required to render the data non-personal or anonymous.[66] Consequently, encrypted data are not anonymous data as such, and even if a government user encrypts data before storing the data with a CSP, EU data protection requirements remain applicable. Furthermore, applying the CJEU ruling in *Breyer v. Germany*, if CSPs have the means 'which may likely reasonably be used' to identify data subjects then that data is likely to be considered personal.[67]

Nonetheless, even if encryption does not eliminate data protection obligations, it is recognized as an important security feature in the GDPR. An additional concept added to the GDPR is pseudonymization, which includes methods of reducing linkability of personal data to a specific data subject.[68] Without additional information, such as an identification key, the data are unintelligible and have the potential to reduce risks to the data subject.[69] Measures such as encryption and pseudonymization will also play an important role in data transfers.

Throughout the GDPR, pseudonymization is recognized as a technique or tool that can be used to meet security and data protection by design and by default (DPbD) requirements.[70] Furthermore, data breach reporting is not required when 'appropriate technical and organizational measures', such as encryption, are in place.[71] For cloud clients, this means avoiding the expense and loss of goodwill that is often associated with a data breach notification. Pseudonymization is also a relevant factor in determining administrative fines under the GDPR. In short, there are many benefits to the public administration, the CSP, and the data subject with the proper implementation of technical and organizational measures.

---

[64] ibid. For further explanation of the use and limits of encryption in cloud computing, see Hon, 'Data Localization Laws and Policy', pp. 284–89.
[65] Hon, Millard, and Walden, 'What is Regulated as Personal Data in Clouds?', pp.184–89.
[66] ibid., 20.
[67] *Breyer v. Germany* (C-582/14) CJEU [2016], [48].
[68] GDPR Art. 4(5). Essentially, the process reduces the risk of direct identification. Bolognini and Bistolfi, 'Pseudonymization and Impacts of Big (Personal/Anonymous) Data Processing', 177. See further GDPR Recital 26 'personal data which have undergone pseudonymisation, which could be attributed to a natural person by the use of additional information should be considered to be information on an identifiable natural person'.
[69] WP29 216 (2014), 20. GDPR Recital 28.
[70] See GDPR Arts. 25(1) and 32(1)(a). Additional areas of application are 'Codes of conduct' Art. 40(2)(d), and additional safeguards in Art. 89. See also GDPR Recitals 26, 28, 29, 75, 85, and 156.
[71] GDPR Art. 34(3)(a).

5.2.1 Jurisdiction and Application of the GDPR

Prior to the adoption of the GDPR, applicable law was particularly significant given the variation in implementation of the Directive among the EU member states.[72] The Directive focused on the location of the controller's establishment to determine the application of data protection law.[73] By applying applicable law criteria to cloud computing under the Directive, a controller established and processing data in multiple EU member states was required to comply with the national law of all of those member states.[74] As processors, CSPs were also required to meet the security obligations of all the EU member states in which they were located.[75]

Article 3 of the GDPR focuses on the territorial scope of application rather than the law applicable to data processing and is critical for determining whether the GDPR applies.[76] While the GDPR includes areas for derogation (e.g. scientific research, public archives, employment, etc.), these derogations are much more limited.[77] However, even if the GDPR provides a more harmonious picture of the data protection law applicable across the EU, applicable law remains relevant.[78] In Sections 5.2.2 and 5.2.3, I provide an overview of applicable law and jurisdictions for CSPs located inside and outside of the EU.

5.2.2 'Inside' of the EU

As a starting point, the GDPR applies to the processing of personal data by controllers or processors in the context of the 'activities of an establishment' in the EU.[79] The law is applicable to this establishment regardless of where the processing activity ultimately takes place. Under the GDPR, both controllers and processors are subject to the laws' territorial scope.[80] To determine the place of establishment, the

---

[72] GDPR Recital 9. Providing that ' ... a difference in levels of protection is due to the existence of differences in the implementation and application of Directive 95/46/EC'.
[73] 95/46/EC Art. 4(1)(a). With the qualification that data processing does not have to occur within the EU for application. Paul de Hert and Michal Czerniawski, 'Expanding the European Data Protection Scope Beyond Territory Article: 3 of the General Data Protection Regulation in its Wider Context' (2016) 6 *International Data Privacy Law* 230–43 at 237. Evaluating Article 4 of the Directive.
[74] WP29 196, 'Opinion on Cloud Computing 05/2012', 7.
[75] 95/46/EC Art. 17(3). This provision was particularly problematic for CSPs as security requirements vary between member states. W. K. Hon, Julia Hörnle, and Christopher Millard, 'Which Law(s) Apply to Personal Data in Clouds?' in Christopher Millard (ed.), *Cloud Computing Law* (Oxford: Oxford University Press 2013), pp. 243–44.
[76] Dan Jerker B. Svantesson, 'Article 3. Territorial Scope' in Christopher Kuner, Lee A. Bygrave, Christopher Docksey, and Laura Drechsler (eds.), *The EU General Data Protection Regulation (GDPR): A Commentary* (Oxford: Oxford University Press 2020), pp. 81 and 84–85.
[77] See generally GDPR Articles 85–91.
[78] Svantesson, 'Article 3. Territorial Scope', p. 85.
[79] GDPR Art. 3(1). See GDPR Recital 22. ibid., 83. Noting that in the EU extends to EEA countries. The United Kingdom will be considered a third country following 'Brexit'.
[80] ibid., 22. The GDPR abandons the 'equipment' criteria in Article 4(1)(c) applied in the Directive for determining jurisdiction. Michał Czerniawski, *Extraterritoriality in the Age of the Equipment-Based*

assessment focuses on 'the effective and real exercise of activity' rather than the legal form or organization of the controller or processor.[81]

The concept of 'establishment' has been analysed by the CJEU in the context of the Directive in several recent cases.[82] In the first CJEU case, a Spanish citizen requested that Google search engine 'remove or conceal' information from search results.[83] The organizational structure of Google Inc. pertinent to the case included having a main location in California ('Google US') and a local office in Spain ('Google Spain').[84] The question before the CJEU was therefore whether Google US processed personal data in the context of its EU establishment, Google Spain, and whether it was therefore subject to EU data protection law.

In its determination and application of the Directive, the CJEU took a broad approach to the concept of 'establishment'. In evaluating whether Google had an EU establishment, the CJEU considered whether the controller exercised 'a real and effective activity – even a minimal one' through 'stable arrangements' in an EU member state.[85] The court found that the advertising services that local offices like Google Spain carried out were 'inextricably linked' to the processing carried out by Google US.[86] That is, without the advertising revenue from its global subsidiaries, Google US would not be economically viable.[87] The operation of Google's search engine, controlled and managed by Google US, could not be separated from its global advertising network of subsidiaries – including Google Spain.[88]

In *Weltimmo s.r.o. v. Nemzeti Adatvédelmi és Információszabadság Hatóság*, the CJEU evaluated the application of establishment and weighed the ability of the Hungarian DPA's authority to impose fines on a company registered in Slovakia.[89]

Society: Do We Need the 'Use of Equipment' as a Factor for the Territorial Applicability of the EU Data Protection Regime? (Cambridge: Intersentia 2017), pp. 221–40 at 234.

[81] GDPR Recital 22. GDPR Art. 4(16). EDPB, 'Guidelines 3/2018 on the Territorial Scope of the GDPR (Article 3) – Version for Public Consultation' (Adopted on 16 November 2018), 4–8. https://edpb.europa.eu/sites/edpb/files/consultation/edpb_guidelines_3_2018_territorial_scope_en.pdf. Based on EDBP draft guidance, this inquiry includes: (1) an establishment in the Union, (2) processing of personal data carried out 'in the context of the activities of' an establishment, (3) plication of the GDPR to the establishment of a controller or a processor in the Union, regardless of whether the processing takes place in the Union or not.

[82] Svantesson, 'Article 3. Territorial Scope', pp. 79–81. Providing an evaluation of additional cases relevant to territorial scope and application of the GDPR.

[83] Case C-131/12, *Google Spain v. AEPD and Mario Costeja Gonzalez* [2014], [14]–[15].

[84] WP29 179, 'Update of Opinion 8/2010 on Applicable Law in Light of the CJEU Judgment in Google Spain' (2015), 2.

[85] *Google Spain* [2014], [58]. Focusing on 'stable arrangements' in jurisdictional determinations. See also Case C-230/14, *Weltimmo s.r.o. v. Nemzeti Adatvédelmi és Információszabadság Hatóság* [2015], [33]. Following Google Spain.

[86] *Google Spain* [2014], [56].

[87] WP29 179, 'Update in Light of the CJEU Judgment in Google Spain', 3.

[88] ibid., 3–4. Dan Jerker B. Svantesson, 'Extraterritoriality and Targeting in EU Data Privacy Law: The Weak Spot Undermining the Regulation' (2015) 5 *International Data Privacy Law* 229. Providing that '[t]here are numerous examples of globally active Internet intermediaries seeking to avoid the jurisdiction of courts by referring to the particular corporate structure they have adopted'.

[89] Case C-230/14, [2015], para. 14.

In its decision applying the Directive, the CJEU determined that the notion of establishment is both broad and flexible and not limited to legal form or organization.[90] The CJEU provided further that the concept of establishment '... extends to any real and effective activity – even a minimal one – exercised through stable arrangements'.[91] In *Weltimmo*, this included targeted websites in the local language.[92] The CJEU also determined that by uploading personal data onto a webpage, Weltimmo processed personal data in the context of the activities of its Hungarian establishment.[93]

In *Google Inc. v. CNIL*, the CJEU again considered the boundaries of the right to erasure ('right to be forgotten').[94] The Court determined that the EU legislature did not provide for the right to erasure set out in the GDPR to go 'beyond the territory of the Member States'.[95] Therefore, Google Inc. was not obligated to apply the right on a global basis thereby limiting the territorial application of the GDPR.[96] However, the CJEU left open the possibility of individual member states to apply delisting more broadly when protecting their citizens' fundamental rights.[97] Thus, although *Google Inc. v. CNIL*, limits territorial application at an EU-wide level, the case left open the possibility of a more global – and less harmonized – approach at the member state level.

If a controller not subject to EU law (based on the aforementioned criteria) uses a CSP processor in the EU, the controller will not be subject to the GDPR as the processor 'is merely providing a service'.[98] However, in addition to GDPR processor obligations provided in the regulation, the EDPB guidance further states that the processor must ensure that operations remain lawful and the processor must report to the controller if the processor CSP believes an instruction violates the GDPR.[99] Therefore, although a controller not otherwise subject to the GDPR will not fall under its jurisdiction by choosing an EU-based CSP, its operation may nevertheless be impacted by the GDPR. Thus, a data controller wishing to avoid the GDPR completely should generally not choose an EU-based CSP.

5.2.3 'Outside' of the EU

The GDPR relies on the 'principle of territoriality' for controllers and processors located in the EU and the 'effects principle' for determining jurisdiction when they

---

[90] ibid., [29]. See also WP29 179, 'Update in Light of the CJEU Judgment in Google Spain', 3.
[91] ibid., [31]. Citing *Google Spain* [2014], [48].
[92] *Weltimmo* [2015], [32]. The CJEU also found it significant that Weltimmo had a mailing address and representatives in Hungry. ibid., [33].
[93] ibid., [38] and [41].
[94] Case C-507/17, *Google v. Commission Nationale de l'Informatique et des Libertés (CNIL)*, ECLI:EU: C:2019:772.
[95] ibid., [62].
[96] ibid., [73].
[97] *Google Inc. v. CNIL*, [38].
[98] EDPB, 'Guidelines 3/2018 on the Territorial Scope of the GDPR (Article 3)', 10–11.
[99] ibid., 11–12.

are not.[100] That is, the GDPR is applicable to non-EU controllers and processors if they process personal data concerning data subjects who are in the EU. This is justified where non-EU controllers or processors are 'offering goods or services' or 'monitoring' the behaviour of data subjects who are in the EU.[101] The point of taking an effects approach when applying the GDPR is to provide data subjects who are in the EU with a level of protection and to ensure that controllers and processors cannot easily avoid responsibility for compliance.[102] The GDPR provides two primary bases for subjecting non-EU controllers and processors to the GDPR.

The first basis or nexus focuses on commercial activity and applies when a controller or processor not established in the EU offers goods or services to data subjects located in the EU.[103] Applying a directing/targeting test is novel in EU data protection law.[104] Based on experiences in the consumer and e-commerce context, directing or targeting EU consumers generally requires an affirmative step beyond simply having a website that is accessible in the EU.[105] However, the processing of personal data follows a different format than an online sale. That is, a CSP providing advertising sales to a third party is a very different transaction than a contract entered into by a consumer purchasing goods from a website.[106]

EDPB guidance provides a list of potential factors for evaluating targeting in the data protection context. Factors include the nature of the activity, references to member states in the offering, contact information to be used by EU customers, the use of EU top-level domains, use of langue or currency other than generally used in the trader's country, and an EU location for delivering goods.[107] The EDPB notes that alone these factors may have little targeting significance. However, when combined they may show a clear indication or intention of a data controller to offer goods and services in the EU. Although mere accessibility is insufficient, a combination of concrete actions – even if minor – may rise to the level of targeting.[108]

A second basis for application of the GDPR by a controller or processor located outside of the EU occurs when the provider 'monitors' the behaviour of data subjects who are in the EU.[109] To determine if a processing activity reaches the level of

[100] WP29 179, 'Update in Light of the CJEU Judgment in Google Spain', 6.
[101] GDPR Art. 3(2)(a–b). Svantesson, 'Extraterritoriality and Targeting in EU Data Privacy Law', 89. Explaining that 'free' services are also included.
[102] Czerniawski, 'Extraterritoriality in the Age of the Equipment-Based Society', p. 224. Further arguing that the overall scope of extraterritorial application in GDPR Art. 3(2) is much more limited. ibid., 235.
[103] GDPR Art. 3(2)(a).
[104] de Hert and Czerniawski, 'Expanding the European Data Protection Scope', 238.
[105] GDPR Recital 23.
[106] Svantesson, 'Article 3. Territorial Scope', p. 89. Arguing that targeting is appealing in theory, it will be difficult to apply in the context of GDPR Art. 3(2).
[107] EDPB, 'Guidelines 3/2018 on the Territorial Scope of the GDPR (Article 3)', 15–16.
[108] ibid., 16. See GDPR Recital 23.
[109] GDPR Art. 3(2)(b).

monitoring, the analysis focuses primarily on ' ... whether natural persons are tracked on the internet ... '.[110] This monitoring may occur through the use of 'cookies' or other 'web-tracking' technologies.[111] Therefore, while the use of equipment (e.g. cookies) is not required to form this nexus, it remains a factor in the overall monitoring analysis.[112] A central factor is whether the controller has the specific purpose to collect and reuse data (i.e. behavioural advertising, geo-localization for marketing, etc.).[113]

The 'effects principle' approach to jurisdiction in the GDPR is an expansion of the 'territorial' approach taken in the Directive. As argued by de Hert and Czerniawski, the GDPR approach ' ... is based on a straightforward rationale you might be targeted by EU law only if you target [data subjects who are in the EU]'.[114] For example, if a US-based CSP advertises its platform by actively claiming it provides the best PaaS system for European municipalities and records and tracks visits from EU IP addresses with the intention of later placing targeted advertisements, the CSP is quite clearly targeting EU-based cloud clients. On the other end of the spectrum, a CSP advertising 'the best government PaaS in the world' is not specifically targeting the EU. However, there are many shades of grey between these two examples.

5.3 LAWFUL PROCESSING OF PERSONAL DATA

European data protection law broadly requires a legal basis for *any* processing of personal data.[115] For processing to be lawful, the processing party must have a lawful basis for the duration of the processing.[116] The legal basis must be determined at the beginning of processing and there is little flexibility for amendment after processing has begun.[117] Overlap between or among these grounds is possible and data

---

[110] GDPR Recital 24.
[111] de Hert and Czerniawski, 'Expanding the European Data Protection Scope', 238.
[112] Eduardo Ustaran, 'The Scope of Application of EU Data Protection Law and Its Extraterritorial Reach' in Noriswadi Ismail and Edwin Lee Yong Cieh (eds.), *Beyond Data Protection: Strategic Case Studies and Practical Guidance* (Heidelberg: Springer 2013), pp. 135–56 at 148. https://link.springer.com/content/pdf/bfm%3A978-3-642-33081-0%2F1.pdf.
[113] EDPB, 'Guidelines 3/2018 on the Territorial Scope of the GDPR (Article 3) Version Adopted after Public Consultation' (2018), 18. https://edpb.europa.eu/our-work-tools/our-documents/guidelines/guidelines-32018-territorial-scope-gdpr-article-3-version_en. Svantesson, 'Article 3. Territorial Scope', p. 90. Arguing there is no 'intention requirement' and unintentional monitoring may also serve as a jurisdictional nexus.
[114] de Hert and Czerniawski, 'Expanding the European Data Protection Scope', 238. Citing GDPR Recitals 23 and 24.
[115] GDPR Art. 6(1)(a–f). For further explanation of legal basis in EU data protection compliance see Samson Esayas, 'The Idea of "Emergent Properties" in Data Privacy: Towards a Holistic Approach' (2017) 25 *International Journal of Law and Information Technology* 139–78 at 141–42.
[116] GDPR Art. 6.
[117] ibid. See also WP29, 'Guidelines on Consent under Regulation 2016/679' Guideline 259 Rev.01 (10 April 2018), 23.

processing activities may be justified based on one or more of the aforementioned legal grounds in Article 6 (or 9).[118] For example, personal data collected by a CSP related to subscription and billing (e.g. name, email address, bank information) could be processed under the legal basis 'performance of a contract'.[119] Processing data necessary for ensuring network security and for the reduction of fraud could be processed under the basis 'legitimate interest'.[120] The cloud client might also consent to additional processing by the CSP that fall outside of 'legitimate interest' and 'performance of a contract'.[121]

A legal basis applicable in one situation will not necessarily be appropriate or available in all others. For example, a core requirement of consent is that it must be freely given and contain an element of genuine choice.[122] In some situations, the imbalance of power is so great that consent will not be valid.[123] This is the case with both public authorities and employers.[124] For governments or public administrations, processing under the 'performance of a task carried out in the public interest or the exercise of official authority ... ' is the most likely basis for the majority of data processing.[125] If a public administration or government agency processes data on the cloud (or otherwise) it must have a legal basis.

5.4 PRINCIPLES RELATING TO DATA QUALITY AND THEIR APPLICATION TO CLOUD COMPUTING

The following section evaluates the application of the principles for the protection of personal data in the cloud computing context. While this section focuses on Article 5 of the GDPR, the principles have a much more extensive history.[126] The following principles are at the heart of GDPR compliance and are evaluated separately in the sections later.

---

[118] WP29, 'Opinion 15/2011 on the Definition of Consent' 187 (2011), 8.
[119] GDPR Art. 6(1)(b).
[120] GDPR Art. 6(1)(f) and Recitals 47 and 49.
[121] GDPR Art. 6(1)(a).
[122] GDPR Art. 4(11). For the conditions for obtaining consent, see GDPR Art. 7. See further WP29, 'Guidelines on Consent under Regulation 2016/679' 259 (2017), 1–30 and 4 and 7–8.
[123] ibid., 7.
[124] ibid., See WP29, 'Opinion 2/2017 on Data Processing at Work' 249 (2017), 6–7. Providing that '[e]mployees are almost never in a position to freely give, refuse, or revoke consent from any work related monitoring'.
[125] GDPR Art. 6(1)(e). This basis also requires specific obligations under national law. GDPR Art. 6(3). General statements of public necessity – without a clear national legal obligation – will be insufficient.
[126] Kenneth A. Bamberger and Deirdre K. Mulligan, *Privacy on the Ground: Driving Corporate Behavior in the United States and Europe* (Cambridge, MA: MIT Press 2015), p. 22. Describing the FIPs as providing '.the backbone for data protection laws in Europe and a key touchstone for American information privacy regulation'.

5.4.1 *Data Must Be Processed Fairly, Lawfully, and Transparently*

Of particular import is the principle that data must be 'processed lawfully, fairly and in a transparent manner ... '.[127] Despite its somewhat vague character, this principle is fundamental to data protection and is applicable to all other principles described in this section.[128] Considering the first element, for processing to be lawful the controller must follow the legal requirements set out in the GDPR, for instance, having a lawful basis for data processing under GDPR Article 6. If a CSP acts outside of the terms of its contract with the data controller or clearly breaches a requirement of the GDPR, such as a prohibited international data transfer, the CSP is acting in an unlawful manner.

When compared to 'lawfulness', 'fairness' is a rather abstract concept. Fairness requires that the party processing personal data (e.g. the controller or processor) does not act unreasonably and takes into account the interests and rights of the data subject.[129] What is required or what is deemed 'fair' is an evolving concept.[130] For example, failing to provide the data subject with adequate information regarding the processing, thus reducing their ability to control and make decisions about the processing, is likely unfair. Repurposing, selling, or reusing data in a manner that goes beyond the consent provided by the data subject is clearly unfair.

As a key concept running throughout the GDPR, the element of 'transparency' is essential to the fair and legitimate processing of data.[131] At the concept's core is the notion that the data subject must be provided with adequate and accurate information regarding processing activities.[132] In the cloud computing context, this essentially requires that the controller provide the cloud client with information regarding the basis for the processing, the extent of the processing, and the categories or recipients with access to data (e.g. subprocessors and subcontractors).[133] Challenges related to cloud computing supply chains and subcontracts are examined further later.

5.4.2 *Purpose Limitation Principle*

In addition to having a defined 'legal basis', as described earlier, the controller must provide a set 'purpose' for data processing.[134] The purpose limitation principle is

---

[127] GDPR Art. 5(1)(a) (lawfulness, fairness and transparency principle).
[128] Bygrave, 'Data Privacy Law: An International Perspective', p. 146. Describing the principle as primary to all principles of data privacy law.
[129] ibid. Essentially, the controller 'cannot ride roughshod over the' data subject.
[130] ibid.
[131] WP29, 'Guidelines on Transparency under Regulation 2016/679' 260 (2016), 1–35 at 5 ('WP29 260'). Further, transparency is ' ... intrinsically linked to fairness and the new principle of accountability under the GDPR'. Transparency provisions in the GDPR are primarily located at Art. 12. However, the GDPR has additional transparency requirements at Articles 13–14, 15–22, and 34.
[132] WP29 196, 'Opinion on Cloud Computing 05/2012', 10–11.
[133] ibid.
[134] WP29, 'Opinion 03/2013 on Purpose Limitation' 203 (2013), 1–70 at 7–8. The Council of Europe's Convention 108 at Articles 5 and 9, ECD Guidelines on the Protection of Privacy and Transborder Flows of Personal Data, and the Directive at Art. 6(1)(b).

a foundation of data protection law.[135] Without setting a purpose, applying the other data protection principles is essentially unworkable.[136] By setting a clear purpose, the principle provides for greater transparency, accountability, and user control.[137] Further, by stating a specified purpose, it becomes easier to ascertain when the data collected exceeds what is necessary to fulfil that purpose.[138] Given the role of purpose specification in setting the scope for applying all other principles, the purpose must be set prior to the collection of personal data.[139]

In terms of the text of the GDPR, the principle requires that data be collected for ' ... specified, explicit and legitimate purposes and not further processed in a manner that is incompatible with those purposes ... '.[140] Broken down, the principle has two main elements. The first element requires that when data are collected it is limited to 'specified, explicit and legitimate purposes'.[141] For instance, without providing additional information, very general purposes such as 'marketing', 'improving user experience', or 'information security' are unlikely to be sufficiently explicit or legitimate.[142] The second element requires that further use of the data remains compatible with the original purpose.[143] After stating the purpose, the processing of personal data that follows must be necessary to fulfil that process.[144] If data are processed in a manner that is incompatible with the purpose for which it was initially obtained (i.e. 'repurposed'), the processing is unlawful.[145]

Complex supply chains, particularly those used in 'free' public cloud services supported by advertising, threaten compliance with the purpose limitation principle.[146] The primary risk is that subcontractors or subprocessors will process the cloud client's data for purposes that are incompatible with the original purpose (e.g. advertising or creating new services).[147] However, even if cloud computing supply chains create challenges, compliance with this principle is not diminished or waived because a controller chooses a cloud-based solution over a more traditional

---

[135] ibid., 7. For a history of the purpose limitation principle, see Nikolaus Forgó, Stefanie Hänold, and Benjamin Schütze, 'The Principle of Purpose Limitation and Big Data' in Marcelo Corrales, Mark Fenwick, and Nikolaus Forgó (eds.), *New Technology, Big Data and the Law* (Singapore: Springer 2017), pp. 17–42 at 23–26. https://link.springer.com/chapter/10.1007%2F978-981-10-5038-1_2.
[136] Forgó, Hänold, and Schütze, 'The Principle of Purpose Limitation and Big Data', p. 26.
[137] WP29, 'Opinion 03/2013 on Purpose Limitation',13.
[138] ibid., 15. An additional aspect of the purpose specification principle is therefore to provide a level of foreseeability. Bygrave, 'Data Privacy Law: An International Perspective', p. 153.
[139] Forgó, Hänold, and Schütze, 'The Principle of Purpose Limitation and Big Data', p. 28.
[140] GDPR Art. 5(1)(b) and GDPR Recital 39.
[141] GDPR Art. 5(1)(b). WP29, 'Opinion 03/2013 on Purpose Limitation', 12.
[142] ibid., 16. For medical research exceptions, see further GDPR Art. 89 and Recital 33.
[143] WP29, 'Opinion 03/2013 on Purpose Limitation', 12–13.
[144] Forgó, Hänold, and Schütze, 'The Principle of Purpose Limitation and Big Data', p. 27.
[145] GDPR Art. 6(4). In evaluating the Directive, the WP29 determined that an incompatible purpose (i.e. 'repurposed') data cannot be later legitimized by changing to a new legal basis. WP29, 'Opinion 03/2013 on Purpose Limitation', 36.
[146] WP29 196, 'Opinion on Cloud Computing 05/2012', 11.
[147] ibid.

or bespoke IT outsourcing service.[148] The controller must ensure that 'personal data are not (illegally) processed for further purposes by the cloud provider or one of his subcontractors'.[149]

5.4.3 Data Minimization

In addition to attaching a specific purpose to data collection, the principle of data minimization requires that data collected be 'adequate, relevant and limited to what is necessary in relation to the purposes for which they are processed'.[150] This principle aligns closely with purpose specification in that the scope of what is necessary or relevant will depend on the purpose of the data collection. Simply stated, this principle requires that controllers limit the amount of data they collect.

Although compliance with this principle is perhaps one of the most straightforward conceptually, it is at odds with the general approach taken by many entities regarding data collection and the development of technologies. Many industries, governments, and other institutions have taken the opposite approach – that is, the aim has been to collect as much data as possible.[151]

5.4.4 Data Accuracy

EU data protection law also requires that data be 'accurate and, where necessary, kept up to date'.[152] If data are not accurate, the data must be erased or corrected.[153] If the data are inaccurate, the data subject has a right to have the data rectified or even object to the processing of data concerning them. One of the challenges of accuracy in cloud computing is locating and correcting or deleting incorrect information that is stored or mirrored across the cloud infrastructure. Processor requirements oblige CSPs as processors, 'insofar as this is possible', to support data subjects' rights, including the right to rectification and the right to erasure, among others.[154]

5.4.5 Storage Limitation

Even when the data stored are accurate and up to date, it should not be kept in a form that identifies the data subject for ' ... longer than is necessary for the

---

[148] ibid.
[149] ibid.
[150] GDPR Art. 5(c).
[151] Esayas, 'The Idea of Emergent Properties', 143. See Lee A. Bygrave, 'Data Protection by Design and by Default: Deciphering the EU's Legislative Requirements' (2017) 2 *Oslo Law Review* 105–20 at 119.
[152] GDPR Art. 5(d).
[153] ibid.
[154] GDPR Art. 28 (3)(d).

purposes for which the personal data are processed … '.[155] If other legal regulations limit the ability of the controller to erase the data, such as legal requirements that the data be stored for accounting purposes, the data must be secured appropriately and erased when it becomes legally possible.[156] Retention periods may vary depending on the purpose of the initial collection. However, the duty of erasure applies whether the data are stored on a local hard drive or a global server farm with infrastructure located around the globe.[157]

Deleting data must also be done sufficiently, either by destruction of the medium or sufficient overwriting of the file.[158] If the files are stored around the globe for backup purposes, obtaining verification that destruction has taken place is more difficult than simply destroying a local hard drive. This requires that all copies of the data, including temporary files and file fragments, be erased irretrievably.[159] To do so often requires reliance on a third party or auditor that can provide certification or verification that the information has been deleted.[160] In that regard, deletion of data stored with a CSP requires not only trust but also verification.[161]

5.4.6 Confidentiality and Integrity

Parties with access to personal data must exercise confidentiality in processing or handling such data ' … in a manner that ensures appropriate security of the personal data, including protection against unauthorized or unlawful processing and against accidental loss, destruction or damage … '.[162] Pseudonymization of data through encryption or other means has the potential to 'significantly contribute' to meeting this principle in the cloud environment.[163] The CSP often manages encryption in a SaaS deployment. In an IaaS deployment, cloud clients may use their own security and encrypt their data before sending it to the CSP or governments and other users with sensitive data; this has the advantage of eliminating the CSP's access. Furthermore, as provided in the controller contract obligations, a duty of confidentially must be included in the contract and imposed on all subprocessors and subcontractors.[164]

---

[155] GDPR Art. 5(e). For purposes in the public interest, including archives, personal data may be stored for longer periods pursuant to GDPR Art. 89(1).
[156] WP29 196, 'Opinion on Cloud Computing 05/2012', 12.
[157] ibid.
[158] ibid.
[159] ibid.
[160] ibid.
[161] GDPR Art. 28(3)(g). The GDPR specifies that deletion or return requirements must be contained in the controller/processor contract.
[162] GDPR Art. 5(f).
[163] WP29 196, 'Opinion on Cloud Computing 05/2012', 15. The WP29 further suggests that data should be encrypted 'in transit and when available at rest'.
[164] GDPR Art. 28(3)(b).

5.4.7 Accountability Principle

The earlier principles remain consistent between the Directive and the GDPR. However, under the GDPR the controller is now required to 'demonstrate compliance' with the earlier principles.[165] Although this principle has existed in practice in some member states and is already an element of data privacy law internationally, it is an addition to the GDPR.[166] To meet this principle, cloud clients will be required to document their compliance with the earlier principles.[167] However, the overall responsibility for compliance with these principles will depend on the categorization of either controller or processor.

5.5 DATA PROCESSORS AND DATA CONTROLLERS: ROLES AND RESPONSIBILITIES

Two of the most central designations in EU data protection law are those of the data 'processor' and the data 'controller'.[168] The concepts have not changed under the GDPR and remain the primary means to allocate responsibilities between or among parties.[169] Understanding these concepts and their interactions is essential to applying the GDPR to cloud computing.[170] In particular, the distinction between them affects the legal requirements that actors have and their liability for breach of data protection law. The roles are defined in the GDPR as:

' controller' means the natural or legal person, public authority, agency, or other body which, alone or jointly with others, *determines the purposes and means* of the processing of personal data ... ;
' processor' means a natural or legal person, public authority, agency or other body which *processes personal data on behalf of the controller* ...'[171]

Under the GDPR, data controllers have the primary responsibility of treating the personal data entrusted to them in conformance with the law in addition to demonstrating compliance.[172] The primary component necessary to meet the

---

[165] GDPR Art. 5(2). See also GDPR Articles 24 and 25.
[166] See Jenna Lindqvist, 'New Challenges to Personal Data Processing Agreements: Is the GDPR Fit to Deal with Contract, Accountability and Liability in a World of the Internet of Things?' (2017) International Journal of Law and Information Technology 13. WP29, 'Opinion 3/2010 on the Principle of Accountability'173 (2010), 1–19 at 6 ('WP29 173').
[167] See GDPR Art. 24(1).
[168] GDPR Art. 4 (7) and (8), respectively.
[169] EDPB, 'Guidelines 07/2020 on the Concepts of Controller and Processor in the GDPR', 9.
[170] W. K. Hon, Christopher Millard, and Ian Walden, 'Who is Responsible for Personal Data in Clouds?' in Christopher Millard (ed.), Cloud Computing Law (Oxford: Oxford University Press 2013), p. 193. Finding the distinction 'both complex and critical'.
[171] GDPR Art. 4 (7) (8). Emphasis added.
[172] WP29, 'Opinion 1/2010 on the Concepts of "Controller" and "Processor"', WP 169 (2010), 17. https://ec.europa.eu/justice/article-29/documentation/opinion-recommendation/files/2010/wp169_en.pdf. EDPB, 'Guidelines 07/2020 on the Concepts of Controller and Processor in the GDPR', 8.

controller designation is that the natural or legal person makes a specific determination regarding 'the purposes and means' of data processing.[173] In evaluating whether a party determines the purposes and means of processing, the level of influence they have over the processing activities is critical.[174] Specifically, does the actor determine the 'how' and the 'why' of data processing?[175] If an actor makes primary decisions about the purpose for which data are processed, access requirements, and length of storage, among other core control elements, they are acting as a data controller.[176]

If the purpose and means of processing are determined by various entities working in concert, they may be considered joint controllers.[177] The EDPB specifies that in an evaluation of joint controllership, the focus should be 'a factual, rather than a formal, analysis' considering the actual arrangement rather than a designation in law or contract.[178] In particular, an evaluation of 'converging decisions' where 'the processing would not be possible without both parties' participation in the sense that the processing by each party is inseparable, i.e. inextricably linked'.[179] Citing recent CJEU case law, EDPB guidance focuses on the use of plugins, cookies, statistics, or other processing activity that result in a mutual benefit arising from the joint activity as markers of joint controllership.[180]

To qualify as a processor, two conditions must be met. First, the party must be a separate legal entity from the controller.[181] Second, the processor must process data on the controller's behalf.[182] The processor must act only on documented instructions from the controller.[183] The legal relationship is one of delegation rather than agency.[184] For instance, if the cloud client makes decisions regarding the data stored on the cloud service, it will generally be considered the data controller.[185] A government agency using cloud-based storage or other applications will wear the controller hat. The CSP acting on the instructions of the cloud client will be

---

[173] EDPB, 'Guidelines 07/2020 on the Concepts of Controller and Processor in the GDPR', 13–15 (paras. 30–39).
[174] ibid., 9–10. The EDPB provides five elements or 'building blocks' for determining controllership including: (1) the natural or legal person, public authority, agency or other body, (2) determines, (3) alone or jointly with others, (4) the purposes and means, (5) of the processing of personal data.
[175] ibid., 13.
[176] WP29 169 (2010), 15. See Voigt and von dem Bussche, ,'Practical Implementation of the Requirements under the GDPR', p. 18.
[177] GDPR Art. 26. EDPB, 'Guidelines 07/2020 on the Concepts of Controller and Processor in the GDPR', 17 (para. 48). The EDPB defines jointly as 'together with' or 'not alone'.
[178] EDPB, 'Guidelines 07/2020 on the Concepts of Controller and Processor in the GDPR', 17.
[179] ibid., 18.
[180] ibid., 19.
[181] WP29 169 (2010), 25. EDPB, 'Guidelines 07/2020 on the Concepts of Controller and Processor in the GDPR', 24.
[182] ibid.
[183] GDPR Art. 28(3)(a). See also Lindqvist, 'New Challenges to Personal Data Processing Agreements', 9.
[184] EDPB, 'Guidelines 07/2020 on the Concepts of Controller and Processor in the GDPR', 24.
[185] WP29 196, 'Opinion on Cloud Computing 05/2012', 7.

deemed the processor. However, if the CSP begins processing personal data for its own purposes or goes beyond the instructions set by the controller, it will become the controller for those purposes.[186] The more influence the CSP has over the processing decisions, the more likely it is to be the data controller or a joint controller.[187]

Although cloud clients will most often be considered controllers and CSPs processors, this designation in not always clear.[188] Given the broad definition of controller contained in the GDPR and the extensive application of the concepts of controller and joint controller in recent CJEU decisions in *Google Spain* and *Unabhängiges Landeszentrum für Datenschutz Schleswig-Holstein v. Wirtschaftsakademie Schleswig-Holstein GmbH* (henceforth *Wirtschaftsakademie*) and *Fashion ID GmbH & Co. KG v. Verbraucherzentrale NRW eV* (henceforth 'Fashion ID') a great deal of processing activity will now meet the threshold.[189]

For example, in the CJEU decision in *Google Spain*, the search engine provider Google was determined to be a controller.[190] Even if much of Google's data processing was essentially automated and largely organizational, the court determined that Google was still making determinations regarding the purpose and means of the processing of personal data as defined under the Directive. In particular, the court focused on record/data retrieval and the organization of results.[191] Similarly, SaaS and PaaS providers often make comparable determinations regarding data organization and storage in addition to functionality and user access and interfaces. Following the CJEU decision in *Google Spain*, CSPs outside of the IaaS model may find it more difficult to retain their role as processors.

In the 2018 case of *Wirtschaftsakademie*, the CJEU further broadened the remit of controller and joint controller.[192] In the case, *Wirtschaftsakademie* used a Facebook fan page to promote its educational services.[193] The Facebook solution was procured on non-negotiable standard contract terms.[194] Facebook provided its fan pages without requiring monetary compensation. However, when fans visit a fan page, Facebook installs a cookie on the hard disk of the visitor, which remains active for a two-year period.[195] The consequence of this arrangement is that the fan page

---

[186] EDPB, 'Guidelines 07/2020 on the Concepts of Controller and Processor in the GDPR', 25. Hon, Millard, and Walden, 'Who is Responsible for Personal Data in Clouds?', p. 210.
[187] Voigt and von dem Bussche, ,'Practical Implementation of the Requirements under the GDPR', p. 239.
[188] Peter Blume, 'Controller and Processor: Is There a Risk of Confusion?' (2013) 3 *International Data Privacy Law* 140–45 at 140–41.
[189] Case C-210/16, *Unabhängiges Landeszentrum für Datenschutz Schleswig-Holstein v. Wirtschaftsakademie Schleswig-Holstein GmbH* [2018]. Case C-40/17, *Fashion ID GmbH & Co. KG v. Verbraucherzentrale NRW eV* [2019] ECLI:EU:C:2019:629.
[190] *Google Spain*, [33].
[191] ibid., [28].
[192] *Wirtschaftsakademie*, [75].
[193] ibid., [15].
[194] ibid.
[195] ibid., [33].

5.5 *Data Processors and Data Controllers: Roles and Responsibilities*   113

operator or administrator effectively provides Facebook with the data of its fans by directing them to the Facebook page.[196]

In *Wirtschaftsakademie*, the CJEU determined that the administrator of a Facebook fan page, even when such a page is essentially designed, operated, and controlled by Facebook, may be deemed a controller or joint controller.[197] In the case, the CJEU also evaluated the concept of controller or joint controller, finding that the role of data controller may include several actors.[198] In its determination that *Wirtschaftsakademie* could be considered a joint controller, the CJEU focused in particular on *Wirtschaftsakademie*'s role in bringing its fans to Facebook and the ability it had to use filters and tools provided by Facebook to determine the categories of data that Facebook would receive including age, sex, relationship, and occupation.[199] The administrator of the fan page therefore takes part in defining the perimeters of processing, contributing to the overall processing that takes place.[200]

In *Fashion ID*, the CJEU followed the low-threshold approach for controllership. In that case, the CJEU focused on the website operators' participation in determining the purpose and means of processing by embedding a social plugin that optimized the publicity of its goods, focusing on whether the joint controller obtained a benefit in using a plugin.[201] Thus, the shared economic interest also played into the controller designation. Governments accepting 'take-it-or-leave-it' cloud computing contracts may also become joint controllers when the CSPs they select affect the rights of data subjects by contributing 'to the processing of the personal data'.[202] Like *Fashion ID* and *Wirtschaftsakademie*, it might take place through relatively 'passive' actions affirmed in standard contract terms (e.g. installing cookies).

5.5.1 *Data Processors and Data Controllers: Contractual Designations*

An additional aspect of the 'controller' and 'processor' distinction in cloud computing is the relatively common practice of CSPs to designate these roles in their standard contract terms. For example, in a US FOIA contract to provide SaaS and IaaS services for the Department of Energy, Google's contract provided that the '[c]ustomer agrees that . . . .Google is merely a data-processor'.[203] However, these terms are ineffective because they do not negate the requirements set out by EU data

---

[196] ibid., [34]. This data is used to help Facebook improve its system of advertising.
[197] ibid.
[198] ibid., [27–29].
[199] ibid., [35–36].
[200] ibid., [39]. However, even if the administration of key aspects of the fan page resulted in controller responsibility, the CJEU noted that that responsibility was not necessarily equal. ibid., [43].
[201] *Fashion ID*, [78]–[80].
[202] *Wirtschaftsakademie*, [36].
[203] Google Inc. and Battelle Energy Alliance, 'Google Apps for Government and Postini via Reseller Agreement, "BEA-DOE Contract" US Gov't No. DE-AC07-05ID14517' (25 August 2011), §2.2.

protection law.[204] Although contract terms are relevant in a factual assessment of the roles parties have in the service, they are not determinative.[205] The GDPR places requirements on parties based on their actual roles or conduct in data processing operations and not simply on the labels they give themselves.[206] Ultimately, the 'controller' or 'processor' designation, and compliance responsibilities, will be based on conduct, not a contract.

For public administrations, in addition to an evaluation of contracts and conduct, legislation also plays a key role. In some cases, the governmental entity will be required by law to share personal data with another entity – public or private – by statute. The public administration will generally be considered a data controller for execution of that obligation.[207] For example, a tax administration may be required to share data on income with a welfare administration. In such a case, the data sharing will be controller-to-controller, leaving a clear break in responsibility.[208] Even in controller-to-controller transfers required by legislation, there is often a data processor facilitator (e.g. a CSP) used transfer data from one public administration to the other.

5.5.2 *Data Controller Obligations and Contracts with Processors*

As the controller, the cloud client has the ultimate responsibility for meeting the requirements of data protection law.[209] When adopting cloud, the controller must assess the cloud structure and evaluate the CSP's ability to comply with data protection obligations.[210] The assessment and its thoroughness will vary to some extent depending on the type of data collected (e.g. sensitive data) and overall processing measures.[211] Given the opaque structure of many cloud services, this can be a difficult task.[212] This is particularly true in the public cloud setting, where

[204] Hon, Millard, and Walden, 'Who is Responsible for Personal Data in Clouds?', pp. 207–08.
[205] EDPB, 'Guidelines 07/2020 on the Concepts of Controller and Processor in the GDPR', 12 . Providing that in 'many cases, an assessment of the contractual terms between the different parties involved can facilitate the determination of which party (or parties) is acting as controller'.
[206] ibid. GDPR Art. 4 (7–8) defining the concepts. GDPR Articles 24, 26, and 28 explaining requirements and duties.
[207] EDPB, 'Guidelines 07/2020 on the Concepts of Controller and Processor in the GDPR', 11.
[208] ibid., 22 (para. 68). Providing an example of a controller-to-controller transfer where a private employer is required to transfer certain personal data to the national taxauthorities.
[209] GDPR Art. 24(1). Requiring that the controller will ' ... ensure and be able to demonstrate that processing is performed in accordance with this Regulation'. WP29 196, 'Opinion on Cloud Computing 05/2012', 7–8. Describing controller requirements for cloud computing under the Directive. See also Hon, Millard, and Walden, 'Who is Responsible for Personal Data in Clouds?', p. 195.
[210] GDPR Art. 24(1). Brendan Van Alsenoy, 'Liability under EU Data Protection Law: From Directive 95/46 to the General Data Protection Regulation' (2017) 7 *Journal of Intellectual Property, Information Technology and e-Commerce Law* 271–88 at paras. 39–40.
[211] ibid., s40. Noting that the notion of 'risk' is an important factor in determining appropriate measures and liability.
[212] Hon, Millard, and Walden, 'Who is Responsible for Personal Data in Clouds?', p. 199.

5.5 Data Processors and Data Controllers: Roles and Responsibilities

services are dynamic and cloud clients generally retain very little contractual control over the acts of the CSPs and their subcontractors.

Specific controller requirements under the GDPR include choosing a data processor that provides 'sufficient guarantees' regarding their ability to meet legal requirements and implements 'appropriate technical and organizational measures'.[213] Furthermore, a data processing contract or other binding agreement specifying processor compliance requirements is also compulsory.[214] These contractual obligations under Article 28 of the GDPR include the following points:[215]

- Processing must be governed by a contract or other legal act.
- The processor processes personal data only on documented instructions from the controller (including terms on subject matter, duration, nature of the processing, type of personal data, and categories of data, obligations, and rights of the controller).
- The processor is committed to confidentiality requirements (statutory or contractual obligation).
- The processor follows security measures as required per GDPR Article 32.
- The processor only engages a subprocessor with 'prior specific or general written authorisation of the controller'.[216]
- The processors must also assist the 'controller in ensuring compliance with the obligations', including security, data breach, and data protection impact assessments (DPIAs).[217]
- The processor deletes or returns all the personal data to the controller after the relationship ends.[218]
- The processor makes information available to the controller to assist with audits and inspections.

---

[213] GDPR Art. 28(1). Choosing a processor compliant with a code of conduct or certification scheme under GDPR Articles 40 or 42 may provide a more practical means for meeting this obligation.

[214] GDPR Art. 28(3). Generally, the parties will enter into a contract. However, the legislation also provides for the use of '... [an]other legal act that is binding on the processor ...'. Perhaps this could include a data processing agreement that does not meet the formalities of a contract (e.g. lacks consideration) but is recognized as binding.

[215] Requirements are based on GDPR Art. 28(3)(a–c). EDPB, 'Guidelines 07/2020 on the Concepts of Controller and Processor in the GDPR', 33–34. Expanding and providing examples of each of the elements listed in the bullet point.

[216] GDPR Art. 28(2).

[217] GDPR Art. 28(3)(f). Requiring assistance with GDPR Articles 32 to 36. WP29, 'Guidelines on Data Protection Impact Assessment (DPIA) and Determining Whether Processing is "Likely to Result in a High Risk" for the Purposes of Regulation 2016/679, WP 248 Rev.01' (2017), 1–22 at 8 ('WP29 248'). In assisting with the DPIA, the '... processor should share useful information without either compromising secrets or leading to security risks by disclosing vulnerabilities'.

[218] GDPR Art. 28(3)(g). This end of contract requirement applies '... unless Union or Member State law requires storage of the personal data'.

Although room for interpretation exists, the contractual requirements contained in GDPR Article 28(3) are extremely prescriptive.[219] In other words, the GDPR occupies areas that would normally fall under the 'freedom of contract' between professional parties by providing such specific obligations.[220]

Overall, controller compliance with GDPR Article 28 will require accommodation from CSPs. However, unlike other areas of the GDPR, such as Article 25 that only provides a relatively vague privacy and data protection by design obligation Article 28 provides a clear recipe including the specific ingredients or elements necessary for compliance. The EDPB has also approved a standard data processing agreement that controllers and processors can use to meet the requirements of Article 28.[221] If the standard agreement is adopted without material amendments, the substance contract will be considered compliant with Article 28 across the EU.[222]

Although expansive and arguably paternal, the contractual requirements in Article 28 are a response to the current reality of much of the contracting that takes place in cloud procurement. In the case of traditional IT outsourcing, where contracts 'flowed in the same direction', obtaining compliant terms was likely easier for controllers and allowed them to evaluate the systems they were adopting.[223] In the cloud computing scenario, the idea that the cloud client has the power to instruct a processor such as Google or Microsoft and dictate contract terms is out of touch with market realities and current practices.[224] At the same time, an imbalance in information and difficulty in negotiating compliant contract terms does not absolve the cloud client controller from meeting legal requirements and protecting the interests of the data subject.[225] The EDPB provides the following example of a municipality adopting cloud:

> [A] cloud service provider has offered a standardized service that is offered worldwide. The municipality however must make sure that the agreement in place complies with Article 28(3) of the GDPR, that the personal data of which it is

---

[219] GDPR Art. 28(5). Contractual requirements under the GDPR will likely be expressed as certification schemes or standards.

[220] WP29 196, 'Opinion on Cloud Computing 05/2012', 12–14.

[221] EDPB, 'Opinion 14/2019 on the Draft Standard Contractual Clauses Submitted by the DK SA (Article 28(8) GDPR)', 12 July 2019. https://edpb.europa.eu/our-work-tools/our-documents/stanovisko-vyboru-cl-64/opinion-142019-draft-standard-contractual_en.

[222] Christopher Millard and Dimitra Kamarinou, 'Article 28. Processor' in Christopher Kuner, Lee A. Bygrave, Christopher Docksey, and Laura Drechsler (eds.), *The EU General Data Protection Regulation (GDPR): A Commentary* (Oxford: Oxford University Press 2020), p. 606.

[223] Paul M. Schwartz, 'Information Privacy in the Cloud' (2013) 161 *University of Pennsylvania Law Review* 1623–62 at 1630. Stating that '[i]n the past model, a processing decision occurred at a discrete moment and involved a unidirectional transfer of data. Companies would also finalize data processing plans in advance. Today, networked series of data processes allow the decentralization of decisions about information processing'.

[224] Blume, 'Controller and Processor', 142. See Lindqvist, 'New Challenges to Personal Data Processing Agreements', 1–19 at 10. Discussing Google's dominant processor role.

[225] EDPB, 'Guidelines 07/2020 on the Concepts of Controller and Processor in the GDPR', 26–27 (para. 82).

controller are processed for the municipality's purposes only. It must also make sure that their specific instructions on storage periods, deletion of data etc. are respected by the cloud service provider regardless of what is generally offered in the standardized service.[226]

If CSPs want access to users with compliance obligations – or those concerned with compliance – CSPs will also have to provide flexible contract terms or risk losing users in those markets. Although such an approach will be advantageous for controllers, it may also result in contractual shifts. For example, CSPs have begun to require indemnities from cloud clients to cover or reimburse them for any administrative fines imposed under the GDPR.[227] Additionally, CSPs are also requiring warranties from controllers and demand guarantees about the data they are receiving. For example, requiring an affirmative statement that the controller has a legal basis for the data that will be processed using the cloud service.

The GDPR excuses a controller from liability when it can prove that '... it is not in any way responsible for the event giving rise to the damage'.[228] However, this liability exclusion is relatively narrow in scope. For instance, it would likely excuse a cloud client when a force majeure event occurs which gives rise to the damage suffered, assuming the CSP has met all other legal requirements.[229] Selecting a CSP that does not provide adequate contractual guarantees would not likely qualify as being 'not in any way responsible' under the GDPR in the same way that force majeure does not generally excuse liability based on clearly foreseeable events.

5.5.3 Data Processor Obligations and Liability

For a CSP, being deemed a data processor has several advantages. Principal among them is the apportionment of liability. As long as the CSP processes personal data under the instruction of the controller, the CSP has reduced liability in many areas and most of the responsibility resides with the controller.[230] However, while the concept of processer remains effectively the same, the GDPR places direct legal obligations on data processors.[231] Among other obligations, processors must implement appropriate technical and organizational security measures, report data

---

[226] ibid.
[227] ibid., para. 13 and Annex C. Providing that United Kingdom agencies should not accept such indemnities and doing so undermines 'better performance and enhanced protection for personal data' under the GDPR.
[228] GDPR Art. 82.
[229] Alsenoy, 'Liability under EU Data Protection Law', para. 44.
[230] EDPB, 'Guidelines 07/2020 on the Concepts of Controller and Processor in the GDPR', 24–25 (para. 77–79). For an overview of the legal obligations of data processors, see also Rolf H. Weber and Dominic Staiger, *Transatlantic Data Protection in Practice* (Berlin Heidelberg: Springer 2017), pp. 33–35.
[231] GDPR Art. 28.

breaches, appoint data protection officers in some circumstances, and may be held directly liable for violations of the GDPR by data subjects.[232]

Prior to the GDPR, the controller/processor relationship was wholly contractual and required the cloud client to negotiate all CSP obligations. Processor liability was also limited to the terms of the contract. Under the GDPR, processors now have direct statutory liability.[233] For example, DPAs can now impose administrative fines on processors directly in addition to other penalties for violating the GDPR, albeit in limited areas.[234] In other words, the GDPR does not impose joint and several liability between the processor and the controller for *all* processing activities.[235] When it comes to damages, the legislation provides that ' ... [e]ach controller or processor shall be held liable for the *entire damage* in order to ensure effective compensation of the data subject'.[236]

However, the GDPR provides that processors are liable 'only where' the processor has violated their obligations under the GDPR or acted outside of the controller's instructions.[237] As a result, the clarity and completeness of controller instructions will be an important factor in determining liability and ultimately damages. However, a processor that is only partially liable for the event that gives rise to the damages may nevertheless be responsible for the entire amount.[238] To hold a processor liable, the data subject must prove (1) failure to comply with the processor obligations under the GDPR; (2) damages; and (3) a causal relationship between (1) and (2).[239]

Furthermore, the GDPR requires processors to provide technical and organizational measures to ensure the security of personal data, keep records of processing activities, and even designate a data protection officer in some instances.[240]

---

[232] GDPR Articles 32, 33(2), 37, and 82, respectively. See Millard and Kamarinou, 'Article 28. Processor', p. 605. Describing the significance of this change.

[233] GDPR Art. 58(1)(a) requiring processors to provide information to DPAs upon request. GDPR Articles 83–84. For an overview of processor legal obligations see Weber and Staiger, 'Transatlantic Data Protection in Practice', pp. 33–34.

[234] GDPR Articles 83–84. For guidance on the assessment of fines, see WP29, 'Guidelines on the Application and Setting of Administrative Fines for the Purpose of the Regulation 2016/679', 253 (2017), 1–17 ('WP29 253').

[235] Alsenoy, 'Liability under EU Data Protection Law', 52–53. Arguing that the GDPR provides a 'proportional liability model' pursuant to GDPR Art. 82(2).

[236] GDPR Art. 82(4). Emphasis added. See also GDPR Recital 146. 'Where controllers or processors are involved in the same processing, each controller or processor should be held liable for the entire damage'.

[237] GDPR Art. 82(2). Hon, Millard, and Walden, 'Who is Responsible for Personal Data in Clouds?', p. 198. Discussing the difficulty of applying the 'giving instructions' requirement in cloud. For example, were the parties to agree to a standard service levels, one party is not necessarily instructing the other. Millard and Kamarinou, 'Article 28. Processor', pp. 609–10. Finding that DPAs deem CSPs to be 'at least a data processor'.

[238] Alsenoy, 'Liability under EU Data Protection Law', para. 53.

[239] ibid., 57.

[240] See GDPR Art. 28(3)(c). Requirements on security measures should also be in the contract between the controller and processor. GDPR Art. 30(2) requires that processors keep records of processing

Processors are now required to inform controllers when they experience data breaches 'with undue delay'.[241] Additionally, if processors receive instructions from the controller that they believe violate EU data protection law, they are required to inform the controller.[242] In short, under the GDPR, processors – including CSPs – have a more active role in protecting data subjects.

5.5.4 Data Processors and Audit Obligations

Although many of the processor requirements cited earlier place additional burdens on CSPs, the audit requirement has been particularly controversial because it requires that the processor ' ... contribute to audits, including inspections, conducted by the controller or another auditor mandated by the controller'.[243] As noted by the WP29, allowing many individual audits can themselves pose security risks for CSPs and their cloud clients.[244] CSPs have traditionally been unwilling to provide detailed information on security practices or allow physical inspections of shared infrastructure for security reasons.[245] EDPB guidance suggests that inspections and audit obligations should be set out in the contract between the parties and that 'parties should cooperate in good faith and assess whether and when there is a need to perform audits on the processor's premises'.[246] In practice, accommodating requests for on premise audits – particularly if they receive many at once – creates serious logistical and security challenges for CSPs with many customers.

The UK FCA has provided guidance on CSP audits and determined that financial firms are required to allow effective access to data for auditors and regulators.[247] To that end, the FCA broadly construes an audit requirement and a cloud client cannot limit the number or timing of requests the regulator can make.[248] On that basis, it seems an audit report provided by a third party will be insufficient for the

---

activities. GDPR Art. 31 requires that the processor cooperate with supervisory authorities. GDPR Art. 33(2) requires that the processor notify the controller of a data breach. GDPR Art. 37(1) requires that processors appoint a data protection officer in certain cases. WP29, 'Guidelines on Data Protection Officers ('DPOs') WP243 Rev.01' (2017), 1–25 at 9–10.

[241] GDPR Art. 33(2). Although the term 'undue delay' creates some ambiguity, the overall obligation is clear. Under the Directive, without a contractual term to the contrary, a CSP could suffer a data breach and not inform its cloud clients.

[242] GDPR Art. 28(3)(h). However, the GDPR does not provide guidance on the situation where the controller disagrees with the processor's assessment.

[243] ibid.

[244] WP29 196, 'Opinion on Cloud Computing 05/2012', 22. Providing that '[i]ndividual audits of data hosted in a multi-party, virtualized server environment may be impractical technically and can in some instances serve to increase risks to those physical and logical network security controls in place'.

[245] Hon, Millard, and Walden, 'Who is Responsible for Personal Data in Clouds?', p. 202.

[246] EDPB, 'Guidelines 07/2020 on the Concepts of Controller and Processor in the GDPR', 38 (para. 141).

[247] Financial Conduct Authority (FCA), 'FG16/5: Guidance for Firms Outsourcing to the "Cloud" and Other Third Party IT Services' (2016), 8–10. www.fca.org.uk/publication/finalised-guidance/fg16-5 .pdf. Guidelines first published in 2016 and last updated in September 2019.

[248] ibid.

FCA. Moreover, under the FCA guidance the regulator retains the right to visit a CSP's business premises without notice.[249]

At the EU level, the European Banking Authority (EBA) takes a more flexible position on audits. Although the EBA requires broad rights to audit, including the right to access and inspect head offices and operations centres, it also allows for 'pooled audits' and third-party certifications.[250] The European Insurance and Occupational Pensions Authority (EIOPA) has adopted specific guidance on outsourcing to CSPs that will also allow for third-party certifications and pooled audits.[251] The EBA provides that the right to audit '... should not be impeded or limited by contractual arrangements'.[252] However, both the EIOPA and the EBA guidance acknowledge the reality that site audits of CSPs are inconsistent with the way cloud computing services are delivered globally.

The flexibility of the EBA advice makes cloud adoption much more achievable. The EBA advice therefore puts a great deal of weight on the functions being outsourced, material (i.e. critical or core operations) or non-material, and the overall level of risk.[253] If data are lost or the system goes down, the EBA advice suggests that the institutions are in a better position to understand the overall threat and the potential impact on their contingency plans.[254] Although this approach is pragmatic, it is important to consider the industry broadly and the market on a longer-term basis. In a competitive market, institutions may skimp on contingency plans as a means to reduce operating expenses. Requiring a baseline standard across the industry, through specific guidance, may go a long way in counteracting a race to the bottom. That is, if all institutions are required to have systems in place, it will not create a burden for responsible actors.

5.5.5 Subcontracting and Subprocessing in Cloud Computing

An important aspect of the controller/processor relationship is retaining transparency and accountability throughout the cloud computing supply chain. The detached organizational structure of many CSPs results in long 'chains' of primary, sub, and sub-subcontractors.[255] The result is a collection of actors operating in

---

[249] ibid., 10.
[250] The European Banking Authority (EBA), 'Recommendations on Outsourcing to Cloud Service Providers' EBA/REC/2017/03 (2017), 1–78 at 13–14. Providing that the rights to audit and access should not be limited contractually.
[251] European Insurance and Occupational Pensions Authority (EIOPA), Final Report on public consultation No. 19/270 on Guidelines on outsourcing to cloud service providers 21–23 (31 January 2020). www.eiopa.europa.eu/content/guidelines-outsourcing-cloud-service-providers_en.
[252] ibid., 14.
[253] ibid., 13–14.
[254] ibid., 18–19.
[255] Isabell Conrad and others, 'Cloud Computing Contracts – Discussion Paper on Subcontracting' (2014) *EU Expert Group on Cloud Computing Contracts*, 3. Maintaining that cloud computing for 'consumers and Small & Medium Enterprises (SME) has become unthinkable without subcontracting'. See also W. K. Hon and Christopher Millard, 'Cloud Technologies and Services' in

5.5 Data Processors and Data Controllers: Roles and Responsibilities

different parts or layers of the cloud service infrastructure.[256] These arrangements may include a diverse group of software and storage providers, or other network providers. Although the term 'partners' is often used in cloud computing contracts, infrastructure, and other providers are not necessarily under the same corporate or organizational umbrella as the CSP. Furthermore, the parties tend to change frequently, may be located in different countries, and are potentially governed by the laws of multiple jurisdictions at the same time.[257]

The contract between the CSP and the cloud client does not always contain detailed information regarding partners or subcontracted parties that will provide the core infrastructure used in the service.[258] This is often the case in highly standardized or one-size-fits-all public cloud services in particular.[259] For example, the CSP may be outsourcing all of its storage to third parties located in countries outside of the cloud client's home jurisdiction. Subcontractors storing data on behalf of the CSP may further outsource storage to secondary data centres for backup or other purposes, including help desks or other IT maintenance functions.[260]

Given the many layers of cloud services, obtaining prior consent from a controller every time part of the CSP's infrastructure is subcontracted is impracticable, if not effectively impossible.[261] The GDPR allows for some flexibility here. The GDPR requires 'prior specific consent' for a processor to add a subprocessor, suggesting very little room to manoeuvre.[262] However, this is immediately followed by an 'or' clause, providing for the much more flexible 'general written authorization of the controller'.[263] This suggests that a controller can agree to a certain group or even a category of subprocessor at the beginning of the service and will not have to confirm or consent to every subcontracting change.[264] However, the WP29 has recommended that processors obtain written consent when transferring data outside of the EEA.[265]

Christopher Millard (ed.), *Cloud Computing Law* (Oxford: Oxford University Press 2013), pp. 15–16. Explaining the 'layers' or 'chains' common in cloud services.

[256] WP29 196, 'Opinion on Cloud Computing 05/2012', 6. See also EBA, 'Recommendations on Outsourcing to Cloud Service Providers', 17. Discussing the risks of subcontracting.

[257] Scott Bender, 'Privacy in the Cloud Frontier: Abandoning the "Take It or Leave It" Approach' (2012) 4 *Drexel Law Review* 487–522 at 489.

[258] WP29 196, 'Opinion on Cloud Computing 05/2012', 6.

[259] ibid., 8.

[260] ibid., 9. Samuel Gibbs, 'Typo Blamed for Amazon's Internet-Crippling Outage', *The Guardian Online*, 3 March 2017. www.theguardian.com/technology/2017/mar/03/typo-blamed-amazon-web-services-internet-outage. As evaluated earlier in Chapter 2.

[261] WP29 196, 'Opinion on Cloud Computing 05/2012', 10. Providing that ' . . . a contract should be signed between cloud provider and subcontractor reflecting the stipulations of the contract between cloud client and cloud provider'.

[262] GDPR Art. 28(2).

[263] ibid. Further, the difference between 'consent' and 'authorization' is not made explicit.

[264] Dimitra Kamarinou, Christopher Millard, and Isabella Oldani, 'Compliance as a Service' (2018) *Queen Mary School of Law Legal Studies Research Paper No. 287/2018*, 10–11. SSRN: https://ssrn.com/abstract=3284497. Finding that the majority of surveyed CSPs post an overview of subprocessors on their website combined with a mechanism to receive notifications when new subprocessors are added.

[265] Kamarinou, 'Article 28. Processor', p. 605.

However, the GDPR also requires that 'the processor shall inform the controller of any intended changes concerning the addition or replacement of other processors, thereby giving the controller the opportunity to object to such changes'.[266] This will perhaps necessitate an ongoing dialogue between the controller or processor requiring a system for updates of a CSP's processors and a time frame for controllers to object.[267] In either case, the processor will be required to obtain some level of acquiescence from the controller, even if the level of information that must be provided varies. Although the instructions in the processing contract must include 'the nature and purpose of the processing' and 'the type of personal data',[268] the GDPR does not appear to require much more information than the names of the subprocessors. For example, stating the role or purpose of the processor and their necessity or function in the purpose of processing is not obligatory.

In addition to obtaining consent, if a subprocessor is added, the processor – still acting on behalf of the controller – must include ' ... the same data protection obligations as set out in the contract ... between the controller and the processor ... '.[269] In other words, the processor is required to flow-down the terms it has with the controller to the agreements it has with the subprocessors. Furthermore, the processor remains liable for the subcontractors or subprocessors it engages.[270] Depending on how broadly this 'flow-down' requirement is applied (i.e. which parties are deemed subprocessors), it may become unwieldy for cloud providers.

The structure and timing of the contracts create one barrier to implementation. If the contract is already in place, then flowing down terms would likely require reopening contract negotiations. Another issue that remains unclear is the scope of the actors that might be considered subprocessors. If essentially every supplier that participates in the operation of a cloud service, regardless of location, is required to apply EU-specific terms, then this will create a substantial barrier. In addition to requiring that terms flow down, the GDPR creates a clear liability chain, thereby making the original processor liable for the acts of the subprocessors.[271]

5.5.6 Data Protection by Design and by Default

Research and discussion on privacy by design has been a global conversation for some time.[272] The central concept or idea behind privacy by design is simple: software, hardware, and other systems should not only be secure, but they should

---

[266] GDPR Art. 28(2).
[267] Kamarinou, Millard, and Oldani, 'Compliance as a Service', 10–11.
[268] GDPR Art. 28(3).
[269] GDPR Art. 28(4).
[270] ibid.
[271] ibid. However, this liability is further qualified per GDPR Art. 82(3). See further GDPR Recital 146.
[272] Lee Bygrave, 'Hardwiring Privacy' in Roger Brownsword, Eloise Scotford, and Karen Yeung (eds.), *The Oxford Handbook of Law, Regulation and Technology* (Oxford: Oxford University Press 2017), pp. 754–62. Providing a history of the concept of PbD dating back to work in the mid-1990s.

5.5 Data Processors and Data Controllers: Roles and Responsibilities

also safeguard privacy by default. Arguments for requiring the technological implementation of privacy obligations are centred on privacy laws' dependence on the design of software and systems.[273] However, even if software and systems are seen as crucial, much of privacy by design's potential has yet to be realized.[274] As noted by Schartum, the general vagueness of EU legislation is a limiting factor or hindrance to privacy by design generally.[275]

The GDPR places a direct – albeit qualified – duty on data controllers to implement DPbD measures to protect the rights of data subjects. Under the GDPR, implementation of DPbD is mandatory and applies specifically to data controllers, requiring that they put in place appropriate technical and organizational measures.[276] Thus, the GDPR provides legislative support for DPbD, taking it out of the sphere of voluntary compliance and making it an EU-wide obligation.[277]

Data controllers are required to consider data protection aspects from the design phase of any system or service and continue that focus throughout the life cycle of the technology's development, deployment, and operation. A core aspect of this process includes applying the data protection principles in GDPR Article 5. Like many other areas of the GDPR, DPbD measures are scalable and follow a risk-based approach. This requires that data controllers take account of the state of the art, the cost of implementation, and the nature, scope, and purposes of the processing as primary factors.[278] DPbD goes beyond the technical aspects and also applies to organizational measures like managerial and business processes.[279]

In cloud computing, application of DPbD will depend to some extent on the service (e.g. SaaS, IaaS, and PaaS). If the use of the cloud service follows the general deployment, where the cloud client is the data controller and the CSP is the data processor, GDPR obligations fall primarily on cloud clients or public administration procuring the service.[280] However, the GDPR also provides that 'the principles of DPbD should also be taken into consideration in the context of

---

[273] Dag Wiese Schartum, 'Making Privacy by Design Operative' (2016) 24 *International Journal of Law and Information Technology* 151.
[274] ibid., 152.
[275] ibid., 152. See also Bygrave, 'Hardwiring Privacy', pp. 767–68. Noting the difficulty in replicating data privacy law into computer code. Michael Veale, Reuben Binns, and Jef Ausloos, 'When Data Protection by Design and Data Subject Rights Clash' (2018) 8 *International Data Privacy Law* 105–23 at 117–18. Criticizing the GDPR for providing little guidance to evaluate the trade-offs or conflicts between data subject rights and DPbD obligations.
[276] GDPR Article 25 and Recital 78. Generally, data processors will not be in a position to assist data controllers with data protection by design requirements. However, GDPR Article 25, Articles 28 and 32 contain security and organizational measures directed at data processors.
[277] Bygrave, 'Hardwiring Privacy', p. 768. Noting that privacy by design requirements have traditionally struggled to gain legislative backing.
[278] GDPR Art. 25(1). See also GDPR Art. 35(1) for data controller obligations in high-risk processing assessments.
[279] Bygrave, 'Data Protection by Design and by Default', 113–14.
[280] GDPR Article 25 and Recital 78. However, GDPR Articles 28 and 32 contain security and organizational measures are primarily directed at data processors.

public tenders'.[281] Thus, governments procuring a cloud service must consider DPbD when deciding to award a bid to a CSP.[282] Even if governments are not designing the systems, they have the potential to positively influence DPbD through purchasing decisions.

5.5.7 The Role of Data Security in Data Privacy Law and the GDPR

As a point of departure, it is important to note that the concept of data protection is separate from that of data security. Although security requirements are found throughout the GDPR, including in the core principles, GDPR compliance requires more than secure systems.[283] Privacy cannot be achieved simply by managing security.[284] Compliance with the GDPR is not a problem that can be 'solved' with encryption technology. Although data protection necessitates security, it also focuses on the data subject's 'privacy-related interests'.[285] In other words, data security serves as a means of safeguarding broader privacy interests, but it is not a substitute for it.[286]

Data security focuses on practices or processes to prevent loss of CIA. However, many privacy violations occur when data *are secure*, and no loss of CIA has occurred. To provide an example, a system designed to collect massive amounts of personal data and store that information indefinitely may be secure and functioning as designed. However, because the design violates data privacy law, the privacy violation is a by-product of the design, not the lack of security.[287] Moreover, because the activity is part of the system design, information security models will not necessarily measure the data protection violation as a threat or vulnerability. After all, the data

---

[281] GDPR Recital 78. The EU Public Sector Directive 2014/24/EU Recital 77 further requires '[w]hen drawing up technical specifications, contracting authorities should take into account requirements ensuing from Union law in the field of data protection law, in particular in relation to the design of the processing of personal data (data protection by design)'. Emphasis added.

[282] EDPB, 'Guidelines 4/2019 on Article 25 Data Protection by Design and by Default' (20 October 2019), 5. https://edpb.europa.eu/our-work-tools/our-documents/guidelines/guidelines-42019-article-25-data-protection-design-and_en. Providing that 'public administrations should lead by example'.

[283] GDPR Art. 5(1)(f) requiring ' ... appropriate security of the personal data ... '. As noted in the earlier section, the GDPR requires increased accountability and data governance obligations on several fronts, including: Responsibilities of Controller Art. 24; Increased Processor Responsibilities Art. 28; Accountability Principle Art. 5(2); Privacy by Design Art. 25; Increased Records of Processing Activities Art. 30; Security of Processing Art. 32; Notification of Data Breach Articles 33–34; Privacy Impact Assessments Articles 35–36; and Designation of the Data Protection Officer Art. 37; among other obligations.

[284] NIST, 'An Introduction to Privacy Engineering and Risk Management in Federal Systems' (2017), 1–49 at 9.

[285] Bygrave, 'Data Privacy Law: An International Perspective', p. 2.

[286] WP29, 'Statement on the Role of a Risk-based Approach in Data Protection Legal Frameworks' 218 (2014), 3–4.

[287] ibid. Such a design would violate privacy by design and privacy by default requirements under Art. 25.

collection taking place *is authorized* by the system.[288] Therefore, appropriate data security is only one aspect of the compliance picture.

The GDPR requires that personal data be processed securely. However, it does not provide one security requirement that will apply to all users. The legislation approaches information security broadly, requiring both technical and organizational measures. As provided earlier, 'integrity and confidentiality' requires confidentiality in processing or handling of personal data ' ... in a manner that ensures appropriate security of the personal data, including protection against unauthorized or unlawful processing and against accidental loss, destruction or damage ... '.[289] Meeting this principle broadly requires that a government or organization has adequate organizational policies, undergoes risk assessments, and puts in place technical measures to protect and ensure the availability of personal data.[290]

To determine what is appropriate or necessary security, GDPR Article 32 provides that controllers must take account of a number of factors including 'the state of the art, the costs of implementation' in determining the appropriate technical and organizational measures necessary to 'ensure a level of security appropriate to the risk ... '.[291] Thus, GDPR security requirements are scalable and will vary depending on the type of data processed, processing operations, and the overall risk to data subjects. Among other aspects, this requires that controllers choose processors that also offer adequate security and organizational measures.[292] Controllers cannot outsource their responsibility for data security under GDPR Article 32 to third parties.[293]

It may be difficult for a CSP to know and concretely enumerate all of the different security practices employed at the beginning of the service. For example, if subcontractors are delivering different parts of the cloud service, they may use varied security practices in their respective roles. Although varied, the different components of the service may provide adequate security even if approached differently at the various levels. Further, updating contract terms to reflect security changes made by partners during the service provides an additional challenge. The data security landscape changes rapidly. A system that is secure – and meets industry standards – when the contract is entered into might not be secure six months or a year later if it is not monitored and updated. After all, data security includes a lot of moving parts

---

[288] ibid.
[289] GDPR Art. 5(1)(f).
[290] Including GDPR Articles 32–34. Bygrave, 'Data Privacy Law: An International Perspective', pp. 164–65.
[291] See also CNIL, 'Security of Personal Data Report/Guidance' (2018), 1–24. www.cnil.fr/sites/default/files/atoms/files/cnil_guide_securite_personnelle_gb_web.pdf. Practical or operational guidance from the French DPA on GDPR security requirements.
[292] GDPR Art. 32(1)(a-d).
[293] See Wolters, 'The Security of Personal Data under the GDPR', 165–78 at 169. Discussing CSP obligations under the GDPR and the NIS Directive. WP29 253 (2017), 1–17 at 13. Whether a controller or processor has implemented technical and organizational measures implemented by them pursuant to Articles 25 and 32 will also be relevant in assessing fines.

from the logical side to the physical and requires an understanding of not only the technical aspects but also the people and places where the system is provided and operated.[294]

In a study of contract terms carried out by the CLP at QMUL, researchers found that the contract terms used to express security practices varied among CSPs.[295] However, relatively non-specific terms were common, including 'generally accepted', 'industry standard', 'reasonable' or 'commercially reasonable'.[296] The QMUL study further noted that specific terms for data security were not always easy to locate within the contractual framework, and the user was often required to seek out specific pages, consult online help centres, or read the CSP's privacy policy.[297] In other words, data security policies or practices were not always accessible, and even when found they provided unclear descriptions.

The reason for providing little information can be explained to some extent by the nature of data security. Although common elements and approaches do exist, data security is provided on something of a sliding scale. For large-scale state users, whether a CSP has adequate capacity and is flexible or 'scalable' is also a central consideration.[298] One plan or standard for all users is neither commercially viable nor practical.[299] Users storing highly sensitive personal information, such as medical or financial data, require (and are often willing to pay for) a more advanced system of protection.[300] At the other end of the spectrum, many users are not interested in the 'how' behind data security – they just want to know that the system they are using is secure. In any case, terms like 'standard' and 'generally accepted' are difficult to assess when industry practices or standards vary considerably.

5.5.8 Conclusion on Data Processing Obligations

Prior to the GDPR, CSPs have generally disclaimed all liability for their services, thereby placing the burden of complying with regulatory requirements on cloud clients.[301] GDPR requirements seem to acknowledge the situation found in many cloud computing scenarios where the controller/cloud client has very limited influence over the processing taking place. Article 28 attempts to rectify that imbalance by

---

[294] Peter Sloan, 'The Reasonable Information Security Program' (2014) 21 *Richmond Journal of Law & Technology* 2–92 at 4.
[295] Dimitra Kamarinou, Christopher Millard, and W. K. Hon, 'Cloud Privacy: An Empirical Study of 20 Cloud Providers' Terms and Privacy Policies – Part II' (2016) 6 *International Data Privacy Law* 170–94 at 178–79. https://doi.org/10.1093/idpl/ipw004.
[296] ibid., 179.
[297] ibid., 178–79.
[298] Scott Paquette, Paul T. Jaeger, and Susan C. Wilson, 'Identifying the Security Risks Associated with Governmental Use of Cloud Computing' (2010) 27 *Government Information Quarterly* 245–53 at 250. Citing problems with scalability in the FBI's 'Virtual Case File' system, among others.
[299] Sloan, 'The Reasonable Information Security Program', para. 21.
[300] ibid., para. 22.
[301] Hustinx, 'Opinion of the European Data Protection Supervisor', 10.

placing direct obligations on the CSP. Guidance from the EDPB also acknowledges the current imbalance, noting that 'the chains of subcontracting are becoming increasingly complex' and that as links to the chain are added, so are obligations under the GDPR.[302]

Contractual and liability requirements under Article 28 of the GDPR have the potential to remedy the compliance needs of cloud clients, or at least bring them to the forefront.[303] By creating additional and independent processor responsibilities under the GDPR, CSPs have direct responsibilities that they cannot escape by simply leveraging their stronger bargaining position. If the data processor CSP is in a better position to prevent data loss or other harms related to unlawful processing by subcontractors or other third parties with access to cloud clients' data, the prescriptive approach in GDPR Article 28 makes sense. This adjustment has the potential to increase compliance in the areas where CSPs have the most control. Moreover, given the imbalance in the bargaining relationship and the lack of information regarding the many layers of cloud computing services, placing the balance of liability on the cloud client has negative consequences for trust in the cloud and ultimately the uptake and use of the services.

5.6 CROSS-BORDER TRANSFERS OF DATA: WHAT ARE THE RULES AND HOW MIGHT CSPS COMPLY?

In cloud computing, international data transfers are often an inherent and inseparable part of the service.[304] Given the structure of cloud services and the location of the infrastructure, a transfer from a cloud client to a CSP in the same country will often result in an international data transfer.[305] Because of the relatively opaque structure of services, a cloud client is rarely in a position to be able to know where the data are located, stored, or transferred – at least in real time.[306] Consequently, international transfers of data are not only effortless in cloud computing but also inadvertent in many cases.[307] In the cloud scenario, transfers to third countries likely include

---

[302] EDPB, 'Guidelines 07/2020 on the Concepts of Controller and Processor in the GDPR', 39 (para. 147).
[303] W. Kuan Hon, Christopher Millard, and Ian Walden, 'Negotiated Contracts for Cloud Services' in Christopher Millard (ed.), *Cloud Computing Law* (Oxford: Oxford University Press 2013), p. 85. Describing treatment by processors/CSPs under the Directive as ' ... ill-defined, misunderstood, or poorly accommodated by providers'.
[304] W. K. Hon and Christopher Millard, 'How Do Restrictions on International Data Transfers Work in Clouds?' in Christopher Millard (ed.), *Cloud Computing Law* (Oxford: Oxford University Press 2013), p. 255. Providing that within many CSP arrangements ' ... data may be replicated to equipment located in other countries, including third countries'.
[305] Christopher Kuner, *Transborder Data Flow Regulation and Data Privacy Law* (Oxford: Oxford University Press 2013), p. 3.
[306] WP29 196, 'Opinion on Cloud Computing 05/2012', 17.
[307] ibid.

- An EU-based cloud client using a CSP established within the EU/EEA using servers outside of the EU/EEA.
- An EU-based cloud client using a CSP with data centres inside and outside of the EU, wherein data from the EU/EEA data centres is transferred to those located in the third country.
- A foreign cloud client transfers data from a third country to the EU, where it is processed, and then attempts to transfer the data back to the third country.
- An EU/EEA-based cloud client using an EU/EEA-based CSP with a parent company (CSP) located in a third country, where the non-EU/EEA parent company has the technical means to access data stored with the EU/EEA subsidiary. This could happen through remote technical or customer support or if the EU/EEA- subsubsidiary is required to transfer personal data to its parent company to meet compliance obligations in that jurisdiction

Based on a lack of stable location arrangements, the cloud client may be unaware that they are transferring data to a third country or that their national CSP stores their cloud clients' data on the infrastructure of a provider in a third country. Therefore, having adequate technical and contractual measures in place to either limit or make transfers GDPR compliant is a primary challenge for cloud adoption and use by governments.

Overall, the GDPR follows the previous approach under the Data Protection Directive regarding data transfers.[308] Data transfers within the EU/EEA are deemed to have an adequate level of protection and are therefore permitted.[309] Absent additional safeguards, the GDPR prohibits data transfers to third countries that do not provide an adequate level of protection.[310] The rationale for this approach is to ensure that international transfers do not undermine the level of protection guaranteed in the GDPR for data subjects.[311]

The term 'transfer' is not defined in the GDPR.[312] Transfers generally concentrate on the physical location of infrastructure (i.e. the CSP's servers where the data are stored) and any movement to or from those points.[313] In the CJEU case *Bodil Lindqvist*, the court determined that loading personal data onto a webpage or blog

---

[308] Chapter 5 of the GDPR Arts 44–50. Voigt and von dem Bussche, 'Practical Implementation of the Requirements under the GDPR', pp. 116–17.
[309] GDPR Art. 1(3). See Bygrave, 'Data Privacy Law: An International Perspective', p. 191.
[310] In some cases, derogations may be applicable under GDPR Art. 49.
[311] GDPR Art. 44 and Recital 101. Bygrave, 'Data Privacy Law: An International Perspective', pp. 190–91.
[312] ibid., 192, fn 3. Arguing that it is especially unfortunate that the GDPR does not clarify uncertainty regarding data transfer.
[313] Hon, 'Data Localization Laws and Policy,' pp. 69–71. See also Hon and Millard, 'International Data Transfers in Clouds', pp. 257–60. A transfer of data to a server outside of the EU is considered a data export.

fell short of a data transfer.[314] However, as argued by the EDPS and others, the CJEU's interpretation of the term 'transfer' in the *Lindqvist* case has limited application in that it is difficult to apply broadly to complex data processing operations.[315] The EDPS has suggested that data transfer has wider applicability and focuses on 'moving' or allowing data to 'move' between different users.[316] The EDPS's definition of transfer includes deliberate transfers and permitted access (e.g. remote access) but excludes illegal actions such as hacking.[317]

Although legislators acknowledge that transferring data to third countries is often necessary, such transfers also have the potential to undermine the protections afforded to data subjects who are in the EU.[318] The GDPR restricts transfers or 'exports' of personal data outside of the EEA to third countries that do not ensure an ' ... an adequate level of protection'.[319] If a third country proves it offers an adequate level of data protection, it may also receive data from the EU. However, any additional 'onward transfer' from that third country to another country or organization must also meet legal requirements (e.g. adequacy or additional safeguards).[320]

The aim of controlling the chain of transfers is to maintain a high level of protection and clear chain of responsibility to wherever data might be transferred. Outside of an adequacy determination, international transfers are only allowed when adequate safeguards are in place or when the transfer meets the requirements of certain derogations. These methods are evaluated in the sections later.

5.6.1 *Adequacy Determinations and Means of Transfer*

The EC is responsible for making adequacy determinations regarding the privacy protections available in third countries. In its evaluation, the EC considers factors including ' ... the rule of law, respect for human rights and fundamental freedoms, [and] relevant legislation ... ', among others.[321] In addition to relevant legislation, the EC also considers the ability of the third country to enforce that legislation, including an assessment of whether the country has a functioning and independent

---

[314] Case C-101/01, *Bodil Lindqvist* [2003] ECR I-12971, [70–71]. See Bygrave, 'Data Privacy Law: An International Perspective', pp. 191–92. Supplying that the CJEU's most convincing justification for this finding was that deciding otherwise would broaden the scope of data transfers immensely.
[315] European Data Protection Supervisor, 'The Transfer of Personal Data to Third Countries and International Organisations by EU Institutions and Bodies' (2014), 6.
[316] ibid.
[317] ibid.
[318] GDPR Art. 44. Expanded further in Rec. 101.
[319] GDPR Art. 45. WP29, 'Adequacy Referential', WP 254 rev.01 (2018), 3. https://ec.europa.eu/news room/article29/items/614108/en.
[320] GDPR Art. 44 and Recital 101.
[321] GDPR Art. 45(2)(a). Recital 104. GDPR Art. 45(2)(b). The European Commission has so far recognized Andorra, Argentina, Canada (commercial organizations), Faroe Islands, Guernsey, Israel, Isle of Man, Japan, Jersey, New Zealand, Switzerland, and Uruguay as providing adequate levels of protection.

supervisory authority.[322] Further, the EC also places weight on whether the third country is a party to international conventions focusing on data protection, among other rights.[323]

To have an 'adequate' level of protection, the third country does not have to adopt legislation identical to the GDPR. However, the legislation of the third country must contain the essential or core requirements of EU data protection law.[324] In particular, the third country's legislation should at least contain some expression of the data protection principles evaluated earlier.[325] The EC's adequacy determination goes beyond the written legislation.[326] The EC also evaluates the system in place to enforce the rules and the remedies available to data subjects.[327] This requires that the EC analyse both the *content* and *application* of data protection law in the country on an ongoing basis.[328] If a third country no longer provides an adequate level of protection, the EC can revisit or repeal the adequacy determination.[329] By requiring countries outside of the EU to prove adequacy, the requirements have an extraterritorial impact.[330]

The United States is not among the list of countries that the EC deems to offer an adequate level of data protection.[331] As a result, personal data cannot flow freely from the EU to the United States, requiring that the controller or processor provide 'appropriate safeguards'.[332] Until 2015, the EC accommodated transatlantic data transfers through the Safe Harbour Framework.[333] The Safe Harbour Framework was a self-regulatory mechanism negotiated between the EC and the US Department of Commerce. Although the Safe Harbour principles have long been subject to criticism, they provided a means of transfer.[334] For example,

---

[322] ibid.
[323] GDPR Art. 45(2)(c).
[324] WP29 254 (2017), 3.
[325] ibid., 5–7.
[326] ibid., 3.
[327] ibid.
[328] ibid., 3–4. This monitoring must take place on an ongoing basis to evaluate developments that might influence adequacy. The WP29 suggests this should take place at least every four years. See GDPR Art. 45(4).
[329] GDPR Art. 45(5). See also GDPR Recital 107.
[330] Christopher Kuner, 'Extraterritoriality and Regulation of International Data Transfers in EU Data Protection Law' (2015) 5 *International Data Privacy Law* 235–45 at 241. Hon and Millard, 'International Data Transfers in Clouds', p. 254.
[331] GDPR Art. 45(3).
[332] GDPR Art. 46(1). See also Recital 108.
[333] Hon, 'Data Localization Laws and Policy,' pp. 162–63. See Finding of adequacy for Safe Harbour effective on 30 November 2000, under Commission Decision of 26 July 2000 pursuant to Directive 95/46/EC of the European Parliament and of the Council on the adequacy of the protection provided by the safe harbour privacy principles and related frequently asked questions issued by the US Department of Commerce, 2000/520/EC [25 August 2000] OJ L215/7. https://eur-lex.europa.eu/legal-content/EN/TXT/?uri=CELEX%3A32000D0520.
[334] Bygrave, 'Data Privacy Law: An International Perspective', p. 195. Describing the Safe Harbour principles as 'considerably watered down' when compared with those contained in the Directive. Prior to the *Maximillian Schrems v. Data Protection Commissioner* [2015] C-362/14 decision,

many CSPs relied on Safe Harbour to transfer data from the EU/EEA to the United States.[335]

The Safe Harbour Framework met its end in the landmark case of *Maximillian Schrems v. Data Protection Commissioner (Schrems I)*. In the case, Schrems, an Austrian citizen, filed a complaint with the Irish Data Protection Commissioner regarding data transfers to the United States. Schrems argued that when his personal data were transferred from Facebook Ireland to Facebook US, it did not receive an adequate level of protection.[336] More specifically, Schrems asserted that once EU/EEA data were transferred to the United States, intelligence and LEAs obtained nearly unrestricted access to the EU/EEA data.[337] Thus, Schrems maintained that data transfers made pursuant to Safe Harbour did not amount to an adequate level of protection.[338]

Among other holdings, the CJEU invalidated the Safe Harbour Framework as a transfer mechanism.[339] The CJEU reasoned that data transferred to the United States under Safe Harbour lacked protections from access by US intelligence and law enforcement services, failed to provide EU citizens with adequate legal remedies, and violated core principles of EU data protection law.[340] The CJEU further provided that

> ... the term 'adequate level of protection' must be understood as requiring the third country in fact to ensure, by reason of its domestic law or its international commitments, a level of protection of fundamental rights and freedoms that is essentially equivalent to that guaranteed within the European Union by virtue of Directive 95/46 read in the light of the Charter.[341]

Thus, while the receiving third country does not have to mirror EU legislation, the level of protection it provides must be 'essentially equivalent'.[342]

Although the decision in *Schrems I* was perhaps expected, it was nevertheless controversial and resulted in a great deal of uncertainty regarding trans-border data

---

commentators called into question the adequacy of the Safe Harbour scheme. Hon and Millard, 'How Do Restrictions on International Data Transfers Work in Clouds?', pp. 263–66.

[335] Hon, 'Data Localization Laws and Policy,' p. 170. Safe Harbour was widely used by US CSPs. Hon and Millard, 'International Data Transfers in Clouds', pp. 270–71.
[336] *Schrems* [2015], C-362/14 [27].
[337] *Schrems* [2015], [28].
[338] ibid., [28].
[339] ibid., [106].
[340] ibid., [94]–[95]. Tuomas Ojanen, 'Rights-Based Review of Electronic Surveillance after Digital Rights Ireland and Schrems in the European Union' in David Cole, Federico Fabbrini, and Stephen Schulhofer (eds.), *Surveillance, Privacy and Trans-Atlantic Relations*, vol 1 (Oxford: Hart 2017), pp. 13–29 at 18–27.
[341] *Schrems* [2015], [73].
[342] ibid., [96]. c.f. David Bender, 'Having Mishandled Safe Harbor, Will the CJEU Do Better with Privacy Shield? A US Perspective' (2016) 6 *International Data Privacy Law* 117–38 at 119–30. Arguing that US intelligence data processing is much more privacy sensitive than as depicted in the CJEU decision.

flows. The decision was seen by some as a 'vindication of privacy as a fundamental right ... '.[343] Others suggested that it was nothing more than a misunderstanding of the actual protections provided by US privacy law.[344] Regardless of the commentator's position, following the CJEU decision in *Schrems I*, transfers via Safe Harbour became unlawful.[345] Thus, CSPs had to find alternative transfer mechanisms, such as standard contractual clauses (SCCs), which are evaluated further later.[346] Before evaluating those instruments, I briefly consider the successor to Safe Harbour – the Privacy Shield Framework.[347]

5.6.2 Privacy Shield

Following the decision in *Schrems I*, the EU and United States developed the Privacy Shield Framework.[348] Privacy Shield also requires self-certification and is in many ways an expanded version of Safe Harbour including, among other aspects, a new oversight mechanism for national security interference with data transfers. Privacy Shield aimed to improve on some of the points that were fatal to the Safe Harbour Framework in the CJEU's assessment, such as by providing more rigorous monitoring, purportedly limiting national security and law enforcement access to EU/EEA data, and strengthening the rights of EU individuals.[349] Unlike Safe Harbour, Privacy Shield also included an ombudsperson to bolster accountability and legal redress for violations.[350]

In addition to promises made by US authorities and (arguably) improved structures, changes were made to US intelligence-gathering practices.[351] The combination of US

---

[343] Ojanen, 'Rights-Based Review of Electronic Surveillance', p. 16.
[344] Bender, 'Having Mishandled Safe Harbor', 125. Arguing that the EU focus on US surveillance was '... .grossly exaggerated if not entirely unfounded'.
[345] *Schrems* [2015], [61]–[63].
[346] Hon and Millard, 'International Data Transfers in Clouds', pp. 263–66.
[347] Commission Implementing Decision (EU) 2016/1250 of 12 July 2016 pursuant to Directive 95/46/EC of the European Parliament and of the Council on the adequacy of the protection provided by the EU–US Privacy Shield (notified under document C (2016) 4176) (Text with EEA relevance) C/2016/4176. http://data.europa.eu/eli/dec_impl/2016/1250/oj (hereinafter 'Privacy Shield').
[348] Holly Kathleen Hall, 'Restoring Dignity and Harmony to United States-European Union Data Protection Regulation' (2018) 23 *Communication Law and Policy* 125–57 at 152.
[349] European Commission, 'Report from the Commission to the European Parliament and the Council on the First Annual Review of the Functioning of the EU–U.S. Privacy Shield' COM (2017) 611 final (2017), 1–7 at 1–2. See also WP29, 'Opinion 01/2016 on the EU – U.S. Privacy Shield Draft Adequacy Decision' 238 (2016), 1–58 at 4.
[350] Tzanou, 'Fundamental Right to Data Protection', pp. 244–46. Arguing that whether the ombudsperson role rises to the level of effective judicial redress is debatable. See also Gert Vermeulen, 'The Paper Shield: On the Degree of Protection of the EU–US Privacy Shield against Unnecessary or Disproportionate Data Collection by the US Intelligence and Law Enforcement Services' in Dan Svantesson and Dariusz Kloza (eds.), *Trans-Atlantic Data Privacy Relations as a Challenge for Democracy*, vol 4 (Cambridge: Intersentia 2017), p. 145. Asserting that the ombudsperson is largely irrelevant.
[351] Peter Swire, 'US Surveillance Law, Safe Harbour and Reforms Since 2013' in Dan Svantesson and Dariusz Kloza (eds.), *Trans-Atlantic Data Privacy Relations as a Challenge for Democracy*, vol 4 (Cambridge: Intersentia 2017), pp. 94–106.

intelligence access alterations, added protection, and perhaps rebranding was enough to receive the EC's stamp of approval.[352] In July 2016, the EC issued an adequacy decision finding that Privacy Shield provides an adequate level of protection, thereby allowing data transfers to the United States under the framework.[353]

5.6.2.1 Standard Contractual Clauses

If a third country does not offer an adequate level of protection, data transfers can be accomplished using contracts.[354] That is, the parties to the transfer can contractually commit to provide an adequate level of protection.[355] Although contracts can be tailored and adopted on an ad hoc basis for individual approval, SCCs drafted by the EC have become an essential tool for international data transfers to third countries.[356] The EC has adopted three sets of SCCs: two focus on controller-to-controller transfers and the third focuses on controller-to-processor transfers.[357]

The SCCs drafted by the EC essentially function as standard contracts or even contracts of adhesion rather than model agreements.[358] The agreements must be adopted in full. Altering or partially adopting SCCs invalidates the 'adequacy' protection they provide.[359] Although SCCs can be combined or presented as part of a larger contract, the SCC terms cannot be materially changed. As a result, SCCs provide little flexibility.

For example, one of the B2B CSP contracts obtained outside of the FOIA study for this book provided that ' ... the Parties agree to be bound by the SCCs *with the following modifications* that are required to take into account the special requirements of cloud computing and its uniform offering to all customers'.[360] Amendments included changes to liability, governing law, and consent to

---

[352] Vermeulen, 'The Paper Shield', pp. 135–36. Arguing that while 'Safe Harbor principles' were renamed 'privacy principles', their content remained similar.
[353] Commission Implementing Decision (EU) 2016/1250 of 12 July 2016 pursuant to Directive 95/46/EC of the European Parliament and of the Council on the adequacy of the protection provided by the EU-US Privacy Shield (notified under document C (2016) 4176) (Text with EEA relevance) C/2016/4176.
[354] GDPR Art. 46 (3)(a).
[355] Voigt and von dem Bussche, 'Practical Implementation of the Requirements under the GDPR', p. 199.
[356] Kuner, 'Extraterritoriality and Regulation of International Data Transfers', 238. Evaluating appropriate contractual clauses under the Directive. GDPR Art. 46(2).
[357] Controller-to-controller clauses: (1) Commission Decision of 15 June 2001 on standard contractual clauses for the transfer of personal data to third countries, under Directive 95/46/EC (2001/497/EC), [4 July 2001] OJ L181/19. (2) Commission Decision of 27 December 2004 amending Decision 2001/497/EC as regards the introduction of an alternative set of standard contractual clauses for the transfer of personal data to third countries (2004/915/EC), [29 December 2004] OJ L385/74. Controller-to-processor clauses: Commission Decision of 27 December 2001 on standard contractual clauses for the transfer of personal data to processors established in third countries, under Directive 95/46/EC (2002/16/EC), [10 January 2002] OJ L6/52.
[358] Voigt and von dem Bussche, 'Practical Implementation of the Requirements under the GDPR', p. 120.
[359] WP29 196, 'Opinion on Cloud Computing 05/2012', 18–19.
[360] Emphasis added. Confidential contract on file with the Author.

subcontracting.[361] Based on the requirement that SCCs are not modified, unless a local DPA approved such changes, I am of the opinion that the contract term examined falls outside of SCC protection.

Currently, the EC is in the process of amending and updating the SCCs. The SCCs currently in use are almost ten-years old, obviously predating the GDPR, and still reference the now repealed Data Protection Directive. Given the recent CJEU decision in *Schrems II* (discussed earlier) an update is much needed. The EC had not issued its final SCCs at the time this book was finalized.

5.6.2.2 Binding Corporate Rules

In addition to SCCs, Binding Corporate Rules (BCRs) provide a means to transfer data within a corporate group.[362] Although certain actors in the group may be located in third countries which lack adequacy, the group as a whole offers an adequate level of protection. Unlike the Directive, the GDPR specifically recognizes BCRs.[363] At first blush, BCRs might seem an attractive alternative for CSPs. However, as noted by Hon and Millard, BCRs are a poor fit for many CSPs.[364] In particular, the process for approval is time consuming and expensive.[365] Moreover, if the CSP uses subprocessors or subcontracts aspects of its infrastructure (i.e. a SaaS using IaaS infrastructure), those providers must also agree to the contract terms.[366] This may require that an IaaS, such as AWS, change its contract terms.[367] Although large CSPs such as Microsoft, AWS, and Google may be able to obtain such concessions, for smaller CSPs this is an unlikely prospect.[368]

5.6.3 *Data Protection Commissioner versus Facebook* (Schrems II)

Maximillian Schrems, the same plaintiff in the *Schrems I* case evaluated earlier, again challenged the adequacy of data transfers to the United States, requesting that the Irish Data Protection Commissioner order the suspension of data transfers by Facebook Ireland to Facebook US.[369] In C-311/18 *Data Protection Commissioner v. Facebook Ireland Ltd and Maximillian Schrems* (*Schrems II*), Mr. Schrems argued that data transfers made to the United States were invalid, asserting that SCCs did

---

[361] ibid.
[362] Lokke Moerel, *Binding Corporate Rules: Corporate Self-Regulation of Global Data Transfers* (Oxford: Oxford University Press 2012), pp. 101–30. Describing the different types of BCRs and procedural requirements.
[363] GDPR Art. 47. Outlining approval process and requirements. WP29, 'Working Document Setting up a Table with the Elements and Principles to be found in Processor Binding Corporate Rules' (2018), 1–22 at 2–3 ('WP29 257 rev.01').
[364] Hon and Millard, 'International Data Transfers in Clouds', p. 268.
[365] ibid.
[366] ibid.
[367] ibid.
[368] ibid.
[369] *Schrems II*, para. 77.

5.6 Cross-Border Transfers of Data

not, and were not capable of, providing an appropriate safeguard for data transfers from Facebook Ireland to Facebook US.[370] His argument centred on the obligation Facebook was under to make user data available to the US government for processing in various surveillance programs.[371]

The case was referred to the Irish High Court. Writing for the Irish High Court, Ms. Justice Costello concurring with the Irish Data Protection Commissioner provided '... there are well founded grounds for believing that the SCC decisions are invalid ...'.[372] The Irish High Court then referred a number of specific questions to the CJEU.[373] The essence of the questions focused on:

1) Whether the Privacy Shield Decision constitutes a finding that the United States ensures an adequate level of protection within the meaning of EU data protection law?
2) Do transfers based on SCCs violate EU data protection law or Articles 7, 8 and/or 47 of the EU Charter?

In *Schrems II*, the CJEU again evaluated data transfers from the EU/EEA to the United States. Before moving to those specific questions, the Court settled several initial topic areas. Of relevance to cloud computing, application of the GDPR to international data transfers. There the Court provided:

> It follows that the operation of having personal data transferred from a Member State to a third country constitutes, in itself, processing of personal data within the meaning of Article 4(2) of the GDPR, carried out in a Member State, and falls within the scope of that regulation under Article 2(1).[374]

Further, the Court also found the fact that a data transfer made for commercial purposes that undergoes processing for purported national security interests does not remove the transfer from the scope or application of the GDPR.[375] The CJEU went on to then examine the core legal issues including the validity of the Privacy Shield Decision and the EC decision on SCCs.

5.6.3.1 Standard Contractual Clauses after *Schrems II*

A central consideration before the CJEU in *Schrems II* was whether data transfers to the United States under Privacy Shield Decision were lawful. That is, whether the

---

[370] ibid., para. 57.
[371] ibid., paras. 60–65. Citing the Irish High Court's evaluation of US legislation regulating intelligence activity.
[372] *Data Protection Commissioner v. Facebook Ireland Limited and Maximillian Schrems* [2017] IEHC 545, 338. www.bailii.org/ie/cases/IEHC/2017/H545.html.
[373] *Schrems II*, para. 68.
[374] ibid., para. 83.
[375] ibid., paras. 86–89. The CJEU also found that additional exceptions that might remove the transfers from falling under the jurisdiction of the GDPR, including application of the 'household exception' and transfers between states were not applicable.

Privacy Shield scheme provides data subjects with an adequate level of protection.[376] In its evaluation, the CJEU evaluated US surveillance programs and the legal regimes providing a legal basis for such programs to take place. The CJEU focused Section 702 of the FISA and on EO 12333 finding that the legal instruments do not require or ensure proportionality in processing personal data transferred from the EU.[377] The CJEU further determined that Section 702 of the FISA does not limit surveillance programs such as PRISM or UPSTREAM in ensuring that individuals under surveillance are specifically targeted.[378]

In addition to wide-ranging and indiscriminate data collection, the CJEU focused on the lack of redress data subjects have in the United States. In particular, the fact that data subjects who are in the EU do not have actionable rights in US courts against US authorities to challenge surveillance or the processing of personal data for intelligence purposes.[379] The primary avenue for judicial review or the pursuit of individual legal remedies for non-US persons is the Privacy Shield Ombudsperson. The CJEU evaluated the ombudsperson's powers and determined that the position lacked the requisite level of independence and general authority to meet an adequacy threshold.[380] Specifically, that the ombudsperson is 'not a tribunal within the meaning of Article 47 of the Charter, US law does not afford data subjects who are in the EU with a level of protection essentially equivalent to that guaranteed by the fundamental right enshrined in that article'.[381] In short, data subjects who are in the EU effectively lack actionable rights in US courts to challenge surveillance activities by US government agencies or cooperation by private providers.[382]

By granting such unrestrained access, US authorities failed to provide an adequate level of data protection.[383] Privacy Shield's adequacy failure occurs on several levels. The reality is that bulk collection remained possible under Privacy Shield. Such bulk collection violates proportionality and necessity requirements of EU data protection law.[384] The CJEU determined that US processing of personal data for surveillance purposes had not been limited to what is strictly necessary to achieve that purpose.[385] Moreover, Privacy Shield protections focused a great deal on the use

---

[376] ibid., para. 168. As required under GDPR Art., 'read in the light of the fundamental rights guaranteed in Articles 7, 8, and 47 of the Charter'.
[377] ibid., paras. 178–79. For further discussion of these programs, see Chapter 4.
[378] ibid., para. 180.
[379] ibid., para. 181. To that point, the court noted specifically that ' ... legislation not providing for any possibility for an individual to pursue legal remedies in order to have access to personal data relating to him or her, or to obtain the rectification or erasure of such data, does not respect the essence of the fundamental right to effective judicial protection, as enshrined in Article 47 of the Charter ... '. ibid., 187.
[380] ibid., paras. 195–97.
[381] ibid., para. 67.
[382] ibid., para. 197. Finding Privacy Shield also lacked a private right of action for data subjects.
[383] ibid., para. 183. The CJEU also found significant that US law allows for bulk collection of data – much of which is not subject to any judicial review.
[384] ibid., para. 184.
[385] ibid.

or processing of data but provide little protection in terms of data collection – violating core GDPR requirements and the general prohibition on processing personal data absent a sufficient legal basis.

In its determination of the adequacy of data transfers made under Privacy Shield, the CJEU found that obligations under US domestic law – specifically national security legislation – fatally limited the protection of person data as required under EU law. As a consequence of interference with the fundamental rights of persons whose data are transferred to the United States, the CJEU deemed the Privacy Shield decision invalid.[386] Transfers from the EU to the US based on Privacy Shield are now illegal and companies continuing to transfer personal data on the basis of the invalid mechanism risk a penalty of €20 million or 4 per cent of their global turnover.[387]

5.6.3.2 Standard Contractual Clauses after *Schrems II*

In evaluating SCCs, the CJEU focused on whether the contracts, in practice, provided a sufficiently effective mechanism to ensure an adequate level of protection for transfers of personal data. When transferring data to the US based on SCCs, the data will be subject to the same US legal instruments supporting surveillance that were central to the invalidation of Privacy Shield. However, the CJEU did not find transfers made under SCCs to be categorically unlawful. As a result, unlike Privacy Shield, transfers to the US based on SCCs are not illegal.

The CJEU interpreted GDPR Articles 46(1) and 46(2)(c) as requiring that data subjects have enforceable rights and effective legal remedies required when their personal data are transferred to a third country.[388] If SCCs are used as a transfer mechanism, they must be capable of providing an 'essentially equivalent' level of protection to that guaranteed within the EU. This requires both an evaluation of the contractual terms entered into between the EU/EEA data exporter and the third country data importer. Additionally, the data exporter must evaluate the ability of the public authorities in the third country to access the personal data transferred. The controller or processor exporting data based on SCCs must also consider aspects of the legal system where the data are being transferred. The CJEU suggests assessment should consider effectively the same elements used in an adequacy decision (rule of law, legislation, human rights, etc.).[389]

There are several difficulties for the continued use of SCCs going forward. In particular, SCCs are not binding on the state authorities of the countries to which data are exported, unless those authorities are parties to the contract.[390] Read in light of the rest of the *Schrems II* decision, this point is particularly important regarding

---

[386] ibid., para. 201.
[387] GDPR Art. 83(5)(c) GDPR.
[388] *Schrems II*, para. 105 citing in GDPR Art. 45(2).
[389] ibid., para. 105.
[390] ibid., para. 125.

the limits of SCCs as a means to remedy the lack of an adequate level of data protection. That is, any promises made in the contract between the parties are limited to parties to the agreement and will not limit or reduce state surveillance.[391] In many cases, the investigating agency will have a duty to conduct surveillance under the law. The parties to an SCC cannot avoid mandatory national surveillance laws by agreeing among themselves – via contract – that the laws do not apply to their service.[392]

The limits of contractual protections have long been an issue. Prior to the *Schrems II* decision, Padova argued that given the surveillance mechanisms and requirements under US law, corporations are required to produce the data of non-residents in ways that violate the terms of the SCCs.[393] Given such requirements, Padova argued that

> ... an American data processor, strictly speaking, should not even be able to enter into a contract based on standard clauses. Indeed, it would not be in a position to 'warrant' the European company that the US legislation does not prevent it from respecting the contractual obligations provided by the said clauses.[394]

If the warranties provided under SCCs clearly conflict with statutory disclosure obligations under US law then the contractual promises are of little value. This does not change post *Schrems II*. Absent a change in US law, the processor remains in the same position and cannot warrant that the obligations under the SCCs will be fulfilled.

It would appear that in many cases, data transfers to the US based on SCCs would not provide an adequate level of protection. Following the logical path of the CJEU's determination regarding Privacy Shield, if SCCs cannot sufficiently limit the powers US authorities have to processes personal data, they cannot provide an essentially equivalent level of protection. Even with SCCs in place, data subjects will lack actionable rights and redress for unlawful processing with regard to US authorities. A contract cannot remedy this deficiency.[395] In guidance on additional or supplementary measures to ensure the adequacy of data transfers, the EDPB guidance suggests a combination of legal, technical, and organizational measures.[396]

---

[391] ibid., para. 132. EDBP, 'Recommendations 01/2020 on Measures that Supplement Transfer Tools to Ensure Compliance with the EU Level of Protection of Personal Data' (10 November 2020), 18. https://edpb.europa.eu/sites/edpb/files/consultation/edpb_recommendations_202001_supplementarymeasurestransferstools_en.pdf.

[392] ibid.

[393] Yann Padova, 'The Safe Harbour is Invalid: What Tools Remain for Data Transfers and What Comes Next?' (2016) 6 *International Data Privacy Law* 139–61 at 152–53.

[394] ibid., 153.

[395] *Schrems II*, paras. 125–27. Providing that ' ... it is common ground that those clauses are not capable of binding the authorities of that third country, since they are not party to the contract'.

[396] EDBP, 'Supplement Transfer Tools', 15. Providing that a combination of 'diverse measures in a way that they support and build on each other may enhance the level of protection and may therefore contribute to reaching EU standards'.

Technical measures, such as encryption, will play a key role as organizational and legal measures are unlikely to be sufficient on their own. If data are encrypted in the EEA before a transfer, it will in theory be unintelligible to US authorities minimizing access and therein further processing for surveillance purposes. However, technical measures are not static and will require reassessment. If at some point US intelligence agencies obtain the ability to bypass such encryption measures, the effectiveness of such technical measures will also be compromised and will no longer meet the adequacy standard.

EDPB guidance provides several examples that are instructive for CSPs. For example, the guidance suggests that data transfers for 'backup and other purposes that do not require access to data in the clear' are still possible.[397] However, to maintain adequacy the exporter must use state of the art encryption, encrypt personal data before it is transferred, and the keys must be properly managed and reside in the EEA.[398] US-based CSPs operating in the EEA will generally face significant challenges in meeting all the EDPB guidance.

For example, in many cases a CSP can provide support without ever accessing personal data. However, there are support situations, 24/7 or otherwise, where the people that are able to solve certain problems are located outside of the EEA. Access to personal data by technicians in the United States would violate EU data protection law, based on the EDPB's guidance. Similarly, even if the encryption keys are managed and kept in the EEA, many of the largest CSPs still fall under US jurisdiction. How should cloud clients assess the possibility that those CSPs (Microsoft, Google, AWS, Apple) might be compelled to provide access to personal data stored in the EEA? The EDPB guidance does not prohibit the use of US-based CSPs. However, as was demonstrated in the *Microsoft Warrant* case in Chapter 4, the US government has the ability to apply pressure on companies that are on US soil. Although the company might be able to challenge the warrant and fight disclosure, SCCs will likely fare poorly against a valid order issued from a domestic court. Will executives in the United States require their EEA offices to provide access to encryption keys under the threat of sanctions or even imprisonment from the US government? How should this type of risk be assessed? Is it even possible to take a risk-based approach?

Although global providers with offices in the EEA will likely be able to comply with many of the measures provided by the EDPB, US-based CSPs without global infrastructure – and the European CSPs based on those services – will face additional challenges. In an example provided for 'transfer to cloud services providers or other processors which require access to data in the clear' the EDPB found that 'considering the current state of the art' the EDPB was 'incapable of envisioning an effective technical measure to prevent that access from infringing on data subject

---

[397] EDBP, 'Supplement Transfer Tools', 22.
[398] ibid., 22–23.

rights'.[399] The EDPB concluded 'where unencrypted personal data is technically necessary for the provision of the service by the processor, transport encryption and data-at-rest encryption even taken together, do not constitute a supplementary measure that ensures an essentially equivalent level of protection if the data importer is in possession of the cryptographic keys'.[400]

Although SCCs remain a possible means of lawful data transfer, they may not be a very viable means for many CSPs. Even if many CSPs used SCCs as a mechanism to continue data transfers after *Schrems I* invalidated the Safe Harbor agreement, *Schrems II* suggests that SCCs will not allow CSPs to 'continue business as usual' to the same extent. It would seem that some type of infrastructure in the EEA, or another country with an adequacy decision under GDPR Article 45, is more important than ever. However, it is unclear if this is enough. The *Schrems II* ruling, combined with the EDPB guidance, creates significant challenges for US-based CSPs. BCRs are also likely to face adequacy challenges similar to those for SCCs and will require similar supplementary measures.

5.6.4 Derogations

The GDPR also allows for the possibility of international transfers of data to third countries lacking both 'adequacy' and the 'appropriate safeguards' evaluated earlier.[401] In certain limited situations, data can be transferred to third countries based on explicit consent, the performance or conclusion of a contract, or when the transfer 'is necessary for important reasons of public interest', among others.[402] However, such transfers have limited applicability and should only take place when other means (e.g. adequacy) are unavailable and affect 'a limited number of data subjects'.[403]

In its Article 49 guidelines, the EDPB specifically provided that derogations are appropriate for non-repetitive transfers that do not rely on the derogations on a systematic basis.[404] In other words, although the exception is available for the occasional transfer, controllers should not build their global data management plans for a large number of users around these derogations. Although some CSPs will likely apply these derogations following the CJEU decision in *Schrems II*, the derogations do not provide long-term solutions for CSPs or cloud clients.

---

[399] ibid., 26.
[400] ibid., 26–27.
[401] GDPR Art. 49.
[402] GDPR Art. 49(1)(a–f). See Padova, 'The Safe Harbour is Invalid', 151. Providing that based on advice from the WP29 and the French DPA CNIL, '... repeated, massive and structural data transfers...' should not rely on derogations.
[403] GDPR Art. 49.
[404] European Data Protection Board (EPDP), 'Guidelines 2/2018 on Derogations of Article 49 under Regulation 2016/679' (Adopted on 25 May 2018), 1–17 at 8, 12, 15. https://edpb.europa.eu/sites/edpb/files/files/file1/edpb_guidelines_2_2018_derogations_en.pdf.

5.6.4.1 Schrems II Conclusion

It is clear that *Schrems II* has created a difficult situation for both CSPs and cloud clients. However, given the CJEU's decisions in *Google Spain, Breyer v. Germany,* and *Schrems I* evaluated earlier, it is clear that the CJEU places little weight on commercial considerations or the more practical consequences when evaluating the right to privacy. *Schrems II* in many ways goes further than *Schrems I* in limiting transfers and requiring real systemic changes in protecting data before making transfers to the third countries.

Unlike the CJEU invalidating Safe Harbor in *Schrems I*, *Schrems II* does not leave CSPs with the opportunity to enter into SCCs on a mass scale to allow transfers to lawfully continue with minor interruption. *Schrems I* provided for a grace period. *Schrems II* did not. *Schrems I* also left the EC and the United States with a more open canvas with which to create Privacy Shield. It seems difficult to image that a third attempt (e.g. 'privacy fence') will meet the substantial legal obligations surrounding data transfers outlined by the CJEU in *Schrems II*. In my opinion, absent significant changes in US surveillance law and practices, any additional mechanism seems likely to face the same end.

5.7 US APPROACH TO DATA PRIVACY

In the United States, unless a prohibition applies, the processing of personal data are generally considered lawful. This stands in stark contrast to the EU approach where the processing of personal data is categorically unlawful, absent a legal basis.[405] At least from the European perspective, US data privacy law is often deemed inadequate or lacking.[406] Specific criticisms of the US approach include its sectoral focus and lack of a more central data privacy regulation.[407] In some cases, US privacy regulation is based on statute, while in others self-regulation is the primary means.[408] Criticisms of this approach generally revolve around the fact that it results in 'gaps' in coverage, responds poorly to technological change, and the rules are difficult to

---

[405] Schwartz, 'Information Privacy in the Cloud', 1634–35.
[406] Bamberger and Mulligan, 'Privacy on the Ground', p. 48. See Bygrave, 'Data Privacy Law: An International Perspective', p. 110. Providing that the US approach is ' ... less restrictive than the European' and '[r]eflects a piecemeal legislative strategy'.
[407] Tzanou, 'Fundamental Right to Data Protection', p. 138. Arguing that the US data privacy law is ' ... fragmented, ad hoc, narrowly targeted ... decentralized and uncoordinated'. Chris Jay Hoofnagle, 'New Challenges to Data Protection Study – Country Report: United States' (May 2010) *European Commission Directorate-General Justice, Freedom and Security Report*, 1–56 at 1. The sectoral regulatory approach is a 'hallmark' of the US approach at the federal level. See, for example, Bank Secrecy Act (BSA) of 1970, Pub. L. 91–508, 84 Stat. 1114; Fair Credit Reporting (FCR) Act of 1970, 15 USC. §§ 1681; Financial Services Modernization Gramm-Leach-Bliley Act, 15 USC. §§ 6801–09 (2000).
[408] Shawn Marie Boyne, 'Data Protection in the United States' (2018) 66 *American Journal of Comparative Law* 299–343. Providing a detailed overview of statutory regulation and major US cases.

apply when more than one regulated sector is involved.[409] The US system also allows data subjects to contract out of core data privacy rights, which is generally prohibited in the EU.[410]

Although the present means of regulation taken in the United States and the EU may have drifted apart, initially the EU and the United States took a similar approach to the legal principles underlying privacy regulation. The fair information practice (FIPs) principles adopted by the United States with the Department of Health, Education, and Welfare have clear similarities and connection to the approach taken in the EU.[411] As argued by Hartzog, '[t]he FIPs model of privacy regulation has been adopted by nearly every country in the world that has decided to take data protection seriously'.[412] Hartzog maintains that the FIPs have become so ingrained in privacy regulation that many countries '... speak substantially similar languages when it comes to data protection'.[413] While Hartzog argues that the FIPs are ill-equipped for and do not scale well when addressing new technologies, they continue to play an important role in data privacy regulation.[414]

In addition to inclusion in the early US Department of Health, Education, and Welfare, Secretary's Advisory Committee report on privacy, the FIPs have been further developed and expanded in a broader international context,[415] particularly as part of the OECD Guidelines on data protection in 1980 and later the Council of Europe's Convention on data protection in 1981.[416] The FIPs are not standardized or uniform, and the scope of adoption varies among states. For example, in the US context, the FIPs (as adopted) are often characterized as less comprehensive than the approach taken in the EU and elsewhere.[417] Nevertheless, the FIPs provide a connection or link of sorts for comparing aspects of the GDPR to US data privacy

---

[409] Hoofnagle, 'New Challenges to Data Protection Study', 21–22.
[410] Lee A. Bygrave, *Internet Governance by Contract* (Oxford: Oxford University Press 2015), pp. 118–19.
[411] US Department of Health, Education and Welfare, Secretary's Advisory Committee on Automated Personal Data Systems: *Records, Computers, and the Rights of Citizens* (US Government Printing Office 1973). See GDPR Art. 5. For application of the principles in the cloud computing context, see WP29 196, 'Opinion on Cloud Computing 05/2012', 10.
[412] Woodrow Hartzog, 'The Inadequate, Invaluable Fair Information Practices' (2017) 76 *Maryland Law Review* 952–83 at 953.
[413] ibid., 960.
[414] ibid., 954, 966–67. See also Esayas, 'The Idea of Emergent Properties', 140–42. Criticizing the 'individualistic approach' in applying data protection principles to each processing activity as unrealistic or out of touch with modern data processing.
[415] Hartzog, 'The Inadequate, Invaluable Fair Information Practices', 957. See Bygrave, 'Data Privacy Law: An International Perspective', p. 34. Arguing that although later CoE provisions were more comprehensive than the US FIPs, the FIPs provided a basis for later developments.
[416] OECD, Guidelines Governing the Protection of Privacy and Transborder Flows of Personal Data, adopted on 23 September 1980. Bamberger and Mulligan, 'Privacy on the Ground', p. 22. See also Council of Europe, Convention for the Protection of Individuals with regard to Automatic Processing of Personal Data (ETS No 108) adopted on 28 January 1981. Bygrave, 'Data Privacy Law: An International Perspective', pp. 31–41. Evaluating and comparing CoE Convention 108 with national and international data protection instruments.
[417] Bamberger and Mulligan, 'Privacy on the Ground', p. 49.

law. In particular, the FIPs form the foundation of the US Privacy Act of 1974, which is applicable to US federal agencies storing and processing personal data.[418] Federal agencies adopting cloud computing services as part of the FedRAMP program are thereby responsible for ensuring compliance with these principles.

Although US data privacy law might be chaotic and lack consistent application and coverage, there is overall no lack of regulation. In addition to focusing on the subject matter of one sector, such as banking, healthcare, or even video rentals, the United States also takes an *actor*-specific approach. In other words, the laws are administered by separate government agencies. In some cases, laws are administered by multiple agencies simultaneously. As many different regulators are responsible for diverse sectors of commerce, they often take different approaches to data privacy, thereby setting dissimilar requirements, such as data security obligations and enforcement standards. Although the legislative, judicial, and executive branches of the US government are all involved in the regulation of data privacy, much of the rule making and enforcement takes place in the executive branch.[419] Because the approach lacks one central set of rules, is enforced by different entities, and includes many different rule makers, the US system has the potential to lead to conflict. For instance, the US approach has led to different interpretations of core terms, including multiple definitions of 'personal data'.

Adding a further layer of complexity is the US federal/state relationship. Many US states regulate and enforce data privacy law at the state level.[420] That is, where the US federal government has not pre-empted the states and provided fully harmonized legislation, the US state government is free to legislate. From the perspective of harmonization, this creates the potential for significant differences to occur in data privacy requirements across US states.

The following section highlights core legal requirements within the 'patchwork' of US data privacy law at the federal level.[421] These legal requirements originate

---

[418] Hartzog, 'The Inadequate, Invaluable Fair Information Practices', 957. The Privacy Act of 1974 reflects the FIPs and regulates the collection of personal data by the US federal government. See Matthew Metheny, *Federal Cloud Computing: The Definitive Guide for Cloud Service Providers* (Burlington, MA: Syngress 2012), p. 77. See also Orla Lynskey, *The Foundations of EU Data Protection Law* (Oxford: Oxford University Press 2015), p. 17. Describing the Privacy Act of 1974 as the 'most comprehensive' attempt to regulate data processing in the US public sector.

[419] Hoofnagle, 'New Challenges to Data Protection Study', 2.

[420] ibid., 1. See also Danielle Keats Citron, 'The Privacy Policymaking of State Attorneys General' (2016) 92 *Notre Dame Law Review* 747–816 at 755–58. Maintaining that '[i]n the past fifteen years, a core group of states have taken the lead on privacy enforcement: California, Connecticut, Illinois, Indiana, Maryland, Massachusetts, New Jersey, New York, North Carolina, Ohio, Pennsylvania, Texas, Vermont, and Washington'.

[421] Samantha Diorio, 'Data Protection Laws: Quilts Versus Blankets' (2015) 42 *Syracuse Journal of International Law and Commerce* 485–513 at 491. Describing the American system of privacy law as a 'patchwork'. For instance, US privacy law includes the following: The Electronic Communications Privacy Act of 1986, Pub. L. 99–508, § 201, 100 Stat. 1848, 1860–68 (codified as amended at 18 USC. §§ 2701–11). Children's Online Privacy Protection (COPPA) 15 USC. §§ 6501–06; Pub. L. 105–277. Gramm-Leach-Bailey Act Pub. L. 106–02, 113 Stat. 1338, (codified in relevant part at 15 USC. §§ 6801–09 and §§ 6821–37. Uniting and Strengthening America by Providing Appropriate Tools Required to

from many sources. While some sectors are heavily regulated, other sectors have no individualized or mandatory requirements. This allows the parties to negotiate and determine the legal requirements largely by contract. Additional requirements, including those related to data breach notification, originate from state law as well as federal law, but vary by sector and data type (among others). For federal agencies, additional 'patches' are added to this regulatory quilt by administrative requirements, internal agency standards, and federal IT security requirements.[422] This makes US privacy law flexible but also somewhat chaotic.[423]

Given the multi-layered nature of US data privacy law, I do not attempt to provide a complete analysis of the subject. Rather, this section focuses on some of the main laws applicable to cloud computing and areas that are of particular relevance to US federal agencies' procuring services under the FedRAMP program. This section also incorporates analyses and arguments from the CLOUD Act and the ECPA that were introduced in Chapter 4.

5.7.1 Constitutional Privacy Protections

Despite references to the 'right to privacy' in political discourse, the US Constitution does not contain an enumerated right as such.[424] Nevertheless, the US Supreme Court has held that the US Constitution protects privacy in certain areas.[425] These constitutional guarantees are found primarily in the First, Third, Fourth, Fifth, and Ninth Amendments to the US Constitution.[426]

In particular, the Fourth Amendment protects citizens against state interference in the form of unreasonable searches and seizures by government actors.[427] This protection extends to areas where citizens have a 'reasonable expectation of privacy' and that expectation is of the type that society accepts as reasonable.[428] If a government search

---

Intercept and Obstruct Terrorism (USA Patriot Act) Act of 2001, Pub. L. 107–56, 115 Stat. 272 (2001). Fair Credit Reporting Act (FCRA) 15 USC § 1681b(f), among others.

[422] Kevin McGillivray, 'FedRAMP, Contracts, and the U.S. Federal Government's Move to Cloud Computing: If an 800-pound Gorilla Can't Tame the Cloud, Who Can?' (2016) 17 *Columbia Science and Technology Law Review* 336–401, 359 and fn 94. Providing an overview of computing and privacy requirements for the US federal government.

[423] Justin Brookman, 'Protecting Privacy in an Era of Weakening Regulation. The Consumer Always has Rights: Envisioning a Progressive Free Market' (2015) 9 *Harvard Law & Policy Review* 355–74 at 357–59.

[424] Samuel D. Warren and Louis D. Brandeis, 'The Right to Privacy' (1890) 4 *Harvard Law Review* 193–220 at 195. Arguing that the common law must protect the individual's right to solitude.

[425] Hoofnagle, 'New Challenges to Data Protection Study', 6–7. See *Griswold v. Connecticut*, 381 US 479, 484–86 (1965).

[426] ibid.

[427] US Constitution, Amendment 4. Tzanou, 'Fundamental Right to Data Protection', p. 139. Evaluating the main components of the Fourth Amendment as (1) Substantive – protections from state interference, and (2) Procedural – requiring a valid search warrant. *Katz v. United States* [1967] 389 US 347. In *Katz*, the US Supreme Court established the 'reasonable expectation of privacy' test.

[428] Francesca Bignami, 'The US Legal System on Data Protection in the Field of Law Enforcement. Safeguards, Rights and Remedies for EU Citizens' (2015) *Study for the LIBE Committee*, 10.

is to take place in an area where an individual has a reasonable expectation of privacy, a warrant is generally required.[429] As applied in the cloud computing scenario, cloud clients present a strong argument that they have a reasonable expectation of privacy in terms of the information they store with a CSP.[430] Unlike a public website, cloud clients do not intend the information they store with CSPs to become widely available.

However, an exception to Fourth Amendment protection significantly reduces the protection of cloud clients. Under the 'third-party doctrine', individuals do not have a reasonable expectation of privacy when they voluntarily turn information over to third parties in the general course of business.[431] The third-party doctrine was initially aimed at areas such as banking or telephone records.[432] The doctrine is also applicable to information supplied to CSPs by cloud clients.[433] Under the doctrine, when cloud clients voluntarily provide data to a third-party CSP, they lose their reasonable expectation of privacy in the storage of their data.[434] If the third-party doctrine applies widely, then the Fourth Amendment protection that might have been available to cloud clients is significantly limited.[435] As argued by Harris, under the widely sweeping doctrine, '[d]igital privacy simply disappears'.[436]

The third-party doctrine is not without limits. For example, the US Supreme Court has not held that all information turned over to a third party loses Fourth Amendment protection. For instance, an individual may have a reasonable expectation of privacy in terms of the information they place in a safety deposit box, even if they do not have such an expectation for their general bank records.[437] The distinction hinges on whether information is turned over for safekeeping rather than disclosure or normal business uses.[438] It is not a stretch to argue that data stored with a CSP is meant for safekeeping rather than disclosure.[439] Cloud computing services are generally password protected, and many services make statements that give the impression that customer data are kept safe, access is limited, and security measures such as encryption are applied to user data. Furthermore, users of many services do not anticipate that CSPs will have access to or use cloud client data.[440]

[429] ibid.
[430] E. Johnson, 'Lost in the Cloud: Cloud Storage, Privacy, and Suggestions for Protecting Users' Data' (2017) 69 *Stanford Law Review* 867–909 at 885–86. Concluding that cloud storage is subject to protection under the Fourth Amendment.
[431] Tzanou, 'Fundamental Right to Data Protection', p. 141. The seminal US Supreme Court cases establishing the doctrine are *United States* v. *Miller* [1976] 425 US 435 and *Smith* v. *Maryland*, 442 US 735 (1979).
[432] David A. Harris, '*Riley* v. *California* and the Beginning of the End for the Third-party Search Doctrine' (2016) 18 *University of Pennsylvania Journal of Constitutional Law* 895, 898.
[433] ibid., 897–98.
[434] Johnson, 'Lost in the Cloud', 882.
[435] ibid., 879.
[436] Harris, '*Riley* v. *California* and the Beginning of the End', 898.
[437] Johnson, 'Lost in the Cloud', 882–85. Citing *Couch* v. *United States*, 409 US 322, 337 (1973).
[438] ibid.
[439] ibid., 892.
[440] ibid., 892.

A US Supreme Court decision on the application of the third-party doctrine to cloud computing remains outstanding.[441] However, in the 2014 case of *Riley v. California*, the topic was raised, even if no determination was made.[442] In the case, the SCOTUS determined that law enforcement officers were required to obtain a warrant before searching a smartphone taken from a suspect placed under arrest. Although US law permits police to conduct searches under exigent circumstances, particularly when the search can be justified by a risk to the officers or the destruction of evidence, in the *Riley* case the court determined that a search of the contents of the digital devices possessed by those under arrest requires a warrant.[443] The court reasoned that smartphones have immense storage capacity and potentially contain thousands of pages of text, GPS data, and photographs, in addition to other very private information.[444] In *Riley*, the court provided:

> To further complicate the scope of the privacy interests at stake, the data a user views on many modern cell phones may not in fact be stored on the device itself. Treating a cell phone as a container whose contents may be searched incident to an arrest is a bit strained as an initial matter. But the analogy crumbles entirely when a cell phone is used to access data located elsewhere, at the tap of a screen. That is what cell phones, with increasing frequency, are designed to do by taking advantage of 'cloud computing.' Cloud computing is the capacity of Internet-connected devices to display data stored on remote servers rather than on the device itself. *Cell phone users often may not know whether particular information is stored on the device or in the cloud, and it generally makes little difference.* Moreover, the same type of data may be stored locally on the device for one user and in the cloud for another.[445]

The *Riley* decision indicates that while the court was aware of issues surrounding the privacy implications of searches conducted on cloud services, it did not overrule the third-party doctrine.[446] Given its broad application in the digital age and the role of cloud storage expressed by the court in *Riley*, the doctrine is on increasingly shaky ground.[447]

Following *Riley*, in *Carpenter* v. *US* the SCOTUS considered whether the government conducts a Fourth Amendment search.[448] In Carpenter, accesses to historical cell phone records provided a comprehensive chronicle of the subscriber's movements.[449] In the case, US law enforcement suspected Carpenter,

---

[441] ibid., 883.
[442] *Riley* v. *California*, 134 S. Ct. 2473 (2014).
[443] Harris, '*Riley* v. *California* and the Beginning of the End', 899–901. Discussing exceptions to the warrant requirement based on 'search incident to a valid arrest'.
[444] *Riley* v. *California*, 134 S. Ct. 2473, 2489 (2014).
[445] ibid., 2491–92. Emphasis added and internal citations omitted.
[446] Harris, '*Riley* v. *California* and the Beginning of the End', 898.
[447] *US* v. *Jones*, 565 US 400, 417 (2012). In her concurring opinion Justice Sotomayor provided that '[t]his approach is ill suited to the digital age'.
[448] *Carpenter* v. *United States*, 138 S. Ct. 2206 (2018).
[449] ibid., 2211.

and others, of committing a string of robberies. Law enforcement obtained cell-site location information (CSLI) from Carpenter's wireless carriers.[450] The court provided '... when the Government tracks the location of a cell phone it achieves near perfect surveillance, as if it had attached an ankle monitor to the phone's user'.[451]

The court determined that in 'mechanically applying' the third-party doctrine, law enforcement failed to account for the revealing nature of CSLI. The court found that Carpenter did not knowingly share his data with his mobile provider in the same way that an individual shares information regarding bank records. Although a person does not have a legitimate expectation of privacy in information that she voluntarily provides to third parties, the *decision to share* must be voluntary.[452] The only concrete step Carpenter took to share his location information with a third party was to turn on his cell phone and have it on his person. Following the SCOTUS opinion in *Riley*, the *Carpenter* decision continues to recognize that carrying a cell phone has become a requirement for participating in modern society.[453] Even though the court supplied that the ruling was to be narrowly construed, *Carpenter* has clear implications and limits the third-party doctrine.[454]

Carpenter's effect on cloud computing can also be debated. As described by Schwartz, 'it is, therefore, an open question whether the Fourth Amendment [post Carpenter] applies to information stored in a cloud, either extraterritorially or domestically'.[455] Assuming privacy protections will be increased as a result of the SCOTUS decision in *Carpenter*, they will be limited to government searches, as evaluated in Chapter 4. Additionally, non-US persons will continue to have more limited protection under the Fourth Amendment.[456]

In sum, the more invasive a search is, and the less voluntary the use, the more likely the data are to receive Fourth Amendment protection. It seems clear that the SCOTUS is willing to critically evaluate the impact of new technologies and consider privacy implications, at least through the lens of the Fourth Amendment.[457][458] Given the approach of the court to recent cases considering

---

[450] ibid., 2212.
[451] ibid., 2218.
[452] ibid., 2216. *Smith v. Maryland*, 442 US 735, 743–44 (1979).
[453] ibid., 2211. Noting that in a country of 326 million people there are 396 million cell phone service accounts.
[454] Susan Freiwald and Stephen Smith, 'The Carpenter Chronicle: A Near-Perfect Surveillance' (2018) 132 *Harvard Law Review* 205–35 at 230–31.
[455] Paul M. Schwartz, 'Legal Access to the Global Cloud' (2018) 118 *Columbia Law Review* 1681–762 at 1711.
[456] ibid., 1712–13. Evaluating probable cause requirements for non-US persons.
[457] *Carpenter v. United States*, 138 S. Ct. 2206, 2219 (2018). Finding that 'the Government's position [regarding application of the third-party doctrine] fails to contend with the seismic shifts in digital technology that made possible the tracking of not only Carpenter's location but also everyone else's, not for a short period but for years and years'.
[458] *Riley v. California*, 134 S. Ct. 2473, 2491–92 (2014).

technological surveillance, I think it is likely that a warrantless search of a cloud service would be difficult to justify under the third-party doctrine. Following *Carpenter*, such a search would likely be considered a Fourth Amendment violation.

5.7.2 *Federal Statutory Data Privacy Law*

The US federal government has also developed certain statutory schemes aimed at protecting citizen/consumer privacy by filling gaps that exist in the common law and constitutional privacy protections.[459] Although many of the privacy statutes look promising from a distance, like the constitutional protections evaluated earlier, they often have such wide exceptions that they provide minimal privacy protection in reality for cloud computing users. Overall the primary focus of much of US privacy law is on the principle of data security.[460]

The financial sector has been the recipient of several sector-specific regulations focusing on the disclosure and confidentiality of financial information.[461] Healthcare and medical data have also been the subject of federal regulation including the Health Insurance Portability and Accountability Act (HIPAA) of 1996.[462] In addition to information security requirements, HIPAA also provides individuals with access rights, confidentiality requirements, and the ability to limit disclosures. Amendments to HIPAA also include data breach notification requirements.[463] The HITECH Act requires data breach notification when medical information is unlawfully accessed.[464]

If a federal agency stores personal data, it is required to comply with the Privacy Act of 1974 (Privacy Act) and the E-Government Act of 2002, among others.[465] The

---

[459] Hoofnagle, 'New Challenges to Data Protection Study', 10–11.
[460] ibid., 26.
[461] Right to Financial Privacy Act of 1978 (RFPA) Pub. L. 95–630, 92 Stat. 3697 (1978) (codified as amended at 12 USC §§ 3401 to 3422). The Gramm–Leach–Bliley Financial Modernization Act (GLB) Pub. L. 106–102, 113 Stat. 1338 (codified at 15 USC §§ 6801–09 (2012)). Bank Secrecy Act, Pub. L. 91–508, Titles I, II, 84 Stat. 1114 to 1124 (1970) (as codified at 12 USCA § 1951–59. Fair Credit Reporting Act of 1970 (FCRA) Pub. L. 91–508, tit. VI, 84 Stat. 1114, 1127–36 (1970) (as codified as amended at 15 USC §§ 1681-1681x (2012)).
[462] Pub. L. 104–191, 110 Stat. 1936. See also Hoofnagle, 'New Challenges to Data Protection Study', 14.
[463] 42 USC § 17932 (2012). Genetic Information Nondiscrimination Act of 2008 (GINA) Pub. L. 110–233, 122 Stat. 881 (2008) (codified at 42 USCA §§ 2000ff et seq). Prohibiting the use of genetic information for discrimination in the areas of health insurance and employment. HITECH Act § 13402, 42 USC § 17932 (2012).
[464] HITECH Act § 13402, 42 USC § 17932 (2012). For analysis of its application in the US healthcare sector see Nicolas P. Terry, 'Regulatory Disruption and Arbitrage in Health-care Data Protection' (2017) 17 *Yale Journal of Health Policy, Law, and Ethics* 183–208.
[465] See Pub. L. 93–579, 88 Stat. 1896 (1974) (codified at 5 USC § 552a (2012)). Providing principles for data privacy focusing on factors including 'collection limitation, data quality, purpose specification, use limitation', (among others). Similarly, the E-Government Act of 2002, Pub. L. 107–347, 116 Stat. 2899, requires federal agencies to protect and ensure the security of the PII of US citizens. The E-Government Act also requires federal agencies to conduct privacy impact assessments (PIAs) in some circumstances.

objective of the Privacy Act is to safeguard the personal data of citizens and require that the federal government limit data collection.[466] On that basis, the Privacy Act protects federal records containing personal data such as Social Security numbers. Like the FOIA, the Privacy Act applies across federal agencies and sectors.[467] The Privacy Act also incorporates FIPs into the statute and requires that federal agencies provide notice of data processing in addition to applying purpose 'specification and limitation' to the data processed.[468] Citizens have the right to sue the government if it is in violation of the Privacy Act, which carries criminal penalties for the officials responsible.[469]

The Privacy Act is among the most comprehensive data privacy statutes applicable in the United States.[470] Nevertheless, it has significant limitations and provides limited protections. As a starting point, the Privacy Act is only applicable to a system of records.[471] In addition to being limited to governmental agencies and departments, the Privacy Act contains exceptions and exclusions that reduce its overall protections. For instance, if 'routine uses' and 'blanket routine uses' are disclosed to the public at the time a system is created, the agency is not prevented from sharing the records.[472] Under the routine uses exception, if the use of the records is compatible with the purpose for which they were collected, the limitation to the prohibition on sharing data outside of the agency does not apply.[473] According to Hoofnagle, the result is 'any system of records, no matter its content or context, can be disclosed to law enforcement, counterterrorism, [and] historical archives', among others.[474]

Additional sources of US privacy law primarily focus on law enforcement/wiretapping regulation and education.[475] US data privacy law also contains extremely narrow protections in some areas. For instance, in the video rental business, specific

[466] Hall, 'Restoring Dignity and Harmony', 136.
[467] Freedom of Information Act of 1966 (FOIA) 5 USC § 552 (2012).
[468] Bignami, 'The US Legal System on Data Protection', 11.
[469] ibid.
[470] ibid., 10. See also Tzanou, 'Fundamental Right to Data Protection', pp. 142–43.
[471] Bignami, 'The US Legal System on Data Protection', 11–12. Further noting that the Privacy Act only provides protection to lawful aliens and US citizens.
[472] ibid., 11. See also Hoofnagle, 'New Challenges to Data Protection Study', 12. Hoofnagle is particularly critical of the 'routine uses' exception.
[473] Privacy Act at 5 USCA § 552a(b)(3). See Bignami, 'The US Legal System on Data Protection', 11.
[474] Hoofnagle, 'New Challenges to Data Protection Study', 12. See further Christine N. Cimini, 'Hands Off Our Fingerprints: State, Local, and Individual Defiance of Federal Immigration Enforcement' (2014) 47 *Connecticut Law Review* 101–66 at 161. Finding that ' ... the DOJ has published several blanket routine uses that apply to every existing FBI Privacy Act system of records'.
[475] Electronic Communications Privacy Act of 1986, Pub. L. 99–508, 100 Stat. 1848 (codified at 18 USCA § 2510 (2012)). Computer Fraud and Abuse Act (CFAA) 18 USCA § 1030 (2012). Family Education Rights and Privacy Act of 1974 (FERPA) Pub. L. 93–380, 88 Stat. 484 (1974) (codified at amended at 20 USC § 1232g). Focusing on rights and restrictions regarding the access of educational records. Children's Online Privacy Protection Act (COPPA), Pub. L. 105–277, 112 Stat. 2681 (1998) (codified at 15 USC § 6501 (2012)). COPPA requires parental consent before obtaining personal information regarding children.

legislation under the Videotape Privacy Protection Act (VPPA) applies to the disclosure of personal data regarding video rentals.[476] Although the traditional video rental business is obviously not a major industry in 2021, the language of the VPPA is sufficiently broad to cover video streaming services such as Netflix or Hulu.[477] The VPPA also provides a broad right to bring an action by ' ... any person aggrieved by any act of a person in violation of this section'.[478]

5.7.3 The Federal Trade Commission and US Privacy Law

The US Federal Trade Commission (FTC) is a quasi-judicial federal agency with jurisdiction to regulate unfair business practices from a consumer protection and a competition/antitrust perspective. As part of its consumer protection mandate, Section 5(a) of the FTC Act gives the FTC the authority to regulate unfair or deceptive trade practices.[479] The terms 'unfairness' and 'deceptive' are broad concepts, and the FTC has been given – or has carved out – a wide scope of authority in the data privacy/data security sphere. Pushing its ability to regulate unfair or deceptive practices to what is perhaps the limit, the FTC has become the primary privacy regulatory agency in the United States, enforcing unfair practices related to consumer privacy and data security.[480]

Notably, the FTC is not a data protection authority or data protection supervisor, as seen in the EU.[481] However, as Bygrave notes, the FTC has the ability to apply penalties that 'go far beyond the sanctions that are ordinarily available to European DPAs'.[482] Hoofnagle describes the FTC's powers as 'extraordinary'.[483] The FTC has the broad authority to bring cases against private companies; it may seek monetary

---

[476] Video Privacy Protection Act ('VPPA') Pub. L. 100–618, 102 Stat. 3195 (1988) (codified at 18 USC § 2710 (2012)). See Daniel L. Macioce, Jr., 'PII in Context: Video Privacy and a Factor-Based Test for Assessing Personal Information (personally identifiable information)' (2017) 45 *Pepperdine Law Review* 331–403, paras. 351–62.

[477] The Harvard Law Review Association (HLRA), 'Developments in the Law More Data, More Problems: Chapter Three the Video Privacy Protection Act as a Model Intellectual Privacy Statute' (2018) 131 *Harvard Law Review* 20, 1770. Arguing that the statutory language ' ... or similar audio visual materials' moves application beyond videotapes.

[478] ibid., 169. Citing 18 USC § 2710(c)(1). For further analysis, see *Ellis v. Cartoon Network, Inc*, 803 F.3d 1251 (2015).

[479] Federal Trade Commission Act, 15 USCA § 45(a). See 15 USC §§ 41–58, as amended. For additional statutory authority and explanation, see FTC, 'A Brief Overview of the Federal Trade Commission's Investigative and Law Enforcement Authority' (2008), Appendix A. www.ftc.gov/about-ftc/what-we-do/enforcement-authority.

[480] Boyne, 'Data Protection in the United States', 334. See also Chris Jay Hoofnagle, *Federal Trade Commission Privacy Law and Policy* (Cambridge: Cambridge University Press 2016), pp. 75–81. Providing a history of the move the FTC into the internet and data privacy sphere. ibid., 168–69. Evaluating the limited role of the Federal Communications Commission (FCC) in regulating privacy.

[481] Bygrave, 'Data Privacy Law: An International Perspective', pp. 110–11.

[482] ibid., 111.

[483] Hoofnagle, 'Federal Trade Commission Privacy Law and Policy', p. 98.

penalties through civil suits, and it has the ability to fine companies for violations of the FTC Act.[484] Moreover, the FTC may file administrative complaints and obtain injunctions, among other remedies.[485] For companies that enter into settlement agreements with the FTC, they are not inconsequential or trivial affairs.[486] Such agreements typically last twenty years and carry with them significant fines or other penalties for violation of the orders.[487]

In practice, FTC privacy enforcement and 'privacy law' result from the complaints filed by the FTC and consent decrees entered into by the company subject to the complaint.[488] As a result, much of the FTC's regulation of privacy law comes from enforcement actions rather than rulemaking.[489] The FTC establishes acts that are unfair through litigation on a case-by-case basis.[490] Consequently, the expectations and in effect the rules governing privacy and data security are formed as a result of *ex post* enforcements rather than *ex ante* rules.

As Solove and Hartzog note, 'the FTC has been more of a standard codifier than a standard maker. Instead of blazing a trail by creating new norms and standards, the FTC has waited until norms and standards have developed and then begun enforcement'.[491] For example, requirements imposed by the FTC are often taken from industry self-regulation. Building on precedents and expertise in false advertising cases, the FTC 'regularly borrows norms developed from the self-regulatory systems of industries and incorporates standards from statutory information privacy law to set standards under the FTC Act'.[492] Once the FTC makes an enforcement based on a self-regulatory or industry standard, 'that standard achieves a new level of legitimacy and formality' and effectively becomes law.[493]

This reality is likely a result of the gaps in US privacy protections and the fact that there is no single omnibus federal law requiring data security.[494] Stegmaier and

---

[484] ibid., 113–17.
[485] ibid.
[486] Bygrave, 'Data Privacy Law: An International Perspective', p. 115. Noting that Google was fined $22.5 million for violating the terms of a settlement agreement.
[487] Hoofnagle, 'Federal Trade Commission Privacy Law and Policy', p. 167. Violation a consent decree cares a fine of $16,000 per violation, per day. Federal Trade Commission, 'LifeLock to Pay $100 Million to Consumers to Settle FTC Charges it Violated 2010 Order', *Press Release*, 17 December 2015. www.ftc.gov/news-events/press-releases/2015/12/lifelock-pay-100-million-consumers-settle-ftc-charges-it-violated.
[488] Hoofnagle, 'Federal Trade Commission Privacy Law and Policy', p. 159.
[489] Daniel J. Solove and Woodrow Hartzog, 'The FTC and the New Common Law of Privacy' (2014) 114 *Columbia Law Review* 583–676 at 583.
[490] *LabMD, Inc.*, v. *FTC*, 894 F.3d 1221, 1232 (2018).
[491] Daniel J. Solove and Woodrow Hartzog, 'The FTC and Privacy and Security Duties for the Cloud' (2014) 13 BNA *Privacy & Security Law Report* 577 1–4 at 2.
[492] Hoofnagle, 'Federal Trade Commission Privacy Law and Policy', p. 146.
[493] Solove and Hartzog, 'The FTC and Privacy and Security Duties for the Cloud', 2.
[494] Gerard M. Stegmaier and Wendell Bartnick, 'Psychics, Russian Roulette, and Data Security: The FTC's Hidden Data-security Requirements' (2013) 20 *George Mason Law Review* 673–720 at 673. Justin C. Pierce, 'Shifting Data Breach Liability: A Congressional Approach' (2016) 57 *William and Mary Law Review* 975–1017 at 984–93.

Bartnick explain that the US focus is on 'criminalizing unauthorized access'.[495] An FTC publication on the standard of data security that ought to be provided simply states:

> [t]he [data security] standard is straightforward: Companies must maintain reasonable procedures to protect sensitive information. Whether your security practices are reasonable will depend on the nature and size of your business, the types of information you have, the security tools available to you based on your resources, and the risks you are likely to face.[496]

As a concept, reasonableness is well established in US information security law.[497] However, the FTC standard as provided gives CSPs little information with which to understand the steps necessary for compliance. In the case of cloud computing, the FTC will continue to regulate CSPs that employ unfair or deceptive trade practices. Such practices may result from inadequate data security practices. Although there is little in the way of cloud-specific guidance, certain actions by CSPs, such as making data available to a wide variety of users through data leakage, ineffective password protection, and disclosure of personal data to third parties, among others, can be considered unfair practices under Section 5(a) of the FTC Act.[498]

Moreover, as Solove and Hartzog explain, CSPs may potentially face liability as third-party 'data stewards'.[499] In effect, by collecting and processing cloud clients' data, Solove and Hartzog argue that the FTC may impose a duty on CSPs to apply adequate contractual, technical, and administrative safeguards.[500] In many ways, this seems to be the next logical step. If privacy and data security requirements are to have any meaning in real-world applications, they must obligate CSPs to make certain that the third parties they choose adequately protect consumer data. If the FTC takes this route, it would also align with the data processor obligations discussed in Section 5.5.4, wherein processors are required to apply certain security and organizational measures.

5.7.4 FedRAMP and US Data Privacy Law

Although they arguably have a less demanding data privacy regulation to comply with than their European counterparts, CSPs providing services under the FedRAMP scheme must comply with myriad laws in the areas of data privacy and

---

[495] Stegmaier and Bartnick, 'Psychics, Russian Roulette, and Data Security', 673.
[496] ibid., 695.
[497] Sloan, 'The Reasonable Information Security Program', para. 131. *FTC v. Wyndham Worldwide Corp.*, 799 F.3d 236, 256 (2015). Providing substantial monetary penalties for inadequate data security practices. C.f. *LabMD, Inc., v. FTC*, 894 F.3d 1221, 1236 (2018). Finding an FTC's order unenforceable and limiting application of FTC sanctions.
[498] *FTC v. Wyndham Worldwide Corp.*, 799 F.3d 236 (2015).
[499] Solove and Hartzog, 'The FTC and Privacy and Security Duties for the Cloud', 1–4 at 4.
[500] ibid.

data security.[501] For CSPs offering services, the substantive compliance picture quickly becomes complex.[502] This section highlights additional requirements for contracting under the Federal Acquisition Regulation (Acquisition Regulation), along with other requirements prescribed for federal information systems.[503]

The Acquisition Regulation covers the uniform policies and procedures for acquiring services by contract for all executive agencies.[504] The Acquisition Regulation requires that the contracting officer ensure agency contracts safeguard the interests of the United States.[505] This obligation includes examining contracts entered into by federal agencies to make certain they meet regulatory requirements. The Acquisition Regulation is applicable to federal agencies storing information relating to citizens and other types of government data with CSPs.[506]

The point of departure in determining the applicability of data privacy regulations in the United States generally hinges on whether the data can be considered personally identifiable information (PII).[507] If PII is stored on the service, the agency must account for data privacy requirements.[508] The designation of whether a federal agency stores PII is therefore central in evaluating applicable compliance requirements.[509] In the context of federal agencies, PII has been defined as:

> Any information about an individual maintained by an agency, including (1) any information that can be used to distinguish or trace an individual's identity, such as name, social security number, date and place of birth, mother's maiden name, or biometric records; and (2) any other information that is linked or linkable to an

---

[501] Schwartz, 'Information Privacy in the Cloud', 1638. Discussing the complexity of applying privacy law to the cloud in the European Union.
[502] Jonathan J. M. Seddon and Wendy L. Currie, 'Cloud Computing and Trans-border Health Data: Unpacking US and EU Healthcare Regulation and Compliance' (2013) 2 *Health Policy and Technology* 229–41. Providing examples of this complexity, particularly when adding in both US and EU regulations as they apply to the healthcare sector. See Erika McCallister, Timothy Grance, and Karen A. Scarfone, 'Guide to Protecting the Confidentiality of Personally Identifiable Information (PII)' (2010) *Special Publication (NIST SP) 800-122*, §2.3. Providing that in addition to protection during storage, PII must also be 'collected, maintained, and disseminated in accordance with Federal law'.
[503] Wayne Jansen and Timothy Grance, 'NIST Guidelines on Security and Privacy in Public Cloud Computing' (2011) *Special Publication (NIST SP) 800-144*, 16. The main source of federal procurement rules is the Federal Acquisition Regulation (FAR), which is issued by the Secretary of Defence (for defence procurement) and the administrator of NASA (non-defence procurement). In addition, federal agencies may issue their own supplements within the scope of specific agency needs. Anne C. L. Davies, *The Public Law of Government Contracts* (Oxford: Oxford University Press 2008), p. 58.
[504] Steven Feldman, *Government Contracts in a Nutshell* (Saint Paul, MN: West Academic 2015). US federal procurement is primarily governed by two main statutes: (1) the Federal Property and Administrative Services Act of 1949 and (2) the Federal Armed Services Procurement Act of 1948.
[505] 48 CFR § 1.602-2 (2013).
[506] 48 CFR § 24.101 (2014).
[507] Schwartz, 'Information Privacy in the Cloud', 45–46. Evaluating the threshold for application of data privacy laws in the US and the EU.
[508] Privacy Act of 1974 § 552a(m)(1).
[509] Bygrave, 'Data Privacy Law: An International Perspective', p. 129.

individual, such as medical, educational, financial, and employment information.[510]

However, even the definition of what is considered PII varies depending on the regulations being applied or the industry being regulated.[511]

The Acquisition Regulation applies to a wide variety of information stored on the cloud and requires the 'protection of individual privacy' for records containing PII such as health data and financial information, among others.[512] The Acquisition Regulation takes a relatively expansive view of the kind of data considered PII. Data stored by an agency on a system of records is considered 'personal' in the context of an executive agency contracting where 'any records under the control of any agency' use 'the name of the individual' or an 'identifying number, symbol, or other identifying particular assigned to the individual'.[513] If PII will be stored in the service, the Acquisition Regulation requires that the agency's systems meet security and privacy requirements above those that are required for non-personal data.[514] For the purposes of criminal liability and penalties, agency officers and employees may also be held liable under the Acquisition Regulation.[515] Criminal liability extends beyond agency employees to contractors and their employees.[516] On this basis, CSPs providing cloud computing to federal agencies may also face liability.[517]

5.7.5 Conclusions on US Data Privacy Law

Although the baselines for privacy protection in the United States and in the EU are different, data privacy law in the United States is multifaceted and in some areas very

[510] Metheny, 'Federal Cloud Computing', pp. 181–82. Providing examples of data that likely qualify as PII in a US context. See also Bygrave, 'Data Privacy Law: An International Perspective', pp. 129–39. Examining factors in evaluating whether data is 'personal' and falls under the protection of EU data privacy law.
[511] Paul M. Schwartz and Daniel J. Solove, 'Reconciling Personal Information in the United States and European Union' (2014) 102 *California Law Review* 887–916 at 888. This determination also varies by legal system and within legal systems. Bygrave, 'Data Privacy Law: An International Perspective', p. 101. Providing that even within the EU, members have their 'own unique mix of rules'. Compared to the United States, the European approach to defining what is considered personal data is generally considered more expansive.
[512] 48 CFR § 24.101 (2014). Under the Acquisition Regulations, the term 'record' includes 'any item, collection, or grouping of information about an individual' that is maintained by an agency.
[513] ibid. § 52.224–2(c)(1)–(3) (2013). See also Privacy Act § 552 a (a)(4)–(5) (2013).
[514] 48 CFR § 24.101 (2014). Metheny, 'Federal Cloud Computing', pp. 83–84. Distinguishing 'privacy', 'security', and 'confidentiality' as interrelated but separate aspects of data management. Pursuant to the Acquisition Regulations and requirements under the Privacy Act, contractors must also ensure that notice of Privacy Act compliance requirements is included in 'every solicitation and resulting subcontract'. See 48 CFR § 52.224–2(2). In addition to general civil liability, the Acquisition Regulations provide for criminal liability for violations. 48 CFR § 24.102(b) (2014).
[515] ibid.
[516] ibid., § 24.102(b) (2014)
[517] Chief Information Officers (CIO) and others, 'Creating Effective Cloud Computing Contracts for the Federal Government Best Practices for Acquiring IT as a Service' (2012), 17.

effective. Although this changes with the GDPR, US sector-specific laws have generally allowed for sanctions that are much more punitive – monetarily and otherwise – than privacy laws in the EU.[518] Currently, a major issue is all the areas where data privacy law does not apply, namely, the consumption of data by private entities that fall outside of sector-specific regulations. Equally problematic are the areas where a sector is regulated, but broad exceptions make that regulation effectively superficial. Finally, attitudes towards data privacy in the United States are somewhat different than they are in the EU.[519] This is also reflected in the means and methods applied to regulation of privacy.

5.8 CONCLUSION

Although a flexible cloud structure may be economically efficient, allocation of responsibility and control over the various actors in the chain is less clear than in traditional outsourcing. In addition to the possibility of diluted accountability, the various providers making up this chain affect other issues, including security and compliance with data privacy laws. Even if flexibility is an important asset, in many services it has come at the expense of trust and certainty. As a result, many users, particularly those in highly regulated sectors such as governments, have been largely excluded from adopting cloud computing. This group of cloud clients offers some of the greatest untapped potential as new users both numerically and financially and may also represent some of the largest beneficiaries of the economy of scale offered by cloud computing.

Guidance from regulators for cloud adoption is increasingly available. However, it is often difficult to align with the commercial reality. As argued by the CLP at QMUL, ' ... if the recommendations contained in WP196 [Opinion on Cloud Computing] were to be followed to the letter, it would be impossible for data controllers to use public cloud computing for processing personal data'.[520] Although the design and implementation of technological mechanisms or tools for data privacy compliance are improving, they have not yet provided the level of certainty that most governments require. Even with the combination of guidance, research, and technology, using cloud computing while complying with EU data protection law is fraught with uncertainty.

Although the GDPR is not government specific, it is highly relevant for states. I am of the opinion that the GDPR is generally a step in the right direction. It provides certain default rules in areas where data subjects have traditionally had

---

[518] Bygrave, 'Data Privacy Law: An International Perspective', pp. 114–15. See further Omer Tene, 'Privacy Law's Midlife Crisis: A Critical Assessment of the Second Wave of Global Privacy Laws. The Second Wave of Global Privacy Protection' (2013) 74 *Ohio State Law Journal* 1217–62 at 1260. Arguing that in the EU, 'enforcement [of the Directive] has been fickle and sanctions weak'.
[519] Bygrave, 'Data Privacy Law: An International Perspective', pp. 112–13.
[520] Hon, Millard, and Walden, 'Who is Responsible for Personal Data in Clouds', p. 205.

weak protection and limited rights. For instance, placing statutory requirements directly on processors will likely help cloud clients minimize contractual and information asymmetry.[521] In turn, this requirement sets the stage for a clearer chain of responsibility and accountability that does not require a strong negotiation position. As provided in Section 5.5.3, the GDPR also takes other affirmative steps in protecting privacy by requiring aspects of DPbD. Whether such affirmative steps are understood to the extent that they will be applied is a more difficult question to answer.

There are many additional requirements that cloud clients as controllers must comply with that will leave cloud adoption unclear. Although this chapter developed some of those issues under the GDPR and their overall impact on cloud, how governments will evaluate them and whether they help or hinder cloud adoption remains to be seen. As data controllers, governments will likely find meeting their obligations under the GDPR even more difficult than under the Directive. Moreover, the current uncertainty regarding what GDPR compliance actually means, particularly regarding data transfers, is unlikely to help governments sort out their legal obligations and begin to adopt cloud computing on a broad basis.

As governments and other cloud clients begin to entrust CSPs with increasing amounts of personal data, the risks that cloud computing pose will only increase. Nowhere is the old adage 'you can't un-ring a bell' truer than on the Internet. Lost, repurposed, or republished data are not recoverable in the traditional sense. Information is now copied, saved, stored, and reused in ways that were simply not possible pre-Internet. Cloud computing is often compared to necessary utilities like electricity or water. In most states, governments regulate such important utilities, at least to some extent. Resources that are of high importance to the national economy, even those operated privately, require some oversight. The cloud is no different. Therefore, laws like the GDPR requiring minimum standards will not destroy cloud computing. In fact, the opposite is likely true – particularly in terms of its use by government.

[521] GDPR Art. 28.

PART III

Private Ordering and Cloud Computing Contracts

This part, containing two chapters, moves from the legal requirements and other obligations for governments adopting cloud computing services to the primary means and methods of procuring such services. The primary focus is on the contract terms that are frequently challenging for CSPs to provide and for governments to operate without. Because of the largely domestic character of contract law, to some extent, application of the law of contracts to cloud agreements varies according to jurisdiction and legal tradition. Therefore, Chapters 6 and 7 do not establish or set *the* contract law applicable to cloud computing; rather, they evaluate and apply general contract principles to cloud computing contracts.

Contract principles are selected using the following approach. First, I evaluate contract principles emanating from restatements, treatises, and pertinent contract law cases to form a general rule. Second, I evaluate research reports on cloud computing generally, focusing largely on European Commission studies and reports. Third, I also evaluate specific guidance provided by various governments on cloud computing contracts, focusing particularly on guidance from the United Kingdom, the United States, and Norway.

The contract principles are then applied to cloud computing contract terms. Much of this analysis is based on specific terms used by states identified in the FOIA research conducted as part of this book. Chapter 7 draws global conclusions on the government contract study. In addition to an analysis of what is contained in existing cloud computing contracts, I conclude by offering recommendations to governments to obtain more compliant contracts. Chapter 8 provides a final conclusion.

6

Contracts Used to Procure Cloud Services I

Study on Contract Structure and Negotiated Terms

In contrast to the standard contracts aimed at consumers and SMEs, governments have generally negotiated their cloud contracts. As a result, government contracts vary considerably in terms of format and content. In many cases, there are multiple contracts underlying the cloud services involving a range of providers. Government contracts are often for much longer terms, and their values range from tens of thousands to millions of dollars. In short, government contracts differ from the standard terms in their scope, functionality requirements, and overall value. However, at their core, the deployments for governments often use the same infrastructure and cloud providers as non-government users. In some cases, the contract terms are also similar, particularly when evaluating the boilerplate and other non-price or technical provisions offered by global providers, such as Google or AWS.

To evaluate the 'law of the parties' applicable to cloud computing services, this chapter evaluates final or operational contracts entered into between CSPs and government users. In analysing the contents of these contracts, this chapter does the following. First, it provides an overview of the contracts evaluated in this book. Second, it provides an overview of the method and contracts obtained as part of the FOIA study. Based on both the studies and secondary surveys, I have selected a subset of contract terms for analysis. Third, it applies the legal framework to those specific government contract terms. Finally, following the analysis of specific contract terms, I evaluate the effectiveness of the procurement systems or plans applied in FedRAMP and G-Cloud.

6.1 STANDARD CLOUD COMPUTING CONTRACT STUDIES

Regardless of jurisdiction, the terms of standard cloud computing contracts for services aimed at consumers and SMEs are relatively standardized among CSPs. The CLP at QMUL have demonstrated this point with an analytical evaluation of cloud computing contracts.[1] The CLP at QMUL research determined that between the 2010 and 2013 studies, the market stabilized in a sense, leading to more uniformity in cloud contracts. In 2016, the CLP at QMUL completed an additional empirical study of the privacy policies of twenty CSPs.[2] The CLP's results were consistent with those of other research projects.[3] This result is not particularly surprising. As CSPs aim at a global audience and attempt to provide a standard service to many users, they also use similar contracts globally.

Studies of contract terms by the CLP at QMUL provide a good overview of the content of contract terms in cloud computing services. This context is important to understanding the overall complexity of the agreements. However, many of the studies focus less on the substance of the terms and more on the general makeup or content of cloud computing contracts. In the following section, I focus on terms that are both *essential* for adoption by states and/or terms that have been particularly *troublesome* points for governments as cloud clients more generally.

Table 6.1 represents the contracts I have obtained from various US federal agencies by making FOIA requests. In acquiring the sample, I placed a great deal of emphasis on including a variety of agencies adopting a range of cloud services. To identify agencies with potential cloud computing contracts, I focused on US federal audits (e.g. by the Governmental Accountability Office), technical documents, and government and industry reports or plans for adopting cloud computing services.

6.2 GOVERNMENT CONTRACTS STUDY

Before progressing to an analysis of the contracts, note that the US FOIA sample is not without constraints or limitations. While access to many agreements was obtained, in some cases parties to the agreements (CSPs and/or subcontractors)

---

[1] Simon Bradshaw, Christopher Millard, and Ian Walden, 'Standard Contracts for Cloud Services' in Christopher Millard (ed.), *Cloud Computing Law* (Oxford: Oxford University Press 2013), pp. 37–71. See also W. Kuan Hon, Christopher Millard, and Ian Walden, 'Negotiated Contracts for Cloud Services' in Christopher Millard (ed.), *Cloud Computing Law* (Oxford: Oxford University Press 2013), pp. 37–104. See further W. Kuan Hon, Christopher Millard, and Ian Walden, 'Negotiating Cloud Contracts: Looking at Clouds from Both Sides Now' (2012) 16 *Stanford Technology Law Review* 79–130. Dimitra Kamarinou, Christopher Millard, and W. Kuan Hon, 'Cloud Privacy: An Empirical Study of 20 Cloud Providers' Terms and Privacy Policies – Part I' (2016) 6 *International Data Privacy Law* 79–101. See also Dimitra Kamarinou, Christopher Millard, and W. Kuan Hon, 'Cloud Privacy: An Empirical Study of 20 Cloud Providers' Terms and Privacy Policies – Part II' (2016) 6 *International Data Privacy Law* 170–94. Johan David Michels, Christopher Millard, and Felicity Turton, 'Contracts for Clouds, Revisited: An Analysis of the Standard Contracts for 40 Cloud Computing Services' (2020) *Queen Mary School of Law Legal Studies Research Paper No. 334/2020*, 1–79. SSRN: https://ssrn.com/abstract=3624712.

[2] Bradshaw, Millard, and Walden, 'Standard Contracts for Cloud Services', p. 47. Regarding contract terms for choice of law, CLP researchers found that 'by 2013 a significant evolution was seen'.

[3] Jay P. Kesan, Carol M. Hayes, and Masooda N. Bashir, 'Information Privacy and Data Control in Cloud Computing: Consumers, Privacy Preferences, and Market Efficiency' (2013) 70 *Washington and Lee Law Review* 341–472.

objected to disclosure under FOIA and the contracts were redacted. The extent of the redaction varied considerably, which may reflect different agency cultures. Additionally, it may also demonstrate that some CSPs were more effective than others in objecting to full disclosure under the US FOIA regime.

TABLE 6.1 *US government FOIA contracts*

US agency name	Number of contracts/ documents	Number of pages	Date provided	Request completed/ fulfilled
Agency for International Development (US Aid)	0	0	N/A	No
Bureau of Ocean Energy Management	1	55	10 Dec 2015	Yes
Consumer Financial Protection Bureau (CFPB)	2	109	27 May 2015	Yes
Department of Commerce (DoC)	1	184	17 July 2015	Yes
Department of Energy (DoE)	10	147	14 April 2016	Yes
Department of the Interior (DoI)	5	400	23 Oct 2015	Yes
Department of Labor (DoL) Office of Inspector General	1	72	10 Aug 2017	Partial
Department of Transportation (DoT)	8	276	21 Dec 2015	Yes
Environmental Protection Agency (EPA)	16	279	23 Aug 2017	Yes
Federal Aviation Administration (FAA)	3	139	26 Apr 2016	Yes
Federal Housing Finance Agency (HUD)	1	17	29 Oct 2015	Yes
Geological Survey Department of the Interior	2	84	1 June 2015	Partial
National Aeronautics and Space Administration (NASA)	2	50	28 May 2015	No
National Endowment for the Humanities (NEH)	2	72	8 June 2015	Yes
Office of Personnel Management (OPM)	15	554	2 May 2015	Partial
US Postal Service (USPS)	6	172	29 May 2015	Yes
Total: sixteen agencies	75	2,610		

However, in a side-by-side comparison of the documents, the contrast and level of transparency between them are stark in some cases. To illustrate this point, the document below on the left is a disclosure from the US Postal Service, which included one of the most heavily redacted disclosures provided by any of the US agencies. In its

FOIA disclosure, the US Postal Service essentially removed all price terms, names, and explanations of technology. On the right is a disclosure from the US Department of Energy (DoE), essentially providing the terms in full. The contracts are both for cloud services and were provided based on effectively the same FOIA request (Figure 6.1).

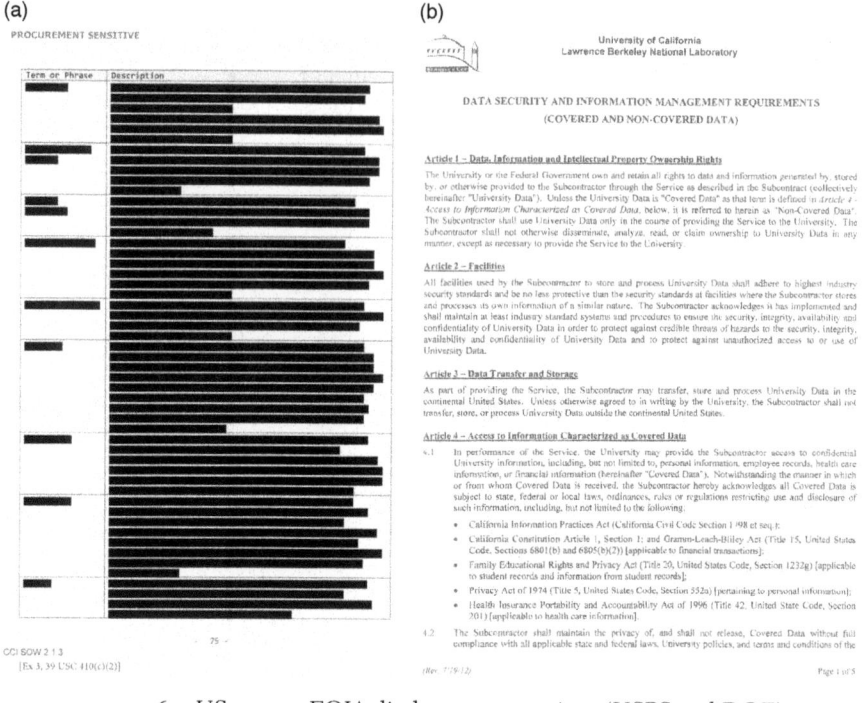

FIGURE 6.1 US agency FOIA disclosure comparison (USPS and DOE)

Although I challenged, and in some cases appealed, redactions made by agencies, significant redactions remain a reality of the contract sample. In addition to the (in)completeness of the contracts, some of the agreements were concluded in different years and the overall monetary value of the contracts also differs. Disclosure by some federal agencies was more limited or slower than others, taking from several months to over three years. In some cases, a response was never given. Therefore, some agencies are overrepresented in the sample as they provided a greater number of, more relevant, or more complete contracts.

While I have obtained numerous negotiated contracts from the US government, I obtained fewer contracts from European governments. The much larger sample of US contracts in this research is to some extent a result of the US government adopting cloud computing much earlier than European governments. Although I compare aspects of standard contracts from EU governmental actors in addition to the Norwegian Digitalisation Agency, I have primarily analysed G-Cloud contracts in the public sphere following UK FOIA requests.[4] The G-Cloud contract sample is limited primarily to contracts entered into by municipalities or smaller governmental units.[5] These final contracts are evaluated along with model or standard terms of use for procuring cloud computing services under the UK G-Cloud program, also represented in Table 6.2.

TABLE 6.2 *UK G-Cloud FOIA contracts*

G-Cloud customer/cloud adopter	Number of contracts/ documents	Number of pages	Date of contract	Contract type
British Library	1	23	20 February 2014	Call Off Contract
Police and Crime Commissioner for Avon & Somerset – and Iken Business Limited	2	74	17 March 2014	Framework Agreement and Call Off Contract
Sprint II Model Contract (Framework Agreement) Thames Valley Police Authority – and – Specialist Computing Services	2	173	21 March 2012	Framework Agreement
UK Crown Commercial Service (CCS) (Standard Contract)	1	34	8 May 2017	G-Cloud 9 Framework Agreement[6]
UK CCS (Standard Contract)	1	39	8 May 2017	G-Cloud 9 Call-Off Contract
UK CCS (Standard Contract)	1	27	23 Oct 2015	N/A
UK CCS (Standard Contract)	1	9	8 May 2017	Collaboration agreement
UK CCS (Standard Contract)	1	3	8 May 2017	Alternative clauses
UK CCS (Standard Contract)	1	6	8 May 2017	Standard Guarantee
Total: Contracts	11	388		

Because the G-Cloud system contains standardized agreements, the contracts are largely identical. Therefore, although the UK sample is much smaller than the United States, it provides good representation of the terms used in G-Cloud contracts. The impact that these limitations or constraints may have on the generalization of the research

---

[4] Norwegian Agency for Public Management and eGovernment (Difi), 'Agreement concerning Ongoing Purchase of Services via the Internet (SSA-L)'. www.anskaffelser.no/verktoy/avtale-om-lopende-tjenestekjop-ssa-l.
[5] UK Freedom of Information Act 2000. www.legislation.gov.uk/ukpga/2000/36/contents.
[6] During finalization of this Book, G-Cloud Moved to its 12th Framework. www.gov.uk/guidance/what-to-do-and-when-for-g-cloud-12.

results is further noted in the 'Lessons from the Government Contract Study' in the Chapter 7.

6.3 CONTRACTUAL AND LEGAL FRAMEWORK

Whether moving documents around the globe by ship or transferring them between global server parks, commerce depends on contracts.[7] The constructive function of contracts provides a flexible means to establish responsibilities and apportion economic risks and liabilities among parties.[8] Contracts play a number of important roles, such as signifying a commitment that a deal has been made, acting as a tool or means of containing risk, regulating behaviour and providing the parties to an agreement with a declaration that lets them 'know where they stand' in their relationship.[9] Entering into a contract also brings with it legal obligations when an agreement is formed.[10]

Fundamentally, a contract is a legally enforceable agreement based on an underlying promise between or among parties.[11] The law of contract determines the circumstances in which a promise should be binding.[12] Under the principle of the freedom of contract, parties have the right to choose to enter into a contract, select the parties they wish to contract with and have the ability to bargain for contract terms.[13] They also have the freedom not to contract. The principle of freedom of contract necessitates that individuals and business can order their own obligations and provides a means to impose sanctions for failing to meet agreed-upon contractual obligations.[14] In addition to providing the freedom to enter into an agreement, the agreements are enforceable against the parties to them. This provides the parties with a level of certainty that commitments will be met.[15] Although legislative enactments limit or override the ability of parties to enter into contracts in some areas – particularly concerning consumers – the general principle is that parties have the freedom to contract.[16]

Contracts have wide application and utility. They provide an accessible means to fill gaps in regulations using 'private legislation' agreed to by the parties to the contract. By creating 'the law' on a contractual basis, parties to contracts are able

---

[7] Jack Beatson, Andrew Burrows, and John Cartwright (eds.), *Anson's Law of Contract*, 30th ed. (Oxford: Oxford University Press 2016), p. 1.
[8] ibid., 3.
[9] Emily M. Weitzenböck, *A Legal Framework for Emerging Business Models Dynamic Networks as Collaborative Contracts* (Cheltenham and Northampton, MA: Edward Elgar 2012), p. 150.
[10] Beatson, Burrows, and Cartwright, 'Anson's Law of Contract', pp. 4–5.
[11] See, for example, Restatement (Second) of Contracts § 1 (1979).
[12] Beatson, Burrows, and Cartwright, 'Anson's Law of Contract', pp. 1–2.
[13] Carolyn Edwards, 'Freedom of Contract and Fundamental Fairness for Individual Parties: The Tug of War Continues' (2009) 77 *University of Missouri-Kansas City Law Review* 647–96 at 654.
[14] Weitzenböck, 'A Legal Framework for Emerging Business Models', pp. 151–56. Evaluating the role of sanctions.
[15] ibid. Finding that the main reasons parties enter contracts is to ' ... signify commitment, to contain risk and to provide a measure of certainty'.
[16] Beatson, Burrows, and Cartwright, 'Anson's Law of Contract', p. 4.

to map their various responsibilities, set standards, and choose where and how rules will be applied, albeit with limits. One of the most useful aspects of contract is its 'flexibility, simplicity, and predictability, not least relative to statute'.[17] On that basis, contracts have the 'binding force of law' between the parties, even if it is limited to that specific relationship.[18]

6.3.1 Contracts Applied to Cloud Computing: Function and Limits

In many ways, the role of cloud computing contracts starts down the well-worn path utilized when an emerging global technology meets existing regulations. The regulatory frameworks, including privacy regulations (as evaluated in Chapter 5), vary considerably between or among states. For the most part, these regulations are organized around national boundaries. At the same time, cloud computing technology operates largely independently of physical location. Applying all of the laws applicable to the service is not only difficult or impracticable, but also often impossible. Thus, the problem of a 'borderless world' meeting a mesh of national regulations is immediately apparent for global CSPs.[19]

If CSPs could adhere to only one law or international treaty, the situation would be much more manageable.[20] However, in many instances, a clear means of compliance does not exist. This creates the potential for conflict to occur between the laws of various jurisdictions and may lead to substantial difficulty in deploying cloud technology. As noted by Reed, '[i]f more than one state makes laws for cloud governance, it is almost certain that those laws will differ'.[21] Therefore, like other technologies delivered over the Internet, cloud computing relies heavily on the instruments of private law, with contracts playing a seminal role. In addition to the 'usual' role of contracts in cementing the rules and relationships between the parties, contracts are also used to some extent as a tool of harmonization between or among jurisdictions.

Contract law is largely domestic law and varies by jurisdiction. Although there are important differences in the application of general principles of contract law among jurisdictions, common ground can also be found.[22] The contract study in this chapter therefore focuses on contract terms frequently included in cloud computing agreements and evaluates how they might be construed in applying general contract

---

[17] Lee A. Bygrave, *Internet Governance by Contract* (Oxford: Oxford University Press 2015), p. 136.
[18] Weitzenböck, 'A Legal Framework for Emerging Business Models', p. 150.
[19] See generally Dan Jerker B. Svantesson, *Extraterritoriality in Data Privacy Law* (Copenhagen: Ex Tuto 2013), pp. 89–111.
[20] Lokke Moerel, *Binding Corporate Rules: Corporate Self-Regulation of Global Data Transfers* (Oxford: Oxford University Press 2012), pp. 63–64. Finding that there is ' ... no treaty, convention, or other instrument that is legally binding and which regulates data protection on a global basis'.
[21] Chris Reed, 'Cloud Governance: The Way Forward' in Christopher Millard (ed.), *Cloud Computing Law* (Oxford: Oxford University Press 2013), p. 363.
[22] Beatson, Burrows, and Cartwright, 'Anson's Law of Contract', p. 23.

principles. By applying general principles and a cross section of the rules in the EU and the United States, the overall framework allows for a broader means of analysis. On that basis, although the analysis in this chapter is not specific to the legal system of one country in particular, it does allow for some generalization when evaluating cloud computing contracts.

In deriving general contract principles applicable to cloud computing, the chapter takes the following approach. First, particular contract terms are selected based on their relevance for governments. Then a general definition or explanation of each contract term is applied and, where possible, form a general or 'global' rule based on authoritative sources. These sources include restatements of contract law, treatises, and cross-border studies aimed at extracting common principles of EU contract law, including the EU Draft Common Frame of Reference (DCFR),[23] the US Restatement of Contracts,[24] and law journals and other academic sources.[25] Where a judicial decision or statute on a given term is available, it is also included and analysed for its applicability to cloud computing.

Moving from the more *general* contract analysis to evaluating *specific* cloud computing terms, I also examine research on cloud computing contracts at the European level. Given the EC's emphasis on contracts used in cloud computing, a great deal of resources, including the funding of research and studies, has been allocated to better understanding cloud computing contracts. A particularly useful source in this regard is the annexes to the *Comparative Study on Cloud Computing Contracts* commissioned by the European Commission. Totalling over 1,000 pages, the annexes contain a detailed analysis of cloud contract issues in all twenty-eight EU member states and the United States.[26] Key aspects of that research, including additional EC studies and EU research project results along with audit reports, such as the Government Accountability Office (GAO) in the United States and the Information Commissioner's Office (ICO) in the United Kingdom are also analysed. Additionally, the chapter also relies on the seminal cloud contract research conducted by the CLP at QMUL.

---

[23] Christian von Bar and others, *Principles, Definitions and Model Rules of European Private Law: Draft Common Frame of Reference (DCFR): Vol. 1*, full ed. (Munich: Sellier 2009).
[24] Restatement (Second) of Contracts § 30 (1981).
[25] See generally Richard Morgan and Kit Burden, *Morgan and Burden on Computer Contracts*, 8th ed. (London: Sweet & Maxwell Thomson Reuters 2009).
[26] European Commission, 'Comparative Study on Cloud Computing Contracts' (2015), 1–60. Henceforth 'EC Contract Study (2015)'. The EC study also includes the following annexes: 'Country Report Overview Work Package 1' (2015), 1–429. Henceforth 'EC Contract Study: Annex 1'. 'Final Report – Annex 2: Methodology and Sample Country Selection Work Package 2' (2015), 1–28. Henceforth 'EC Contract Study: Annex 2'. 'Final Report – Annex 3: Template Questionnaire with Information Note Used to Gather Input for Work Package 3' (2015), 1–12. Henceforth 'EC Contract Study: Annex 3'. 'Final Report – Annex 4: Country Report Overview Work Package V' (2015), 1–120. Henceforth 'EC Contract Study: Annex 4'. EC Contract Study and Annexes are https://publications.europa.eu/en/publication-detail/-/publication/40148ba1-1784-4d1a-bb64-334ac3df22c7.

6.4 WHAT IS INCLUDED IN A CLOUD CONTRACT?

For governments, one of the first issues encountered in adopting a service is determining the scope of the terms included in the cloud computing contract. Terms that are an integral part of the agreement, such as price, are often clearly integrated into the contract. Additional 'boilerplate' terms, such as access to data, warranties and indemnification, choice of law and forum, rights and liabilities at the termination of the service, are included in almost all cloud contracts.[27]

The terms included in a cloud computing agreement are not standardized. As noted by Bygrave in reference to contracts for online services, 'the nomenclature is somewhat bewildering, especially as it is often used imprecisely and interchangeably'.[28] Contract terms with similar functions are often combined or labelled differently, depending on the provider. European academics often characterize privacy policies as part of the contract for cloud computing and other digital services.[29] In the US context, some scholars consider privacy policies separate documents.[30] Further complicating this categorization, many providers attach the same privacy policy to several services.[31] This creates the additional challenge of matching continually updated privacy policies to the services and underlying contracts.[32]

Most of the longer-term and larger-value contracts evaluated in this book are in paper format and include all terms within the four corners of the contract. However, even when provided in a paper format, finding all terms and rectifying or applying them consistently was not a straightforward process. This was particularly true in the case of US federal agencies using integrators or many layers of subcontractors. This confusion was exacerbated by heavy redaction on the part of some agencies, making connections between the various agreements difficult to establish. The complexity of these agreements creates challenges for understanding the contract and interpreting content, particularly for municipalities and smaller governmental units lacking a legal department and IT contracting expertise.

---

[27] Chief Information Officers (CIO) and others, 'Creating Effective Cloud Computing Contracts for the Federal Government Best Practices for Acquiring IT as a Service' (2012), 6–7.
[28] Bygrave, 'Internet Governance by Contract', p. 38.
[29] ibid., 37–38. Bygrave refers specifically to the use of ToS, end-user licence agreements (EULAs), terms of use (ToUs), and 'Statements of Rights and Responsibilities', in addition to privacy policies.
[30] Daniel J. Solove and Woodrow Hartzog, 'The FTC and the New Common Law of Privacy' (2014) 114 *Columbia Law Review* 583–676 at 590. For example, Solove and Hartzog provide '[t]oday, scholars and practitioners almost take for granted that a privacy policy is a separate document, not a contract or even a set of privately enforceable promises, ... '. See also Chris Jay Hoofnagle, *Federal Trade Commission Privacy Law and Policy* (Cambridge: Cambridge University Press 2016), p. 157. Noting that in the 1990s 'some lawyers recommended that sites not adopt a privacy policy to short-circuit claims that any privacy promises were made'.
[31] Kamarinou, Millard, and Hon, 'Cloud Privacy: An Empirical Study of 20 Cloud Providers' Terms and Privacy Policies – Part I', 79–101 at 80–83.
[32] Chris Jay Hoofnagle and Jan Whittington, 'Free: Accounting for the Costs of the Internet's Most Popular Price' (2014) 61 *University of California Los Angeles Law Review* 606–70 at 611.

Although there are instances in consumer contracts where contract terms are implied by courts, this is atypical in government-to-CSP agreements.[33] Therefore, it is up to governments to make certain that the contract contains terms that are adequate for their needs and cannot rely on courts to 'improve' a contract negotiated with a CSP.[34] Barring an obvious exclusion or conflicting mandatory rule (or in some cases implied terms), the individually agreed-upon terms of service (ToS) will govern the relationship between the government and the CSP.

6.4.1 Contracting Cloud and IT Outsourcing: More Alike than Different

A persistent theme in analysing cloud computing in the United States and the EU has been its relationship to IT outsourcing from both an organizational and operational perspective. In approaching that issue, I agree with the statement made by Maconick that '[w]hile there are important differences between the cloud-based service models and traditional outsourcing, they should be seen as part of the same continuum, rather than opposing ends in a binary decision tree'.[35] Specifically, cloud computing and IT outsourcing share many of the same legal and compliance issues, even if the service models and processes for procuring the services differ to some extent. Although retaining control may be more difficult in cloud, it is also a well-known problem in IT outsourcing. Therefore, the experience and compliance methods used in IT outsourcing are particularly relevant for governments adopting cloud computing. Instead of comparing cloud computing to the 'perfect' in-house solution a more realistic comparison is with existing outsourced services.

In many outsourcing models, either online or offline, one supplier may not be able to fulfil all of a customer's needs. Accordingly, various suppliers with assorted specialties are used to bridge these gaps, offering diverse attributes or unique contributions. Subcontractors fill many roles and may provide physical infrastructure including servers or other pieces of hardware, software, and even physical connections to networks. Like cloud computing, potentially many independent providers are used to deliver an IT outsourcing service to a customer, resulting in a long and complex supplier chain. In some cases, the IT outsourcing provider manages this chain. In others, the customer manages it. Two common models for IT outsourcing are the single-sourcing model and the multi-sourcing model.[36]

---

[33] Beatson, Burrows, and Cartwright, 'Anson's Law of Contract', p. 161.
[34] The Council of the Inspectors General on Integrity and Efficiency (CIGIE), 'The Council of the Inspectors General on Integrity and Efficiency's Cloud Computing Initiative' (2014), 9. In the US government cloud audit of federal agencies' use of TOCs, auditors found that 22 contracts did not contain TOS provisions adequately defining responsibilities.
[35] Emma Maconick, 'Climate Change: Cloud Sourcing as the New Normal for IT Outsourcing Transactions' (2014) WL 1600650 Aspatore, 1, 2.
[36] George S. Geis, 'Business Outsourcing and the Agency Cost Problem' (2007) 82 Notre Dame Law Review 955–1004 at 989–90. In addition to single sourcing, a similar variant termed 'co-sourcing' the outsourcing customer takes part in managing the operations and has more oversight.

In the single-sourcing IT model, the provider essentially assumes responsibility for the entire service, leaving the customer with only one provider or contractor for the entire scope of the services it outsources. On the trust side, single-sourcing providers have access to a great deal of their customers' information. For instance, in a SaaS deployment, CSPs often manage all aspects of the service. In many ways, the SaaS looks like the single-sourcing model from the customer's perspective. Although the service is essentially turnkey, from the cloud clients' perspective, knowledge between the SaaS CSP and the cloud client is much more asymmetrical. The cloud client does not have the close relationship often seen in the single-sourcing model.

Under the multi-sourcing model, the customer contracts with multiple service providers that will provide a part of the service, allowing the customer to take advantage of the strengths of different suppliers.[37] However, such flexibility comes with its own challenges forcing the customer to assume the role of project manager and integrator, with responsibility for steering several parties that may have little incentive to cooperate or work together.[38] Additional disadvantages lie in the details of a much more complex contracting structure where roles become less clear and the outsourcing client's risk and responsibility increase.[39] Unlike single-sourcing, the outsourcing client does not always have a clear path to a single liable party in the case of a problem with the system. If the failure is a result of the actions of several suppliers, apportioning liability and pursuing legal remedies will be costly and time consuming.

In both single-sourcing and multi-sourcing, the contracting time frame is often substantial.[40] In some cases, the negotiation may take place over a period of a year or more.[41] The contractual aspects managing the complex deployments are seen as being particularly important as they ' ... can attenuate the leeway for opportunism, prohibit moral hazards in a cooperative relationship, and protect each party's proprietary knowledge'.[42] Broadly stated, the primary contractual components in either model include confidentiality agreements, master service agreements (MSAs) or framework agreements, statements of work (SOWs), and SLAs.[43] These contracts, with some variations, allow the parties to work together, from engaging in less specific

---

[37] Michael J. Brito, 'Cloud Computing, Multi-Sourcing Create New Challenges in Outsourcing' (2014) West Law number 1600655 Aspatore, 2–6.
[38] Geis, 'Business Outsourcing and the Agency Cost Problem', 974.
[39] Brito, 'Cloud Computing, Multi-Sourcing', 6. These challenges are typically addressed with a governance structure to obtain cooperation and coordination between and among the various service providers.
[40] George Kimball, Outsourcing Agreements: A Practical Guide (Oxford: Oxford University Press 2010), pp. 1–527 at 11.
[41] ibid.
[42] Petter Gottschalk and Hans Solli-Sæther, 'Critical Success Factors from IT Outsourcing Theories: An Empirical Study' (2005)105 Industrial Management & Data Systems 685–702 at 687–88.
[43] Geis, 'Business Outsourcing and the Agency Cost Problem', 984. See also Ian Ferguson, 'Outsourcing Contract Structures' in Herald Jongen (ed.), International Outsourcing Law and Practice (Alphen aan den Rijn: Kluwer Law International 2008), pp. 6–8.

initial negotiations during the pre-contract stage to agreeing on specific services, methods to measure delivery, and the penalties for failing to meet those requirements.

Governments procuring cloud computing borrow a great deal from traditional IT outsourcing, including contract templates or precedents. This is clear from the US FOIA contracts obtained from the US government. For example, in an IaaS and PaaS service entered into between the US Federal Aviation Administration (FAA) and a CSP, the contract was limited to ten years, required status reports from the CSP, multiple reviews and audits, and required that the CSP coordinate the subcontractors.[44] Much like the single-sourcing model outlined earlier, the contract generally required a great deal of cooperation with the US government. In other words, the FAA cloud computing contract contained many aspects that one would expect to find in an IT outsourcing agreement, even if the parties were clearly contracting for a cloud service.[45]

Although cloud computing raises specific concerns, the content, structure, and concepts are similar in cloud contracts and IT outsourcing agreements. Additionally, in areas where updates and changes are necessary, such as developing standards and certifications, a great deal of progress has been made.[46] However, even if I argue that there are a great number of similarities, when there are differences, they are important. The following section focuses primarily on those areas.

6.5 CLOUD COMPUTING CONTRACTS: CHARACTERISTICS AND ORGANIZATION

In long-term contracting arrangements, it is reasonable to expect changes to take place over time in the technology used, applicable regulations, the parties providing the service, and even the price. Therefore, many of the contracts reviewed in this study contained the means for addressing changes while also emphasizing the core requirements. In the contracts used by US agencies, these agreements were designated MSAs. In the UK G-Cloud program, the more general or overarching terms were included in the framework agreement. Although the legal background for the designation differs, in the contracts reviewed for this study, the umbrella-type terms play a similar role.

6.5.1 *Master Service Agreement*

Generally, the MSA sets out the global or universal rules that will apply to all other contracts over the life of the service. MSAs commonly contain central or comprehensive terms that will apply to all contracts or sub-agreements made between the parties.

---

[44] FAA and Computer Sciences Corp. Contract DTFACT-15-D-0003 1–81 (26 August 2015), §§ F.3, C.4.13., C.4.23 (respectively).

[45] ibid., § C.4.1.1. Providing requirements for cooperation of the parties providing the service, much like an operating-level agreement.

[46] Trevor W. Nagel and Elizabeth M. Kelley, 'The Impact of Globalization on Structuring, Implementing, and Advising on Sourcing Arrangements' (2007) 38 *Georgetown Journal of International Law* 619–44 at 632.

The primary components include aspects relating to the work timeline, governance, change procedures, superiority of terms, and methods for resolving disputes among suppliers.[47] In some cases, MSAs are supplemented with schedules for different services or regions as a means of accommodating local compliance requirements.[48]

Consequently, MSA terms are generally framed broadly. Although MSAs do not assume a standardized form, they create a base or platform that allows details to be added or changed over time. This not only builds in flexibility but also allows for an overall plan and continuity in contract terms. In the event of a conflict with another contract or term, MSAs set out the hierarchy, thereby allowing the parties to determine which term will have precedence.[49] For example, an MSA might specifically require that data be stored in one geographic area or that all individuals working with that data are located in a specific jurisdiction. The MSA can set these requirements while omitting details like the type of server to be used, the exact location in the region, or the specific contractor to perform the task.

Although MSAs are often associated with IT outsourcing, they are also used in cloud computing services, including those negotiated by governments. In the US FOIA contracts, some had a clear MSA or master agreement, while others assumed a more hybrid model. Generally, there was an agreement that set out general terms and provided a clear process or mechanism for amending the agreements. Statements regarding the overall purpose or goal of the contract were often contained in other instruments. Therefore, although the US FOIA contracts were influenced by the MSA structure, the application was not always clear. In some cases, this made it difficult to understand how certain contracts fit together.

6.5.2 Framework Agreements and Call-off Contracts

As noted in Chapter 3, contracts between CSPs and governments are subject to a host of public procurement obligations.[50] Depending on the value of the contract,

---

[47] Geis, 'Business Outsourcing and the Agency Cost Problem', 985. See also Cloud Select Industry Group (C-SIG), 'Cloud Service Level Agreement Standardisation Guidelines' (Brussels 2014), 9. https://ec.europa.eu/digital-single-market/en/news/cloud-service-level-agreement-standardisation-guidelines. Providing that SLAs are sometimes made part of the MSA. For example, one US FOIA contract contained a specific procedure for updating systems one month before new legislation became effective. US Department of the Treasury on Behalf of the Consumer Financial Protection Bureau (CFPB) and Deloitte Consulting LLP, Contract No TDP-CFP-12-C-0008 (23 May 2012), § 28.

[48] Peter Burns and Matt Karlyn, 'What Companies Need to Know About Outsourcing Contracts' (2014) WL 1600656 *Aspatore*, 1, 5.

[49] Erin O'Hara O'Connor, Margaret M Blair, and Gregg Kirchhoefer, 'Outsourcing, Modularity, and the Theory of the Firm' (2011) 2 *Brigham Young University Law Review* 263–314 at 291. See also Ferguson, 'Outsourcing Contract Structures', p. 8. Including the statements of work (SOW), service schedules, and SLAs, among others.

[50] Gian Luigi Albano and Caroline Nicholas, 'The Design of Framework Agreements' in Caroline Nicholas and Gian Luigi Albano (eds.), *The Law and Economics of Framework Agreements: Designing Flexible Solutions for Public Procurement* (Cambridge: Cambridge

governments must comply with rigid notice and award procedures.[51] Even where public contracts fall under a set threshold, they remain subject to EU obligations of transparency and non-discrimination.[52] In other words, governments are not free to contract on the same basis as private parties.

Meeting the extensive requirements of the EU public procurement structure brings with it a set of considerations and complications that could be the subject of a book in their own right. Therefore, to provide the 'short version', public procurement has become increasingly complex, time consuming, and expensive.[53] To combat this trend and reduce transaction costs and procedural burdens, governments have introduced measures, such as framework procurements, for acquisitions of relatively standard goods and items subject to repeat purchase.[54] In 2014, the EU adopted changes to public procurement requirements through a series of directives that EU member states were required to adopt domestically by 2016.[55] The goal of these reforms is to simplify the procurement process wherever possible.[56]

A framework agreement is essentially an umbrella agreement designed to set out general terms or requirements for entering into a contract with public agencies.[57] Framework agreements outline the subject matter, time frame, and boundaries for the procurement of the goods or services without requiring the parties to come to a final agreement. Rather than get into the 'nitty-gritty' of a final contract, the government can set out its core requirements, and the contracting parties can then

---

University Press 2016), p. 311. There are many layers of obligations applicable in public procurement, from general policy statements and internal rules to primary law and statutory regulations.

[51] Niamh Gleeson and Ian Walden, '"It's a Jungle Out There"?: Cloud Computing, Standards and the Law' (2014) 5(2) *European Journal of Law and Technology* 1–12.

[52] ibid.

[53] Gian Luigi Albano and Caroline Nicholas, 'Introduction' in Caroline Nicholas and Gian Luigi Albano (eds.), *The Law and Economics of Framework Agreements: Designing Flexible Solutions for Public Procurement* (Cambridge: Cambridge University Press 2016), pp. 3–7.

[54] Albano and Nicholas, 'The Design of Framework Agreements', p. 5. Providing that ICT and technology supplies are particularly suitable for such agreements. Directive 2014/24/EU of the European Parliament and of the Council of 26 February 2014 on public procurement and repealing Directive 2004/18/EC (Text with EEA relevance) (OJ L 94, 28 March 2014) Art. 33.

[55] These include Directive 2014/24/EU on public procurement, Directive 2014/25/EU on procurement by entities operating in the water, energy, transport and postal services sector, and Directive 2014/23/EU on the award of concession contracts. http://ec.europa.eu/growth/single-market/public-procurement/rules-implementation_en.

[56] Niamh Gleeson and Ian Walden, 'Placing the State in the Cloud: Issues of Data Governance and Public Procurement' (2016) 32(5) *Computer Law & Security Review* 683–95 at 693. https://doi.org/10.1016/j.clsr.2016.07.004.

[57] Directive 2014/24/EU Art. 33. A framework agreement is defined as ' ... an agreement between one or more contracting authorities and one or more economic operators, the purpose of which is to establish the terms governing contracts to be awarded during a given period, in particular with regard to price and, where appropriate, the quantity envisaged'. W. Kuan Hon, Christopher Millard, and Ian Walden, 'Public Sector Cloud Contracts' in Christopher Millard (ed.), *Cloud Computing Law* (Oxford: Oxford University Press 2013), p. 113. Providing that '[a] framework agreement is simply an umbrella agreement, setting up the overall contractual structure, terms and producers ... '.

determine whether they meet the requirements without having to submit a complete application or contract.[58]

Frameworks have two stages. In the first, the government and supplier enter into a framework or master agreement for future supply.[59] In the second, the parties enter into a final, more specific, call-off contract within the scope of the framework agreement. The call-off contract provides specific and binding contractual terms.[60] There has been some discussion as to whether a framework agreement is a binding contract or simply ' ... an agreement to agree in the future', and thus not contractually binding.[61] The categorization of a framework agreement as an 'agreement' or a 'contract' is important because the designation of a contract or a procurement contract may influence the procedures or regulations applicable.[62]

Determining whether a framework meets the legal formalities of a contract will depend on the terms of the framework agreement in addition to domestic law.[63] However, on a general basis, I am of the view that a framework agreement does not constitute a binding contract.[64] Although framework agreements are often relatively detailed, they generally clarify that the agreement is not intended to be a binding contract between the parties. For instance, framework agreements may even provide that they are 'an invitation to tender' and do not carry with them the power of acceptance. In other words, the agreements function as a necessary 'ticket' to a marketplace, not an offer to enter into a binding contract.[65] However, even if they do not constitute a binding contract, framework agreements are binding in the sense that a CSP agreeing to the framework will be unable to introduce inconsistent terms in the call-off phase.[66] In that sense, the framework agreement 'binds' the CSP and affects any eventual contract between the parties.

When applying this process to G-Cloud procurements, the first agreement that a CSP must enter into is a framework agreement to supply services. This gives the CSP access to the cloud marketplace. Under the G-Cloud scheme, the framework agreement provides the terms that control the relationship between the CSP and the governmental authority: the Crown Commercial Service (CCS). The CSP cannot alter or negotiate framework terms. In other words, if the CSP wants access to the G-Cloud marketplace, it must accept its framework terms. Therefore, all CSPs have

---

[58] Rick Canavan, 'Public Procurement and Frameworks' in Christopher H. Bovis (ed.), *Research Handbook on EU Public Procurement Law* (Cheltenham and Northampton, MA: Edward Elgar 2016), p. 120. In essence, framework agreements create an 'approved suppliers list'.
[59] Albano and Nicholas, 'The Design of Framework Agreements', p. 5.
[60] Canavan, 'Public Procurement and Frameworks', pp. 123–25. There are variations to this structure, particularly when it needs to account for many actors.
[61] ibid., 121.
[62] Albano and Nicholas, 'The Design of Framework Agreements', pp. 90–93.
[63] ibid.
[64] Canavan, 'Public Procurement and Frameworks', p. 121.
[65] Gleeson and Walden, 'Placing the State in the Cloud', 689.
[66] ibid.

to agree to the framework terms to offer their services. However, they are not bound to provide any services at that point.

In G-Cloud, the actual contracting occurs during the second step: the call-off phase. In the call-off phase, the CSP and the government agency finalize the contract after entering into an agreement. The call-off agreement is more flexible and allows for some bargaining to take place between the government agency and the CSP.[67] For instance, in this phase, the CSP can add its own contract terms. However, the terms of the call-off contract cannot contradict or depart from the terms set out in the framework agreement. If there is a conflict, the terms in the framework agreement take precedence.[68] The combination of these agreements essentially forms the basis for offering and adopting cloud services under G-Cloud.

Although this structure shares some similarities with the MSA contracting structure traditionally used in IT outsourcing, it is in many ways more rigid. In framework agreements, statutory requirements guide the process and timelines.[69] For instance, although the framework can be open for a period of four years, there are strict requirements on the timelines for entering into the agreement and changing its terms. In an EC study on public cloud computing adoption, researchers considered the general public procurement framework to be a barrier to implementation.[70] In particular, EC researchers pointed out that once CSPs enter into a framework agreement, they cannot adjust their contract terms.[71] This restriction undermines the flexibility that is one of the benefits of cloud services.[72]

G-Cloud has attempted to address this problem by opening new frameworks every six to nine months.[73] While this means that CSPs' contracts and offerings must be 'locked' during that period, they are still provided with relatively frequent opportunities for updates. Although the framework/call-off structure has been efficient in the G-Cloud setting, it still imposes limits on cloud clients and CSPs. Even if the duration of the agreement is short, the parties lose the flexibility to change the terms and perhaps add new partners. In particular, it requires both parties to contract repeatedly. Furthermore, new CSPs are only able to join the framework at certain times.

An additional issue related to framework agreements is their need to meet policy requirements and address supply chain concerns in public contracting. In addition

---

[67] UK Government Digital Service, 'Guidance: Terms and conditions of Digital Marketplace frameworks' (18 April 2016). www.gov.uk/guidance/terms-and-conditions-of-digital-marketplace-frameworks.
[68] ibid.
[69] Canavan, 'Public Procurement and Frameworks', p. 119, fn 1.
[70] European Commission, '"Analysis of Cloud Best Practices and Pilots for the Public Sector" and "Annex to the Final Report: Country Files"' (13 November 2013) A *Study Prepared for the European Commission DG Communications Networks, Content and Technology*, 1, 22. https://ec.europa.eu/digital-single-market/en/news/analysis-cloud-best-practices-and-pilots-public-sector. Henceforth 'EC Public Sector Study (2013)'.
[71] ibid. See also Gleeson and Walden, 'Placing the State in the Cloud', 691.
[72] ibid.
[73] ibid.

to a more responsive and cost-effective procurement process, framework agreements can also be used to address sustainability, labour, and environmental concerns.[74] As noted by Andrecka, the supply chains used to deliver government services are complex and often difficult to follow.[75] Although a primary contractor might appear to adhere to the labour or environmental standards of the country procuring the services, its subcontractors may not.[76] There are practical challenges in enforcement and application, but contracting authorities under the EU framework may now require transparency in the chain of subcontracting suppliers.[77] Although these liability provisions are more generally aimed at tangible goods, they might also be used to address subcontracting concerns in cloud computing, specifically, to determine whether subcontractors are adhering to EU privacy law.

Given the increased focus on data protection compliance, this issue will likely attract attention, as governments must take into account aspects of EU data privacy law when procuring services.[78] Specifically, the GDPR provides in a recital that 'the principles of data protection by design and by default should also be taken into consideration in the context of public tenders'.[79] Furthermore, the Public Sector Directive 2014/24/EU provides the following requirement:

> When drawing up technical specifications, contracting authorities should take into account requirements ensuing from Union law in the field of data protection law, in particular in relation to the *design of the processing of personal data (data protection by design).*[80]

A comparable provision requiring incorporation of data protection by design is also included in the updated directive on procurement by entities operating in the water, energy, transport, and postal services sectors.[81] Similar guidance is also included as part of the UK Government Digital Service Technology Code of

---

[74] Marta Andrecka, 'Sustainable Public Procurement under Framework Agreements' in Beate Sjåfjell and Anja Wiesbrock (eds.), *Sustainable Public Procurement under EU Law: New Perspectives on the State as Stakeholder* (Cambridge: Cambridge University Press 2015), pp. 114–37 and 193–240. Citing specifically Recitals 2, 41, 47, 91, 93, 95, 96, 123 and Arts 2(22), 18(2), 42(3)(a), 43, 62, 68, 70 of Public Sector Directive 2004/24/EU.
[75] ibid., 148.
[76] ibid., 149.
[77] ibid. For further evaluation of 'contracting authorities', see Clarke Charles, 'Public Procurement and Contracting Authorities' in Christopher Bovis (ed.), *Research Handbook on EU Public Procurement Law* (Cheltenham and Northampton, MA: Edward Elgar 2016), pp. 60–65.
[78] GDPR Recital 78.
[79] ibid. See also EDPB, 'Guidelines 4/2019 on Article 25 Data Protection by Design and by Default', *Guidelines 4/2019*, 1–31 at 5. Providing that 'Despite all controllers having the duty to integrate DPbDD into their processing activities ... public administrations should lead by example'. Citing obligations in GDPR Recital 78.
[80] Directive 2014/25/EU of the European Parliament and of the Council of 26 February 2014 on procurement by entities operating in the water, energy, transport and postal services sectors and repealing Directive 2004/17/EC. Emphasis added.
[81] ibid., Recital 86.

Practice.[82] In other words, procuring solutions that are privacy-friendly – or as privacy friendly as possible – is an obligation that many governments now face.[83]

In order to meet data protection by design requirements, governments adopting cloud services will have to begin addressing these issues in the contracting phase. This will require that they understand how cloud technology functions, the composition of cloud computing supply chains, and, in some cases, they may need to limit the subcontracting infrastructure. Framework agreements appear to be a useful vehicle in getting data protection obligations into contracts and subsequently into cloud computing technology. For example, in the EDPS's guidelines on the use of cloud computing, it suggests using framework agreements/contracts as a means to include data protection requirements as procurement criteria.[84]

Although the use of framework agreements in G-Cloud is often seen as a model, the procurement model has been called into question following two CJEU cases.[85] In the cases of *Tirkkonen* and *Falk Pharma*,[86] the CJEU held that when framework agreements are issued on effectively an open basis – without applying sufficient selection criteria – the procurements would fall outside of the public contracting framework. In *Tirkkonen*, the CJEU found that the award criteria were based on qualifications and experience to perform the contract rather than on economically advantageous bids.[87] Furthermore, the *Tirkkonen* Court found that the framework did not meet 'public contract' requirements of the directive and therefore could not use the framework scheme.[88]

If the G-Cloud system does not meet public contracting requirements, based on insufficient framework agreements, then call-off contracts are also invalid. In other words, if entry into the G-Cloud scheme is too 'open' regarding its selection under framework agreements, the scheme will not qualify as a framework under the directive. In a report on developing a 'cloud store' for public administrations, the Norwegian Agency for Digitalization (Digdir) has advised against following the G-Cloud scheme.[89]

---

[82] UK Government Digital Service, 'Guidance: Make Privacy Integral' (6 November 2017). www.gov.uk/guidance/make-privacy-integral.

[83] Lee A. Bygrave, 'Data Protection by Design and by Default: Deciphering the EU's Legislative Requirements' (2017) 2 *Oslo Law Review* 105–20 at 111. Maintaining ' . . . data protection by design and by default is an essential part of a state's positive obligations to secure respect for the right(s) laid down in ECHR Article 8, at least in relation to safeguarding the confidentiality of health data, its precise status under EU law remains somewhat unclear'.

[84] European Data Protection Supervisor, 'Guidelines on the Use of Cloud Computing Services by the European Institutions and Bodies' (16 March 2018), 14–15. https://edps.europa.eu/data-protection/our-work/publications/guidelines/guidelines-use-cloud-computing-services-european_en.

[85] Victoria Moorcroft and Roger Bickerstaff, 'Choosing Not to Choose – the Procurement Loophole that Threatens G-Cloud?', *Blog: Law Firm of Bird&Bird*, 5 May 2018. www.twobirds.com/en/news/articles/2018/uk/choosing-not-to-choose-the-procurement-loophole-that-threatens-G-cloud.

[86] Case 410/14, *Dr. Falk Pharma GmbH v. DAK-Gesundheit* [2016] 399.

[87] Case C-9/17, *Tirkkonen v. Maaseutuvirasto* [2018] CJEU 142.

[88] ibid., 41–42.

[89] Steffen Sutorius and others, 'Innkjøpsordning/markedsplass for skytjenester Forprosjektrapport' (2018), 59–60 ISSN 1890-6583. www.difi.no/sites/difino/files/innkjopsordning-markedsplass-for-skytjenester-difi-rapport-2018-6.pdf.

Following *Tirkkonen* and *Falk Pharma*, Digdir assesses the framework agreements as inadequate to meet public contract agreements under the directive. Given the ruling in *Tirkkonen*, G-Cloud could face a real challenge on its relatively wide-open framework contract. Much of this will depend on how G-Cloud applies selection criteria. As it stands, G-Cloud criteria does not seem to be particularly selective.

EU governments creating cloud stores must require that entrance to their frameworks involve a sufficiently competitive award procedure if they intend to use the framework option and avoid applying the more burdensome public procurement requirements for each cloud contract. This can be accomplished by applying a scoring system that takes account of economic benefits, assesses applicants based on competitive criteria (rather than simply being able to complete the task), or provides competitive selection requirements for entry into the marketplace. If all who apply are entered into the marketplace without a review of tenders, the framework runs the risk of being invalided following CJEU precedent in *Tirkkonen* and *Falk Pharma*.

6.6 TERMS FOCUSED ON PERFORMANCE: METRICS AND MEASUREMENTS IN CLOUD CONTRACTS

6.6.1 *Statements of Work*

As a starting point, SOWs are terms used to describe what a service must accomplish. SOW terms can be most generally characterized as functionality requirements. For example, specifying that certain applications must be created (e.g. webmail) or that a service provider host a particular website. Essentially, the SOW contains commercial requirements necessary to complete the contract and meet the services description as defined in the contract.[90]

Although the SOW contents oblige the parties to meet certain requirements, many of the core legal terms and agreements remain in the MSA or others parts of the contract. Keeping the SOW terms separate, often as an attachment to the overall agreement, allows for changes to be made throughout the lifetime of the service. Although adaptations to the SOW will generally be required following a change, according to the procedure set out in the MSA, the parties do not have to renegotiate the entire agreement. A flexible SOW structure allows the CSP and cloud client to incorporate new technologies or functionalities without renegotiating the entire agreement. Stated differently, much of the core legal substance of the contract is set in the MSA, while the technical necessities flow down through the SOW and service schedules.

---

[90] Geis, 'Business Outsourcing and the Agency Cost Problem', 985–86. See generally David W. Tollen, *The Tech Contracts Handbook: Cloud Computing Agreements, Software Licenses, and Other IT Contracts for Lawyers and Businesspeople* (Chicago, IL: American Bar Association 2016).

For example, the US DoE adopted a SaaS deployment, 'Messaging Replacement', for sharing information among research centres.[91] The applicable SOW required very specific functional requirements for the solution, such as '... the ability to permanently delete specific messages from servers and all mailboxes within the end user accessible portion of the system ... [and] provide a means for administrators to change a user's name within the system, e.g., when a user gets married'.[92] Furthermore, the Messaging Replacement SOW also contained very specific software and hardware requirements in addition to open application programming interfaces (APIs) and encryption requirements.[93] Other SOWs in the US FOIA sample also included references to, or portions of, NIST documents and were often highly technical and subject to change with advancements in technology. While often described as having separate functions, I found a great deal of overlap between the SOWs and MSAs in the US FOIA sample. This is likely a combination of variance among the practices of government agencies as well as CSPs.

6.6.2 Service Level Agreements

SLAs are used to define, measure, and ultimately regulate the level of service provided to a cloud client. SLAs play an important role in describing the CSP's expectations and responsibilities, ranging from terms focusing on the quality of the service to privacy requirements.[94] Defined broadly, an SLA 'is a formal, [sometimes] negotiated document that defines (or attempts to define) in quantitative (and perhaps qualitative) terms the service being offered to a customer'.[95] In other words, the SLA details the obligations the CSP has to the cloud client using a specific measuring stick. This measuring stick is comprised of metrics that can be applied to the operation of the cloud service. If the SOW describes 'what' must be done, the SLA describes 'how well' it must be accomplished.[96]

SLAs generally contain three types of promises made between or among the parties to the contract. First, there are the promises the CSP makes to its cloud client. Second, there are exclusions or promises the CSP explicitly *is not* making. Third, there are the obligations the cloud client has to the CSP.[97] Although many SLAs focus on availability and promises regarding the performance of the service, others look much more like

---

[91] Idaho National Laboratory, 'Messaging Replacement Statement of Work (SOW)' (26 March 2012) Document ID: SOW-9406, 1–28, § 1.1.1.
[92] ibid., s. 3.3.1.
[93] ibid., s. 3.3.8.2. Providing specific hardware and software requirements.
[94] European Commission, 'Content and Technology Unit E2 – Software and Services, Cloud Computing Service Level Agreements: Exploitation of Research Results (2013)'. https://ec.europa.eu/digital-agenda/en/news/cloud-computing-service-level-agreements-exploitation-research-results. Henceforth EC, 'SLA (2013)'. See also EC, 'Contract Study (2015)', 22.
[95] EC, 'SLA (2013)', 1.
[96] Geis, 'Business Outsourcing and the Agency Cost Problem', 985–86.
[97] Lee Badger and others, 'Cloud Computing Synopsis and Recommendations' (2012) *National Institute of Standards and Technology (NIST)*, §§ 3.1–3.3. https://nvlpubs.nist.gov/nistpubs/Legacy/SP/nistspecialpu

typical ToS or boilerplate contracts focusing primarily on disclaimers of liability or warranties.[98] Even though certification schemes and standards are evolving, the contents of SLAs currently vary considerably.

On the side of the promises made to the cloud client, SLAs generally address four elements: availability, remedies for failure to perform, data preservation, and legal obligations regarding the cloud client's information.[99] On these points, SLAs are often relatively specific, defining roles and responsibilities ranging from delivery requirements to compliance metrics. In some cases, SLAs also provide requirements or a means to audit in order to assess the delivery of the cloud service.[100] These requirements are generally based on a formula to calculate availability and provide remedies to the cloud client, often in the form of service credits, if the CSP does not meet the SLA targets.[101]

SLA requirements generally have a different focus than boilerplate provisions of the contract, including both functional requirements (i.e. requirements related to the technical functionality of the service) and nonfunctional requirements (i.e. requirements to evaluate the service operation).[102] The primary functional requirements contained in an SLA generally include what a system is supposed to do, including availability, scalability, cost calculation, configuration of services, and security.[103] Nonfunctional requirements include privacy requirements, general customer care, service provisioning, and so forth.[104]

6.6.3 Why are SLAs so Important in Cloud Computing?

SLAs are neither unique nor specific to cloud computing and are commonly used in other technology contracts as well, including software, hosting, and traditional IT outsourcing. However, even if SLAs are not novel to cloud computing, they are integral to increasing the adoption of cloud computing services in both the public and private sectors for several reasons. First, SLAs serve multiple functions, from easing user concerns to protecting the CIA security triad. Specifically, by providing explicit promises rather than very general statements (i.e. 'best efforts') regarding the security and availability of services, cloud clients can better assess the risks related to

---

blication800-146.pdf. These terms might include uses of the service or rights regarding the CSP's intellectual property, among others.

[98] ibid., § 3.1. The exclusions CSPs generally include in their SLAs are (1) scheduled outages, (2) force majeure events, (3) contract variation, (4) security breaches, and (5) changes to programming interfaces (APIs). Nayan B. Ruparelia, *Cloud Computing* (Cambridge, MA: MIT Press 2016), pp. 1116–23.

[99] Badger and others, 'Cloud Computing Synopsis and Recommendations', § 3.1.

[100] ibid.

[101] ibid., iv.

[102] Mohammed Alhamad, Tharam Dillon, and Elizabeth Chang, 'Conceptual SLA Framework for Cloud Computing' (2010) *Digital Ecosystems and Technologies (DEST) 4th IEEE International Conference*, 606–10 at 607.

[103] ibid.

[104] ibid.

availability.[105] Particularly in regulated sectors, specific measurable promises are helpful in satisfying certification or standards auditors, internal security officers, and, perhaps most importantly, regulators. Second, they provide the potential to objectively measure whether the user is obtaining value for the services they have purchased. Additionally, they provide a remedy, or at least the possibility of a remedy, when a CSP fails to deliver a service adequately.

Compared to services offered on a wholly take-it-or-leave-it basis, negotiated SLAs provide clear promises that flow from the CSP to the cloud client. Although the level of specificity is not uniform, the cloud client has some idea of what they can expect and an objective measure to apply if they believe the service is underperforming. This approach diverges sharply when compared to many standard cloud contracts available to municipalities, SMEs, and consumers, where CSPs generally go to great lengths to avoid making any promises.

However, core aspects of the benefits described earlier often remain in the potential or aspirational category rather than the operational. There are several aspects of SLAs that have been and continue to be problematic. Principal among these is the lack of widely adopted standards and commonly understood SLA metrics.[106] SLAs vary considerably among providers, and interpretations of the terms used in contracts lack consistency.[107] For example, to define reliability, CSPs use different terms, including 'uptime, resilience, or availability', which may not be synonymous.[108] Specifically, what must be available, and the overall functionality a service must maintain to retain the designation of being 'available', varies by SLA.[109] Guaranteed access or uptime is often promised in the range of 98 per cent to 100 per cent each month.[110] Customers that require a service with few interruptions might pay a premium to achieve a level closer to, or at, 100 per cent availability.

SLAs generally contain exclusions from uptime guarantees for routine maintenance, emergency repairs or outages, and situations beyond the direct control of the CSP, including loss of network connection or force majeure situations. In addition to planned or force majeure downtime, for a service to be considered down or unavailable, it may

---

[105] Alassafi and others, 'Security in Organisations: Governance, Risks and Vulnerabilities in Moving to the Cloud' in V. Chang and others (eds.), *Enterprise Security: Second International Workshop, ES 2015, Vancouver, BC, Canada, November 30–December 3, 2015, Revised Selected Papers* (Springer International 2017), pp. 248–51. Summarizing cloud security principles as 'confidentiality, availability, and integrity (CIA)'.

[106] T. Noble Foster, 'Navigating Through the Fog of Cloud Computing Contracts' (2013) 30 *Journal of Information Technology & Privacy Law* 13–30 at 19–20. A perceived lack of standards in SLAs has created a lack of confidence among cloud adopters.

[107] Fang Liu, Michael Hogan, Annie Sokol, and Jin Tong, 'NIST Cloud Computing Standards Roadmap' (2011) *Special Publication 500–291*, 38. Finding that 'SLA ambiguities leave the customer at risk'.

[108] ibid.

[109] Kevin McGillivray, 'FedRAMP, Contracts, and the U.S. Federal Government's Move to Cloud Computing: If an 800-pound Gorilla Can't Tame the Cloud, Who Can?' (2016) 17 *Columbia Science and Technology Law Review* 336–401 at 368–70.

[110] Michels, Millard, and Turton, 'Contracts for Clouds, Revisited', 53–54.

have to be unavailable for a significant amount of time before the service disruption qualifies for a service credit. For example, if an SLA provides that downtime only begins after an interval of 20 minutes, a 19-minute service interruption is not considered 'down'. If multiple failures of less than 19 minutes occur consecutively, with only a few minutes of availably in between, the cloud client will have greatly reduced availability of access to the service.[111] However, even if the service is effectively unavailable from the cloud client's perspective, the CSP will not be in breach of the contract.

An additional issue is how much of the service must be down before the downtime calculation starts. Does the SLA provide for services that experience slowdowns that result in greatly reduced functionality? For example, if a user is able to view their inbox but unable to open or respond to emails, is the SaaS service considered unavailable? The answer is 'it depends'. What the CSP must provide and when a CSP has breached an SLA is determined by the contract. From the CSP's perspective, it is often preferable to generally define service levels and limit remedies for such breaches to service credits or a total amount of liability based on the contract price.[112] A service that performs poorly on a low-value contract may leave the cloud client with little recourse. If service levels are not met, the CSP may only provide service credits rather than a tangible monetary refund. If a cloud client is dissatisfied with the service they have been provided, receiving 'free' or discounted cloud services that continue to be inadequate is unappealing.

The potential negative impact of an inadequate SLA on a government is abundantly clear. For example, in a US federal agency audit of service levels used in SLAs, auditors found that the Environmental Protection Agency (EPA) and the DoE's cloud contracts lacked SLAs. EPA contracts did not provide specific service levels that contractors were required to uphold in providing the services.[113] Essentially, the contracts only obliged the CSPs to host the application, and did not require a specific standard of performance to be upheld.[114] Similarly, the DoE entered into a contract with a CSP that provided some service requirements but failed to specify uptime percentages, service outages, and remedies for failing to meet service requirements.[115]

This does not mean that the EPA or the DoE's CSPs were free to act in bad faith.[116] Contract law in the United States requires that each party to the agreement

[111] Roger Clarke, 'Data Risks in the Cloud' (2013) 8(3) *Journal of Theoretical and Applied Electronic Commerce Research (JTAER)* 60–74. www.rogerclarke.com/II/DRC.html. Noting that '[e]ven a 99% uptime commitment permits a 7-hour outage each month without recompense'.
[112] EU SLALOM Project, 'Final Legal Terms for Adoption D2.2' (2016) *SLALOM Legal Model Terms*, 19. http://slalom-project.eu/node/176. Henceforth 'SLALOM Terms (2016)'.
[113] US Environmental Protection Agency Office of Inspector General, 'EPA is Not Fully Aware of the Extent of Its Use of Cloud Computing Technologies' (2014) *Report No 14-P0323*, 8. www.epa.gov/office-inspector-general/report-epa-not-fully-aware-extent-its-use-cloud-computing-technologies. Henceforth EPA OIG, 'EPA Needs to Improve the Recognition and Administration of Cloud Services'.
[114] ibid.
[115] Gregory H. Friedman, 'The Department of Energy's Management of Cloud Computing Activities' (2014) *Department of Energy (DoE) Office of Inspector General, Office of Audits and Inspections*, Audit Report 2.
[116] Andrea M. Matwyshyn, 'Privacy the Hacker Way' (2013) 87 *Southern California Law Review* 1–68 at 54–56. Providing that performance may be considered 'bad faith' in a wide variety of circumstances,

perform its obligations in good faith.[117] However, it would be difficult to argue that a CSP providing 90 per cent uptime was not acting in good faith, even if the EPA was anticipating (and paying for) an uptime closer to 99 per cent. Moreover, if a CSP fails to provide a service at the level agreed upon, there is often a service credit or other discount available to the user. If the agency has no practical means with which to measure performance, knowing when the agency is eligible for service credits or discounts is very difficult.[118] In addition, without the means to measure SLA performance, proving that a CSP is in breach of the contract and terminating the agreement on that basis is also problematic.

Contracts negotiated by some agencies with CSPs contained aspects of SLAs, but lacked important parts including audits and e-discovery obligations, as required by law.[119] In other cases, SLA terms were not specific enough to protect the government investment.[120] For example, United States Department of Agriculture (USDA) contracts did not contain uptime percentages required of the CSP.[121] Other USDA contracts did not provide how uptime would be calculated, thereby making any enforcement for non-performance against the CSP difficult.[122]

In evaluating US FOIA contracts, the promises CSPs made to federal agencies, and the means in place to enforce or monitor those promises, auditors found that while the contracts may have provided an SOW, the SLA was often missing. This is a significant oversight. Without a reliable measuring stick, federal agencies are at the mercy of the CSP to determine whether a service is being performed adequately. In making this determination, CSPs are not a neutral party. Consequently, federal government auditors recommend that all agencies should have an SLA with 'clearly defined terms, definitions, and penalties for failure to meet SLA performance measures'.[123]

---

including inaction. Conduct considered to be in 'bad faith' may be that which violates the written contract directly or actions that violate the implied covenant of good faith and fair dealing more generally. ibid., 55, fn 239.

[117] Restatement Second § 205. Providing that 'every contract imposes upon each Party a duty of good faith and fair dealing in its performance and its enforcement'.

[118] EPA Office of the Inspector General, 'Cloud Oversight Resulted in Unsubstantiated and Missed Opportunities for Savings, Unused and Undelivered Services, and Incomplete Policies' (2014) *Report No 14-P-0332*, 7. www.epa.gov/sites/production/files/2015-09/documents/20140815-14-p-0332.pdf.

[119] ibid., 6–7. See 48 CFR § 52.203–13 (2010) (requiring contractors to cooperate with law enforcement investigations by disclosing certain information); 48 CFR § 52.239–1 (1997) (allowing agency access to a CSP's facilities); 48 CFR § 52–215–2 (2010) (allowing the Office of Inspector General to access the contractor's facilities and personnel, among other sources, for audit).

[120] Office of Inspector General, United States Department of Agriculture (USDA), 'USDA's Implementation of Cloud Computing Services' (2014) *Audit Report 50501–0005–12*, 7. Henceforth 'USDA (2014)'.

[121] ibid., 7.

[122] ibid. With no means to measure noncompliance, it is also difficult for the USDA to make claims for service credits.

[123] CIGIE, 'The Council of the Inspectors General on Integrity and Efficiency's Cloud Computing Initiative', 7.

6.6 Terms Focused on Performance 183

The FedRAMP issued a best practice guide for contracting onto the cloud that provides that penalties for failing to meet SLA requirements should be included in the contract with the CSP to provide 'a credible consequence' for failure to meet the agreed upon service level.[124] Without these credible consequences, CSPs risk little by offering a subpar performance.

Following an audit, the GAO established a list of ten SLA practices for federal agencies to include in their contracts with CSPs.[125] These practices focus primarily on roles and responsibilities, performance measures, security, and consequences.[126] In its report, the GAO defines the role of SLAs, providing that, in addition to ensuring value and security, they help agencies avoid conflict and resolve disputes.[127] In 2016 and 2019 audits, the GAO found that improvements had been made in federal contracts for cloud services including SLAs.[128] The key factor for the best performing agencies was the adoption of clear guidance on contracts and SLAs.

In the US FOIA sample obtained for this book, one agency had particularly detailed requirements and definitions for SLAs. The FAA provided an attachment or rider to be included in all cloud computing contracts.[129] The FAA attachment contained specific definitions of reliability which, in addition to defining uptime and downtime, also included a calculation to determine the mean time between outages (MTBO), addressing the problem of when a service is down, but not for a period of time long enough to be considered an outage (e.g. down 19 minutes when downtime starts at 20 minutes).[130] Furthermore, the FAA attachment provides that where a supplemental feature of the service does not meet performance requirements ' . . . it also constitutes an outage of the associated service'.[131] This addresses the problem of when a service is not technically down, but much of the service's functionality is unavailable.

In a SaaS and PaaS service procured by the FAA, SLA requirements (as provided in the FAA attachment) are incorporated by reference in the contract.[132] However, the heavy redaction of the negotiated SLA provided as part of the FAA FOIA request made it difficult to determine whether the parties followed the FAA schedule requirements (see

---

[124] CIO Council, 'Creating Effective Cloud Computing Contracts for the Federal Government', 8. See also ENISA, 'Survey and Analysis of Security Parameters in Cloud SLAs Across the European Public Sector' (2011) *Final Report*, 6. www.enisa.europa.eu/publications/survey-and-analysis-of-security-parameters-in-cloud-slas-across-the-european-public-sector. Henceforth 'ENISA, Cloud SLAs Across the European Public Sector'. Finding service levels linked with penalties in only 44 per cent of cases.
[125] GAO, 'Cloud Computing: Agencies Need to Incorporate Key Practices to Ensure Effective Performance' (2016) GAO-16-325, 12–13. www.gao.gov/assets/680/676395.pdf.
[126] ibid., 13–14.
[127] ibid., 9.
[128] ibid., 16. GAO, 'Cloud Computing: Agencies Have Increased Usage and Realized Benefits, but Cost and Savings Data Need to Be Better Tracked' (2019) GAO-19-58, 13–14. www.gao.gov/assets/700/698236.pdf.
[129] FAA, 'Cloud Services DTFACT-15-D-00003, Attachment J-1 Cloud Computing Services Description 1-40' (21 August 2015). The FAA attachment is required and has precedence over other terms in CSP agreements with the FAA. ibid., § 2.3.
[130] ibid., § 3.
[131] ibid., § 3.1.
[132] FAA and Computer Sciences Corp. Contract DTFACT-15-D-0003 1–81 (26 August 2015), § C.4.8.

184   Contracts Used to Procure Cloud Services I

FAA SLA in Figure 6.2).[133] Therefore, how the CSP applied the requirements and how such expansive and specific SLA requirements might have affected costs are unclear.

DTFACT-15-D-00003	Attachment J-6
August 21, 2015	Service Level Agreement

Attachment J-6 Service Level Agreement (SLA)

1.0 Introduction
This attachment defines the proposed Service Level Agreement (SLA) pertaining to the delivery and operation of Colocation Services, Cloud Computing Services, non- VM Services, and Storage Services. The SLA is consistent with FAA recommendations and offers relevant measurements to demonstrate reliability, availability, and responsiveness for services ordered. Besides identifying the metrics Team CSC will measure and report, this SLA Attachment

FIGURE 6.2 FAA SLA

[133] ibid.

Furthermore, whether the remedy for a breach of the SLA provisions included monetary penalties is also uncertain.

Moving from FedRAMP to G-Cloud, if the individual government cloud clients are not able to negotiate better terms, G-Cloud users may experience similar uncertainties. The G-Cloud standard contracts provide little in the way of SLA requirements, monitoring, or audits. Although the call-off contract agreement provides a very general definition of service level, it does not define specific terms or metrics.[134] The CSP and cloud client must essentially work these out in their negotiation and contracting process. Similarly, the framework agreement generally refers to the role of service levels in the cloud client's selection process, but provides no independent or specific guidance.[135] This is an area of potential improvement for the G-Cloud contracts. Like FedRAMP, along with implementing more specific metrics, the G-Cloud framework should also have a system that monitors and enforces SLAs in addition to making certain they are in place.

In the US context, after evaluating the contracts between federal agencies and CSPs, a very different reality than the one described in the best practice guide emerged. It was not a matter of SLAs providing vague or ambiguous terms or failing to provide adequate monitoring tools, rather, SLAs were entirely *absent* from many of the agreements. In fact, of the seventy-seven contracts evaluated in one US federal audit, valued at approximately $317 million, forty-two contracts failed to detail how the performance of CSPs would be monitored or measured.[136] If no SLA is in place, the CSP cannot be in breach for failing to provide an adequate performance absent a showing of bad faith.

6.6.4 Legislative Landscape in the EU – Regulating the SLA

In considering the current regulatory landscape, there is little, if any, EU legislation providing cloud-specific SLAs or other detailed cloud computing requirements, for that matter. However, there are rules in many EU member states that apply to the SLAs used in cloud services, even if they are not directly aimed at cloud computing regulation. In other words, the content of SLAs is limited by national mandatory rules impacting *all contracts* in areas such as unfair business practices (B2B and B2C), obligations of good faith, and other mandatory provisions of national law.

---

[134] G-Cloud Framework 12, 'Call-off Contract' (11 September 2020) RM1557.12, 6.
[135] G-Cloud Framework 12, 'Framework Agreement' (19 October 2020) RM1557.12, § 3.20.
[136] CIGIE, 'The Council of the Inspectors General on Integrity and Efficiency's Cloud Computing Initiative', 7.

For example, under English law, the Supply of Goods and Services Act (SGSA) may also be relevant in the SLA context as it imposes a general standard of care on the CSP.[137] If a cloud service is continually unavailable and the CSP possesses the ability to remedy the problem, the CSP may be in breach of this implied SGSA warranty.[138] Furthermore, the SGSA warranty provision might also be applied to a CSP that does not put adequate security in place or create reasonable backups of data.[139]

Acknowledging the difficulty users have in decoding SLAs and the limits this has placed on cloud adoption on an EU-wide basis, the EC has dedicated substantial efforts to mapping the legal requirements affecting SLAs, the possible standardization of SLAs, and the technical means of implementing cross-border SLAs.[140] An array of initiatives and research projects have emerged and created multiple model or standard SLAs that might be adopted by users. Specifically, ENISA,[141] the Cloud Select Industry Group on SLAs,[142] SLA-Ready,[143] and SLALOM[144] have created standards, model contracts, and certifications.[145] Although the level of guidance has increased substantially in the EU, it is often difficult to tell how the projects differ in substance and untangle the results of the various EU projects.

6.7 PARTNERS AND SUBCONTRACTORS – CONTRACTUAL ROLES AND LIMITS

As introduced in Chapter 2, cloud computing services are dynamic and often outsource critical parts of the service infrastructure, resulting in multi-layered service offerings.[146] Wide-ranging contractual networks in cloud computing services raise issues regarding the responsibility and liability of third-party providers/partners and the rights or claims that governments may have against such third-party subcontractors. Although standards

---

[137] EC Annex 4, 'Comparative Study on Cloud Computing Contracts: Final Report – Annex 4: Country Report Overview Work Package 3' (2015), 2. https://publications.europa.eu/en/publication-detail/-/publication/13f8fb54-f159-4ff1-ba72-a8478a33a072/language-en. Henceforth ('EC Annex 4 (2015)'). Citing Supply of Goods and Services Act 1982 § 13 providing that '... where the supplier is acting in the course of a business, there is an implied term that the supplier will carry out the service with reasonable care and skill'.
[138] ibid.
[139] ibid.
[140] See generally EU Project 'SLA Ready' <www.sla-ready.eu/about-sla-ready>.
[141] ENISA, 'Procure Secure: A Guide to Monitoring of Security Service Levels in Cloud Contracts' (2012). www.enisa.europa.eu/publications/procure-secure-a-guide-to-monitoring-of-security-service-levels-in-cloud-contracts.
[142] https://ec.europa.eu/digital-single-market/en/cloud-select-industry-group-service-level-agreements.
[143] www.sla-ready.eu/.
[144] http://slalom-project.eu/.
[145] See also European Commission, 'Measuring the Economic Impact of Cloud Computing in Europe' (Final Report 2016), 12–13. https://ec.europa.eu/digital-single-market/en/news/measuring-economic-impact-cloud-computing-europe.
[146] Hon, Millard, and Walden, 'Public Sector Cloud Contracts', pp. 123–24.

6.7 Partners and Subcontractors – Contractual Roles and Limits

and certification mechanisms have the potential to play an important role in modelling behaviour and building trust in cloud computing services, contracts remain the primary means for organizing and managing subcontracting risks.

In cloud computing agreements, the primary contract generally sets the requirements, obligations, and rights for use of the service. However, layering a service by using third-party providers is a widespread practice. Although this is not uncommon in IT outsourcing, the scope of subcontracting in cloud computing contributes to potentially more tenuous connections between primary contractors and subcontractors than in other types of IT outsourcing agreements used by government agencies.[147] The result is often that major aspects of the cloud service are not visible to end users and are performed by third-party subcontractors.[148] Consequently, the primary contractor may have a reduced level of technical control over its subcontractors.

Although contractual obligations must generally be completed as required in the contract, this does not mean that the contracting party must be the one to discharge them.[149] The party completing the contract often has the ability to use third parties, unless the contract requires that a specific party perform the agreement or the contract requires consent for substitution.[150] In short, vicarious performance or subcontracting is generally permissible. Nevertheless, the primary contractor will remain liable for performance of the contract and will be liable for the performance of its subcontractors.[151]

Ideally, the government user flows down their terms to all subcontractors and partners, ensuring a clear chain of control and liability throughout the services, such as by using 'back-to-back' contracts. However, given the relationships between primary contractors and subcontractors in cloud computing arrangements, this is often a difficult proposition. For example, if an integrator uses AWS or Google on an IaaS basis, it shares that infrastructure with millions of other users. It would be extremely difficult for AWS or Google to apply different contract terms for all of their users (integrators and others) and still provide a standard offering. Additionally, negotiating terms with AWS or Google is difficult given their market dominance and strong bargaining position. After all, cloud computing is about standardization and

---

[147] European Parliament, 'Fighting Cyber Crime and Protecting Privacy in the Cloud' (2012) *Committee on Civil Liberties, Justice, and Home Affairs*, 1, 31. www.europarl.europa.eu/RegData/etudes/etudes/join/2012/462509/IPOL-LIBE_ET(2012)462509_EN.pdf. Describing cloud computing arrangements as a 'complex mesh of contracts that are primarily concerned with abstracting the details of where and how processing actually takes place, in the interest of economic efficiency'.

[148] Primavera De Filippi and Smari McCarthy, 'Cloud Computing: Centralization and Data Sovereignty' (2012) 3(2) *European Journal of Law and Technology* 1–18 at 11.

[149] Beatson, Burrows, and Cartwright, 'Anson's Law of Contract', p. 465.

[150] ibid. FAA and Computer Sciences Corp. Contract DTFACT-15-D-0003 1–81 (26 August 2015), § 3.12–14(e). Providing that ' ... the Contracting Officer will consider case-by-case exceptions to this [Subcontracting] requirement for individual subcontracts'.

[151] Beatson, Burrows, and Cartwright, 'Anson's Law of Contract', p. 712.

economies of scale. Negotiating and applying millions of separate contract terms is in direct conflict with that goal.

In addition to scale, the timing of the contracting might also prohibit 'flowing-down' primary contract terms to all subcontractors. This is particularly true in cases where subcontractors are working on a contract that is separate from or predates the contract between the government user and the CSP providing the cloud service. For example, if a SaaS provider has a long-standing or pre-existing contract with an infrastructure provider, such as AWS or Google, the SaaS CSP must make adjustments in that contract to ensure the terms governing the infrastructure match the contract between the SaaS provider (or integrator) and the government client.[152] Although infrastructure providers, such as AWS or Google, are increasingly providing additional options for government clients, it is still a challenge to account for very specific or special arrangements and maintain the needed scale.[153]

However, this difficulty does not affect the concerns governments have when it comes to subcontracting – that is, maintaining accountability, and to some extent transparency, throughout the 'layers' of the supply chain. For governments, such a wide network of subcontractors may also be unsuitable given the security requirements and other rules applicable to government data.[154] If a government user does not have a contractual relationship with all suppliers of the service and is unable to obtain contractual assurances such as infrastructure location, audit requirements, or confidentiality guarantees it may be difficult, if not impossible, to meet regulatory requirements. This is particularly true where the nature of the data on the service requires a certain level of control (e.g. health or financial data).[155] Many contract terms used by CSPs make scant reference to the role, authorization, or limits of the subcontractors they employ.[156]

In the EU, subcontracting in cloud services is also a common practice. In the EC's comparative cloud computing contract study, subcontracting is primarily considered a problem in the context of data protection.[157] Various EC legal experts found that the subcontracting common in cloud services would not conflict with the

---

[152] Defense Information Systems Agency (DISA), 'Department of Defense (DoD) Cloud Computing Security Requirements Guide' (2015), 7. Henceforth 'DISA (2015)'. See Weitzenböck, 'A Legal Framework for Emerging Business Models', p. 290.
[153] See generally Amazon Web Services, 'Compliance Programs'. https://aws.amazon.com/compliance/programs/.
[154] ibid.
[155] CIO Council, 'Creating Effective Cloud Computing Contracts for the Federal Government', 9, 35, 38. Providing that 'roles and responsibilities for all parties need to be clearly defined' when adding subcontractors or integrators. See also Financial Conduct Authority (FCA), 'FG16/5: Guidance for Firms Outsourcing to the "Cloud" and Other Third-Party IT Services' (2016) *Finalized Guidance*, 10. www.fca.org.uk/publication/finalised-guidance/fg16-5.pdf.
[156] Jan Tore Sanner, 'Cloud Computing Strategy for Norway' (2016) *Norwegian Ministry of Local Government and Modernisation, Publication Number: H-2365 E*, 10. Noting that CSPs use ' ... multiple subcontractors without this being clearly stated in the service specification'.
[157] EC, 'Contract Study: Annex 1', 76. See also EC, 'Contract Study: Annex 2', 9.

6.7 Partners and Subcontractors – Contractual Roles and Limits

principles of general contract law. To take one example, in Denmark, the EC legal expert responded that '[g]enerally, a party can use subcontractors without consent unless it can be deduced from the contract that the obligation must be performed by the party himself'.[158] Similarly, English law allows subcontracting unless 'the proper inference to be drawn from the contract itself, the subject matter of it and other material surrounding circumstances suggests otherwise'.[159] Based on the EC comparative cloud contract report, subcontracting is permitted in most EU member states.[160]

Although subcontracting was determined to be widely permissible in most EU jurisdictions, EC research showed that not all EU member states take such an open approach. In some jurisdictions, adding or changing subcontractors to a service requires additional steps. For instance, in France, researchers submitted that subcontracting is heavily regulated and ' ... subcontractors and the method of their payment must be approved individually by the client before the conclusion of any agreement with the contractor'.[161] Researchers in Lithuania came to a similar conclusion, providing that ' ... a contract as a whole (entailing both obligations and claims) cannot be transferred without the consent of all parties involved'.[162]

Moving from national EU requirements to the impact on governments, in the G-Cloud scenario the issue of subcontracting is confronted directly by placing strict limits on its use. In the G-Cloud call-off contract, very specific information is required regarding the names of subcontractors, including a list of all of the CSP's subcontractors and partners, together with details regarding the subcontractors that will be delivering the cloud service.[163] The call-off contract further requires that the CSP obtain ' ... *prior written consent* from the Buyer to transfer Buyer Personal Data to any other person (including any Subcontractors) for the provision of the G-Cloud Services'.[164]

The G-Cloud framework agreement is also very clear on subcontracting, requiring that the CSP must have the cloud client's approval for any subcontracting to take place. Furthermore, the framework agreement states that subcontracting will not ' ... relieve the Supplier of its duties under this Framework Agreement'.[165] The framework agreement further provides that subcontracting without consent is considered a material breach under the contract.[166] This default or standard position in

---

[158] ibid., 76. This response was relatively typical in the Commission study. However, in some countries, such as Estonia, there were additional caveats and limitations. See ibid., 103.
[159] ibid., 88. Citing the case of *Davies* v. *Collins* [1945] 1 All ER 247. A similar position was taken by the European Commission's expert in Irish law. ibid., 201.
[160] ibid., 88.
[161] ibid., 138.
[162] ibid., 243.
[163] G-Cloud Framework 12, 'Call-off Contract', 8, 39.
[164] ibid., 39. Emphasis added.
[165] G-Cloud Framework 12, 'Framework Agreement', § 8.34–8.37. Further that '[t]he Supplier is responsible for the acts and omissions of its Subcontractors and Supplier Staff as though they are its own'.
[166] ibid., 44.

G-Cloud contracts is consistent with the contracts I have examined from G-Cloud FOIA disclosures. Additionally, when subcontracting does take place, the government user retains authority to access its assets and to inspect subcontractor premises.[167] Even in earlier versions of the G-Cloud standard agreements, where the G-Cloud call-off terms were adopted with little change, strict requirements on subcontracting were also in place.[168]

In the United States, the contractual approach to subcontracting for US agencies was less uniform. Following US audits of the FedRAMP program, several agencies failed to meet established best practices in their contracts regarding the use of subcontractors. In particular, the EPA failed to require contract terms allowing the agency to audit – or seek damages from – subcontractors used to provide the service.

In moving its permit management oversight system ('permit system') to the cloud, the EPA entered into a contract with a CSP (primary contractor) that met many of the requirements of FedRAMP.[169] However, the agreement did not appropriately restrain or place limits on the use of subcontractors through 'back-to-back' or 'flow-down' clauses.[170] In the EPA contracting scenario, the primary contractor is using a subcontracted CSP to host the permit system cloud application. In the EPA's contract, it has accepted a term wherein the subcontracted CSP, the party actually hosting the EPA's permit system, includes a disclaimer that could limit or block any agency recourse in the event of a malfunction, loss of data, or even for failing to provide basic functionality.[171] Specifically, the contract term provides:

> You acknowledge and agree that your use of the services is solely at your own risk, and that except as expressly provided herein the services are provided on an 'as is' and 'as available' basis. [The subcontractor hosting the permit system application] *expressly disclaims any and all warranties and conditions of any kind*, express, implied, or statutory, including, without limitation, the implied warranties of title, non-infringement, merchantability, and fitness for a particular purpose and any warranties arising from a course of dealing, usage or trade practice.[172]

Given the contract term, it would potentially be difficult for the EPA to recover losses from the subcontractor for its misuse of agency data. Although the EPA would

---

[167] Sprint II Model Contract (Framework Agreement) Thames Valley Police Authority and Specialist Computing Services, 'Contract Relating to the Provision of IT Products and Services VISAV Ltd (Model Contract v 1.00)' (2012), §§ 2.1, 2.8.
[168] British Library and Bravo Solutions UK Ltd (10 February 2014) Ref # FIN 8895, 1–23, § CO-16.1, requiring written approval before assignment or subcontracting. Similar terms contained in a contract between the Police and Crime Commissioner for Avon & Somerset and Iken Business Limited, 'Relating to the Provision of G-Cloud Services' (Call-off terms, 17 March 2014), § CO-16. Henceforth 'Somerset and Iken Contract (2014)'.
[169] EPA OIG, 'EPA Needs to Improve the Recognition and Administration of Cloud Services'.
[170] Jörn Zons, 'The Minefield of Back-to-Back Subcontracts' (2010) 5 *Construction Law International* 11–17 at 11.
[171] EPA OIG, 'EPA Needs to Improve the Recognition and Administration of Cloud Services', 5.
[172] ibid. Emphasis added.

likely have a cause of action against the primary contractor, it is not uncommon in the cloud scenario that the party with the 'deep pockets' is the subcontractor (e.g. AWS, Google, etc.).

The lack of certainty that a term like the EPA contract creates is problematic for federal agencies because they need to have accountability throughout the entire structure. As noted in the FedRAMP best practice guide on contracting:

> As a best practice, cloud contracts should not *permit a CSP to deny responsibility* if there is a data breach within its environment. Federal agencies should make explicit in cloud computing contracts that CSPs indemnify Federal agencies if a breach should occur and the CSP should be required to provide adequate capital and/or insurance to support their indemnity.[173]

In the case of the permit system application, the contract terms specifically limit the liability of the subcontractor hosting the application. If the CSP has also included a similar clause limiting their liability for the acts of their subcontractors, then the EPA will have very little recourse in the event of a malfunction or even a service that does not perform or meet the needs of the agency.[174] Given this contract term, the EPA has done little to impose 'credible consequences' for subcontractors mishandling or misusing important agency data.[175] If the permit system application malfunctions or a data breach occurs, the EPA will be in a difficult position to claim any damages from a service provided on an 'as-is' and 'as-available' basis.

Although such disclaimers might be expected and even appropriate with free services, for the EPA, the service was not without cost. In fact, the audit found that the EPA paid $2.3 million for services that were not fully delivered or did not comply with federal requirements.[176] Given the EPA's purchasing power and mandate, the primary contractor should have had guidance limiting its ability to enter into such a contract term. Under this agreement, the EPA has contracted for a service that has no guarantee of being fit for the purposes stated and will be used on an 'as-is' basis.

6.7.1 *Privity of Contract*

Outside of clear contract terms, there are still questions regarding the remedies available for a government user or its citizens when they are not directly named or in privity of contract with the provider.[177] Under the traditional doctrine of privity, 'a person cannot acquire rights or be subject to liabilities arising under a contract to

---

[173] CIO Council, 'Creating Effective Cloud Computing Contracts for the Federal Government', 14. Emphasis added.
[174] ibid.
[175] ibid., 8. See also ENISA, Cloud SLAs Across the European Public Sector', 6.
[176] EPA OIG, 'EPA Needs to Improve the Recognition and Administration of Cloud Services', 7.
[177] Beatson, Burrows, and Cartwright, 'Anson's Law of Contract', p. 647. See De Filippi and McCarthy, 'Cloud Computing', 11.

which he is not a party'.[178] Under the traditional common law approach, courts were unwilling to allow parties that had not contracted directly to enforce aspects of the contract. The reasoning or justification for the rule was based on lack of consideration paid by the third party, that the third party could sue but not to be sued to enforce contractual obligations, and the impact or interference with the rights of the contracting parties, such as limiting liability.[179]

Although the common law provided a bright-line rule initially, there has been significant reform of the common law doctrine of privity in both the United States and the United Kingdom.[180] As noted by Beatson, Burrows, and Cartwright, the traditional common law doctrine disallowing a third party to acquire rights under a contract was subject to significant criticism by judges, law reform bodies, among others.[181] Even where the doctrine had exceptions, their applicability was complex and technical, leading to 'artificiality and uncertainty'.[182] Reform has taken place with expanded common law exceptions and statutory intervention aimed at providing clearer applications of the rule.[183] In the United States and the United Kingdom, intended third-party beneficiaries have contractual recourse, even if they are not part of or named in the contract.[184]

Even with reforms, applying the third-party beneficiary doctrine is not straightforward.[185] The general rule is that 'intended' third-party beneficiaries to a contract can recover losses while 'incidental' beneficiaries cannot.[186] The requirement that a third-party beneficiary must be an intended beneficiary makes application of the doctrine difficult and creates uncertainty. That is, courts will consider whether the parties to a contract intended to create legally enforceable rights for a third party. If a third party is substantially removed from the contemplation of the parties or 'incidental' to the benefits of the contract, owing liability to that party becomes less likely. Making that determination is based on whether the party was intended to have any rights under the contract.

---

[178] G. H. Treitel, *The Law of Contract*, 8th ed. (London: Sweet & Maxwell 1991), p. 538.
[179] Beatson, Burrows, and Cartwright, 'Anson's Law of Contract', pp. 656–58.
[180] See generally Contracts (Rights of Third Parties) Act 1999 in the United Kingdom.
[181] Beatson, Burrows, and Cartwright, 'Anson's Law of Contract', p. 657.
[182] ibid.
[183] ibid., 647. For analysis of the statutory intervention in the UK Contracts (Rights of Third Parties) Act 1999, see ibid., 659–70.
[184] Restatement (Second) of Contracts, 'Intended and Incidental Beneficiaries' (1981), § 302. See also David Epstein and others, 'An "App" for Third Party Beneficiaries' (2016) 91 *Washington Law Review* 1663–703 at 1672–82.
[185] Weitzenböck, 'A Legal Framework for Emerging Business Models', p. 310. In evaluating the application of the doctrine of privity of contract in an empirical study of dynamic and primarily inter-firm networks, the author found that the contracts are a 'major stumbling block' in allowing members of virtual networks to hold other members (suppliers etc.) accountable.
[186] Restatement Second Contracts (1979), § 302. For further analysis of the 'intent to benefit' approach, see David Summers, 'Third Party Beneficiaries and the Restatement (Second) of Contracts' (1982) 67 *Cornell Law Review* 880–99 at 887–99.

6.7 Partners and Subcontractors – Contractual Roles and Limits

If the primary CSP has sufficient capital or insurance to cover losses, the cloud client can be made whole without seeking damages from the subcontractor. However, if a CSP suffers a major loss and cannot cover its liabilities to its cloud clients, cloud clients may attempt to recover damages from other layers of the service (e.g. the IaaS provider). This is particularly true in cases where the subcontracting IaaS provider was the source of the data loss, such as a data breach or deletion of data, or the cause of substantial unavailability. If a cloud client is not an intended (or direct) beneficiary under this analysis, then the IaaS subcontractor does not owe any liability to the cloud client.[187] However, a strong argument could be made that the cloud client was an intended beneficiary of the contract between the CSP and the IaaS provider. On the other hand, a customer of the cloud client would likely be deemed an incidental beneficiary and would be too far removed for recovery.

Making this determination would require an analysis of the *intention* of the parties.[188] Given the widespread use of non-beneficiary or similar clauses, CSPs and their subcontractors make their intention clear, which is that the contract benefits do not extend beyond the parties named. In cases where the primary SaaS provider's funds are limited but the subcontracted IaaS's effectively are not (e.g. AWS or Google), the difference between being able to recover damages from a subcontractor, rather than the primary contractor, could be substantial when it comes to obtaining a remedy. For instance, under US law it is possible for a CSP to transfer liability to its subcontractors. However, such a transfer requires the consent of both the cloud client and the subcontractor.[189] As a result, this type of transfer is both uncommon and unlikely.

An additional question in the government cloud or outsourcing context is the rights that citizens have as third parties. On the one hand, citizens in a sense purchase the services through their taxes and the fees they pay to process permits and applications, among other means of indirect financing. Although also indirect, the contracts that governments enter into are also for the benefit of their citizens. On the other hand, allowing citizens to enforce rights as third parties under government contracts is seemingly limitless in scope.[190] On that basis, suits by citizens as third parties to government contracts are limited. Generally, even if they would benefit from a public contract or expenditure, the public is not considered an intended beneficiary.

Exceptions to the general rule exist (1) where the terms of the contract allow for liability and (2) when the contract performance was not rendered and the damages are specific and consistent with the terms of the contract and the policy of the law.[191]

---

[187] In some cases, the terms 'incidental', 'donee', or 'creditor' beneficiary are used.
[188] Weitzenböck, 'A Legal Framework for Emerging Business Models', pp. 303–04.
[189] EC, 'Contract Study: Annex 4', 111–12. See Beatson, Burrows, and Cartwright, 'Anson's Law of Contract', pp. 712–13. Providing that a novation must also be supported by a new consideration.
[190] Wendy Netter Epstein, 'Contract Theory and the Failures of Public-Private Contracting' (2012) 34 *Cardozo Law Review* 2211, 2257.
[191] Restatement Second Contracts (1979), § 313(2)(a–b). Is often read as a presumption against third-party liability of governments, unless (1) the contract terms provide for such liability, or (2) assigning

Meeting these exceptions will often require a well-defined group of citizens with specific interests that the government intends to protect. As noted previously, many of the cloud contracts examined in this study contained specific clauses limiting beneficiaries to the parties to the contract. These clauses critically limit any exception. Remembering the *Indiana* v. *IBM* case in Chapter 3, citizens that were denied Medicare sued IBM because of the damages they suffered as a direct result of IBM's failure to adequately provide the service. However, their claims were dismissed by an Indiana court as the contract contained '... an explicit no third parties beneficiaries clause'.[192]

Even if governments essentially act on behalf of the public, making private parties that contract with the state liable to citizens as third-party beneficiaries under the contract is largely an unworkable solution. Therefore, even if the general rule allows third-party beneficiaries to enforce contracts when they are not parties, this is a difficult prospect in the government–citizen relationship.[193] As noted by Epstein, it is very difficult for a third-party citizen to '... gain standing to sue under a government contract'.[194] Epstein further notes that '[t]his is particularly so where there is an express clause disclaiming the intention to benefit third parties, as is often the case in such contracts'.[195] In my review of US FOIA contracts, such disclaimers were common in essentially all agreements with integrators and infrastructure providers.

Nonetheless, Aman and Dugan have argued that citizens should be allowed to bring actions to a much greater degree than they do so currently. They argue that increasing enforcement over contracts by third parties will increase overall accountability. Specifically,

> ... if contractors are aware that they can no longer hide behind the guise of privity, immunity ... or any of the other mechanisms they presently employ to avoid liability and to dodge their contractual responsibilities, they are likely to be more conscientious with respect to the policies they implement, the employees they hire and train, and the activities they undertake.[196]

For government cloud clients, it is important to have an understanding of the parties that will actually be providing the service. The contracts that govern the service should reflect this complexity. Although there are situations where it may be impracticable – or from a negotiation standpoint impossible – to flow down all terms, governments may face challenges in enforcing terms against subcontractors.

    liability is consistent with the terms of the contract and with the policy of the law authorizing the contract.
[192] ibid., 2224.
[193] ibid., 2257.
[194] ibid.
[195] ibid. Noting that '"[n]o third-party beneficiary clauses are almost always controlling"'.
[196] Alfred C. Aman and Joseph C. Dugan, 'The Human Side of Public-Private Partnerships: From New Deal Regulation to Administrative Law Management' (2017) 102 *Iowa Law Review* 883–937 at 929.

This is particularly the case where the contract specifies the intent. For citizens, it is difficult to bring suit directly against subcontractors. Therefore, it is up to the government to ensure adequate terms are in place.

6.8 CONCLUSION

Cloud computing contracts and the procurement of cloud computing services by governments are similar to more traditional IT outsourcing. In addition to the structure of the agreements, including both negotiated or 'prime' terms and standard or boilerplate contractual provisions, both IT outsourcing and cloud computing face similar contracting challenges. In particular, the subcontracting structure and uncertainty surrounding SLA agreements are perceived as additional risks for governments adopting cloud computing services.

Maintaining an adequate level of control throughout the contracting chain and making certain that SLAs provide an appropriate means to measure performance are more difficult given the more fluid or flexible relationships between and among the parties. Comparing the US FedRAMP to the UK G-Cloud program, the G-Cloud approach was more prescriptive. For instance, the G-Cloud framework agreement and call-off contracts contained very specific consent obligations for adding or removing subcontractors. The FedRAMP agreements left this aspect much more open to the agency procuring the service. On the US side, the result was much greater variance in terms and in some cases clear oversights.

By comparing the results of and secondary data from studies of cloud computing contracts, some clear trends in the terms emerge. In Chapter 7, I evaluate more standard or boilerplate terms as adopted as part of the UK and US cloud computing procurement programs. Chapter 7 will further draw global conclusions from the contract study presented in this chapter.

7

Contracts Used to Procure Cloud Services II

Standard Terms, Impact on Governments, and Lessons Learned

This part of the contract study focuses on terms that are generally considered standard in cloud computing agreements. Following the method outlined in Chapter 6, contract terms are drawn from US and UK FOIA disclosures, among other sources. The contract terms are divided into four main groups: (1) terms related to confidentiality and disclosure; (2) terms related to liability and warranties; (3) terms related to contract variation; (4) terms related to location and jurisdiction; and (5) terms related to termination of services and problems related to users being able to 'walk away' with their data. Following an evaluation of the contract terms and based on the results of the study, I examine how governments might create better cloud computing contracts.

7.1 CONFIDENTIALITY AND DISCLOSURE

In the following section, I evaluate the contract terms obligating CSPs, and in some instances cloud clients, to either produce information or keep it confidential. For governments, legislative FOIA requirements often mandate disclosure of information.[1] Governments using cloud services must therefore make certain that the CSP with which they contract has the ability to fulfil such requests. At the same time, whether imposed by contract or statute, governments are also required to maintain the confidentiality of certain information. Although these goals are not necessarily in conflict, governments must procure systems capable of balancing these requirements.

7.1.1 Non-disclosure Agreements

Confidentiality terms play an essential role at different points of the contracting process. Throughout the life of a cloud computing service, parties need assurances that the information they share will not be disclosed. If the parties engage in pre-

---

[1] In addition to access and disclosure requirements under GDPR Art.15.

contractual discussions, confidentiality clauses play an essential role in allowing for an open dialogue and provide a measure of security in the event that the parties do not reach a contract.[2] In other words, if one of the parties backs out, the other has some assurance that the information they have disclosed will remain protected, or at least that damages will be recoverable in the case of a breach of the non-disclosure agreement (NDA).[3] In line with the broad promises of confidentiality, NDAs generally survive the term of any contract ultimately reached by the parties.

Unlike requiring confidentiality in data management or security, NDAs generally focus on the disclosure of confidential information to third parties by humans rather than machines. For example, an NDA would likely cover a situation in which a cloud client shares confidential CSP price information or intellectual property with a third party, but not necessarily a data breach.[4] Furthermore, NDAs vary considerably in their level of detail. Some dedicate many pages to defining the information they deem confidential, including specific schedules and means of identifying and limiting the dissemination of that information. This might include information that is commercially sensitive, trade secrets, and IP-protected material, among others.[5] Other services provide very general NDAs focusing on general disclosures.

Of course, parties to an NDA often have competing objectives. While CSPs tend to focus on keeping information regarding technologies and price confidential, the cloud client is often more focused on the actual information being stored in the cloud service, such as personal data.[6] From the cloud client's point of view, the need for very specific terms might depend on how the service is delivered. For example, the SaaS delivery model generally provides the CSP with a greater level of control over, and thereby access to, cloud client data than does an IaaS model. If the cloud client encrypts their data before uploading it onto the IaaS infrastructure, the risk of disclosure can be minimized, particularly when they do not use the CSP's tools or technology to encrypt the information and do not share decryption keys with the CSP. In other words, with proper security in place, CSP employees and partners will have less opportunity to view or access the data and thereby reduce the possibility of breaching confidentiality obligations.

As for any commercial actor, protecting confidentiality is important for governments moving their data to cloud services. In the G-Cloud framework agreement, both parties have a general duty to treat the other Party's information as confidential and safeguard it accordingly.[7] This includes setting specific limits on disseminating

---

[2] Richard Morgan and Kit Burden, *Morgan and Burden on Computer Contracts*, 8th ed. (London: Sweet & Maxwell Thomson Reuters 2009), s. 1.1.
[3] Andrea M. Matwyshyn, 'The Law of the Zebra' (2013) 28 *Berkeley Technology Law Journal* 155–226 at 222.
[4] GDPR Articles 33–34 also require that data breaches involving personal data be reported in some cases. Further, data breaches are often covered by a separate contract term.
[5] ibid., 43.
[6] ibid., 40.
[7] G-Cloud Framework 12, 'Call-off Contract' (11 September 2020) RM1557.12, s. 6.

or sharing data without consent.[8] Although the G-Cloud framework agreement does not provide exhaustive terms, the call-off contract includes confidentiality requirements on multiple levels, such as indemnifying the cloud client for all losses, expenses, and legal fees resulting from a breach of data protection requirements by the supplier.[9] The CSP is also required to notify the government cloud client in the case of any breach of security involving confidential information.[10]

In the United States, federal agencies engaging the services of private contractors often require them to sign NDAs.[11] The contracts focused not only on protecting non-public data on citizens but also on information that could impact data security. US federal guidance on cloud contracting places particular weight on the ability of the federal agency to enforce NDAs against CSPs.[12] Notwithstanding explicit guidance, in early US government cloud adoption, the NDA requirement was rarely met. In one federal audit, thirty-three of the seventy-seven contracts examined did not have an NDA in place.[13] This oversight may also be in conflict with the requirements of the Federal Acquisition Regulation (FAR) that mandates that contractors keep certain information private.[14] Even in cases where the FedRAMP NDA requirement was not wholly disregarded, NDAs were not applied throughout the infrastructure.

In some cases, it would be impractical if not impossible for all subcontractors to a service to enter into NDAs with cloud clients. Requiring all employees and subcontractors of the largest CSPs to sign specific NDAs every time they contracted with a government would create a substantial barrier. Amazon, Microsoft, and Google employees would spend a substantial period of their days reviewing signing such agreements. However, when the contract is for millions of dollars and concerns vital information, if the agency cannot flow down the NDA through its primary contractor, then the agency ought to avoid the service.

7.1.2 *Freedom of Information Act and Governmental Disclosure*

Although governments might wish to keep information confidential, they often have transparency requirements compelling them to make information available to

---

[8] ibid. Also providing general (e.g. the information becomes public knowledge or must be disclosed under a 'legal obligation') and specific (e.g. 'examination under s. 6(1) of the National Audit Act 1983') exceptions. ibid., ss. 8.85–8.86.
[9] Cloud Framework 12, 'Call-off Contract', s.10.1.
[10] ibid., 58.
[11] ibid., Some US agency contracts included an extensive NDA as part of the contract terms. US Department of the Treasury on Behalf of the Consumer Financial Protection Bureau (CFPB) and Deloitte Consulting LLP, Contract No TDP-CFP-12-C-0008 (23 May 2012) Attachment A.
[12] ibid.
[13] The Council of the Inspectors General on Integrity and Efficiency (CIGIE), 'The Council of the Inspectors General on Integrity and Efficiency's Cloud Computing Initiative' (2014), 8–9.
[14] FAR 52.239–1(a)–(c) (1996).

citizens upon request.[15] Even if there are other countervailing interests, such as data privacy or trade secret legislation that must be balanced against releasing information, disclosure under FOIA legislation is weighted heavily in many democratic states.[16] In many countries, including the United States and Norway, there is a presumption of disclosure.[17] Therefore, even if disclosures are expensive or difficult in cloud systems given scale or customization requirements, such arguments are unlikely to carry much weight in excusing FOIA obligations. As a result, governments must make certain that data remains accessible and retrievable.[18]

At a basic level, governments must therefore ensure that the cloud systems they adopt allow for compliance with FOIA requirements and that they have contract terms in place that require the CSP to make the requested information available. For instance, the G-Cloud framework, requires CSP cooperation in responding to such requests, and even addresses procedural aspects in the contract, such as stating that the CSP may not respond directly to citizens.[19] In G-Cloud contracts made public pursuant to the UK FOIA, this obligation was consistently included in the contracts.[20] In contrast to the US FOIA sample, G-Cloud users appear to have obtained the required terms consistently.

According to US Department of Defense reports, failing to require a CSP to sign an NDA may have additional consequences for a US federal agency.[21] More specifically, under the 'release to one release to all' rule, if a government agency releases information to a contractor without an NDA, it cannot later deny the public access to that information under the FOIA.[22] Therefore, although there may never be a data breach or other security failure, US federal agencies that fail to include NDAs risk that information they intend to keep private will become public through citizen FOIA requests. By making confidentiality obligations clear in the contract, starting with a broad definition of what is to be protected from disclosure under

---

[15] Tanya Aplin, Lionel Bently, Phillip Johnson, and Simon Malynicz, *Gurry on Breach of Confidence: The Protection of Confidential Information* (Oxford: Oxford University Press 2012), pp. 608–09.
[16] ibid., 609–10.
[17] ibid., 610. Although the presumption is rebuttable and many exceptions to disclosure exist (e.g. trade secrets and commercial concerns).
[18] EPA and AVANTI Corporation, Contract #EP-BPA-12-C-0010 (24 January 2012), 4. Requiring the provider to build in functionality to meet FOIA obligations.
[19] Cloud Framework 12, 'Call-off Contract', 25.
[20] Police and Crime Commissioner for Avon & Somerset and Iken Business Limited, 'Relating to the Provision of G-Cloud Services' (Call-Off Terms, 17 March 2014), § CO 4.4.1 and § CO 6.1. Requiring that the CSP assist in meeting FOIA and other regulatory disclosure requests. ibid., s. 18.2.1. British Library and Bravo Solutions UK Ltd (10 February 2014) Call-off terms Ref # FIN 8895, 1–23. s. CO 4.4.1.
[21] See also Defense Information Systems Agency (DISA), 'Department of Defense (DoD) Cloud Computing Security Requirements Guide' (2015), 8.
[22] Inspector General, Department of Defense, 'DoD Cloud Computing Strategy Needs Implementation Plan and Detailed Waiver Process' (2014) *Report DODIG-2015-045*, 'Issue Matrix' Appendix B #3.

FOIA requests, much of the potential problem evidenced in the audit could have been avoided.

7.1.3 E-discovery

In jurisdictions with discovery requirements, government use of cloud computing creates a particular challenge. In the United States, federal agencies can expect to be sued – contract disputes and challenges of procurement awards are commonplace.[23] This reality of unavoidable litigation means that federal agencies must be able to meet the discovery demands that litigation entails when using cloud computing. Specifically, federal agencies must be able to find, preserve, and possibly produce electronically stored information (ESI) and metadata stored with CSPs if so ordered.[24] In addition to discovery requirements, federal agencies must be able to obtain data from CSPs and subcontractors for audits and should consider portability barriers that might inhibit the agency from obtaining their data after a service has ended.[25]

The Federal Rules of Civil Procedure (FRCP) require the party being sued to make certain records available.[26] Pursuant to the FRCP, ESI must be provided in both civil and criminal cases where that information is in the 'possession, custody, or control' of the party from whom data is sought.[27] ESI includes data from a variety of sources beyond email and final agency documents.[28] Moreover, limits to production exist, including instances where producing the ESI carries an undue burden or cost for the disclosing party.[29] However, even if agency data is under the control of a CSP (or a CSP's subcontractor), the agency is still required to produce the ESI.[30] The general standard applied for being able to produce ESI is control over the document, not the location (either domestic or foreign) of the data storage.

Once an agency receives notice of litigation, or if litigation can be reasonably anticipated, the agency is required to take steps to preserve information.[31] If an agency fails to do so, it risks facing sanctions for spoliation or destruction of

---

[23] Chief Information Officers (CIO) and others, 'Creating Effective Cloud Computing Contracts for the Federal Government Best Practices for Acquiring IT as a Service' (2012), 24.

[24] Cindy Pham, 'E-Discovery in the Cloud Era: What's a Litigant to Do?' (2013) 5 *Hastings Science & Technology Law Journal* 139–90 at 157.

[25] Robert H. Carpenter Jr., 'Walking from Cloud to Cloud: The Portability Issue in Cloud Computing' (2010) 6 *Washington Journal of Law, Technology & Arts* 1–14 at 9, 12–14.

[26] CIO Council, 'Creating Effective Cloud Computing Contracts for the Federal Government', 23–25, fn 53. Explaining e-discovery requirements and citing Federal Rules of Civil Procedure, Rule 16, Rule 26(f), Rule 26 (b)(2) on Inaccessible ESI, Rule 33 on ESI Interrogatories, and Rule 34(b) on Form ESI.

[27] Federal Rules of Civil Procedure 26(a)(1)(A)(ii).

[28] United States Postal Service (USPS), 'Cloud Security' Report (2015), 34.

[29] Pham, 'E-Discovery in the Cloud Era', 175–79.

[30] ibid., 156–57.

[31] Daniel Carmeli, 'Keep an I on the Sky: E-discovery Risks Forecasted for Apple's iCloud' (2013) *Boston College Intellectual Property & Technology Forum* 1–11 at 7. http://bciptf.org/wp-content/uploads/2013/02/Daniel-Carmeli-Cloud-Computing.pdf.

7.1 Confidentiality and Disclosure

evidence.[32] If the agency fails to produce or preserve ESI as ordered, severe penalties may be incurred.[33] For federal agencies, this requires them to be able to identify and preserve the information they store with CSPs.[34] Where agency information is stored on infrastructure not owned or operated by the agency, obtaining the necessary ESI to be transferred to a third party requires cooperation with the CSP.[35]

Complying with agency discovery requests may be cumbersome from the perspective of the CSP. More concretely, identifying, locating, separating, and saving ESI for discovery purposes may disrupt operations or affect CSP data retention schedules.[36] While possible, fulfilling discovery requests is particularly problematic in the cloud model.[37] If many users of the infrastructure are making these types of requests, the CSP may have difficulty fulfilling all of them while also operating its infrastructure in an efficient manner. Ultimately, this will impact the effectiveness and quality of the service. Furthermore, when complying with discovery requests, the CSP risks disruption of the service and the inadvertent disclosure of data stored on the service by other customers.[38]

For governments, the discovery process is difficult, time consuming, and expensive. However, it is also an area where cloud computing services are particularly relevant for agencies. In an SOW for an e-discovery SaaS system procured by the USPS, the agency stated the following:

> [c]urrently, lawyers representing the USPS manually review individual documents to identify the relevant and privileged materials. Typical legal matters will require USPS lawyers to review tens of thousands of documents, and for class actions, tens of millions of documents.[39]

Therefore, a system both offering innovative tools and allowing the agency to scale up a service when needed (e.g. during litigation) is attractive, particularly if the alternative is shipping around truckloads of paper documents rather than accessing them instantly via the cloud from multiple locations.

---

[32] ibid.
[33] Federal Rules of Civil Procedure 37(e) and advisory committee notes. See also Dan H. Willoughby Jr., Rose Hunter Jones, and Gregory R. Antine, 'Sanctions for E-Discovery Violations: By the Numbers 2010 Civil Litigation Review Conference' (2010) 60 *Duke Law Journal* 789–864 at 814–15.
[34] Pham, 'E-Discovery in the Cloud Era', 156–57.
[35] Carmeli, 'Keep an I on the Sky', 2. See also M. James Daley, Steven C. Bennett, and Natascha Gerlach, 'Storm Clouds Gathering for Cross-Border Discovery and Data Privacy: Cloud Computing Meets the U.S.A. Patriot Act' (2012) 13 *Sedona Conference Journal* 235–52 at 238.
[36] Pham, 'E-Discovery in the Cloud Era', 172. Preserving ESI also detracts from the CSP's ability to effectively use its resources, raising costs. Alberto G. Araiza, 'Electronic Discovery in the Cloud' (2012) 10 *Duke Law & Technology Review* 1–18 at ¶31–32. https://scholarship.law.duke.edu/dltr/vol10/iss1/8.
[37] Araiza, 'Electronic Discovery in the Cloud', paras. 26–32. See also Pham, 'E-Discovery in the Cloud Era', 158. Arguing that many CSPs did not consider e-discovery in their designs, making compliance difficult.
[38] Araiza, 'Electronic Discovery in the Cloud', para. 26.
[39] USPS and Autonomy Inc, Statement of Work (SOW) for Contract No 1BITSV-11-B-1007 (21 September 2010), s. 1.1.

7.1.4 Contractual Limits on Law Enforcement Agency Access

As discussed in Chapter 4, access by LEAs and intelligence agencies is problematic for government cloud users from a data protection and a data sovereignty perspective.[40] Nonetheless, most, if not all, western countries have procedures that allow governments to access data stored with CSPs. However, the standard for when a CSP will disclose a law enforcement request for information varies between providers.[41] The following section focuses on contract terms allowing cloud clients to be informed and providing them with the opportunity to object to LEA disclosure when possible.

CSPs generally have terms in their agreements to account for LEA access.[42] However, this is an area where the contract terms vary to some extent in their substance. In some cases, contracts provide very broad access rights to LEAs seeking data stored with a CSP, while others promise limited access – particularly when requests are made by foreign LEAs. For example, some CSPs will only provide such disclosure based on a 'good faith belief' or a 'reasonable belief' or if they 'determine [that] the disclosure is reasonably necessary'.[43] Others employ contract language that is much more limiting, such as requiring a binding court order from a specific jurisdiction.[44] Furthermore, in other instances, a request like a subpoena, which may be issued on an *ex parte* basis (without all parties present), provides a sufficient contractual basis for a CSP to provide an LEA with access to a cloud client's data.

In practical terms, the differences between the contractual standards for disclosing information to LEAs are relatively stark. In some terms, the cloud client is given the opportunity to contest the order and present arguments to a court. In others, they may not even be notified, and the CSP is given complete discretion. There are of course instances where legal barriers leave CSPs unable to inform cloud clients of access requests made by LEAs. However, whether the CSP promises to make an effort to inform its users of an LEA request, when it is possible or legal, varies by CSP.

In the United States, FedRAMP contract guidance on this point is explicit. In particular, a CIO report provided that LEA access to US federal data may in some instances violate certain requirements under the Privacy Act.[45] The guidance requires that agency contracts clearly define specific requirements for data storage,

---

[40] This has been a focal point of the discussion around cloud adoption for governments at all levels following the revelations of widespread access to cloud services by the NSA. See generally Judith Rauhofer and Caspar Bowden, 'Protecting Their Own: Fundamental Rights Implications for EU Data Sovereignty in the Cloud' (2013) No 2013/28 *Edinburgh School of Law Research Paper* 1–31 at 11–12.

[41] W. Kuan Hon, Christopher Millard, and Ian Walden, 'Negotiated Contracts for Cloud Services' in Christopher Millard (ed.), *Cloud Computing Law* (Oxford: Oxford University Press 2013), p. 91.

[42] Dimitra Kamarinou, Christopher Millard, and W. Kuan Hon, 'Cloud Privacy: An Empirical Study of 20 Cloud Providers' Terms and Privacy Policies – Part II' (2016) 6 *International Data Privacy Law* 3–5.

[43] ibid. Referencing Google, Spider Oak, and Dropbox, respectively.

[44] ibid., 4. Citing Jotta Cloud.

[45] CIO Council, 'Creating Effective Cloud Computing Contracts for the Federal Government', 22.

including the locations of server infrastructure, and incorporate all required security controls. Additionally, federal agencies are required to 'contractually define a procedure for what CSPs must do in the event of any request for disclosure, subpoena, or other judicial process ... seeking access to agency data'.[46] To limit such access, almost all US FOIA contracts contained a clause requiring that data be stored in the United States. In some cases, there was also a requirement that data be only made accessible to 'US persons'.

7.2 LIABILITY, CONDITIONS, WARRANTIES, AND LIMITING PROMISES

Liability may originate from contractual obligations, be imposed through an adopted standard, arise from tort actions, or be based on legal obligations flowing down from specific regulations.[47] In cloud computing, there are many opportunities for the various parties to a service to find themselves in the position of being liable.[48] In the following section, I examine contractual attempts to limit liability.

Given the multi-tenancy structure of cloud services, CSPs potentially face a great deal of liability. If something goes wrong with the service, such as a data breach, the loss or destruction of data, or an outage, it will generally affect many users. Even if the claims made by each user are relatively moderate, in the aggregate, the damages could be extremely large.[49] If CSPs were to be held liable for all losses related to user data, a substantial outage could put even a major CSP out of business. Such an approach to CSP liability would leave very few companies willing to take on the potential risk of offering cloud services. If a CSP were willing to take such a risk under a full liability scenario, one would also have to question the CSP's financial standing or ability to remunerate users if an incident occurred.

In addition to liability-inducing events that are a direct result of a CSP's actions, reliance on the infrastructure and software of third parties means that many CSPs have little control over certain types of outages. For instance, if a CSP provides a SaaS offering to end users, and is itself an IaaS user, an outage with the CSP's IaaS provider (e.g. AWS or Google) would result in the SaaS service being unavailable. Although the CSP does not have control over the IaaS, without limiting their promise of availability or including some type of exclusion in the contract with their end users, the IaaS CSP could effectively be held liable for an outage beyond its

---

[46] ibid. See also Sasha Segall, 'Jurisdictional Challenges in the United States Government's Move to Cloud Computing Technology' (2013) 23 *Fordham Intellectual Property, Media and Entertainment Law Journal* 1105–53 at 1153.

[47] Rolf H. Weber and Dominic Staiger, 'Cloud Computing: A Cluster of Complex Liability Issues' (2014) 20 *European Journal of Current Legal Issues* 1 online. www.zora.uzh.ch/id/eprint/108609/1/418.

[48] ibid. Focusing in particular on breach of contract from unavailability, non-compliance with privacy rules, and infringing content.

[49] Timothy J. Calloway, 'Cloud Computing, Clickwrap Agreements, and Limitation on Liability Clauses: A Perfect Storm' (2012) 11 *Duke Law & Technology Review* 163–74 at 170–73. Providing examples of potential losses.

control. Consequently, it can be argued that CSPs should have very little liability outside of the immediate role they play in providing the service. In short, CSPs should not be held liable for failures in other parties' systems. This argument, and the current sources and systems for limiting liability, are further analysed in the following section.

The most probable or foreseeable situation resulting in CSP liability is breach of contract.[50] This failure may result from not meeting SLA or SOW requirements, among other breaches. However, a cloud client's opportunity to recover contract damages will be based primarily on the terms of the contract. Although such contracts are limited in many jurisdictions by concepts such as good faith, CSPs generally limit – often extensively – their contractual promises regarding their confidentiality, integrity, or availability obligations to cloud clients.[51]

7.2.1 Limiting or Excluding Contractual Liability

To reduce the pool of potential liability, providers generally take several contractual approaches. One approach is to exclude most or all liability-inducing events by lowering expectations and limiting promises made regarding the service.[52] For instance, even if a CSP promises 100 per cent availability, it will be limited and will not apply to events such as planned service outages, network outages, force majeure, or other downtime events. An additional approach is to specifically exclude, cap, or otherwise limit liability to certain losses or the overall price of the contract – or some combination thereof. Moreover, by making few promises about the quality or security of the service, CSPs attempt to lower the reasonable expectations of the contracting parties using the service further.

For instance, the party providing the good or service offers an assurance or guarantee regarding performance, which is memorialized in the contract. This 'condition' is an essential contract term, the breach of which gives the innocent party the option to discharge the contract.[53] A 'warranty' is a term that is essential to the contract.[54] However, if a warranty is breached, the non-breaching party is generally entitled to damages rather than repudiation of the agreement.[55] To limit

---

[50] Jack Beatson, Andrew Burrows, and John Cartwright (eds.), *Anson's Law of Contract*, 30th ed. (Oxford: Oxford University Press 2016), p. 563.
[51] Simon Bradshaw, Christopher Millard, and Ian Walden, 'Standard Contracts for Cloud Services' in Christopher Millard (ed.), *Cloud Computing Law* (Oxford: Oxford University Press 2013), p. 51. Noting ' … providers continue to firmly place the onus for ensuring data integrity onto consumers'.
[52] Giuditta Cordero-Moss, 'Conclusion: The Self-Sufficient Contract, Uniformly Interpreted on the Basis of Its Own Terms: An Illusion, But Not Fully Useless' in Giuditta Cordero-Moss (ed.), *Boilerplate Clauses, International Commercial Contracts and the Applicable Law* (Cambridge: Cambridge University Press 2011), pp. 36–65. Evaluating the different approaches to drafting warranties clauses in common law and civil law systems.
[53] Beatson, Burrows, and Cartwright, 'Anson's Law of Contract', p. 148.
[54] ibid.
[55] ibid., 148–49, 152.

the risk of repudiation based on the breach of a condition and damages for breach of a warranty, CSPs generally attempt to mitigate both risks through exemptions or other similar clauses. Most standard CSP agreements offer little in the way of guarantees or warranties for services being performed, including disclaimers of indirect or consequential liability.[56] This is generally accomplished through an 'exemption', 'exclusion', or 'exculpatory clause' expressly disclaiming liability.[57]

Although parties are given broad authority to negotiate exclusion clauses, there are limits to the exclusions. In particular, legislation often restricts the parties from excluding liability for negligence.[58] The policy rationale behind limiting such exclusions is that 'it is "inherently improbable" that the innocent party would have agreed to the exclusion of the contract-breaker's negligence'.[59] English contract law places additional requirements on B2B contracts entered into on standard terms.[60] The rationale is that unlike bespoke or customized agreements, in standard agreements one party dictates the terms. Therefore, the contract is not the product of bargaining or negotiation.[61] On that basis, the reasonableness of the term may be examined or assessed.[62] In assessing the reasonableness of a non-negotiated term, courts will consider variables such as the relative bargaining strengths of the parties, customer knowledge of the term, and reasonable expectation of compliance with the term, among others.[63]

In the cloud computing context, the CLP at QMUL found that CSPs have gone from categorically limiting liability and denying that any warranty was in place in 2010 and 2013 to offering some guarantees in 2019.[64] Such warranties include 'commercially reasonable skill and care' or 'professional diligence' when providing services.[65] The CLP at QMUL studies has generally found that both EU and US

---

[56] Andrew Joint and Edwin Baker, 'Knowing the Past to Understand the Present – Issues in the Contracting for Cloud Based Services' (2011) 27 *Computer Law & Security Review* 407–15 at 412–13. See also Bradshaw, Millard, and Walden, 'Standard Contracts for Cloud Services', p. 59. Noting that '[a]lmost without exception, every provider went to considerable, and in some cases extraordinary lengths to deny that any such warranty existed'.

[57] Edward T. Canuel, 'Comparing Exculpatory Clauses under Anglo-American Law: Testing Total Legal Convergence' in Giuditta Cordero-Moss (ed.), *Boilerplate Clauses, International Commercial Contracts and the Applicable Law* (Cambridge: Cambridge University Press 2011), p. 85.

[58] Beatson, Burrows, and Cartwright, 'Anson's Law of Contract', pp. 195–97.

[59] ibid.

[60] European Commission (EC), 'Comparative Study on Cloud Computing Contracts Final Report – Annex 4: Country Report Overview Work Package V' (2015), 1–120 at 11. https://op.europa.eu/en/publication-detail/-/publication/13f8fb54-f159-4ff1-ba72-a8478a33a072/language-en/format-PDF/source-216092933.

[61] ibid.

[62] ibid.

[63] ibid.

[64] Johan David Michels, Christopher Millard, and Felicity Turton, 'Contracts for Clouds, Revisited: An Analysis of the Standard Contracts for 40 Cloud Computing Services' (2020) *Queen Mary School of Law Legal Studies Research Paper No. 334/2020*, 41–44. Bradshaw, Millard, and Walden, 'Standard Contracts for Cloud Services', pp. 58–59.

[65] Michels, Millard, and Turton, 'Contracts for Clouds, Revisited', 44.

CSPs adopted terms to limit direct liability.[66] Although EU CSPs provided more nuanced terms and did not attempt to disclaim all direct liability as was common of US providers, disclaimers were still present.[67] As further noted by QMUL's study of negotiated contracts, it was often difficult for cloud clients to obtain concessions on liability.[68] The CLP at QMUL found that CSPs often treated these terms as non-negotiable. Although CSPs did not disclaim all liability in the US FOIA contracts, it was limited to a great extent in all the contracts I reviewed. Furthermore, in the US FOIA contracts, direct liability was generally limited to the specific enumerated promises made in the contract.

An additional potential source of CSP liability is misrepresentation. In theory, a misrepresentation by a CSP could entitle the cloud client to damages or rescission of the contract. The representation would have to go well beyond the general advertising or 'puffery' common in such services (e.g. 'iCloud does it all automatically').[69] In contract law, parties are generally given a great deal of room to promote, and cloud clients are expected to look out for their own interests.[70] However, if a CSP actively misrepresents their service, their action induces the contract, and the reliance by the cloud client is objectively reasonable, damages or rescission of the contract are a possibility.[71] Nonetheless, in the government procurement setting, a finding of misrepresentation based on advertising or sales seems unlikely.

As a means of reducing some of the uncertainty in categorizing and proving contract damages under common law, parties often rely on indemnity clauses.[72] In the cloud computing context, such clauses are common and are often applied to breaches of intellectual property, confidentiality, or data protection.[73] As noted in the EC comparative contract study, the advantage of an indemnity clause is that ' … the party relying on the indemnity may be able to claim for the prescribed losses on a pound-for-pound basis without the limitations of causation, remoteness and mitigation'.[74] However, the clause must be reasonable under the circumstances.[75] EC researchers provided a hypothetical scenario where a CSP settles a claim with a third party after the CSP's cloud client has violated that third party's intellectual property rights. When the CSP seeks remuneration from its cloud client on that basis, the CSP must show that the settlement it entered was justified based on the strength of

---

[66] Bradshaw, Millard, and Walden, 'Standard Contracts for Cloud Services', p. 60. Further noting that US providers tended to push these terms to the limit, excluding nearly all direct liability.
[67] ibid.
[68] Hon, Millard, and Walden, 'Negotiated Contracts for Cloud Services', pp. 81–82.
[69] Kevin McGillivray, 'Conflicts in the Cloud: Contracts and Compliance with Data Protection Law in the EU' (2014) 17 *Tulane Journal of Technology and Intellectual Property* 217–53 at fn 188.
[70] Beatson, Burrows, and Cartwright, 'Anson's Law of Contract', pp. 318–19.
[71] ibid., 320–26.
[72] EC, 'Contract Study: Annex 4', 10.
[73] Bradshaw, Millard, and Walden, 'Standard Contracts for Cloud Services', p. 62. Finding indemnification terms extremely popular among providers. See also ibid., 10.
[74] EC, 'Contract Study: Annex 4', 10.
[75] ibid.

the third party's claim.[76] In other words, even with what might be unlimited coverage, the CSP is required to mitigate its damages.

7.2.2 Force Majeure and Discharge by Frustration in Cloud Contracts

There are additional circumstances where a contractual performance may be excused, including frustration of purpose, impossibility, and in some jurisdictions, impracticability.[77] Although the doctrine of frustration is not designed to reallocate risks negotiated between parties, changes in circumstances may have rendered the initial purpose of the contract impossible – or at least commercially unreasonable – in light of the contract's agreed-upon purpose.[78] Standard cloud contracts often include clauses that cover frustration and, in particular, events where performance becomes impossible.[79]

Force Majeure clauses' provide a broad basis for excusing performance (e.g. availability) and mitigating or eliminating liability for the nonperforming party.[80] Ultimately, force majeure clauses provide an affirmative contractual defence, and the party asserting the defence has the burden of showing that a force majeure event occurred.[81] Although the events that excuse contractual performance based on force majeure vary by contract, and perhaps also by industry or trade practice, they tend to include language excusing performance based on events such as ' ... acts of God, war, government regulation, terrorism, disaster, strikes ... or any other emergency beyond the parties' control, making it inadvisable, illegal, or impossible to perform'.[82]

Recalling the *State of Indiana* v. *IBM* case introduced in Chapter 3, the court evaluated whether IBM's breach of contract could be excused as a force majeure event.[83] In the case, the state of Indiana contracted with IBM to outsource delivery of its welfare services. After entering the contract, Indiana, like much of the United States, experienced a significant economic recession in 2008. In that year, the unemployment rate in Indiana doubled.[84] For IBM, this meant managing a large

---

[76] ibid.
[77] Uniform Commercial Code (UCC), 'Article 2 – Sales: Breach, Repudiation and Excuse' (2002), ss. 2–615. Providing the standard of impracticability in the US.
[78] Beatson, Burrows, and Cartwright, 'Anson's Law of Contract', p. 497.
[79] ibid., 498.
[80] Morgan and Burden, 'Computer Contracts', pp. 354–55. Providing a standard clause excusing liability for non-performance for delays ' ... caused by circumstances by its [the breaching parties] reasonable control'.
[81] Edwin Peel, 'The Common Law Tradition: Application of Boilerplate Clauses Under English Law' in Giuditta Cordero-Moss (ed.), *Boilerplate Clauses, International Commercial Contracts and the Applicable Law* (Cambridge: Cambridge University Press 2011), p. 175.
[82] Richard A. Lord, *Williston on Contracts*, 4th ed. (London: Sweet & Maxwell 1993), p. 30, s. 77:31. In the US FOIA sample, performance was excused for ' ... acts of God or the public enemy ... fires, floods, epidemics ... ' Battelle Energy Alliance, LLC, and DoE, 'General Provisions for Commercial Items/Services' (29 August 2011) Applicable to Contract No 00109064, 1–20, s. 14.1.
[83] *State of Indiana* v. *IBM*, 51 NE 3d 150 at 164–165 (2016).
[84] ibid., 155.

increase in applications for welfare services. Shortly thereafter, the state of Indiana experienced a series of floods, which again caused the numbers of applications for assistance to increase sharply.[85] The IBM/Indiana MSA defined a force majeure event as a ' ... fire, flood, earthquake, or other act of God or nature ... beyond the reasonable control of the affected party that delay[s] or prevent[s] the Party, directly or indirectly, from performing its obligations under the Agreement'.[86] However, an additional requirement for excusing performance under the force majeure clause was that IBM was required to provide notice of the force majeure event to Indiana state officials. Because IBM failed to provide such notice, it was precluded from using the defence.[87] In addition to the substantive burden, excusing performance may also have strict procedural obligations.

Force majeure clauses often require that the force majeure event was beyond the control of the party asserting the defence and that the asserting party was not at fault or in any way negligent.[88] However, there are significant differences in the perception and application of force majeure.[89] For example, as a well-established principle in Norwegian law, force majeure requires more than diligence and good faith in failing to perform.[90] In the view of Hagstrøm, '"[b]eyond the control" presupposes that some external event has occurred ... that the party could not have reasonably expected to have taken the impediment into account at the time of the conclusion of the contract'.[91]

In the case of cloud computing, force majeure clauses often include service or network outages. Although the exact outage time or severity of an outage is not always predictable, outages are not uncommon and are almost expected to occur. Therefore, I would argue that a CSP has an obligation to prevent facing the consequences of an outage by establishing an alternative power supply or generators. If a CSP takes reasonable backup measures, and all backups fail for reasons beyond the CSP's control, then the CSP has a much better force majeure argument.

Under the G-Cloud framework agreement, force majeure is defined on a relatively open or broad basis, including ' ... events or omissions beyond the reasonable control of the affected party'.[92] Additionally, the framework agreement defines the terms negatively through examples of instances that are *not* force majeure events.[93] These include industrial disputes over a supplier, its staff, or a failure in the

---

[85] ibid.
[86] ibid., 164. However, an outage caused by increased traffic hardly seems to be adequate for a force majeure event.
[87] ibid.
[88] Lord, 'Williston on Contracts', p. 30, s. 77:31.
[89] Viggo Hagstrøm, 'The Nordic Tradition: Application of Boilerplate Clauses Under Norwegian Law' in Giuditta Cordero-Moss (ed.), *Boilerplate Clauses, International Commercial Contracts and the Applicable Law* (Cambridge: Cambridge University Press 2011), pp. 274–75.
[90] ibid.
[91] ibid., 275.
[92] Cloud Framework 12, 'Call-off Contract', s. 11.1.1.
[93] ibid.

supplier's (or a subcontractor's) supply chain, events attributable to a wilful act or failure to take reasonable precautions by the party relying on a force majeure event, and events that were foreseeable by the party enforcing the event when the contract was entered into.[94] Although many security events beyond the reasonable control of the CSP would be excused, they are considerably narrower than many standard terms.

7.2.3 Contract Damages

As a general rule, cloud computing contracts are treated as contracts for services rather than goods. As a consequence, many of the statutory warranty obligations imposed on the sellers of goods are not applicable to cloud computing, given its status as a service. Although there are some requirements to apply reasonable care, statutory obligations imposed by the state are typically more reduced for services than goods.[95] Cloud contracts generally provide an obligation to perform services at a certain level. If the CSP fails to operate the service in a manner that conforms to the contract, it is subject to potential liability for breach and the government using the service is owed a remedy. Remedies for breach of contract generally include compensation, specific performance, or restitution in some circumstances.[96]

Breach of contract in the cloud computing environment could include unavailability of data, a data breach, or a CSP's failure to supply functionality or performance as stated in the contract between the parties. Additional examples include situations where data are incorrectly backed up, corrupted, inadequately deleted, or not returned as required by the contract. If a CSP breaches its contract with the cloud client in any of these areas, the cloud client may seek compensation in the form of damages. The starting point for measuring damages is to compensate for losses incurred rather than punish the breaching party.[97] After a determination of causation has been made, courts must assess the amount of damages for which the breaching party has liability.[98] In most of the EU member states, contractual damages are framed as being either 'direct' or 'consequential', with some variation in interpretation and application.[99]

---

[94] ibid.
[95] ibid., 91. Discussing the requirement to apply 'reasonable care and skill' under English law. See the Unfair Contract Terms Act of 1977 (requiring reasonableness in standard contract terms in B2B relationships as well). See also Directive (EU) 2019/770 of 20 May 2019 on certain aspects concerning contracts for the supply of digital content and digital services, OJ L 136, 22 May 2019, pp. 1–27. Containing both subjective and objective obligations.
[96] Beatson, Burrows, and Cartwright, 'Anson's Law of Contract', pp. 563–64. Remedies for breach of contract generally include compensation, specific performance, or restitution, in some circumstances.
[97] ibid., 564, 570.
[98] ibid., 575.
[99] European Commission (EC), 'Comparative Study on Cloud Computing Contracts' (2015), 44–45. https://op.europa.eu/en/publication-detail/-/publication/40148ba1-1784-4d1a-bb64-334ac3df22c7.

'Direct' damages are those that are foreseeable or naturally emanate from the breach of contract.[100] These damages are 'probable' or 'likely' based on the facts surrounding the contract. In other words, they are of the kind that the parties would normally contemplate when entering into an agreement.[101] Based on this measurement, direct damages tend to focus on objective events and apply reasonableness. The point of departure is that the damages are grounded in losses that are reasonably foreseeable at the time of contracting.[102] In the cloud computing scenario, a refund of contract price, service credits, or other damages related to unavailability are generally of the type considered reasonably foreseeable. Some damages related to data breaches, such as reporting costs, are also arguably direct damages in that they are reasonably foreseeable. However, loss of reputation or lost revenue because of the breach would likely be too remote.

'Consequential' damages are awarded with the aim of returning the party to the position they would have occupied had the contract been performed as agreed.[103] The measure of consequential damages goes beyond the contract price or the direct (i.e. 'usual' or 'natural') damages resulting from a breach.[104] However, this does not mean that all resulting damages will be recoverable.[105] Consequential damages also require evidence that the type of damages that occurred was contemplated by the parties at the time they entered the contract.[106] In many agreements, the parties disclaim consequential damages, thereby limiting the non-breaching party to direct damages.

Assuming that consequential damages were not disclaimed in a contract, they could be applied to the cloud scenario. For instance, if a CSP was very involved in the migration of a government's legacy system, was aware that the government client had no other means of backup, and further understood that the government would be storing extremely valuable data on the CSP's service, then perhaps the argument for a finding of consequential losses would succeed. However, as in the example,

---

[100] Beatson, Burrows, and Cartwright, 'Anson's Law of Contract', p. 575.
[101] ibid., 575–78. Explaining *Hadley* v. *Baxendale* [1854] 9 Ex 341, 156 Eng. Rep. 145 (Court of Exchequer).
[102] Michael Stoolman, 'The Cause of Action for Breach of Data?: The Problem with Relying on Courts When Managing the Risks of Cloud Services' (2018) 70 *Rutgers University Law Review* 717–48 at 731–33. Discussing application of the rule of *Hadley* v. *Baxendale* in US cases.
[103] Beatson, Burrows, and Cartwright, 'Anson's Law of Contract', p. 570. See also Restatement (Second) of Contracts § 344 (1981) (a) 'expectation interest' Providing that the party should be 'put in as good a position as he would have been if the contract had been performed'.
[104] Beatson, Burrows, and Cartwright, 'Anson's Law of Contract', p. 575.
[105] See generally Restatement (Second) of Contracts § 351 (1981) (1). Providing that '[d]amages are not recoverable for loss that the party in breach did not have reason to foresee as a probable result of the breach when the contract was made'.
[106] Beatson, Burrows, and Cartwright, 'Anson's Law of Contract', pp. 575–85. Evaluating the remoteness of damages. See further Andrea M. Matwyshyn, 'Privacy the Hacker Way' (2013) 87 *Southern California Law Review* 55–56. Discussing the difficulty of demonstrating privacy harms in traditional contract doctrine, including 'restitution damages, reliance damages, expectation damages, and punitive damages'.

some special knowledge of the loss at the time of contracting would generally have to be present. Most CSPs head off such enquiries by specifically excluding consequential damages outright in the contract terms.

Based on studies of contractual liability and warranties in the EU, categorization of damages as either direct or indirect are common in both civil and common law countries.[107] However, how they are applied and understood is not always consistent.[108] Some EU member states allow both direct and indirect damages (e.g. England and Wales), while others generally limit parties to direct damages (e.g. France).[109] In other countries, such as Sweden, both types of damages may be recovered, but the distinction as to what constitutes indirect or direct damages is apparently less clear.[110]

In England and Wales, the distinction is very fact-specific. In order to limit the zone of consequential damages, the general approach by parties is to describe exhaustively the damages covered and excluded in the contract.[111] In Germany, EC researchers found that contract exclusions were primarily aimed at limiting consequential damages and disclaiming statutory warranties rather than broad omnibus disclaimers.[112] However, despite some differences between countries, the general approach that CSPs take in the EU is to ' ... regulate in great detail in the contract the classification of certain types of damages along with the rules applicable to each of these classes'.[113] By categorizing what the parties anticipate and deem foreseeable at the time of contracting, CSPs attempt to limit both types of contract damages.

7.2.4 English and US Approach

Although it analyses a more traditional IT outsourcing solution, the case of *GB Gas Holdings Limited* v. *Accenture* illustrates two important points relevant to cloud computing.[114] The first is determining when a breach of contract has occurred. The second is categorizing the damages once a breach has been determined. In the case, Accenture entered into a contract with GB Gas Holdings Limited (GB) to move GB's operations to an automated billing system. The contract called for delivery of the service over five separate phases or deliverables. GB experienced substantial problems with the system after the first two deliverables. Essentially, the software was not billing customers accurately. As a result, GB had to provide compensation to its customers for poor service and, in some cases, overbilling. In others, GB suffered

[107] EC, 'Contract Study (2015)', 45.
[108] ibid.
[109] ibid., 44.
[110] ibid.
[111] ibid., 45. This was also the approach taken in France.
[112] ibid., 44.
[113] ibid., 45.
[114] *GB Gas Holdings Limited* v. *Accenture (UK) Limited and others* [2010] EWCA (Civ.) 912.

losses from under billing and incurred costs related to its additional collection efforts. In some instances, the under billed amounts were uncollectable and resulted in outright losses.

Because of the failed outsourcing, GB renegotiated aspects of the contract to take over maintenance of the billing system after Accenture delivered it. The parties were unable to agree on the scope of the problem, and Accenture denied that the problems amounted to a 'fundamental defect' under the terms of the contract.[115] GB filed suit against Accenture, asserting that Accenture was in breach of both the fundamental and material defects clauses of the contract.[116] In answering the first query, the court first determined that a fundamental breach could occur because of an aggregation of individual minor breaches of the agreement.[117] Essentially, numerous lesser breaches added up to a fundamental defect under the contract terms, giving the plaintiff, GB, additional rights to compensation.

Moving to damages, the contract between Accenture and GB contained a clause limiting certain types of direct contract claims in addition to limiting all indirect, consequential, or punitive claims. Based on this clause, the only damages GB would be able to recover were those that were direct. Applying the division of damages set out in the case of *Hadley* v. *Baxendale*,[118] the court in GB followed the judgment of the lower court, holding that the damages suffered by GB fell ' ... within the first [direct loss] not the second [indirect or consequential loss] limb of *Hadley* v. *Baxendale*'.[119] As a result, GB's damages were recoverable, including its losses in the form of gas distribution charges in the amount of £18,700,000 (based on GB's dealings with third parties), additional borrowing charges, and collection costs.[120] In other words, the court held that all of the damages resulting from the faulty billing software were direct damages and thus recoverable.[121] Therefore, in addition to direct payments for the software, the court also considered many of the connected costs from the poor performance of the software as naturally arising out of the breach.

The court took a broad approach to defining direct damages based on software failure. In particular, it found that GB incurred damages in remunerating its customers for poor service.[122] Although foreseeable, this type of damage is arguably more removed than the more closely connected costs resulting from software providing incorrect billing amounts. Even if this does not necessarily fall under the *indirect* prong of *Hadley*, in my view it moves it closer to the line. Furthermore,

---

[115] ibid., [5–6].
[116] ibid., [16].
[117] ibid., [22]. The lower court provided that ' ... the categories of Material Defects and Fundamental Defects are not mutually exclusive'.
[118] *Hadley* v. *Baxendale* [1854] 9 Exch 341.
[119] *GB Gas Holdings Limited* v. *Accenture* [2010], [29].
[120] ibid., [28–29].
[121] ibid.
[122] ibid., [29].

the case could also have an impact on CSPs migrating legacy systems to cloud solutions. While warranties in cloud are often limited to direct losses, expanding the category of what might reasonably be considered direct could substantially expand a CSP's potential liability.

Following the English case of *Hadley* v. *Baxendale*, the United States takes a similar approach to the foreseeability of damages and also focuses on 'direct' and 'indirect', or 'consequential damages', among other categories.[123] Like other common law jurisdictions, damages under contract require a higher level of certainty than under tort. The rationale for this distinction is essentially that in contract, the parties choose to enter into a relationship with each other. In tort, parties do not choose their tortfeasors or the parties that commit torts against them. Therefore, under contract, the damages that will be available are limited to events that were foreseeable when the contract was entered into.[124] Although requiring that damages be foreseeable does impose some limits, damages can go beyond the contract price and still be considered direct.[125]

How such damages are characterized is extremely fact-specific and may depend on the jurisdiction and ultimately the court. Without a clear statement of what is included (or excluded) from the agreement, there are many categories of damages that could be considered direct. For example, if a SaaS billing solution becomes unavailable, workers in the accounting department are likely to be unable to perform their core employment functions. If medical journals cannot be accessed in a hospital setting, cancellations and rescheduling of patient appointments is a natural consequence. Perhaps this would require staff overtime and adjacent expenses. Even looking at a slightly more removed issue, if a data breach occurs, the resulting reporting costs are likely direct damages.

As a general point, liquidated damages clauses are prohibited under English law if the damages amount to a penalty.[126] On its face, application of the 'penalty rule' potentially raises some questions regarding the use of certain SLA terms requiring damages in the form of service credits for a CSP's failure to perform adequately. That is, if the damages assessed when a CSP violates an SLA are unreasonably high, such a clause may be deemed an unenforceable penalty clause.[127] In that case, the SLA would be unenforceable.

However, if the damages are ' ... a genuine attempt to "liquidate," that is to say, reduce to a certainty, prospective damages of an uncertain amount ... the sum will

---

[123] European Commission (EC), 'Comparative Study on Cloud Computing Contracts: Country Report Overview Work Package 1–Annex 1' (2015), 1–429 at 421. https://op.europa.eu/en/publication-detail/-/publication/c854e3e9-8f7a-4a38-b811-46e799747858/language-en/format-PDF/source-search.

[124] Restatement (Second) of Contracts s. 351 (1981) (1) providing that '[d]amages are not recoverable for loss that the party in breach did not have reason to foresee as a probable result of the breach when the contract was made'.

[125] See generally *Wartsila NSD North America, Inc.* v. *Hill Intern, Inc.*, 436 F. Supp. 2d 690, 697 (2006). Noting that ' ... there is no general rule that direct damages are limited to the difference between the value of the product or service contracted for and the value of the product or service actually provided'.

[126] EC, 'Contract Study: Annex 1', 87–88. See Cordero-Moss, 'Boilerplate Clauses', pp. 362–64.

[127] EC, 'Contract Study: Annex 1', 87–88.

be recoverable'.[128] The 'penalty rule' was evaluated and limited by the Supreme Court of the United Kingdom in the case of *Cavendish Square Holding BV v. Talal El Makdessi* (*Makdessi*).[129] The test, as enumerated by the court in *Makdessi*, determined 'whether the impugned provision is a secondary obligation which imposes a detriment on the contract-breaker out of all proportion to any legitimate interest of the innocent party in the enforcement of the primary obligation'.[130]

Based on the court's ruling in *Makdessi*, as long as the stipulated damage protects legitimate interests, even if it is not a genuine estimate of loss, it is not a penalty when proportional. On that basis, parties may stipulate losses to be paid in the event of a breach of contract, as long as the sum is not a 'penalty' for such a breach.[131] Therefore, if an SLA clause has been negotiated and is not unreasonable (i.e. requiring a 100 per cent service credit for minor downtime of noncritical functions), then service credits will not be deemed a penalty clause.[132]

Under US contract law, 'liquidated damages' generally fall under the freedom of contract, allowing the parties to agree to a pre-determined damage amount if a contract is not preformed.[133] However, such damages must be 'reasonable in the light of the anticipated or actual loss caused by the breach'.[134] Unless the amount of the damage agreed upon is unreasonably large, it will generally be deemed enforceable. US courts might also treat service credits as a price adjustment, reflecting a reduced value of the services provided.[135] Taking that position, the service credits would not be deemed a penalty or even a liquidated damages clause.[136]

7.2.5 G-Cloud and FedRAMP Terms

Even at the level where states are negotiating terms with CSPs, exclusions for consequential, and in many cases direct, damages, are common.[137] Although

---

[128] Beatson, Burrows, and Cartwright, 'Anson's Law of Contract', p. 598. See also Cordero-Moss, 'Boilerplate Clauses', pp. 362–64. Arguing that as long as the clause makes ' … a genuine estimate of the possible damages and is not used as a punitive mechanism, it will be enforceable'.

[129] [2015] UKSC 67, [2015] 3 WLR 1373. Providing that the penalty rule is an 'ancient, haphazardly constructed edifice which has not weathered well'. ibid., [3].

[130] ibid., [32].

[131] ibid.

[132] See EC, 'Contract Study: Annex 4', 12. EC researchers also argue that English courts are reluctant to find a penalty and thus such clauses are often enforceable. See also Cordero-Moss, 'Boilerplate Clauses', pp. 362–64.

[133] Beatson, Burrows, and Cartwright, 'Anson's Law of Contract', pp. 598–99.

[134] Restatement (Second) of Contracts § 356 (1981) (1). In the United States, the ability to agree to such damages falls under the freedom of contract and is enforceable if agreed upon, but is nevertheless limited in situations where the amount is (1) unconscionable, (2) deemed an illegal penalty, or (3) violates public policy. See 'Validity of Provisions for Liquidated Damages', generally, Lord, 'Williston on Contracts', p. 24, s. 65:1.

[135] EC, 'Contract Study: Annex 4', 112.

[136] ibid.

[137] W. Kuan Hon, Christopher Millard, and Ian Walden, 'Public Sector Cloud Contracts' in Christopher Millard (ed.), *Cloud Computing Law* (Oxford: Oxford University Press 2013), p. 115.

7.2 *Liability, Conditions, Warranties, and Limiting Promises* 215

governments and CSPs have a great deal of flexibility when negotiating liability, contract terms excluding liability will face some limits, even in the B2B setting. For example, in the United Kingdom, the Misrepresentation Act of 1967 and the Unfair Contract Terms Act of 1977 apply to non-consumer contracts.[138] While courts are reluctant to interfere with contracts negotiated between professional parties, an overly broad contract exclusion (i.e. excluding liability for fraudulent misrepresentation) might be ineffective.[139] In the FOIA contracts evaluated for this book, disclaimers for damages were common in governmental cloud computing contracts, but they were generally narrowly drawn.

For example, in the G-Cloud framework agreement, the standard contract provides that ' ... neither party will be liable to the other for any ... indirect, special or consequential loss or damages'.[140] Even if states have greater negotiating power, they are often limited to direct losses or those that flow naturally from the breach of contract. Although the G-Cloud framework agreement does not limit all types of liability (e.g. material breaches, regulatory losses, fines, etc.), the call-off contract does allow the parties to limit total costs outright or base total exposure under the contract on a percentage of the contract cost. In G-Cloud contracts, CSPs generally limit total exposure to 125 per cent of the contract price.[141]

In specific G-Cloud procurements, limitations of liability for losses arising from negligence, breach of legislation (e.g. Section 12 of the Sales of Goods Act 1979), fraud, or other sources of liability are not subject to disclaimer by operation of law. In the case of the Thames Valley Police/Sprint contract, liability under the contract is limited to 'direct' losses and capped at £5,000,000, while liability from all sources (e.g. tort) is capped at 125 per cent of the contract price.[142] In addition to disclaiming all 'direct, incidental, punitive or consequential loss or damage', the contract also disclaims all 'loss of profits, business, revenue or goodwill'.[143] Other G-Cloud contracts had similar terms, given their standard nature. However, there were variances in the ability to seek damages for expenses arising from supplier default or failure to deliver a service.[144]

Even in the United States, where parties are generally given wide latitude in disclaiming warranties, there are similar limits to the disclaimer of wilful or illegal

    Initially, G-Cloud contracts did not address liability and those provisions were essentially reserved for CSPs in their agreements.

[138] Beatson, Burrows, and Cartwright, 'Anson's Law of Contract', p. 352.
[139] ibid., 353.
[140] G-Cloud Framework 12, 'Framework Agreement' (19 October 2020) RM1557.12, 12.
[141] G-Cloud Framework 12, 'Call-off Contract', 7.
[142] Sprint II Model Contract (Framework Agreement) Thames Valley Police Authority and Specialist Computing Services, 'Contract Relating to the Provision of IT Products and Services VISAV Ltd (Model Contract v 1.00)' (2012), ss. 13.1–13.1.4. Somerset and Iken Contract (2014), s. 13.4. See also EC, 'Contract Study: Annex 4', 2. In England and Wales, establishing a negligence claim generally requires: (1) a duty of care, (2) a breach of that duty, and (3) a breach causing harm.
[143] Thames Valley Police Contract (2012), s. 13.5.
[144] Somerset and Iken Contract (2014), ss. 11.5–11.5.3.

conduct.[145] Contracts entered into under the FedRAMP program generally contained similar 'public policy' exclusions to those in G-Cloud procurements. In most cases, government contracts exclude certain acts and their resulting damages (e.g. bribery or fraud).[146] Many of these limits are mandatory statutory provisions that cannot be excluded by the parties through contract.[147]

Outside of the limits of disclaiming liability, in some cases US federal agencies agreed to relatively broad disclaimers or limits of liability. In addition to the EPA term evaluated earlier, expressly disclaiming 'any and all warranties and conditions of any kind', the DoE also entered into an agreement with a similar warranty.[148] In that agreement, the DoE's integrator accepted a term from Google providing that

> To the fullest extent permitted by applicable law, except as expressly provided for herein, neither party makes any other warranty of any kind, whether express, implied, statutory or otherwise, including without limitation warranties of merchantability, fitness for a particular use and noninfringement. Google makes no representations about any content or information made accessible by or through the services ...[149]

Although the disclaimer is broad in scope, there are important differences between the DoE contract and the one entered into by the EPA earlier.[150] First, although Google excludes all other third-party beneficiaries, Google makes direct promises to the DoE and its integrator in the agreement.[151] Unlike the EPA, the DoE would be able to bring a direct claim against Google as a subcontractor in addition to the integrator primarily responsible for the service.[152] While liability is limited to direct damages and capped at the amount paid for services 'twelve months prior to the event giving rise to liability', the DoE has the ability to collect damages and enforce rights against Google.[153] Even if the DoE's integrator provided a better guarantee, it

---

[145] EC, 'Contract Study: Annex 1', 420.
[146] G-Cloud Framework 12, 'Framework Agreement', 11.
[147] See generally Restatement (Second) of Contracts s. 178 (1981) (1). Providing that a ' ... term of an agreement is unenforceable on grounds of public policy if legislation provides that it is unenforceable or the interest in its enforcement is clearly outweighed in the circumstances by a public policy against the enforcement of such terms'.
[148] EPA Office of Inspector General (OIG), 'EPA Is Not Fully Aware of the Extent of Its Use of Cloud Computing Technologies' (Report #14-P-0323, 2014), 5. www.epa.gov/office-inspector-general/report-epa-not-fully-aware-extent-its-use-cloud-computing-technologies. Henceforth EPA OIG, 'EPA Needs to Improve the Recognition and Administration of Cloud Services'.
[149] Google Inc. and Battelle Energy Alliance, 'Google Apps for Government and Postini via Reseller Agreement, "BEA-DOE Contract" US Gov't No DE-AC07-05ID14517' (25 August 2011), s. 12.2. See also Battelle Energy Alliance, LLC, and DoE, 'General Provisions for Commercial Items/Services', s. 15.4. Providing a similar broad disclaimer of implied warranties and liability to third-party beneficiaries.
[150] EPA OIG, 'EPA Needs to Improve the Recognition and Administration of Cloud Services', 5.
[151] Google Inc and Battelle Energy Alliance, 'Google Apps for Government and Postini via Reseller Agreement', s. 12.1. No third-party beneficiaries at s. 16.8.
[152] ibid.
[153] ibid., s. 15. Moreover, these limits are not applicable to breach of IP rights.

was also limited at two times the total amount paid for the agreement in the twelve months prior to the claim, or 1,000,000.[154]

7.2.6 Warranties and Limitations in Sum

Contract terms excusing parties from intentional torts or other wilful conduct are often ineffective and generally will not excuse a party from liability in either the United States or the EU.[155] CSP contract terms excluding all types of liability will face some limits, even in the B2B or Business-to-Government (B2G) setting.

While I agree with the general principle that CSPs should not be liable for acts outside of their control, there is another side to that coin. CSPs may not have control over what happens with their infrastructure providers, software suppliers, or other third parties; however, they do have control over the infrastructure provider they select. Moreover, CSPs also have some control over the contract terms they accept or negotiate with infrastructure providers.

Building on the earlier examples of the many partners used to supply a service, the SaaS CSP is in the best position to understand the resilience of the IaaS underlying its SaaS system, at least when compared to the cloud client. In the case of many services, there is little information regarding the sub-providers that supply core elements of the service (or contract terms), making it very difficult – if not impossible – for cloud clients to make an independent evaluation. Therefore, even if the CSP has little control over events that happen to its infrastructure provider, the CSP is the one with the best and perhaps the only opportunity to choose a provider with a proven track record. With the understanding that things can and do go wrong, CSPs should choose third-party providers carefully.

Perhaps the best solution would be to apportion liability between or among the many cloud service providers. Although enticing, such an approach is also problematic. In many IaaS services, the CSP is unaware of the type of data that is being stored on its service. If extremely valuable data are lost, holding the IaaS provider accountable for data it did not know existed is also unreasonable. After all, the cloud client is in a much better position to understand and account for the information it stores on the service, to properly back up data, or to obtain insurance.

7.3 VARIATION AND UNILATERAL AMENDMENT OF TERMS

Cloud computing contracts generally include a 'variation' or 'modification' clause allowing for alteration of the agreement on either a mutual or a unilateral

---

[154] Battelle Energy Alliance, LLC, and DoE, 'General Provisions for Commercial Items/Services', s. A.19. Battelle Energy Alliance also obtained insurance and named the DoE as a beneficiary/insured party. See s. C.4.5 (a).
[155] Restatement (Second) of Contracts § 195 (1981). Providing that '[a] term exempting a party from tort liability for harm caused intentionally or recklessly is unenforceable on grounds of public policy'. Carmeli, 'Keep an I on the Sky', 8.

basis.[156] In non-negotiated cloud computing agreements, CSPs generally reserve a broad right to vary or modify terms on a unilateral basis.[157] In negotiated agreements, CSPs are more likely required to follow a change or notice process before making such amendments. When a notice process is in place, it includes everything from obtaining the cloud client's written consent to posting changes on a provider's website.[158] In addition to differences in how CSPs provide notice, the contracts also vary on how much time is given before the changes become effective.[159]

For CSPs, retaining the right to unilaterally amend specific terms of the contract is often to build in a measure of flexibility for operating the service. Many of these changes are essential, such as allowing for software or security updates that are clearly beneficial to the cloud client. This flexibility may also allow the CSP to implement new technology or react to regulatory changes, such as the GDPR.

However, some variations have the potential to constitute substantial alterations that may jeopardize the cloud client's ability to meet its compliance requirements. In that regard, changes that the CSP considers minor could have a major impact on the cloud client. For a US-based CSP, adding an infrastructure partner (e.g. a data centre) in India might seem to be of little consequence. However, for the CSP's EU-based users, this would result in a breach of data protection rules if proper controls, such as binding corporate rules, were not in place.[160] Although such unilateral changes are to a large extent prohibited under consumer protection legislation in the EU, this is not the case for B2B or B2G contracts. For most governments, open-ended contracts allowing for unilateral modifications with immediate effect are unacceptable.

In addition to having a negative impact on meeting regulatory requirements, if the CSP retains wide latitude or the ability to act unilaterally regarding changes to the contract, the cloud client might have a difficult time assessing the security aspects of the service.[161] Furthermore, if a certification or standard requires that certain controls are in place, and those controls are subject to change at any time, obtaining or keeping the certification might also be difficult.

Under the G-Cloud framework agreement, once the service is included in the catalogue, variations are limited and require approval.[162] If variations are outside of the scope of the framework agreement, they are not permitted.[163] Similarly, in the

[156] Michels, Millard, and Turton, 'Contracts for Clouds, Revisited', 1–79 at 34.
[157] Chris Jay Hoofnagle and Jan Whittington, 'Free: Accounting for the Costs of the Internet's Most Popular Price' (2014) 61 *University of California Los Angeles Law Review* 611.
[158] Bradshaw, Millard, and Walden, 'Standard Contracts for Cloud Services', p. 50.
[159] Michels, Millard, and Turton, 'Contracts for Clouds, Revisited', 36–38. Ranging from immediate effect to several months.
[160] See discussion of international data transfers in Chapter 5, s. 5.6.
[161] EC, 'Contract Study', 54–56. Finding that in their standard terms, many CSPs reserve the right to unilaterally amend contract terms. In the EU, amendments must be limited to actions that are 'reasonable' or not 'surprising or substantially unfair' based on the original agreement.
[162] G-Cloud Framework 12, 'Framework Agreement', 9.
[163] ibid.

7.3 *Variation and Unilateral Amendment of Terms*

call-off contract, variation is limited and puts the burden on the CSP to show that the updates are non-material.[164] Like adding or removing subcontractors, requests must be made in writing, the variation cannot take place immediately, and the government user must have the opportunity to object and to terminate the service.[165] In some of the earlier G-Cloud contracts, the focus on variation is primarily on changes of partners in a subcontracting situation.[166] However, under Framework 12, notice and prior consent requirements are relatively robust.

Looking to procurements under the FedRAMP program, in the case of the EPA, the agency accepted a contract clause allowing the subcontracting CSP hosting the service to unilaterally change the contract.[167] Although the EPA's agreement with the primary contractor contained a clause requiring that '[c]hanges in the terms and conditions of this contract may be made only by written agreement of the parties', this term was not imposed on the subcontracted CSP actually hosting the service.[168] Therefore, the service agreement between the prime contractor and the subcontractor allows the subcontractor to make 'unilateral changes to the terms of the service agreement by posting to the subcontractor's website'.[169] By agreeing to this variation or modification clause, the EPA potentially relinquishes a great deal of control over the terms governing federal data stored by the subcontracted provider.[170] Moreover, the variation clause in the contract does not even require that explicit notices of changes be provided to the EPA.[171]

As noted in many of the studies of cloud computing contracts, is not uncommon for CSPs to reserve the right to modify the terms of the agreement unilaterally in 'free' services or those accepted on standard terms.[172] Nonetheless, it seems unnecessary for a party with significant bargaining power, such as a US federal agency, to accept such terms.[173] Even moving from subjective terms like 'any necessary changes' to the more objective 'commercially reasonable' or 'non-material' standard

---

[164] G-Cloud Framework 12, 'Call-off Contract', 31.
[165] ibid. In earlier frameworks (e.g. 3, 4, and 5), this procedure varies to some extent.
[166] Reviewing specifically: British Library and Bravo Solutions UK Ltd (10 February 2014), Ref # FIN 8895, 1–23 (drafted under 'Giii'). Somerset and Iken Contract (2014), 34, § 5.
[167] EPA OIG, 'EPA Needs to Improve the Recognition and Administration of Cloud Services', 10.
[168] ibid.
[169] ibid.
[170] Giuditta Cordero-Moss, 'Contract Practice and Its Expectations in Terms of the Governing Law' in Giuditta Cordero-Moss (ed.), *International Commercial Contracts: Applicable Sources and Enforceability* (Cambridge: Cambridge University Press 2014), p. 20.
[171] EPA OIG, 'EPA Needs to Improve the Recognition and Administration of Cloud Services', 10. David Krebs, 'Regulating the Cloud: A Comparative Analysis of the Current and Proposed Privacy Frameworks in Canada and the European Union' (2012) 10 *Canadian Journal of Law and Technology* 30, 37. Arguing that 'if terms, such as where data is stored, change without notice compliance with privacy laws vanish'.
[172] Wayne Jansen and Timothy Grance, 'NIST Guidelines on Security and Privacy in Public Cloud Computing' (2011) *Special Publication (NIST SP) 800–144*, 8. Bradshaw, Millard, and Walden, 'Standard Contracts for Cloud Services', pp. 50–55.
[173] For an example from Sweden, see Dan Jerker B. Svantesson, 'Data Protection in Cloud Computing – The Swedish Perspective' (2012) 28(4) *Computer Law & Security Review* 476–80 at 477. In evaluating

provides the cloud client with some additional control. For governments using cloud, the control provided by pre-approval obligations is essential. Comparing the approaches, the G-Cloud procedure provides much clearer coverage of the issue and greater protection for the government user.

7.4 LOCATION, JURISDICTION, AND APPLICABLE LAW: USING CONTRACTS TO MAKE THE WORLD SMALLER

Contract terms addressing the location of data storage are included in many if not most cloud computing agreements.[174] CSPs have taken a range of approaches to setting these boundaries. At one end of the spectrum, CSPs effectively reserve the right to store data in any country where they or their 'partners' are located. On the other end, CSPs guarantee that data will be stored in one specific country, a specific region (e.g. the EU/EEA), or within a larger network of providers.[175] Although CSPs tend to make some promises regarding data storage, the level of specificity and compliance guarantees varies.

As noted in Chapter 3, governments are generally concerned about the location of their data. In the FOIA contracts reviewed for this book, this was particularly evident in US government contracts. Almost all contracts reviewed made some reference – or requirement – regarding data location.[176] Similar assurances were required in the United Kingdom, where the G-Cloud framework agreement specifically provides that 'the Supplier will not transfer Personal Data outside of the EEA unless the prior written consent of the Buyer has been obtained'.[177] The G-Cloud clause further requires that the CSP has appropriate safeguards in place for making such transfers.

In addition to location of data, CSPs and governments also attempt to settle the problem of the uncertain application of choice and law to legal disputes. Almost all CSPs incorporate choice of law and choice of forum clauses into their contracts.[178] Generally, they have considerable discretion in determining the forum and the law

---

the case of a Swedish municipality contracting with Google, Svantesson provides that 'few contractual clauses so strongly indicate a power-imbalance as do clauses allowing one party to unilaterally change the terms of the contract. Indeed, on a general level, it is questionable whether a governmental actor, such as the municipality, ever should enter into a contract containing such a clause'.

[174] Kamarinou, Millard, and Hon, 'Cloud Privacy: An Empirical Study of 20 Cloud Providers' Terms and Privacy Policies – Part II', 170–72. Finding that 16 of the 20 CSPs reviewed in the study provided some information about data location.

[175] ibid.

[176] Google Inc. and Battelle Energy Alliance, 'Google Apps for Government and Postini via Reseller Agreement', s. 1.2. In a contract for a SaaS and IaaS solution between Google and a US Department of Energy integrator, Google provided that when data was 'at rest' it would only be stored in the United States.

[177] G-Cloud 9, 'Framework Agreement' (8 May 2017), s. 33.5.

[178] Michels, Millard, and Turton, 'Contracts for Clouds, Revisited', 71. Finding that the terms thirty-eight of the forty cloud services surveyed asserted that the contract was covered by the laws of a specific jurisdiction. A greater number of CSP contracts chose the law of a European country instead of a US state in 2019.

that will be applied to their dispute. Moreover, in many cases, the parties are free to determine whether they will air their disputes in a traditional court or enter mediation or arbitration proceedings. The choices made in this regard are often based on convenience, expertise in the particular forum, and the favourability of the law in the jurisdiction. In the G-Cloud Framework 12 agreement, parties must agree to 'exclusive jurisdiction of the courts of England and Wales and for all disputes'.[179]

At an EU-wide level, jurisdictional rules are found in the Brussels I regulation.[180] Rome I (contractual) and Rome II (non-contractual) regulations are the primary tools for determining the law applicable to disputes.[181] Parties may elect to apply the law of the forum they choose, but that determination is not mandatory. In certain situations, a court may apply the law of a foreign nation in a cloud computing dispute, depending on the parties' choice of law and forum.

In almost all cases, the parties to a cloud computing service will have entered into a contract for use of the service. At Article 25 (1), Brussels I provides the following:

> [i]f the parties ... have agreed that a court or the courts of a Member State are to have jurisdiction to settle any disputes which have arisen or which may arise in connection with a particular legal relationship, that court or those courts shall have jurisdiction, unless the agreement is null and void as to its substantive validity under the law of that Member State. Such jurisdiction shall be exclusive unless the parties have agreed otherwise.[182]

On that basis, professional parties have wide latitude in determining the choice of forum or the jurisdiction where a dispute will be settled on a B2B or B2G contractual basis.[183]

Although this may reduce some of the confusion and provide greater certainty or predictability, the jurisdictional problems do not go away completely. While there are some relatively straightforward cases (e.g. B2B choice of law and forum on purely contractual matters), non-contractual matters (such as intellectual property claims

---

[179] Cloud Framework 12, 'Call-off Contract', 24.
[180] Regulation (EU) No 1215/2012 of the European Parliament and of the Council of 12 December 2012 on jurisdiction and the recognition and enforcement of judgments in civil and commercial matters (recast) (henceforth 'Brussels I'). https://eur-lex.europa.eu/legal-content/EN/TXT/HTML/?uri=CELEX:32012R1215&from=en.
[181] Council Regulation (EC) No 593/2008 of the European Parliament and of the Council 17 June 2008 on the law applicable to contractual obligations (Rome I). Council Regulation (EC) No 864/2007 of the European Parliament and of the Council of 11 July 2007 on the law applicable to non-contractual obligations (Rome II). Michael Wilderspin, 'Contractual Obligations' in Jürgen Basedow and others (eds.), *Encyclopedia of Private International Law* (Online: Edward Elgar 2017), p. 475. Noting that whether an obligation arises under contract or tort is not always as clear-cut as it may appear in the Rome instruments.
[182] Brussels I at Art. 25(1).
[183] Ellen Wauters, Eva Lievens, and Peggy Valcke, 'Towards a Better Protection of Social Media Users: A Legal Perspective on the Terms of Use of Social Networking Sites' (2014) 22 *International Journal of Law and Information Technology* 254–94 at 272. With some exceptions, in the case of consumers, the general principle of the Brussels I regulation is the place where the individual is domiciled.

or torts) often fall outside of this choice. In the EU, data protection laws are applicable regardless of the contract terms.[184] Furthermore, in the EU, the rights of consumers are prioritized and a more 'protective' approach is taken than in other jurisdictions, such as the United States. Even though the parties are free to contract, EU consumer protection legislation imposes limits on that freedom.[185] The EU approach does not allow consumers to waive certain rights, regardless of the terms they accept in the contracting process. As a result, standard terms offered by CSPs will not necessarily be enforceable.

In the most straightforward cases, contracts choosing law and forum are likely very effective and the parties' choices are respected by national courts. For instance, in most B2B or B2G transactions, the parties can effectively choose the forum and law for contractual matters. However, for governments, the bigger question is whether they are willing to accept contract terms that may require that they settle their disputes in the courts of other sovereign nations. Based on the FOIA study, there appears to be a general unwillingness to do so.

7.5 TERMINATION OF SERVICES, DATA PORTABILITY, AND DELETION

When data are stored on a cloud service, the contract terms will largely define the rights and liabilities of the parties when the agreement ends. Therefore, government users must plan for the eventual dissolution or termination of the cloud service at an early contracting stage.[186] For both CSPs and government users, the term and termination aspect of a cloud computing contract is a central factor in choosing a CSP and one of the most important negotiation points. In the following section, I combine issues related to the term and to termination of a cloud computing service with problems related to portability, or walking away from the cloud service.

7.5.1 Term and Termination

When setting the term of a cloud computing agreement, the parties generally opt for either a fixed-term or a 'pay-as-you-go' model.[187] Users with complex regulatory requirements, including users in the financial industry or heath sector, generally

---

[184] For an evaluation of jurisdiction in the EU data protection context, see Chapter 5.
[185] Michael L. Rustad and Maria Vittoria Onufrio, 'Reconceptualizing Consumer Terms of Use for a Globalized Knowledge Economy' (2012) 14 *University of Pennsylvania Journal of Business Law* 1085–190 at 1116.
[186] Hon, Millard, and Walden, 'Public Sector Cloud Contracts', p. 99. Morgan and Burden, 'Computer Contracts', p. 245. Providing that termination of the outsourcing contract raises difficult problems for both the user and the provider.
[187] Hon, Millard, and Walden, 'Public Sector Cloud Contracts', p. 100. Finding that the more customized the service, the more likely the parties were to agree to a fixed term. Michels, Millard, and Turton, 'Contracts for Clouds, Revisited', 26–29. Providing an overview of termination clauses from termination without reason to termination for cause.

opt for the fixed-term category.[188] Fixed-term users, including governments, often require additional time when switching to a new provider, as they are less able to find 'off-the-shelf' standard services that meet their compliance needs.[189] The term varies, but for users with complex requirements, a contract term of one to three years, with an automatic renewal, is not uncommon.[190] Although cloud clients often have the option to terminate a contract early, doing so typically incurs expensive termination fees.[191]

In addition to their more complex deployment requirements, for governments it is often necessary to run a competitive procurement process with set timetables for placing bids and potentially bid protests. This process can greatly increase the time it takes to adopt a service. Automatic renewals, without a competitive bidding process, may not be an option under the procurement framework. From the perspective of the CSP, government procurement formalities also require a significant time commitment. Thus, longer-term agreements are often more attractive for providers. Therefore, it is not surprising that CSPs also prefer lengthier terms. For both cloud clients and CSPs providing services under the G-Cloud program, the current system of two-year terms is often seen as a barrier.[192] However, the primary reason for setting a two-year limit was to prevent locking government cloud clients into services.[193]

At a European level, EC comparative contract researchers found few specific requirements regarding cloud computing contract terms in the B2B or B2G setting.[194] Essentially, the general rule in all EU member states was that cloud computing contracts could be agreed to on a fixed-term or an ongoing basis.[195] However, a general trend was that parties could not terminate a fixed-term agreement simply for the sake of convenience (i.e. without cause).[196] In both fixed-term and ongoing agreements, setting a means for terminating the agreement is thus imperative. In many jurisdictions, including England and Wales, an ongoing contract for an undetermined period can be terminated if reasonable notice is provided.[197] Determining reasonable notice requires the application of a balancing

[188] ibid. See also Financial Conduct Authority (FCA), 'FG16/5: Guidance for Firms Outsourcing to the "Cloud" and Other Third Party IT Services' (2016), 11.
[189] Hon, Millard, and Walden, 'Public Sector Cloud Contracts', p. 100.
[190] ibid.
[191] ibid.
[192] Stuart Lauchlan, 'G-Cloud's "Biggest Single Barrier" – Two Year Contracts in a World of 13 Year Outsourcing Deals', *Diginomica*, 26 April 2016. https://government.diginomica.com/2016/04/26/g-clouds-biggest-single-barrier-two-year-contracts-in-a-world-of-13-year-outsourcing-deals/>.
[193] Hon, Millard, and Walden, 'Public Sector Cloud Contracts', p. 111.
[194] EC, 'Contract Study (2015)', 52.
[195] ibid. However, member states did have limitations for consumer contracts. Further, in some cases the contract classification (e.g. lease) might provide additional requirements.
[196] ibid. See EC, 'Contract Study: Annex 1', 160. In Germany, the expert provided '[a] service contract with more than a five-year term can be terminated for convenience after five years with a termination period of six months'.
[197] EC, 'Contract Study: Annex 1', 394–95.

test evaluating multiple factors, including market practice, the complexity and term of the relationship among the parties (i.e. standard turnkey service versus bespoke), and the timing of the termination.[198]

Where a contract lacks a termination term, a clear challenge is distilling what is 'reasonable' under the circumstances. As has been noted in other sections, best practices in cloud computing are still emerging. Therefore, reasonableness is subject to some interpretation.[199] A complex deployment where a CSP has been significantly involved in meeting a cloud client's requirements will most likely be treated differently than a standard click-through deployment. Nonetheless, there are many levels of involvement, and therefore determinations of reasonableness, in-between. In any event, if the term and notice of termination are not clearly defined in the contract, a determination of what is reasonable must be made on a less-certain basis. This has the potential to upset either party.

By contrast, contract terms that clearly define how a CSP and cloud client should part ways when the time comes can avoid uncertainty and ultimately prevent disputes during termination. In both paid and free services, CSPs generally reserve the right to suspend or terminate the service.[200] Termination or suspension may be based on non-payment for services, insolvency, or breach of other terms of the agreement (e.g. the acceptable use policy). In some cases, CSPs retain a wide range of options for terminating an agreement by broadly defining the events or actions that are considered material breaches. In the least flexible cases, such termination may take place almost immediately.[201] In others, only certain events will allow for termination and the cloud client will have a greater opportunity to find a new provider and transfer its data.[202]

For cloud clients, the events allowing for termination of the contract vary but include everything from a change of ownership or merger of the provider, insolvency or bankruptcy of the CSP, non-performance of SLA requirements by the CSP, and violations of confidentiality or data protection obligations, among others.[203] The most important aspects of the termination will likely vary depending on the cloud client. For instance, guidance for US agencies advises that they include language allowing them to terminate an agreement as a result of a data breach.[204] For governments, terms allowing the government to terminate the contract if ownership of the CSP changes (e.g. in the event that a foreign operator or government

---

[198] ibid., 93.
[199] ibid., 25. In Belgium, researchers provided that termination of an ongoing contract is a right, but must not be 'abrupt or untimely' and is further evaluated on a 'prudent person standard'.
[200] ibid., 41. In addition to payment obligations, CSPs often include breach of third-party rights and storage of illegal content as grounds for termination.
[201] Hon, Millard, and Walden, 'Negotiated Contracts for Cloud Services', p. 102. Noting that many cloud clients attempt to limit terms that allow for immediate termination following a breach of an AUP requesting terms that allow the cloud client to remedy the breach when possible.
[202] ibid., 101.
[203] ibid. EC, 'Contract Study: Annex 4', 41.
[204] CIO Council, 'Creating Effective Cloud Computing Contracts for the Federal Government', 23.

purchases the service) might be important, whereas this would have little impact on other types of users. For example, if a Russian or Chinese company were to purchase a US-based CSP, a US federal agency may find it necessary to seek out another provider.

A central concern for cloud clients are the options they have available in the case of suspension or termination of their service. Many CSPs provide very short timetables or vague schedules for removing data. In a DoE/Google contract, upon termination, Google provides the cloud client with access to Google's systems with the ability to export their data 'for a commercially reasonable period of time at Google's then-current rates for the applicable services'.[205] However, depending on the needs of the user, having a period of even six months to make the transition could pose a challenge. A requirement that the transfer take place in a shorter period may be logistically impossible.[206]

Disputes following terminations are not limited to technical problems. Applying the example of a transition period from an IT hosting service, the English case of *AstraZeneca v. International Business Machines Corporation* provides an example of the role contracts play in a transition following termination.[207] In that case, the service provider, IBM, and its client, AstraZeneca, entered into a contract for a complex multi-tenant global IT infrastructure service delivering server storage, hosting, network management, and a helpdesk.[208] The IBM solution was similar to a SaaS deployment. Before the scheduled end of the contract term, AstraZeneca terminated a seven-year, $1.4 billion MSA contract.

In addition to disputing whether AstraZeneca was entitled to terminate the service for cause or had terminated the contract for convenience, the parties disputed several aspects of the MSA contract with regard to IBM's obligations at termination.[209] Following termination of the contract, the parties disputed the scope and duration of IBM's obligations to continue to provide IT services to AstraZeneca, along with the overall cost of doing so.[210] In other words, although the MSA was clear on the fact that IBM would have some obligations to AstraZeneca following termination, the specifics of that obligation, such as which aspects of IBM's 'infrastructure' would be open to AstraZeneca and whether AstraZeneca could choose the services it would receive, were unclear.[211] Given the complexity of the global solutions provided by IBM, AstraZeneca was not able to easily transfer its global operations to a

[205] Google Inc. and Battelle Energy Alliance, 'Google Apps for Government and Postini via Reseller Agreement', s. 13.4.
[206] Bradshaw, Millard, and Walden, 'Standard Contracts for Cloud Services', p. 52.
[207] *AstraZeneca v. International Business Machines Corporation* [2011] EWHC 306 (TCC).
[208] ibid., para. 87.
[209] ibid., para. 3.
[210] ibid., paras. 26–28.
[211] ibid., para. 77. Explaining that the use of certain terms, such as what is meant by 'infrastructure', was unclear in the MSA. For instance, 'shared infrastructure' could include 'staff, infrastructure, security', and so forth. ibid., para. 87.

new provider. The court held that IBM was required to provide a broad range of services to AstraZeneca during the termination period.[212]

The takeaway from the IBM/AstraZeneca case is that a clear and well-defined exit plan is essential to preventing disputes and maintaining availability, intervenability and portability of data. The plan should include the scope of the services, the timing, and the end date, in addition to costs. For IBM as the provider, unclear terms in their MSA contract led to the requirement that they provide a much more extensive service on less certain terms during the termination period. Although IBM was required to shoulder much of the expense in that case, it also offers lessons for cloud clients and other users. Namely, they should ensure that the time frame for moving to a new service is adequate in addition to retaining access to services and functionality while the migration takes place. Additional means and contractual requirements for facilitating such a movement are further considered in the Section 7.5.2.

7.5.2 Portability

Apprehension surrounding 'lock-in', or the inability to retrieve data or move to a new service, is a serious obstacle to cloud adoption for many cloud clients, including governments.[213] Data portability refers to the ' ... ability to move applications and data from one computing environment to another'.[214] Portability limits may emanate from different sources and impact data protection, intellectual property rights, and competition law, among others.[215] Although portability issues affect different legal areas, for many users the primary barriers to movement of data from one CSP to another are contractual and technical.[216] In addition to evaluating contractual barriers to portability from the perspective of states, I also evaluate these requirements concerning the movement of personal data under the GDPR. The remit of

---

[212] ibid., para. 121.
[213] European Commission, 'Communication from the Commission to the European Parliament, the Council, the European Economic and Social Committee and the Committee of the Regions. Unleashing the Potential of Cloud Computing in Europe' (2012), 5. https://eur-lex.europa.eu/legal-content/EN/TXT/?uri=CELEX%3A52012DC0529. Stating '[p]roblems with contracts were related to worries over data access and portability, change control and ownership of the data'. Hon, Millard, and Walden, 'Negotiated Contracts for Cloud Services', p. 97. See further ENISA, 'Survey and Analysis of Security Parameters in Cloud SLAs Across the European Public Sector' (2011) *Final Report*, 44. www.enisa.europa.eu/publications/survey-and-analysis-of-security-parameters-in-cloud-slas-across-the-european-public-sector. Providing that 'it is extremely important for governments to avoid any form of "vendor lock-in"'.
[214] Fang Liu, Michael Hogan, Annie Sokol, and Jin Tong, 'NIST Cloud Computing Standards Roadmap' (2011) *Special Publication 500-291*, 38.
[215] W. Kuan Hon and Christopher Millard, 'Control, Security, and Risk in the Cloud' in Christopher Millard (ed.), *Cloud Computing Law* (Oxford: Oxford University Press 2013), p. 26. See also Aysem Diker Vanberg and Mehmet Bilal Ünver, 'The Right to Data Portability in the GDPR and EU Competition Law: Odd Couple or Dynamic Duo?' (2017) 8 *European Journal of Law and Technology* 1–22 at 6–8.
[216] Hon and Millard, 'Control, Security, and Risk in the Cloud', p. 26.

the GDPR analysis is to consider how these requirements might affect the contractual landscape between the CSP and the cloud client.

On the technical or operational side, cloud clients may have a limited ability to move to a new provider as a result of their reliance on a particular CSP. Essentially, if a cloud client's data are stored in a format that is proprietary or unique to one CSP, the data may be effectively unusable if transferred to another CSP, thereby limiting options for migration.[217] On that basis, the format in which a government's data is stored becomes a primary concern. Furthermore, for many states, there is also a cumbersome process of moving from a legacy system to a CSP or other IT-hosting provider.[218] Once data are reformatted and transferred out of a legacy system, it may be difficult to transfer it back, and if it can be transferred back, it may be expensive, particularly if a significant amount of time has passed since the legacy system was abandoned. In other words, once governments commit to a solution, they may have a difficult time moving data back in-house or elsewhere.

In addition to technical barriers, the contract may also impose limits on the cloud client's ability to freely move data. For example, removal of the cloud customer's data may be subject to a 'data hostage clause'.[219] Data hostage clauses generally require that the cloud client pay all debts and/or settle all disputes before data can be transferred from the service. Providing insurance, collateral, or another guarantee could potentially satisfy the requirement in some instances. However, if such options are not available, the cloud client has little choice but to make payment or risk losing access to its data.[220] However, if the contract is explicit on this point, making it clear that the cloud client can obtain the data in an accessible format upon leaving the service, the government user can potentially mitigate transmission delays.

In the EU, comparative contract researchers found 'no clear-cut obligation' for a CSP to return data following the termination of a service under the legislation of EU member states.[221] Although most EU member states have an obligation to delete personal data under data protection law upon termination either by law or operation of law or data processing agreement under GDPR Article 28, this does not extend to a general duty to delete all types of data or assist in moving data to a new provider.[222] The general rule across EU member states is that most portability protections must be negotiated contractually. Other jurisdictions require the CSP to act in good faith regarding the cloud client's data but did not provide any more specific requirements.[223]

---

[217] ibid.
[218] David C. Wyld, 'Moving to the Cloud: An Introduction to Cloud Computing in Government' (2009) *Report for the IBM Center for the Business of Government*, 1–82 at 22. www.businessofgovernment.org/report/moving-cloud-introduction-cloud-computing-government.
[219] Carpenter, 'Walking from Cloud to Cloud', 12–14.
[220] ibid., 3–4, 12–14.
[221] EC, 'Contract Study (2015)', 53.
[222] ibid.
[223] ibid. For example, in France, there is general requirement to act in good faith under such circumstances.

In addition to portability, or removing data from a CSP's system, an added concern is deletion of the cloud client's data from the CSP's system (and the systems of their subcontractors) after the cloud client has moved to a new provider.[224] As provided in a NIST publication, the ' ... data porting process is not complete, however, until the data is removed or erased ... the consumer's ability to delete data *is as essential* to a user's control over that data as the ability to retrieve it'.[225] This concern not only involves the CSP but also extends to the proper deletion of data from the CSP's service and the systems of its subcontractors.[226]

Regulation (EU) 2018/1807 of the European Parliament and of the Council of 14 November 2018 on a framework for the free flow of non-personal data in the European Union became applicable in May 2019. The Regulation applies to data that is not considered personal under the GDPR.[227] In addition to aiming at minimizing localization barriers, a central aspect of the regulation is portability or 'porting of data' targeting vendor lock-in.[228] The regulation does not create a right to portability as such. Rather, it requires the EC to 'encourage and facilitate the development of self-regulatory codes of conduct' to encourage portability practices.[229] These best practices are designed to provide transparent and essential information regarding the process, and technical requirements, for professional users to switch to another provider or move data to internal systems.[230]

Although perhaps a good first step, the free-flow Regulation is weak in two important areas. First, it is difficult to determine exactly when it applies. Second, it does not create a right. The Regulation focuses on the possibility to create best practices and codes of conduct. Although the self-regulatory approach may help to guide some providers to adopt policies that limit lock-in, the Regulation lacks teeth in cases where this guidance is ignored.

7.5.3 GDPR and Portability

In addition to contractual requirements negotiated between parties, the GDPR establishes a right to data portability.[231] Pursuant to this right, data subjects now have the ability to request that their data be provided in a commonly used format for transfer either to the data subject or directly to another controller.[232] This right will

---

[224] Michels, Millard, and Turton, 'Contracts for Clouds, Revisited', 31–34. Finding varied practices regarding deletion obligations including everything from180 days to unspecified.
[225] Liu, Hogan, Sokol, and Tong, 'NIST Cloud Computing Standards Roadmap', 39. Emphasis added.
[226] Hon and Millard, 'Negotiated Contracts for Cloud Services', p. 97.
[227] See Chapter 5. In particular, discussion of the far-reaching definition of personal data under the GDPR and CJEU jurisprudence.
[228] Regulation (EU) 2018/1807 Art. 6.
[229] ibid., Art. 6(1).
[230] ibid., Art. 6(1)(b).
[231] GDPR Art. 20.
[232] Paul Voigt and Axel von dem Bussche, *The EU General Data Protection Regulation (GDPR)* (Cham: Springer 2017), pp. 168–69.

thus eliminate much of the burden carried by data subjects when moving to a new provider. The point of departure of the right is to 're-balance' the relationship between controller and data subject and reduce the ability of controllers to use proprietary formats, or restrictive contract terms, for that matter, as a means of keeping customers.[233] The WP29 makes it clear that the right is not aimed at regulating competition law.[234] Rather, the portability right is intended to increase the free flow of data and foster competition between controllers.[235]

The right to portability includes two specific elements. The first element gives the data subject ' ... the right to receive the personal data ... provided to a controller'.[236] The WP29 guidance notes that 'such storage can be on a private device or a private cloud, without necessarily transmitting the data to another data controller'.[237] The second element gives the data subject the 'right to transmit the data to another controller, without hindrance'.[238] This means that, within technical limitations, the party requesting the transfer is not bound to one format.[239] Controllers are further required to produce information that is 'provided by' the data subject, including both 'data actively and knowingly provided by the data subject' (e.g. account data, name, and address) and 'observed data' (e.g. search history, traffic data, and location data).[240]

The GDPR right deals directly with some of the major portability concerns cloud clients have. For instance, the right to portability takes direct aim at data hostage clauses and preventing lock-in.[241] The WP29 opinion further provides that the ' ... controller should not reject a data portability request on the basis of the infringement of another contractual right (for example, an outstanding debt, or a trade conflict with the data subject)'.[242] Therefore, contracts requiring that all debts be paid prior to a transfer are likely unacceptable. Over and above limits on denying portability for unpaid debts, the right to portability cannot be limited or abrogated by contract terms restricting or bargaining away the right.

The WP29 opinion provides little guidance regarding the obligations of data processors, only requiring that '[t]he data controller should therefore implement specific procedures in cooperation with its data processors to answer data portability

---

[233] WP29, 'Guidelines on the Right to Data Portability 242 Rev. 01' (2017), 4. Paul Voigt and Axel von dem Bussche, 'Practical Implementation of the Requirements under the GDPR' in *The EU General Data Protection Regulation (GDPR)* (Cham: Springer 2017), p. 169.
[234] WP29, 'Guidelines on the Right to Data Portability 242', 3.
[235] ibid.
[236] GDPR Art. 20(1).
[237] WP29, 'Guidelines on the Right to Data Portability 242', 4.
[238] ibid., 5. GDPR Art. 20(1).
[239] ibid., 4. GDPR Art. 20(2). The right to have data transferred to another controller is however limited by what is 'technically feasible'. GDPR Recital 68.
[240] WP29, 'Guidelines on the Right to Data Portability 242', 10.
[241] ibid., 5.
[242] ibid., 12. Citing the requirement that data be provided to the data subject without hindrance. GDPR Art. 20(1).

requests'.[243] As most CSPs will be treated as data processors under the GDPR, the impact and scope that the right to portability will have on a CSP depend largely on the type of service it is offering.[244] In an IaaS deployment, the CSP will most likely be acting solely as a processor and will not be managing or controlling data. Therefore, the IaaS provider will not be required to fulfil portability requests. However, in the case of a SaaS deployment, responsibilities might include providing contact lists for an email provider. For a social media provider, this might include photos or information.[245] In such a deployment, the SaaS CSP will likely have greater responsibility for making such data portable than would an IaaS provider.[246]

The GDPR takes important steps for solving the portability challenge for many cloud clients. However, for most governments it offers little help in meeting their portability needs. First, the right applies only to *personal data* and focuses largely on the data subject. Second, the right only applies in situations where processing is based on *consent* or *contractual necessity*.[247] When states process data they often rely on other bases, such as a legal obligation based on national law.[248] Furthermore, as governments are generally data controllers, they will not be able to utilize the right in the same way that their citizens might request that their SaaS cloud-based email provider transfer their contact information or playlists to a new provider. Therefore, states must focus on obtaining contractual rights to data portability and will generally be unable to fall back on the right as created under the GDPR.

7.5.4 Portability Approach by States

Guidance issued under FedRAMP advises that federal agencies should make certain that when they leave the cloud service, they are able to obtain their data in a format they can access. By making the contract explicit on this point, and providing that the agency is the owner of the data it stores with the CSP, the agency can mitigate transmission delays.[249] If removal of agency data is subject to a data hostage clause, the agency may find itself paying for services that were not performed adequately just to keep operations running.[250]

For the US federal government, the problem of retaining data after the end of a service has not been a purely hypothetical one. The US Department of Labor (DoL) entered into a contract with Global Computer Enterprises (Global Computer) to

---

[243] ibid., 6.
[244] Gabriela Zanfir, 'The Right to Data Portability in the Context of the EU Data Protection Reform' (2012) 2(3) *International Data Privacy Law* 149–62 at 151–52.
[245] WP29, 'Guidelines on the Right to Data Portability 242', 8. In order to fall under the scope of the portability requirement, the data processing must be based on the consent of the data subject. GDPR Art. 6(1)(a) or GDPR Art. 9(2)(a).
[246] ibid.
[247] GDPR Art. 20(1)(a).
[248] GDPR Art. 6(1)(e).
[249] CIO Council, 'Creating Effective Cloud Computing Contracts for the Federal Government', 26.
[250] Carpenter, 'Walking from Cloud to Cloud', 3–4, 12–14.

provide a SaaS cloud computing service for financial management.[251] While providing cloud computing services for several agencies, Global Computer was under investigation by the US Department of Justice and its offices were raided by the Federal Bureau of Investigation.[252] Federal LEAs asserted that Global Computer was employing personnel prohibited from handling federal data due to their citizenship or immigration status. Legal expenses resulting from the FBI investigation played a central role in Global Computer's eventual declaration of bankruptcy, leaving the DoL with uncertain access to its data.[253]

At the time it filed for bankruptcy, Global Computer was processing over $170 billion worth of DoL transactions with its cloud application.[254] In a DoL report evaluating the risks of Global Computer's control over agency data, the DoL's inspector general noted that the DoL had not developed a recovery plan in the case of disruption of access to its financial data, which could result in 'serious consequences'.[255] In other words, the DoL had become overly dependent or locked in to its CSP.[256] Specifically, the DoL failed to 'include language in its contract that required [Global Computer] to create a data extract process and return the data to the DoL in a machine-readable form'.[257] Because the service was so highly customized, the agency was extremely dependent on Global Computer and did not have an alternative provider or the ability to complete the function in-house. The DoL determined that without access to Global Computer's employees, licences, and other intellectual property owned by Global Computer, any transition to a new provider would fail.[258]

---

[251] Debtor's Motion, Memorandum and Affidavit at para. 7, in re: Global Computer Enterprises, Inc., No 14–13290-RGM, 2014 WL 4700821 (Bnkr. ED Va. 2014). See also Jason Miller, 'Labor, GSA Forced to Buy Systems from Bankrupt Vendor', *Fed News Radio*, 8 September 2014. http://federalnewsradio.com/management/2014/09/labor-gsa-forced-to-buy-systems-from-bankrupt-vendor/.

[252] ibid. See Debtor's Motion, Memorandum and Affidavit at para. 13, in re: Global Computer Enterprises, Inc., No 14–13290-RGM, 2014 WL 4700821 (Bnkr. ED Va. 2014) (providing details on the Department of Justice investigation and legal expenses); Adam Mazmanian, 'Cloud Contractor to Pay US $9M to Settle False Claims Charges', *Washington Tech*, 8 May 2015. http://washingtontechnology.com/articles/2015/05/08/gce-false-claims.aspx (stating that GCE settled the case against it for $9 million – money that would come out of its Chapter 11 proceedings).

[253] Debtor's Motion, Memorandum and Affidavit, in re: Global Computer Enterprises, Inc., No 14–13290-RGM, 2014 WL 4700821 (Bnkr. ED Va. 2014), paras. 13–15.

[254] ibid., para. 11.

[255] US Department of Labor, 'Memorandum from Scott S Dahl, Inspector Gen, US Dep't of Labor, to Christopher P Lu, Deputy Sec'y, Dep't of Labor' (15 August 2014), 2. www.oig.dol.gov/public/reports/oa/2014/22-14-007-01-001.pdf.

[256] Bart Perkins, 'Lessons to Be Learned from a Project Nightmare', *Computerworld*, 11 March 2015, 11:00 PM. www.computerworld.com/article/2895066/lessons-to-be-learned-from-a-project-nightmare.html.

[257] ibid.

[258] Debtor's Motion, Memorandum and Affidavit at paras. 33–36, in re: Global Computer Enterprises, Inc, No 14–13290-RGM, 2014 WL 4700821 (Bnkr ED Va 2014). See also US Department of the Treasury on Behalf of the Consumer Financial Protection Bureau (CFPB) and Deloitte Consulting LLP, Contract No TDP-CFP-12-C-0008 (23 May 2012), § 16.5.

As the DoL learned the hard way, unclear contract terms regarding data ownership can cause difficulties for an agency trying to obtain its data if the CSP providing its services goes bankrupt.[259] In the case of the DoL, the SaaS contract terms with its CSP were unclear on whether data must be returned after termination of the service.[260] In its public notice justifying the contract to buy assets held by Global Computer, the agency determined that ' ... at this point in time [Global Computer] is the only source available to perform this service'.[261] Based on that assessment, the DoL did not have the ability to obtain its data or keep the system running without purchasing Global Computer's data – which also happened to be the agency's. To obtain its data and keep its services running, the DoL (and other agencies) spent over $23.5 million. In other words, the DoL spent millions of taxpayer dollars to buy back its own data.

In contrast to the US experience, the UK G-Cloud framework requires a clear 'exit plan'. The framework 12 call-off contract contains detailed requirements for migration including a strategy for exportation of government data and CSP assistance obligations to ensure there is 'no vendor lock-in to the Supplier's Service at exit'.[262] The aims of the G-Cloud obligations are to safeguard continuity of service and limit any adverse impact associated with switching. This standardized approach has clear benefits and would likely help a government agency to avoid the situation the DoL faced in its transition.

7.6 LESSONS FROM THE GOVERNMENT CONTRACT STUDY

In evaluating government cloud adoption, it is evident that certain aspects need improvement. This is particularly true in the context of US federal agencies. In the following section, I consider some of the core problems the US government encountered in procuring cloud and identify methods that ought to be included in procurement plans – specifically contracts – to improve overall cloud adoption by states. As a point of departure, I do not argue that the baby should be thrown out with the bathwater. Rather, there are many aspects of the programs, with some modification, that will provide states with functional tools for adopting cloud computing. Following the 'lessons learned' discussion in this section, I provide recommendations for improving government cloud computing contracts.

---

[259] Jill R. Aitoro, 'The Mysterious Bankruptcy Case of Global Computer Enterprises', *Washington Business Journal*, 12 September 2014, 2:36 PM. www.bizjournals.com/washington/blog/fedbiz_daily/2014/09/the-mysterious-bankruptcy-case-of-government.html (last updated 17 September 2014, 5:55 PM).

[260] Jason Miller, 'Inside the Reporter's Notebook: Labor Pinched by Poor Cloud Contracting; Financial Shared Services Progresses', *Fed News Radio*, 9 December 2013, 6:47 AM. www.federalnewsradio.com/?nid=533&sid=3521104.

[261] Public Notice, Office of the Chief Financial Officer, Department of Labor, 'Justification for Other than Full and Open Competition Financial Data Warehouse (FDW)' (2013) *Data Feed Solicitation Number: 132-1494-791*, 2.

[262] G-Cloud Framework 12, 'Call-off Contract', 26–27. Providing detailed exit plan terms.

7.6.1 FedRAMP and G-Cloud Compliance and Deficiencies

Although federal agencies procured cloud computing services under the FedRAMP program, many either failed to include terms required under the program or did not obtain compliant contracts by program deadlines.[263] In addition to failing to apply specific FedRAMP standards, noncompliance with the FARs – the US federal government's procurement requirements – was also a widespread problem among agencies. Like FedRAMP, compliance with the acquisition regulations is mandatory for federal agencies using cloud computing. The regulations provide that '[c]ontracting officers are responsible for ... necessary actions for effective contracting, ensuring compliance with the terms of the contract, and safeguarding the interests of the United States in its contractual relationships'.[264]

Although the omissions of provisions allowing agencies to inspect or audit CSPs and their subcontractors were particularly widespread, most agencies failed to negotiate other key elements in their cloud contracts as well. For example, the DoE lacked a majority of key terms in its contracts with CSPs.[265] In addition to noncompliance with general acquisition regulation standards, many agencies failed to meet cloud-specific security and organization requirements.[266]

Based on federal audits, one of the most visible agency shortcomings – arguably the most woeful case – was that of the EPA. In addition to deficiencies in meeting acquisition regulations and FedRAMP requirements, EPA contracts were missing SLA agreements, omitted NDAs, and contained contract terms inconsistent with federal best practices. For instance, the EPA failed to use an authorized CSP and did not complete a required audit.[267] An examination of USDA contracts revealed that only four of the six met FedRAMP compliance requirements by the deadline.[268] In the case of the Department of Energy, contracting officials were of the opinion that 'they were not required to comply with FedRAMP'.[269] This assumption was incorrect. As a result, the Department of Energy did not include many FedRAMP requirements in its agreements.

In some cases, the contracting US agencies negotiated terms that complied with FARs in their contract with the primary contractor but failed to impose mandatory

---

[263] Gregory H. Friedman, 'The Department of Energy's Management of Cloud Computing Activities' (2014) *Department of Energy (DoE) Office of Inspector General, Office of Audits and Inspections*, Audit Report 2.
[264] 48 CFR § 1.602-2 (2015).
[265] Friedman, 'The Department of Energy's Management of Cloud Computing Activities', 2.
[266] EPA OIG, 'EPA Needs to Improve the Recognition and Administration of Cloud Services', 18–21. Evaluating non-compliance by the EPA. Instead of supplying a specific term, many contracts contained general obligations, such as exercising 'due diligence' in safeguarding sensitive information.
[267] ibid., 20. FedRAMP requires the use of CSPs from a third-party assessment organization (3PAO).
[268] Office of Inspector General United States Department of Agriculture, 'USDA's Implementation of Cloud Computing Services' (2014) *Audit Report 50501-0005-12*, 11. www.usda.gov/oig/webdocs/50501-0005-12.pdf.
[269] Friedman, 'The Department of Energy's Management of Cloud Computing Activities', 4–5.

contract requirements on other parties, including subcontractors accessing or processing federal data. Missing mandatory requirements in the areas of access, audit, and preservation of federal data were particularly prevalent.[270] Even in areas where agreements were in place with primary contractors, the contract terms were not adequately imposed on the subcontractors actually hosting federal data.

Other agencies, including those with sensitive mandates, placed data on cloud computing systems without including proper protections in their contracts. For example, the OIG found that 'none of' the five contracts that NASA entered into 'came close to meeting recommended best practices'.[271] Among other shortcomings, NASA did not negotiate contract terms with providers and instead accepted standard contract terms.[272] These standard agreements failed to meet cornerstone requirements of FedRAMP, including federal record management, privacy, and security requirements.[273] Considering these points, the audit determined that NASA's contracting missteps had the potential to cause serious disruptions to agency operations.[274]

In short, many US federal agencies failed to account for and understand their legal obligations before adopting cloud. Additionally, they did not secure means of audit or ensure that liability/responsibility applied throughout all layers of the services and extended to the actors actually providing the service. As discussed previously, when contract terms were in place, they were often well off the mark. In the case of early US deployment, deficiencies at many levels were clearly present.

7.6.2 Government FOIA Study Bright Spots

Although I have focused heavily on the problem areas, not all aspects of implementing the US FedRAMP program were as bleak as early audits and contracts might suggest. For instance, FOIA contracts provided by the FAA contained clear requirements to include FedRAMP controls in addition to meeting specific ISO standards.[275] Moreover, the CFPB's contracts with AWS, which used Deloitte's compliance analysis toolkit to monitor contracts and cloud computing for compliance, met FedRAMP requirements in a variety of areas, including SLAs, security, and other federally mandated requirements.[276] The CFPB audit found the contracts

---

[270] Steven VanRoekel, 'Security Authorization of Information Systems in Cloud Computing Environments' (8 December 2011) *Office of Management and Budget*, 5.
[271] NASA Office of the Inspector General, 'Audit Report: NASA's Progress in Adopting Cloud-Computing Technologies' (2013) *NASA Report No IG-13-0213-5*, 12.
[272] ibid., iv.
[273] ibid.
[274] ibid., iii. Finding that on five occasions, NASA failed to address business and security risks in its cloud computing agreements.
[275] FAA and Computer Sciences Corp Contract DTFACT-15-D-0003 1–81 (26 August 2015), s. C.4.91 (FedRAMP Controls) and s. C.4.1.4 (ISO controls).
[276] Consumer Financial Protection Bureau, Office of the Inspector General, 'Audit of the CFPB's Acquisition and Contract Management of Select Cloud Computing Services' (2014) *Audit Report 2014-IT-C-016*, 2. https://oig.federalreserve.gov/reports/cfpb-cloud-computing-services-sep2014.pdf.

included clauses covering important aspect of the parties' relationship, including security and service expectations.[277] However, despite these 'bright spots', deficiencies were still present. First, the contracts did not include penalties if the CSP failed to meet terms in the SLA.[278] Second, the contracts omitted important clauses required for investigative purposes, e-discovery, and federal records requirements.[279]

In many ways, the G-Cloud program has been more effective in generating contracts that meet legal requirements. Although there are areas where G-Cloud could be improved, such as providing clearer SLA principles, overall the program has many positive attributes.[280] In short, the G-Cloud contracts were much more 'fit for purpose' than the FedRAMP agreements. In particular, the program provides units of government with less expertise, and perhaps without a dedicated legal department, to obtain compliant services. Furthermore, allowing CSPs to use their own contracts, or at least aspects of them, in the call-off phase helps to retain a level of flexibility. While the program meets standardized cloud services with contract terms that are obligatory, offering a reverse contract of adhesion of sorts, it still offers scope for adaptation. From the CSP side, it seems the biggest barrier to the public/private contract approach was the strict limit in contract duration.

The more rigid contracting structure contained in G-Cloud plays an important role in obtaining a compliant system. Although G-Cloud leaves some room for negotiation, many of the most important contractual aspects are already in place as part of the framework agreement as default rules. This clear hierarchy addresses central compliance requirements. That is, the most important privacy and security requirements were placed at the top and 'flowed down' throughout all other contracts. Even if the specific call-off agreement between the parties missed certain aspects, they were accounted for in the umbrella encompassing the entire service. Although a government unit might negotiate a contract with a suboptimal SLA, the important structural elements of the contract were in place.

An example of the advantages of using more standardized agreements was apparent in one of the UK FOIA contracts entered into by the British Library.[281] The cloud client (British Library) filling out the standard agreement did not complete many of the boxes including service levels and other information. However, even with those omissions, the contract still included essential terms regarding data protection, variation, and consent for subcontracts/contract changes, termination, and insurance, among other terms. Although the agreement was weak on requiring a certain level of service and could have encountered similar problems to US agencies in ensuring that the British Library was obtaining value for resources, the contract

---

[277] ibid., 3.
[278] ibid., 6.
[279] ibid.
[280] Hon, Millard, and Walden, 'Public Sector Cloud Contracts', p. 114. Noting that at least in the initial phases of G-Cloud, SLAs were to be covered in CSP terms.
[281] British Library and Bravo Solutions UK Ltd., Call-off terms Ref # FIN 8895 (10 February 2014), 1–23.

was not lacking essential terms in multiple areas as was common in the FedRAMP agreements (e.g. NDAs, data privacy protections, and variation limitations).

Although such an approach would be difficult for government units to negotiate individually, if a CSP wants access to UK government buyers, they have little choice but to meet the requirements of the G-Cloud framework. As noted by the CLP at QMUL, Salesforce, a major CSP, submitted 'specially tailored' standard terms to meet G-Cloud contract obligations.[282] A similar approach of negotiating 'must-have terms' with CSPs entering a store or catalogue has proven an effective means of protecting the interests of governments.[283] At the same time, at least in the EU, this method has been one of the few that has moved governments from forming a cloud strategy to actual cloud adoption.

Based on the US FOIA and UK FOIA contracts reviewed, I conclude that the G-Cloud system provides a much better 'default' contract option than FedRAMP. Furthermore, I maintain that many of the US agencies evaluated earlier would have likely obtained services that were more compliant by applying something similar to the G-Cloud framework. However, I also note that there are limitations in comparing the systems. For instance, the scope of cloud adoption under the programs is different. G-Cloud allows for much more limited deployments and adoption of cloud computing focusing on SMEs and arguably less sophisticated deployments or migrations. G-Cloud also has significant limitations with regard to the contract period (length and timing), overall value of the contracts, and the types of government services (and data) being moved to cloud. Agencies contracting under FedRAMP were often intended for more customized and longer-term deployments at the executive rather than the regional level.

Even taking into account the differences between the procurement schemes, I argue that having a clearer or standard framework or MSA agreement for all FedRAMP contracts would have led to a better outcome for federal agencies. Although arguably less flexible, the G-Cloud contracts made the obligations of the procuring parties much clearer. Furthermore, the fact that the US contracts were often higher value and longer term suggests a greater need for a G-Cloud-type approach. After all, the risk of financial and valuable data loss in the FedRAMP agreements was much greater.

Overall, governments have recognized that cloud computing technology raises a great deal of security and technical challenges. The US government has taken these security and organizational challenges seriously. NIST and other agencies have produced clear technical standards and regulations that federal agencies are required to follow. A point that appears to have received less attention is the contracts that would be used to manage legal requirements for federal agencies.[284]

---

[282] Hon, Millard, and Walden, 'Public Sector Cloud Contracts', p. 115.
[283] ibid., 111. Discussing the use of a catalogue in the G-Cloud system.
[284] VanRoekel, 'Security Authorization of Information Systems in Cloud Computing Environments', 3–4.

Guidance in this area has been very general. Therefore, many agencies failed to negotiate contract terms as anticipated in the cloud-first strategy and as required by the FedRAMP program.

Moreover, many of the FOIA contracts I reviewed from US agencies were not designed for procuring cloud services specifically or even computing systems generally. For example, many of the FOIA contracts contained precedents that were likely drafted ten or even fifteen years before.[285] When the contracts did include computer-specific terms, they focused heavily on management and ownership of software licences.[286] These terms were generally irrelevant to the services being provided. That is, in the 'pay-as-you-go' SaaS deployments the agencies were adopting, software licences were not among the services sought.[287]

To take another example, an EPA contract provided detailed requirements on copying, printing, double-sided copying, creating microform files, and other 'analog' elements in its agreement with a CSP.[288] The extreme focus in the contract on hardcopies made little sense when the EPA was contracting a system designed for digital files.[289] In fact, it is entirely possible that the only paper document that would be produced as a result of the procurement was the contract itself. The agreement was made considerably more voluminous and complex by containing terms that had little to do with the actual cloud service being procured. More importantly, despite its complexity, the contract still failed to contain terms necessary for compliance. In that regard, the EPA was not alone. Many of the contracts used by agencies included precedents that predated FedRAMP (and arguably cloud computing) by a decade or more. In other words, although the contracts were extremely lengthy, very little emphasis was placed on relevant points, such as SLAs or data portability.

7.7 CREATING BETTER GOVERNMENT CLOUD CONTRACTS

In the following section, I argue that a more standardized approach to contracting is necessary to obtain compliant government cloud services. Incorporating recommendations based on individual contract terms discussed earlier, I highlight specific steps that governments should take in creating model or standardized agreements drawing from the FOIA contract sample.

7.7.1 Standardizing Legal Requirements in Cloud-Relevant Contracts

When it comes to procuring cloud computing services, potential cloud users are often presented with a complex contract that they must evaluate for compliance

---

[285] USPS and THISMOMENT Inc., Contract #2BTCON-13-B-0075 (30 September 2013), 1–23.
[286] ibid., 20–22.
[287] ibid.
[288] EPA and AVANTI Corporation, Contract #EP-BPA-12-C-0010 (24 January 2012), s. (b–c).
[289] ibid.

based on limited resources. Even with some guidance on what the legal requirements are, understanding and incorporating these requirements in a CSP's infrastructure can be an extremely difficult task that is beyond the capacity of many users.[290] For instance, unlike national or executive government users, most municipalities do not have a full-time legal team with decades of experience in IT system procurement to examine their contracts.

Taking the example of FedRAMP, a great deal of focus is on creating a standardized process that can be applied repeatedly by agencies. However, the template or model contract provided on the FedRAMP website is only partial. When approaching a CSP, the agency has the difficult task of sorting the terms that must be included as part of the FedRAMP program and obligations based on its own internal agency requirements. In addition to applicable standards and FedRAMP guidance, the FedRAMP program provides the following list of legal requirements that federal agencies must include as 'applicable laws and regulations':

- Computer Fraud and Abuse Act [PL 99–474, 18 USC 1030]
- E-Authentication Guidance for Federal Agencies [OMB M-04–04]
- Federal Information Security Management Act (FISMA) of 2002 [Title III, PL 107–347]
- Freedom of Information Act as Amended in 2002 [PL 104–232, 5 USC 552]
- Guidance on Inter-Agency Sharing of Personal Data – Protecting Personal Privacy [OMB M-01–05]
- Homeland Security Presidential Directive-7, Critical Infrastructure Identification, Prioritization and Protection [HSPD-7]
- Internal Control Systems [OMB Circular A-123]
- Management of Federal Information Resources [OMB Circular A-130]
- Management's Responsibility for Internal Control [OMB Circular A-123, Revised 12/21/2004]
- Privacy Act of 1974 as Amended [5 USC 552a]
- Protection of Sensitive Agency Information [OMB M-06–16]
- Records Management by Federal Agencies [44 USC 31]
- Responsibilities for the Maintenance of Records About Individuals by Federal Agencies [OMB Circular A-108, as amended]
- Security of Federal Automated Information Systems [OMB Circular A-130, Appendix III]

Even for a contracting officer with a great deal of experience and expertise, elucidating the rules aforementioned and determining how they must be applied to cloud infrastructure is not a straightforward process. Moreover, if there are multiple contract officers conducting the same analysis, it is likely that they will reach a

[290] Svantesson, 'Data Protection in Cloud Computing', 477. Stating that a contract between a Swedish municipality and Google was effectively so complex that it 'constituted a breach of the applicable [Swedish] law'.

variety of conclusions. The agency must then assess how the FedRAMP requirements ought to fit with the standard contracts offered by CSPs and which aspects they must change to comply with FedRAMP and federal law. Based on agency audits, most agencies have failed to accomplish this. In some cases, US agencies did not even attempt this contract merger and simply accepted standard terms offered by the CSP (e.g. NASA).

One of the aims of FedRAMP was to move from a system of complex and costly individual security authorizations under FISMA to a system where the security authorization could be done once and then applied to many similar deployments. The goal was to move from the pre-FedRAMP scenario where a US agency individually assessed the security levels of each provider to a workflow where if a CSP passes a stringent evaluation, other agencies could procure services from that CSP without conducting a new assessment. To some degree, the same principle can (and ought) to be applied to contracting agreements.

By not providing standard contracts or model contract clauses that can easily be incorporated into contracts, the FedRAMP program risks losing some of its ability to standardize and streamline efforts. It will also require that all agencies have a high level of competence regarding the legal requirements of cloud computing to conduct the same or similar analysis. In addition to the potential for 'patchy' or uneven compliance, this will also reduce the benefits offered by standard cloud offerings. The FedRAMP program would therefore benefit greatly from a 'write once, use many times' approach to contracting.[291]

7.7.2 Incorporate Legal Requirements in Model and Standard Terms

In its audit of SLA terms, the GAO found a strong correlation between agencies that did not provide adequate guidance and contracts that did not meet federal requirements.[292] Even if agencies used third parties to assess requirements or used other tools outside of the GAO's 'key practices', when agencies lacked clear guidance, their contracts excluded or overlooked essential terms.[293] For instance, US Department of Health and Human Services (HHS) officials argued that aspects of the SLAs were unnecessary as they had their own tools, such as a disaster recovery plan, to meet best practices.[294] However, the GAO found that even with such tools, agencies need adequate terms in their contracts to 'ensure agencies have the proper control over their cloud services'.[295]

---

[291] FedRAMP promotes a 'do once, use many times' framework. See 'FedRAMP Branding Guidance' www.fedramp.gov/assets/resources/documents/FedRAMP_Branding_Guidance.pdf.
[292] GAO, 'Cloud Computing: Agencies Need to Incorporate Key Practices to Ensure Effective Performance' (2016) GAO-16-325, 17. www.gao.gov/assets/680/676395.pdf.
[293] ibid., 17–18.
[294] ibid., 18.
[295] ibid.

Governments have not been static on this issue. In the United States, there has been some movement towards more standardized terms in the FedRAMP program, including certain 'Control Specific Contract terms'.[296] While previous terms focused largely on technical aspects of the FedRAMP program, the control-specific terms contain clauses that are more detailed, such as terms that clearly provide that the agency owns government data. Furthermore, terms providing that specific protections must be in place to protect personal and sensitive data are included.[297] Even if the control specific terms are not mandatory or standard, unlike the best practices guide provided by the CIO in 2012, the template provides specific clauses rather than provide a general list of principles. In my judgment, this is a step in the right direction.

7.7.3 Including Core Requirements for Every Contract

In addition to incorporating legal requirements and building better model or standard terms, governments should also include terms that adequately limit CSPs. These limits are necessary to meet data privacy requirements, among others. By separating 'flexible' from 'nonflexible' requirements, states will be in a better position to determine what their contracts must contain. For instance, 'flexible' terms could be drafted as model terms that states would adopt either 'as is' or amend the terms following negotiations with CSPs. 'Nonflexible' terms would be provided as boilerplate or standard terms, requiring adoption without alteration.

Governments might address these terms through a framework/call-off type structure (e.g. G-Cloud), as part of an MSA, or another contract schedule or attachment (e.g. FAA). For instance, following the G-Cloud structure, terms that limit practices that are nonflexible requirements, or 'deal-breakers', from the point of view of the government user would be included in the framework portion. The flexible terms would then be contained in the negotiable portion of the contract. Whatever the contract structure, making certain these core or foundational requirements are in every contract is an elementary requirement, in my view.

Specific examples in this area of 'nonflexible' terms might be those requiring NDAs, statutory obligations incorporating data privacy and other laws, access and geographical limits (including limiting data transfers), notification of data breaches, and audit requirements. These would also include contract terms limiting the ability of CSPs to add or change infrastructure or partners without consent. In addition, other nonflexible areas might include archive or record retention requirements. In the case of US agencies, they might also include model terms requiring specific retention periods of ESI, e-discovery, and other audit requirements making certain

---

[296] FedRAMP Standard Contract Language (27 June 2012). www.fedramp.gov/files/2015/03/FedRAMP_Standard_Contractual_Clauses_062712_0.pdf. See also General Services Administration (GSA), 'FedRAMP Control Specific Contract Clauses: Version 2.0' (6 June 2014).
[297] ibid.

that data are available in the case of litigation as well as for other purposes, such as FOIA requests and archive requirements. For EEA-based public administrations, terms on data transfers and locations for data processing in addition to other GDPR specific obligations.[298]

Flexible terms, or those left open to allow for a greater deal of negotiation, might include those related to functionality, SLAs, delivery timelines, and price. Liability caps, limits on damages, and insurance requirements could also be part of the negotiation. Terms in this category would reflect areas where the cloud client could conduct its own assessment and determine how important uptime or availability would be and negotiate on price accordingly.

7.7.4 Terms That Limit CSPs: Meeting Compliance Requirements

Together with the terms provided for in the FedRAMP program, individual US agencies added additional layers of contract terms applicable to their use of cloud computing. For instance, the DoD and the USPS have released terms containing specific clauses on areas not included in either the FedRAMP control-specific terms or the best practices guide. The USPS has drafted standard terms aimed at protecting agency data from being repurposed for behavioural advertising or other commercial purposes.[299] The term further provides that 'The CP [CSP] must not analyze Postal Service data anonymously and use it for their purposes or share it with third parties'.[300] Here, the USPS makes the point that even if a CSP makes the data 'anonymous', it cannot be repurposed.

The USPS's internal rules require that all servers, including backup servers, reside in the contiguous United States because 'data stored outside of the US cannot be protected under the Privacy Act'.[301] I disagree with the notion that the location of data is determinative of whether privacy protections are adequate.[302] However, if the internal rules of the agency require that this term be included, it ought to be included in a contract. A standard or a model term that clearly elucidates this requirement will likely have a much broader impact on compliance than a document setting out general principles.

The DoD also updated selected contract terms in a class deviation providing terms that must be included in any cloud computing contract.[303] In addition to

[298] Michels, Millard, and Turton, 'Contracts for Clouds, Revisited', 70–71. Finding CSPs are providing more tailored localization clauses for European customers.
[299] USPS, 'Cloud Security', 60.
[300] ibid., 39.
[301] ibid., 41. See Segall, 'Jurisdictional Challenges in The United States Government's Move to Cloud Computing Technology', 1138–39.
[302] W. K. Hon, *Data Localization Laws and Policy: The EU Data Protection International Transfers Restriction through a Cloud Computing Lens* (Cheltenham and Northampton, MA: Edward Elgar 2017), p. 274. Explaining logical and physical security.
[303] US Department of Defense, 'Cloud Computing Security Requirements Guide' (2017), 3–5. https://rmf.org/wp-content/uploads/2018/05/Cloud_Computing_SRG_v1r3.pdf.

being obligatory, the terms generally require a more restrictive use of government data than the control-specific contract terms provided in the FedRAMP template.[304] For instance, the DoD terms include an expanded definition of government data.[305] In addition to broadly defining government data, the term specifically limits processing to 'the operational environment that supports the government data and for no other purpose unless otherwise permitted with the prior written approval of the Contracting Officer'.[306] Like the term added by the USPS, federal agencies are concerned that their data may be repurposed and used for other objectives.[307] These may include targeted advertising, among other commercial uses.[308]

Like the USPS guide, the DoD terms focus on not only limiting use of data to primary contractors but also ensuring that other suppliers and subcontractors with access are bound by the same terms.[309] These additional obligations are designed to ensure that back-to-back contract terms are in place that will flow down and create a chain of clear obligations for security. Moreover, it provides for a clear line of liability if a partner or supplier misuses DoD data. The DoD has also acknowledged the need for privity of contract with CSPs hosting data elsewhere and provides that if subcontracting occurs, the agency should ensure that the prime contractor retains 'operational configuration and control of DoD data'.[310] Similar terms could help to limit oversights like the broad exclusions for CSP subcontractors accepted by the EPA discussed earlier.

Additional terms like those offered by the USPS and the DoD may increase security. However, requiring CSPs to take into account the detailed changes required by each federal agency may have the effect of reducing the cost savings and flexibility the government is trying to achieve in its cloud-first strategy. In particular, the efforts placed on making the FedRAMP strategy flexible and reusable will be diluted if each agency requires significant changes after the CSP overcomes the initial FedRAMP hurdle. Stated differently, agency individualization runs the risk of altering the program from a 'do once, use many times' to simply a 'do many times' authorization and contracting process. Therefore, although I argue later that maintaining flexibility is important, a balance must be struck.

---

[304] ibid., 3–5.
[305] ibid., 3.
[306] ibid., 4. Including 'unauthorized transfer of classified data or controlled unclassified information to an information system that is not accredited for the applicable security level of the data or information'.
[307] Carol M. Hayes, Jay P. Kesan, and Masooda N. Bashir, 'Cloud Services, Contract Terms, and Legal Rights' (2013) 17 *Journal of Internet Law* 244.
[308] Joshua S. Parker, 'Lost in the Cloud: Protecting End-User Privacy in Federal Cloud Computing Contracts' (2012) 41 *Public Contract Law Journal* 385, 407–08. Citing the federal government's failure to obtain contract terms prohibiting CSPs from using personal stored on the services for commercial purposes.
[309] DISA, Cloud Computing Security Requirements Guide', 4.
[310] ibid., 24. For a description of privity of contract in the United States, see Gregory Klass, *Contract Law in the United States*, 2nd ed. (Alphen aan den Rijn: Kluwer Law International 2012), p. 161. Providing generally that a contract confers legal rights and imposes legal obligations only on individuals who are parties to the contract.

7.7.5 Retaining Flexibility

Despite the fact that I advocate for a high level of standardization throughout this book, it is also important to note that an overly standardized approach may be unrealistic, and even undesirable, when applied to the cloud computing market. Even if standardized agreements provide some certainty through uniformity and reduced transaction costs, requiring rigid agreements would limit the flexibility of governments to take advantage of diverse cloud offerings. Although it might be an option for some government programs, generally the approach that one contract must be developed and applied to all transactions is unnecessarily rigid. Therefore, standardization of the agreements must recognize that the mandates of government agencies differ and should therefore contain the requisite flexibility to account for them. For instance, some agencies deal with extremely sensitive data while others do not. In some cases, although it may be confidential, the data the agency stores are not personal data. Therefore, a more clearly defined baseline, or catalogue of several agreements based on sensitivity or presence of personal data, could go a long way in reducing the customization needed by each agency. Raising the floor for all CSPs and providing specific minimum terms, even if within a range, is a starting point.

Agencies contracting for cloud also need a measure of flexibility to address the evolution of cloud technology in addition to changing needs within agencies. Even the best-planned procurement system and accompanying contracts are unable to predict the needs of parties on all sides.[311] This is particularly true if cloud computing services are employed by agencies over many years, as the technology and needs of the users will likely change. If FedRAMP terms become inflexible, they may have the unwanted result of limiting the uptake of cloud computing or significantly reducing the advantages of cloud. Inflexibility, particularly in reference to terms, has been one of the major criticisms of G-Cloud.

Providing core terms that are more specific than the FedRAMP best practices guide has the potential to reduce agency oversights.,. After all, the data being placed in the cloud by governments are extremely valuable, and the risk of loss has significant monetary and privacy implications. But the risks are variable among agencies, and the terms of standard contracts should reflect this.

7.7.6 Audits, Inventories, and Monitoring

If monitoring is adequate, acceptable contractor performance should follow.[312] In reality, adequate monitoring of government contracts is rare as it is expensive and often difficult to conduct.[313] In the opaque structure of cloud, such monitoring (e.g.

---

[311] Hon, Millard, and Walden, 'Public Sector Cloud Contracts', pp. 109–12.
[312] Wendy Netter Epstein, 'Contract Theory and the Failures of Public-Private Contracting' (2013) 34 *Cardozo Law Review* 2211–60 at 2249. Arguing that adequate monitoring rarely takes place in public-private contracting.
[313] ibid., 2249–50.

auditing CSPs) poses additional challenges. Unlike physical goods, in cloud computing, a high level of technical expertise and provider cooperation is required to monitor and ensure performance.

Therefore, in addition to specific promises regarding delivery (SOW, SLAs, etc.), the contract terms should also contain requirements that the CSP actively assist the government in measuring and ensuring performance. This would most likely include keeping records or logs, developing reporting tools, and providing access to such information – either directly to the government or to a third-party auditor. Standards and certification schemes could form the basis for such performance audits.

7.7.7 *The Answer to the Contract is the Contract*

As noted by Epstein, '[t]he prevailing sentiment in the academic literature is that private, profit-maximizing firms should not be entrusted with providing government services absent safeguards because profit-maximizing goals conflict with public service values'.[314] Epstein suggests that the answer to this contractual problem is the contract itself. More concretely, that governments should create a contractual duty of the parties to act 'in the public interest' when carrying out contracted obligations on the government's behalf.[315] Such a mechanism would provide an objective or heightened duty of good faith requiring the supplier to act in good faith on behalf of the government and its citizens.[316]

Many contractual frameworks used by governments include a statement of objectives or general policy statement regarding the agreement.[317] However, Epstein and others suggest taking this a step further. For instance, Aman and Dugan have also suggested that agencies could approach accountability problems by requiring additional procedures at the formation of the contract and embed those values throughout the entire agreement.[318] In particular, they could require that the content of the contract terms require providers to protect individual rights.[319] Furthermore, standard contracts might expand enforceability measures by allowing citizens to bring actions directly against providers as third-party beneficiaries.[320]

Implementing the views of Epstein and others would have a clear impact on cloud computing contracts. Although it might be a difficult negotiation point, requiring

---

[314] ibid., 2215.
[315] ibid.
[316] ibid.
[317] Gian Luigi Albano and Caroline Nicholas, 'The Design of Framework Agreements' in Caroline Nicholas and Gian Luigi Albano (eds.), *The Law and Economics of Framework Agreements: Designing Flexible Solutions for Public Procurement* (Cambridge: Cambridge University Press 2016), p. 311.
[318] Alfred C. Aman and Joseph C. Dugan, 'The Human Side of Public-Private Partnerships: From New Deal Regulation to Administrative Law Management' (2017) 102 *Iowa Law Review* 883–937 at 916.
[319] ibid.
[320] ibid.

CSPs and their subcontractors to act in the interests of citizens would perhaps present the clearest means of protecting those interests. For example, if the contract required that the CSP act as a fiduciary of sorts when considering how citizen data are processed and protected, the CSP would be more inclined to make certain to choose reliable subcontractors and apply terms on a back-to-back basis. Such a term could also include transparency requirements. Additionally, giving the citizen the right to bring suit directly for violations against the provider would provide a means of holding CSPs accountable. This would be particularly useful in areas where government contractors are the beneficiaries of sovereign immunity, and the data subject citizen has little in the means of direct recourse.

The IBM/Indiana case evaluated in Chapter 3 demonstrates the benefits of having a public policy clause in an outsourcing contract. In that case, Indiana terminated its contract with IBM for cause based on a breach of contract theory.[321] A central issue in the case was whether IBM materially breached the contract. In making its determination, the court placed a great deal of emphasis on certain 'policy objectives' enumerated in the contract. The policy objectives focused on providing 'accurate', 'timely', and 'efficient' services to citizens, in addition to general compliance obligations.[322]

The Indiana case is important for governments adopting cloud for a couple of reasons. First, it raises the preliminary question of what types of services (or data) are appropriate for cloud computing. If a government moves services to the cloud that provide the gateway to medical care and food for its neediest citizens, and those systems fail, the consequences are likely to be serious. This is particularly true for needy populations as they are often in the worst position and have the least capacity to assert their rights and inform the government of failures.[323] Second, contract terms are extremely important to protect the interests of citizens. Without clear policy objectives making citizens the focus of the contract, Indiana might have faced a much different situation. Although the citizens were not directly named as beneficiaries in the contract, their rights were included by applying the policy objectives as part of the standard for breach of the agreement.

---

[321] *State v. IBM*, 51 NE 3d 150, 157 (2016).
[322] ibid. The objectives as summarized by the court include: '(i) to provide efficient, accurate and timely eligibility determinations for individuals and families who qualify for public assistance, (ii) to improve the availability, quality and reliability of the services being provided to Clients by expanding access to such services, decreasing inconvenience and improving response times, among other improvements, (iii) to assist and support Clients through programs that foster personal responsibility, independence and social and economic self-sufficiency, (iv) to assure compliance with all relevant Laws, (v) to assure the protection and integrity of Personal Information gathered in connection with eligibility determination, and (vi) to foster the development of policies and procedures that underscore the importance of accuracy in eligibility determinations, caseload integrity across all areas of public assistance and work and work-related experience for Clients in the Programs'.
[323] Aman and Dugan, 'The Human Side of Public-Private Partnerships', 897.

7.8 CONTRACT STUDY CONCLUSION

Accounting for all aspects of the cloud computing life cycle contractually requires careful planning. As early as the pre-contractual phase, governments must consider the eventual dissolution or termination of the cloud computing service they are using. Whether the termination is a result of contract expiration, bankruptcy of a CSP, or even non-performance or breach of contract, the agreement must provide the terms necessary to make a smooth transition of government data back in-house or to another CSP. Vague or missing terms in cloud computing agreements might make a smooth transition, or any transition, difficult. Not only is attempting to address overlooked contractual and security issues retroactively difficult and less effective, but it also carries with it extra risk and expense.

In the audits of US federal agencies, the central question was whether the contracts agencies entered into contained adequate controls to meet agency needs in the areas of data privacy, data security, availability, and access, while at the same time protecting federal investment. The answer for most agencies, at least based on early contracts and agency audits, was a clear 'no'. The audits showed that the vast majority of agencies using cloud computing lacked the necessary contractual mechanisms for monitoring agreements and assessing the delivery of the service. The range of the missing terms, and the laws that certain terms conflicted with, was surprising in the audit. From the failure to define services as cloud computing to incomplete inventories of services, the organization and general communication of the US cloud-first strategy was problematic.

In the case of the UK G-Cloud deployment, the contracting scheme was a central component of the strategy. The framework and call-off contracts provided terms that protected government and citizen interests, but were also flexible enough to ensure that the CSPs were still interested and able to offer their services to government clients. However, as noted in the comparison, G-Cloud deployments were also generally more limited in scope, content, and duration. Expanding G-Cloud offerings and replacing major IT systems with CSP offerings will likely require a contracting structure that is more flexible in duration and in scope than is currently applied in G-Cloud.

This begs the question: what improvements or changes ought to be made in order to increase compliance generally? First, guidance that is more concrete and includes specific requirements should be provided to the government entities or agencies adopting cloud computing services. Part of this package should also include standardized or model contract terms. Such contracts ought to be drafted by the government agencies with the most expertise in procuring cloud computing and then applied widely. This approach has the potential to greatly increase agency compliance and reduce the patchwork of implementation seen in the initial adoption of cloud by US agencies.

Over and above increasing compliance, providing individual governmental units with less discretion in the contracts they use when adopting cloud computing services might also prove an effective tool for negotiation. If agencies are able to offer their terms to CSPs on a take-it-or-leave-it basis, they have a much greater opportunity to influence the market. Reliance on best practice guides or other sets of general principles – instead of mandatory or prepared clauses – appears to have resulted in uneven compliance in the US FedRAMP program. Although the FOIA contract sample was more limited, the UK G-Cloud deployment did not seem to suffer from the same weaknesses. Even where G-Cloud FOIA contracts seemed to be completed haphazardly, they contained essential terms.

Although the initial round of cloud computing adoption under FedRAMP was bumpy, there is cause for optimism. Many of the contracts initially adopted by federal agencies were for relatively short terms, giving agencies the ability to renegotiate their agreements and obtain more compliant services in the near future. While I argue that the G-Cloud system was more successful, at least from a legal/compliance position, it also faced some early hurdles requiring adaptation. As governments become more accustomed to contracting for cloud computing and have better tools with which to obtain compliant contracts, the oversights noted in the initial adoption are less likely to recur. However, as governments expand the use of cloud computing services to perform government functions, contract terms will remain key in not only compliance but also protecting the interests of citizens.

8

Conclusion

This book examined the challenges that governments face when moving to cloud computing solutions. The central question asked was whether governments can adopt cloud computing services and still meet their legal requirements and other obligations to citizens. Assessing this question involved considering the interplay of the technical properties of cloud computing services with the numerous and complex legal requirements applicable to cloud adoption and use. The challenge of addressing contracting and procurement requirements, data privacy, and jurisdictional obligations when using an opaque, global, multi-tenant technology such as cloud computing is sizeable.

Although contracting for cloud computing services differs from more traditional IT outsourcing, it does not radically depart from the contracting models used in IT outsourcing. That is, cloud computing does not necessitate a new or sui generis category of contract. The doctrine of contract in its present form is sufficient to accommodate cloud computing. Even though cloud computing services may be complex and multi-layered, IT outsourcing and construction contracts have long been able to accommodate or to meet the needs of such dispersed networks of partners and subcontractors.

Despite its challenges or problem areas, cloud computing does not break the mould of the contracting model. Thus, although 'blockchain' and 'smart contracts' may very well be of great utility and merit further research in the cloud computing context, the traditional doctrine of contract in its present form is sufficient to meet the needs of governments in procuring cloud computing services. However, the substance of the contract must account for the legal and other obligations governments have. This requires acknowledging that data storage and processing operations differ from the storage of paper documents. In some areas, government contracts failed to account for the unique properties of data.

Given their purchasing power, my initial premise was that government agencies procuring cloud were likely obtaining compliant contract terms that could be transferred into models for municipalities and eventually B2C, B2B, and other agreements. However, this hypothesis was challenged by the findings based on FOIA contracts, particularly those regarding early FedRAMP adoption. In the case of US government procurement, there was a considerable compliance gap between the legal requirements and terms of the contracts.

When it comes to the growth and adoption of cloud, I am of the opinion that it is in many ways the future of IT. In a sense, there is a certain inevitability of cloud computing. That is, the decision to use cloud computing will become less of a choice in the future for many users. In reviewing service offerings, it is often difficult to find a service not built on Amazon, Google, or Microsoft infrastructure. Many software companies are abandoning the traditional model of providing users with a copy of their software, and giving them the responsibility for its installation and management, in favour of a cloud-based delivery model. In short, if a government, or a citizen for that matter, wants access to certain software or applications, they will have no choice but to have that product delivered via cloud computing.

However, unless other necessary conditions such as procurement plans or certification schemes incorporating adequate measures to ensure that legal requirements are in place, the advantages to be gained by having greater purchasing power will not result in states obtaining compliant cloud computing systems. In other words, even with their greater purchasing power, states must recognize and understand how cloud computing diverges from traditional IT outsourcing services and then make plans for obtaining the necessary concessions to accommodate these variances. Although my focus and findings in this area are largely based on US and UK agency contracts, the lessons have wider implications.

Governments must be aware of what they need, what they are buying, and where those two points diverge. If a gap exists, can it be filled with additional security, a contractual guarantee, a code of conduct or standard, or perhaps an assurance from a third-party auditor or cloud access security broker? I am of the opinion that the answer is generally a combination of the aforementioned. That is, states must generally approach these challenges through a combination of contracts, standards, and technological measures. When compared against a 'perfect' solution, moving to cloud computing can be daunting. However, if governments compare moving to cloud from their current outsourcing practices, bridging the gap is much more manageable.

8.1 DATA PRIVACY AND DATA PROTECTION

Many of the technical barriers to cloud computing adoption have been solved. However, legal barriers remain. Contracts will continue to play a central role in filling the gaps where legislation is an inappropriate or inadequate means of governing cloud computing services. In my view, the GDPR will continue to play an important role in assisting cloud computing clients in obtaining better contract terms and an improvement of the services more generally. It will also continue to raise the global standard for privacy. Moreover, it is no longer enough for CSPs to convince cloud clients that they are compliant. Given that the GDPR places direct statutory obligations on CSPs, they are now in a position similar to that of cloud clients. CSPs must also demonstrate to regulators that they meet the requirements of the GDPR. In other words, data protection is no longer solely a marketing challenge for CSPs – it is also a legal one.

On a more general note, if there is a current mantra in the law and IT field, it is that 'data is the new oil'. However, regardless of whether we believe that data actually carries such a high value, it has generally been treated in a manner that is less than befitting. If this new 'oil' is truly a valuable resource, then why is it often very poorly secured, shared widely, and obtained using questionable practices? If data breaches were oil spills, the seas would be black. Unlike oil wells, data subjects – the sources of this 'new oil' – have fundamental rights. These rights often fare poorly when weighed against the economic opportunities that exploitation of the data presents. As demonstrated in recent years, particularly with the Cambridge Analytica scandal, disregarding data privacy and individual rights has broader consequences for democracy and ultimately society as a whole.[1]

Although it might be naïve, I am also hopeful that we are reaching a turning point. As a resource, oil was arguably haphazardly managed during its early exploitation and market development. However, after encountering major spills and other such incidents, the need for greater regulation and changes in how the resource was treated became apparent. Globally, there is now a much wider appreciation for privacy and data protection. This discussion recognizes the importance of treating data carefully and seems to recognize its value both to individuals and the system.

For example, in 1999, Scott McNealy, chairperson of Sun Microsystems, stated '[y]ou have zero privacy anyway. Get over it'.[2] Ten years later, in 2009, former Google CEO Eric Schmidt similarly argued '[i]f you have something that you don't want anyone to know, maybe you shouldn't be doing it in the first place'.[3] Although the statements made by McNealy and Schmidt were controversial in both 1999 and 2009, they were perhaps not uncommon viewpoints. Moving forward another decade, in 2021, there is arguably much less room to make such statements. The overall value of data protection and privacy are much more broadly recognized now. Privacy is no longer viewed as a right that people are not concerned with protecting.

---

[1] Elizabeth Denham, 'Investigation into the Use of Data Analytics in Political Campaigns' (11 July 2018) *United Kingdom Information Commissioner (ICO) Report*, 16–27. https://ico.org.uk/media/action-weve-taken/2259371/investigation-into-data-analytics-for-political-purposes-update.pdf.
[2] Newton Lee, 'Social Networks and Privacy' in Newton Lee (ed.), *Facebook Nation* (New York: Springer-Verlag 2013), p. 13.
[3] ibid.

8.2 GOVERNMENT CLOUD PROCUREMENT

Throughout the book, I point out many of the concerns that are present in outsourcing government data and processes to cloud computing. However, I do not maintain that the process can simply be stopped or that states should reverse this trend and begin building, operating, and running their own dedicated cloud systems. Not only would this be unrealistic given the current trends, but it also would not necessarily provide government users with better security or more control over their information assets. Nonetheless, that does not mean that the processes used to procure cloud systems and the frameworks for holding outsourcing providers accountable are adequate. It also does not mean that *all* types of data should be hosted by CSPs. As in the offline world, some government functions (such as the operation of corrections facilities and providing certain welfare services) are poor candidates for outsourcing.

The focal point for governments ought to be how they can improve upon the cloud computing systems they adopt. This includes accounting for legal constraints, meeting accountability and transparency requirements, and finding service providers that assist governments in adhering to their legal requirements while also minimizing their more systemic data sovereignty risks. After all, the stakes are high for governments. In addition to a loss of availability or access, a loss of control over data may limit a state's ability to carry out its core functions. Thus, governments have a clear obligation to make certain that citizen data are secure and that the privacy rights of citizens are also weighted heavily when making outsourcing decisions. In addition to mitigating concrete risks such as unavailability, governments also have a duty to minimize the risks or harm emanating from providers that are unable or uninterested in supporting democratic norms.

Even if it is an important factor or a necessary condition for implementing legal requirements, technology alone will never be sufficient to obtain compliance. In that regard, contracts will remain an important tool. By improving their application to cloud computing subject matter and implementation, they will continue to provide the primary means of regulating the relationship between the parties.

8.3 LOOKING FORWARD

Cloud computing may eventually result in substantial savings, but this must be preceded by adequate levels of investment. Like the IT hosting services they will potentially replace, good cloud computing systems are complex and must be implemented correctly. While individual consumers may decide to pay for the services they use with their privacy (knowingly or otherwise), governments should not take the same risks with their citizens' personal information. Thus, governments must negotiate contract terms that honour their legal requirements and allow them to fulfil their duty to their citizens. In many cases, cloud computing makes complex data processing easy. However, it is the job of governments to make certain that it is also done correctly.

Based on my observations of contracts and government audits from the time I began researching in this area, I am optimistic. The contracts have become better. Government audit reports, at least in the United States, have shown a great deal of improvement. A focus on security has grown, and the EU has invested significant sums into increasing understanding of and developing tools for implementing privacy into cloud computing services.

However, the stakes are continually being raised. Since I began research in this area in 2012, the move to adopt cloud computing by governments has only intensified. The US Department of Defense has awarded a $10 billion cloud contract called the Joint Enterprise Defence Infrastructure (JEDI) to Microsoft. Under the contract, Microsoft will have the sole responsibility for delivering cloud computing to the Pentagon.[4] The JEDI cloud will be primarily used by the US military, allowing communication among the branches. As noted in Chapter 3, intelligence services in the United States are also spending billions of dollars on cloud solutions. The UK G-Cloud programme has become increasingly popular, and its share of UK public sector users has continued to increase. As governments work to implement their cloud computing strategies and expand their use of cloud, they must also be realistic about the price that must be paid in exchange, not only in terms of legal tender but also privacy, sovereignty, transparency, and accountability.

---

[4] Kate Conger, 'Pentagon Sticks With Microsoft for Cloud Computing Contract', *New York Times*, 4 September 2020. www.nytimes.com/2020/09/04/technology/jedi-contract-microsoft-amazon.html.

References

LEGISLATION

European Legislation

Charter of Fundamental Rights of the European Union [2012] OJ C 326, 391
Directive 95/46/EC of the European Parliament and of the Council of 24 October 1995 on the protection of individuals with regard to the processing of personal data and on the free movement of such data [1995] OJ L 281, 31
Directive 2000/31/EC of the European Parliament and of the Council of 8 June 2000 on certain legal aspects of information society services, in particular electronic commerce, in the Internal Market [2000] OJ L 178, 1
Directive 2002/58/EC of the European Parliament and of the Council of 12 July 2002 concerning the processing of personal data and the protection of privacy in the electronic communications sector (Directive on privacy and electronic communications) [2002] OJ L 201, 37
Directive 2011/83/EU of the European Parliament and of the Council of 25 October 2011 on consumer rights, amending Council Directive 93/13/EEC and Directive 1999/44/EC of the European Parliament and of the Council and repealing Council Directive 85/577/EEC and Directive 97/7/EC of the European Parliament and of the Council Text with EEA relevance [2011] OJ L 304, 64
Directive 2014/25/EU of the European Parliament and of the Council of 26 February 2014 on procurement by entities operating in the water, energy, transport and postal services sectors and repealing Directive 2004/17/EC Text with EEA relevance [2014] OJ L 94, 243
Directive (EU) 2016/1148 of the European Parliament and of the Council of 6 July 2016 concerning measures for a high common level of security of network and information systems across the Union [2016] OJ L 194, 1
Regulation (EC) No 864/2007 of the European Parliament and of the Council of 11 July 2007 on the law applicable to non-contractual obligations (Rome II) [2007] OJ L 199, 40
Regulation (EC) No 593/2008 of the European Parliament and of the Council of 17 June 2008 on the law applicable to contractual obligations (Rome I) [2008] OJ L 177, 6
Regulation (EU) No 1215/2012 of the European Parliament and of the Council of 12 December 2012 on jurisdiction and the recognition and enforcement of judgments in civil and commercial matters (recast) [2012] OJ L 351, 1

Regulation (EU) 2016/679 of the European Parliament and of the Council of 27 April 2016 on the protection of natural persons with regard to the processing of personal data and on the free movement of such data, and repealing Directive 95/46/EC (General Data Protection Regulation) (Text with EEA relevance) [2016] OJ L 119, 1

European Commission Decisions

Commission Decision 2000/520/EC on the adequacy of the protection provided by the safe harbour privacy principles and related frequently asked questions issued by the US Department of Commerce [2000] OJ L215/7

Commission Decision of 15 June 2001 on standard contractual clauses for the transfer of personal data to third countries, under Directive 95/46/EC (2001/497/EC) [4 July 2001] OJ L181/19

Commission Decision of 27 December 2001 on standard contractual clauses for the transfer of personal data to processors established in third countries, under Directive 95/46/EC (2002/16/EC) [10 January 2002] OJ L6/52

Commission Decision of 27 December 2004 amending Decision 2001/497/EC as regards the introduction of an alternative set of standard contractual clauses for the transfer of personal data to third countries (2004/915/EC) [29 December 2004] OJ L385/74

Commission Implementing Regulation (EU) 2015/806 of 22 May 2015 laying down specifications relating to the form of the EU trust mark for qualified trust services (Text with EEA relevance) C/2015/3364

Commission Implementing Decision (EU) 2016/1250 of 12 July 2016 pursuant to Directive 95/46/EC of the European Parliament and of the Council on the adequacy of the protection provided by the EU-US Privacy Shield (notified under document C (2016) 4176) (Text with EEA relevance) C/2016/4176

Council of Europe

Convention for the Protection of Individuals with Regard to Automatic Processing of Personal Data (Convention 108)

European Convention for the Protection of Human Rights and Fundamental Freedoms (European Convention on Human Rights, as Amended) (ECHR) (1950)

United States Legislation

Administrative Procedure Act, Pub. L. No. 79–404, 60 Stat. 237 (codified as amended at 5 U.S.C. §§ 551–706)

Bank Secrecy Act, Pub. L. 91–508, Titles I, II, 84 Stat. 1114 to 1124 (1970) (as codified at 12 U.S.C.A. § 1951–59)

Children's Online Privacy Protection 15 U.S.C. §§ 6501–06, Pub. L. 105–277

Clarifying Lawful Overseas Use of Data Act (CLOUD Act) part of the Consolidated Appropriations Act, 2018, Pub. L. 115–141.

Computer Fraud and Abuse Act, Pub. L. 99–474, 18 U.S.C. § 1030

Electronic Communications Privacy Act of 1986, Pub. L. 99–508, § 201, 100 Stat. 1848, 1860–68 (codified as amended at 18 U.S.C. §§ 2701–12)

Fair Credit Reporting Act of 1970, 15 U.S.C. § 1681

Family Education Rights and Privacy Act of 1974, Pub. L. 93–380, 88 Stat. 484 (1974) (codified as amended at 20 USC § 1232)
Federal Information Security Management Act of 2002, 44 U.S.C. § 3541
Federal Trade Commission Act, 15 U.S.C.A. § 45(a)
Freedom of Information Act, 5 U.S.C. § 552, As Amended by Public Law No. 104–231, 110 Stat. 3048
Genetic Information Nondiscrimination Act of 2008, Pub. L. 110–233, 122 Stat. 881 (2008) (codified at 42 U.S.C.A. §§ 2000ff et. seq.)
Gramm–Leach–Bliley Financial Modernization Act, Pub. L. 106–102, 113 Stat. 1338 (codified at 15 U.S.C. §§ 6801–09)
Right to Financial Privacy Act of 1978, Pub. L. 95–630, 92 Stat. 3697 (1978) (codified as amended at 12 U.S.C. §§ 3401–22)
Stored Communications Act, Codified at 18 U.S.C. Chapter 121 §§ 2701–12
United States Constitution, Amendment IV
Uniting and Strengthening America by Providing Appropriate Tools Required to Intercept and Obstruct Terrorism Act of 2001, Pub. L. 107–156, 115 Stat. 272
US Health Information Technology for Economic and Clinical Health Act, 42 U.S.C. § 17932 (2012)
US Health Insurance Portability and Accountability Act of 1996, Pub. L. 104–191, 110 Stat. 1936
Video Privacy Protection Act, Pub L. 100–618, 102 Stat. 3195 (1988) (codified at 18 U.S.C. § 2710) (2012)

JUDICIAL DECISIONS

European Union Cases

Big Brother Watch and Others v. the United Kingdom (applications nos. 58170/13, 62322/14, and 24960/15) [2018] ECHR
Bodil Lindqvist (C-101/01) [2003] CJEU
Breyer v. Germany (C-582/14) [2016] CJEU
Data Protection Commissioner v. Facebook Ireland Limited and Maximillian Schrems [2017] IEHC 545
Digital Rights Ireland v. Ireland and Kärntner Landesregierung, Tschohl, Seitlinger and Others (C-293/12 and C-594/12) [2014] CJEU
Falk Pharma GmbH v. DAK-Gesundheit (C-410/14) [2016] CJEU
Google LLC v. Commission Nationale de l'Informatique et des Libertés (CNIL) (C-507/17) [2019] CJEU
Google Spain SL, Google Inc. v. Agencia Espannola de Proteccion de Datos (AEPD), Mario Costeja Gonzalez (C-131/12) [2014] CJEU
Heinz Huber v. Federal Republic of Germany (C-524/06) [2008] CJEU
Maximillian Schrems v. Data Protection Commissioner (C362/14) [2015] CJEU
Peter Nowak v. Data Protection Commissioner (C-434/16) [2017] CJEU
Peter Pammer v. Reederei Karl Schlüter GmbH & Co. KG (C-585/08) and *Hotel Alpenhof GesmbH v. Oliver Heller* (C-144/09) [2010] CJEU

Tirkkonen v. *Maaseutuvirasto* (C-9/17) [2018] CJEU
Unabhängiges Landeszentrum für Datenschutz Schleswig-Holstein v. *Wirtschaftsakademie Schleswig-Holstein GmbH* (C-210/16) [2018] CJEU
UsedSoft GmbH v. *Oracle International Corp* (C-128/11) [2012] CJEU
Weltimmo s.r.o. v. *Nemzeti Adatvédelmi és Információszabadság Hatóság* (C-230/14) [2015] CJEU

United Kingdom Cases

AstraZeneca v. *International Business Machines Corporation* [2011] EWHC 306 (TCC)
Cavendish Square Holding BV v. *Talal El Makdessi* [2015] UKSC 67 [2015] 3 WLR 1373
GB Gas Holdings Limited v. *Accenture (UK) Limited and others* [2010] EWCA (Civ) 912
Hadley v. *Baxendale* [1854] 9 Ex 341, 156 Eng Rep 145 (Court of Exchequer)
Nash and others v. *Paragon Finance Plc* [2001] EWCA (Civ) 1466
St Albans City and DC v. *International Computers Ltd* [1996] 4 All ER 481

United States Cases

Amazon Web Services, Incorporated v. *United States*, 113 Fed. Cl. 102 (2014)
American Broadcasting Co., Inc. v. *Aereo, Inc.*, 134 Supreme Court 2498 (2014)
Applied Data Processing, Inc. v. *Burroughs Corp.*, 394 F. Supp. 504 (D. Conn. 1975)
Carpenter v. *United States*, 138 U.S. 2206 (2018)
Couch v. *United States*, 409 U.S. 322 (1973)
EEOC v. *United Parcel Serv., Inc.*, 587 F 3d 136, 139–140 (2d Cir 2009)
Ellis v. *Cartoon Network, Inc.*, 803 F. 3d 1251 (11th. Cir. 2015)
FTC v. *Wyndham Worldwide Corp.*, 799 F. 3d 236 (3d Cir. 2015)
Griswold v. *Connecticut*, 381 U.S. 479 (1965)
Katz v. *United States*, 389 U.S. 347 (1967)
LabMD, Inc. v. *FTC*, 894 F. 3d 1221 (2018)
Microsoft Corporation v. *United States* 829 F.3d 197 (2d Cir. 2016)
Microsoft Corp. v. *United States*, 855 F.3d 53 (2d Cir. 2017)
Re Warrant to Search a Certain Email Account Controlled & Maintained by Microsoft Corp., 15 F. Supp. 3d 446 (2014)
Re Warrant to Search a Certain E-Mail Account Controlled and Maintained by Microsoft Corp., 829 F. 3d 197, 204 (CA2 2016)
Re Search Warrant to Google, 232 F. Supp 3d 708 (2017)
Riley v. *California*, 134 U.S. 2473 (2014)
Smith v. *Maryland*, 442 U.S. 735 (1979)
State of Indiana v. *IBM*, 51 NE. 3d 150 (2015)
United States, Petitioner v. *Microsoft Corporation on Writ of Certiorari to the United States Court of Appeals for the Second Circuit*, 584 U.S. ___ (2018)
United States v. *Miller*, 425 U.S. 435 (1976)
US v. *Jones*, 565 U.S. 400 (2012)
Warshak v. *United States*, 490 F. 3d 455 (6th Cir. 2007)
Wartsila NSD North America, Inc. v. *Hill Intern, Inc.*, 436 F. Supp. 2d 690 (2006)

Miscellaneous

SS Lotus (*France* v. *Turkey*) 1927 PCIJ (ser. A) No 10 (7 September 1927)

Amici Curie

Krishnamurthy V. and M. Kortzus, 'Brief Amicus Curiae of UN Special Rapporteur on the Right to Privacy Joseph Cannataci in Support of Neither Party' in *US v. Microsoft Corporation* (2017)

Vandenberg J., 'Brief for 51 Computer Scientists as Amici Curiae in Support of the Respondent' in *Amici Curie Brief Filed in Microsoft Warrant Case* (2017)

Data Protection Authorities

Thon B. and G. Alhaug, 'Varsel om vedtak – overtredelsesgebyr – Akershus universitetssykehus HF' [Notification of Decision and Fine – Akershus University Hospital] (Datatilsynet [Norwegian DPA]) (2017) www.datatilsynet.no/globalassets/global/regelverk/avgjorelser-datatilsynet/2017/16-01531-53-varsel-om-vedtak–overtredelsesgebyr–akershus-universitetssykehus-hf-222955_3_1.pdf

RESTATEMENTS AND TREATISES

Bar C. and others, 'Principles, Definitions and Model Rules of European Private Law: Draft Common Frame of Reference (DCFR): Vol. 1' (Full ed., Sellier 2009) sec. II

Costello M., 'Data Security Generally' 1 Data Security & Privacy Law Westlaw (2017) sec. 3: 2

Restatement (Fourth) of Foreign Relations Law, 'Jurisdiction Based on Effects' (2016) sec. 213

Restatement (Second) of Contracts, 'Contract Defined' (1981) sec. 1

Restatement (Second) of Contracts, 'Intended and Incidental Beneficiaries' (1981) sec. 302

Restatement (Third) of Foreign Relations Law, 'Bases of Jurisdiction to Prescribe' (1987) sec. 402

Uniform Commercial Code (UCC), 'Article 2 – Implied Warranty of Merchantability' (2002) sec. 2-314-315

Uniform Commercial Code (UCC), 'Article 2 – Sales: Breach, Repudiation and Excuse' (2002) sec. 2-615

DATA PROTECTION AUTHORITIES OPINIONS AND GUIDANCE

CNIL, 'Security of Personal Data' Report/Guidance (2018) www.cnil.fr/sites/default/files/atoms/files/cnil_guide_securite_personnelle_gb_web.pdf

Datatilsynet [Norwegian Data Protection Authority], 'Reply - Use of Microsoft Office 365 Cloud Computing Services - Municipality of Moss' Vol 11/01198-4/LON (2012)

Datatilsynet [Norwegian Data Protection Authority], 'Saken avsluttes - Ny e-postløsning i Narvik Kommune-Google Apps' ['Case Closed- New Email solution for Narvik Municipality – Google Apps'] Vol. 11/00593-18 RTH (2012)

European Data Protection Board, 'Endorsement 1/2018' (25 May 2018) https://edpb.europa.eu/sites/edpb/files/files/news/endorsement_of_wp29_documents_en_0.pdf

European Data Protection Board, 'European Data Protection Board Rules of Procedure' (25 May 2018) https://edpb.europa.eu/sites/edpb/files/files/file1/edpb_rop_adopted_en.pdf

European Data Protection Board, 'Statement of the EDPB on the Revision of the ePrivacy Regulation and its Impact on the Protection of Individuals with Regard to the Privacy and

Confidentiality of their Communications' (25 May 2018) https://edpb.europa.eu/our-work-tools/our-documents/other/edpb-statement-eprivacy-25052018_en

European Data Protection Board, 'Guidelines 4/2019 on Article 25 Data Protection by Design and by Default' Version 2.0 (20 October 2020) https://edpb.europa.eu/our-work-tools/our-documents/guidelines/guidelines-42019-article-25-data-protection-design-and_en

European Data Protection Board, 'Frequently Asked Questions on the Judgment of the Court of Justice of the European Union in Case C-311/18 - Data Protection Commissioner v Facebook Ireland Ltd and Maximillian Schrems 24/ 07/2020' (23 July 2020) https://edpb.europa.eu/our-work-tools/our-documents/ohrajn/frequently-asked-questions-judgment-court-justice-european-union_en

European Data Protection Board, 'Recommendations 01/2020 on Measures that Supplement Transfer Tools to Ensure Compliance with the EU Level of Protection of Personal Data - Version for Public Consultation' (11 November 2020) https://edpb.europa.eu/our-work-tools/public-consultations-art-704/2020/recommendations-012020-measures-supplement-transfer_en

European Data Protection Board, 'Guidelines 3/2018 on the territorial scope of the GDPR (Article 3)- Version for public consultation' (16 November 2018) https://edpb.europa.eu/our-work-tools/public-consultations/2018/guidelines-32018-territorial-scope-gdpr-article-3_en

European Data Protection Supervisor, 'Guidelines on the Use of Cloud Computing Services by the European Institutions and Bodies' (16 March 2018) https://edps.europa.eu/data-protection/our-work/publications/guidelines/guidelines-use-cloud-computing-services-european_en

European Data Protection Supervisor, 'Opinion 5/2018 Preliminary Opinion on Privacy by Design' (2018) https://edps.europa.eu/data-protection/our-work/publications/opinions/privacy-design_en

European Data Protection Supervisor, 'The Transfer of Personal Data to Third Countries and International Organisations by EU Institutions and Bodies' (2014) https://edps.europa.eu/sites/edp/files/publication/14-07-14_transfer_third_countries_en.pdf

Federal Trade Commission, 'ASUS Settles FTC Charges That Insecure Home Routers and "Cloud" Services Put Consumers' Privacy at Risk' Press Release (23 February 2016) www.ftc.gov/news-events/press-releases/2015/12/lifelock-pay-100-million-consumers-settle-ftc-charges-it-violated

Federal Trade Commission, 'Facebook Settles FTC Charges That It Deceived Consumers by Failing to Keep Privacy Promises' Press Release (17 December 2015) www.ftc.gov/news-events/press-releases/2015/12/lifelock-pay-100-million-consumers-settle-ftc-charges-it-violated

Federal Trade Commission and ASUSTeK Computer, Inc., 'Agreement Containing Consent Order File No. 1423156' (2016) www.ftc.gov/system/files/documents/cases/160222asusagree.pdf

Information Commissioner Elizabeth Denham, 'Investigation into the Use of Data Analytics in Political Campaigns' United Kingdom Information Commissioner (ICO) Report (11 July 2018) https://ico.org.uk/media/action-weve-taken/2259371/investigation-into-data-analytics-for-political-purposes-update.pdf

Information Commissioner's Office, 'Guidance on the Use of Cloud Computing 2012100 2 Version: 1.1' (2012) https://ico.org.uk/media/fororganisations/documents/1540/cloud_computing_guidance_for_organisations.pdf

WP29, 'Guidelines on Consent under Regulation 2016/679' 259 rev. 01 (2018)

WP29, 'Guidelines on Consent under Regulation 2016/679' 259 (2017)

WP29, 'Guidelines on Data Protection Impact Assessment (DPIA) and Determining whether Processing Is "Likely to Result in a High Risk" for the Purposes of Regulation 2016/679' 248 rev. 01 (2017)
WP29, 'Guidelines on Data Protection Officers' 243 rev. 01 (2017)
WP29, 'Guidelines on Personal Data Breach Notification under Regulation 2016/679' wp250 rev.01 (2017)
WP29, 'Guidelines on the Application and Setting of Administrative Fines for the Purpose of the Regulation 2016/679' 253 (2017)
WP29, 'Guidelines on the Right to Data Portability' 242 rev. 01 (2017)
WP29, 'Guidelines on Transparency under Regulation 2016/679' 260 (2016)
WP29, 'Letter of Ms Falque-Pierrotin (ART29 WP) to CISPE' (2018)
WP29, 'Opinion 01/2016 on the EU – U.S. Privacy Shield Draft Adequacy Decision' 238 (2016)
WP29, 'Opinion 1/2010 on the Concepts of "Controller" and "Processor"' 169 (2010)
WP29, 'Opinion 2/2017 on Data Processing at Work' 249 (2017)
WP29, 'Opinion 03/2013 on Purpose Limitation' 203 (2013)
WP29, 'Opinion 3/2010 on the Principle of Accountability' 173 (2010)
WP29, 'Opinion 4/2007 on the Concept of Personal Data' 136 (2007)
WP29, 'Opinion 05/2012 on Cloud Computing' 196 (2012)
WP29, 'Opinion 05/2014 on Anonymisation Techniques' 216 (2014)
WP29, 'Opinion 06/2014 on the Notion of Legitimate Interests of the Data Controller under Article 7 of Directive 95/46/EC' 217 (2014)
WP29, 'Opinion 15/2011 on the Definition of Consent' 187 (2011)

BOOKS AND BOOK CHAPTERS

Alassafi M. and others, 'Security in Organisations: Governance, Risks and Vulnerabilities in Moving to the Cloud' in V. Chang and others (eds.), *Enterprise Security: Second International Workshop, ES 2015, Vancouver, BC, Canada, November 30 – December 3, 2015, Revised Selected Papers* (Cham: Springer International 2017)
Albano G. and C. Nicholas, 'The Design of Framework Agreements' in C. Nicholas and G. L. Albano (eds.), *The Law and Economics of Framework Agreements: Designing Flexible Solutions for Public Procurement* (Cambridge: Cambridge University Press 2016)
Alhamad M., T. Dillon, and E. Chang, 'Conceptual SLA Framework for Cloud Computing' (Digital Ecosystems and Technologies [DEST] 4th IEEE International Conference, 2010)
Andrecka M., 'Sustainable Public Procurement under Framework Agreements' in B. Sjåfjell and A. Wiesbrock (eds.), *Sustainable Public Procurement Under EU Law: New Perspectives on the State as Stakeholder* (Cambridge: Cambridge University Press 2015)
Aplin T. and others (eds.), *Gurry on Breach of Confidence: The Protection of Confidential Information* (Oxford: Oxford University Press 2012)
Bamberger K. and D. K. Mulligan, *Privacy on the Ground: Driving Corporate Behavior in the United States and Europe* (Cambridge, MA: MIT Press 2015)
Beatson J., A. Burrows, and J. Cartwright (eds.), *Anson's Law of Contract* (30th ed., Oxford: Oxford University Press 2016)
Bentzen H. and D. J. B. Svantesson, 'Jurisdictional Challenges Related to DNA Data Processing in Transnational Clouds' in D. J. B. Svantesson and D. Kloza (eds.), *Trans-Atlantic Data Privacy Relations as a Challenge for Democracy* (Cambridge: Intersentia 2017)

Bix B., 'History and Sources' in B. H. Bix (ed.), *Contract Law: Rules, Theory, and Context* (Cambridge: Cambridge University Press 2012)

Bock K., 'Data Protection Certification: Decorative or Effective Instrument? Audit and Seals as a Way to Enforce Privacy' in D. Wright and P. De Hert (eds.), *Enforcing Privacy: Regulatory, Legal and Technological Approaches* (Cham: Springer International 2016)

Bovis C., 'The Principles of Public Procurement Regulation' in C. H. Bovis (ed.), *Research Handbook on EU Public Procurement Law* (Cheltenham: Edward Elgar 2016)

Bradshaw S., C. Millard, and I. Walden, 'Standard Contracts for Cloud Services' in C. Millard (ed.), *Cloud Computing Law* (Oxford: Oxford University Press 2013)

Bygrave L., 'Contract vs. Statute in Internet Governance' in I. Brown (ed.), *Research Handbook on Governance of the Internet* (Cheltenham: Edward Elgar 2013)

Bygrave L., *Data Privacy Law: An International Perspective* (Oxford: Oxford University Press 2014)

Bygrave L., *Data Protection Law: Approaching its Rationale, Logic, and Limits* (London: Kluwer Law International 2002)

Bygrave L., 'Hardwiring Privacy' in R. Brownsword, E. Scotford, and K. Yeung (eds.), *The Oxford Handbook of Law, Regulation and Technology* (Oxford: Oxford University Press 2017)

Bygrave L., *Internet Governance by Contract* (Oxford: Oxford University Press 2015)

Bygrave L. and T. Michaelsen, 'Governors of Internet' in L. Bygrave and J. Bing (eds.), *Internet Governance: Infrastructure and Institutions* (Oxford: Oxford University Press 2009)

Bygrave L. and others, 'The Naming Game: Governance of the Domain Name System' in L. Bygrave and J. Bing (eds.), *Internet Governance: Infrastructure and Institutions* (Oxford: Oxford University Press 2009)

Caimi C. and others, 'Implementing Privacy Policies in the Cloud' in F. Cleary and M. Felici (eds.), *Cyber Security and Privacy: 4th Cyber Security and Privacy Innovation Forum, CSP Innovation Forum 2015, Brussels, Belgium April 28–29, 2015, Revised Selected Papers* (Cham: Springer International 2015)

Caimi C. and others, 'Legal and Technical Perspectives in Data Sharing Agreements Definition' in B. Berendt and others (eds.), *Privacy Technologies and Policy: Third Annual Privacy Forum, APF 2015, Luxembourg, October 7–8, 2015, Revised Selected Papers* (Cham: Springer 2016)

Canavan R., 'Public Procurement and Frameworks' in C. H. Bovis (ed.), *Research Handbook on EU Public Procurement Law* (Cheltenham: Edward Elgar 2016)

Canuel E., 'Comparing Exculpatory Clauses under Anglo-American Law: Testing Total Legal Convergence' in G. Cordero-Moss (ed.), *Boilerplate Clauses, International Commercial Contracts and the Applicable Law* (Cambridge: Cambridge University Press 2011)

Charles C., 'Public Procurement and Contracting Authorities' in C. Bovis (ed.), *Research Handbook on EU Public Procurement Law* (Cheltenham: Edward Elgar 2016)

Chesterman S., 'Intelligence Services' in S. Chesterman and A. Fisher (eds.), *Private Security, Public Order: The Outsourcing of Public Services and Its Limits* (Oxford: Oxford University Press 2009)

Cordero-Moss G., 'Conclusion: The Self-Sufficient Contract, Uniformly Interpreted on the Basis of Its Own Terms: An Illusion, But Not Fully Useless' in G. Cordero-Moss (ed.), *Boilerplate Clauses, International Commercial Contracts and the Applicable Law* (Cambridge: Cambridge University Press 2011)

Cordero-Moss G., 'Contract Practice and Its Expectations in Terms of the Governing Law' in G. Cordero-Moss (ed.), *International Commercial Contracts: Applicable Sources and Enforceability* (Cambridge: Cambridge University Press 2014)
Cordero-Moss G., 'The Impact of the Governing Law' in G. Cordero-Moss (ed.), *International Commercial Contracts: Applicable Sources and Enforceability* (Cambridge: Cambridge University Press 2014)
Corthaut T. and others, 'Operationalizing Accountability in Respect of Informal International Lawmaking Mechanisms' in J. Pauwelyn, R. Wessel, and J. Wouters (eds.), *Informal International Lawmaking* (Oxford: Oxford University Press 2012)
Cottrell M., 'Legitimacy and Institutional Replacement' in M. P. Cottrell (ed.), *The Evolution and Legitimacy of International Security Institutions* (Cambridge: Cambridge University Press 2016)
Cunningham A. and C. Reed, 'Consumer Protection in Cloud Environments' in C. Millard (ed.), *Cloud Computing Law* (Oxford: Oxford University Press 2013)
Czerniawski M., 'Extraterritoriality in the Age of the Equipment-Based Society. Do We Need the "Use of Equipment" as a Factor for the Territorial Applicability of the EU Data Protection Regime?' in D. Svantesson and D. Kloza (eds.), *European Integration and Democracy Series*, vol. 4 (Cambridge: Intersentia 2017)
Davies A., *The Public Law of Government Contracts* (Oxford: Oxford University Press 2008)
DiMatteo L., Q. Zhou, and S. Saintier, 'Transatlantic Perspectives' in K. Rowley and others (eds.), *Commercial Contract Law: Transatlantic Perspectives* (Cambridge: Cambridge University Press 2013)
Dobinson I. and F. Johns, 'Qualitative Legal Research' in M. McConville and W. H. Chui (eds.), *Research Methods for Law* (Edinburgh: Edinburgh University Press 2007)
Donahue J., 'The Transformation of Government Work: Causes, Consequences, and Distortions' in J. Freeman and M. Minow (eds.), *Government by Contract: Outsourcing and American Democracy* (Cambridge, MA: Harvard University Press 2009)
Dziminski B. and N. C. Gleeson, 'Legal Aspects of Cloud Accountability' in M. Felici and C. Fernández-Gago (eds.), *Accountability and Security in the Cloud: First Summer School, Cloud Accountability Project, A4Cloud, Malaga, Spain, June 2–6, 2014, Revised Selected Papers and Lectures* (Cham: Springer International 2015)
Egea M. and others, 'Definition of Data Sharing Agreements: The Case of Spanish Data Protection Law' in M. Felici and C. Fernández-Gago (eds.), *Accountability and Security in the Cloud: First Summer School, Cloud Accountability Project, A4Cloud, Malaga, Spain, June 2–6, 2014, Revised Selected Papers and Lectures* (Cham: Springer International 2015)
Esayas S., T. Mahler, and K. McGillivray, 'Is a Picture Worth a Thousand Terms? Visualising Contract Terms and Data Protection Requirements for Cloud Computing Users' in S. Casteleyn, P. Dolog, and C. Pautasso (eds.), *Current Trends in Web Engineering: ICWE 2016 International Workshops, DUI, TELERISE, SoWeMine, and Liquid Web, Lugano, Switzerland, June 6-9, 2016. Revised Selected Papers* (Cham: Springer International 2016)
Fawcett J. J., J. Harris, and M. Bridge, *International Sale of Goods in the Conflict of Laws* (Oxford: Oxford University Press 2005)
Feldman S., *Government Contracts in a Nutshell* (Saint Paul, MN: West Academic 2015)
Ferguson I., 'Outsourcing Contract Structures' in H. Jongen (ed.), *International Outsourcing Law and Practice* (Alphen aan den Rijn: Kluwer Law International 2008)
Forgó N., S. Hänold, and B. Schütze, 'The Principle of Purpose Limitation and Big Data' in M. Corrales, M. Fenwick, and N. Forgó (eds), *New Technology, Big Data and the Law* (Singapore: Springer 2017)

Freeman J. and M. Minow, 'Introduction: Reframing the Outsourcing Debates' in J. Freeman and M. Minow (eds.), *Government by Contract: Outsourcing and American Democracy* (Cambridge, MA: Harvard University Press 2009)
Gandal N. and P. Régibeau, 'Standard-Setting Organisations' in P. Delimatsis (ed.), *The Law, Economics and Politics of International Standardisation* (Cambridge: Cambridge University Press 2015)
Garner B. (ed.), *Black's Law Dictionary* (10th ed., Eagan, MN: Thomson West 2014)
Gellman R. and P. Dixon, 'Failures of Privacy Self-Regulation in the United States' in D. Wright and P. De Hert (eds.), *Enforcing Privacy: Regulatory, Legal and Technological Approaches* (Cham: Springer International 2016)
Georgieva I., 'The EU Principles in Public Procurement. Transparency – Origin and Main Characteristics' in I. Georgieva (ed.), *Using Transparency against Corruption in Public Procurement: A Comparative Analysis of the Transparency Rules and Their Failure to Combat Corruption* (Cham: Springer 2017)
Greenleaf G., *Asian Data Privacy Laws: Trade & Human Rights Perspectives* (Oxford: Oxford University Press 2014)
Hagstrøm V., 'The Nordic Tradition: Application of Boilerplate Clauses under Norwegian Law' in G. Cordero-Moss (ed.), *Boilerplate Clauses, International Commercial Contracts and the Applicable Law* (Cambridge: Cambridge University Press 2011)
Halliday T. and G. Shaffer, 'Transnational Legal Orders' in T. C. Halliday and G. Shaffer (eds.), *Transnational Legal Orders* (Cambridge: Cambridge University Press 2015)
Hippelainen L., I. Oliver, and S. Lal, 'Towards Dependably Detecting Geolocation of Cloud Servers' in Z. Yan and others (eds.), *Network and System Security* (Cham: Springer 2017)
Hon W. K., *Data Localization Laws and Policy: The EU Data Protection International Transfers Restriction through a Cloud Computing Lens* (Cheltenham: Edward Elgar 2017)
Hon W. K. and C. Millard, 'Cloud Technologies and Services' in C. Millard (ed.), *Cloud Computing Law* (Oxford: Oxford University Press 2013)
Hon W. K., C. Millard, and I. Walden, 'Negotiated Contracts for Cloud Services' in C. Millard (ed.), *Cloud Computing Law* (Oxford: Oxford University Press 2013)
Hon W. K., C. Millard, and I. Walden, 'Public Sector Cloud Contracts' in C. Millard (ed.), *Cloud Computing Law* (Oxford: Oxford University Press 2013)
Hon W. K., C. Millard, and I. Walden, 'What is Regulated as Personal Data in Clouds?' in C. Millard (ed.), *Cloud Computing Law* (Oxford: Oxford University Press 2013)
Hon W. K., J. Hörnle, and C. Millard, 'Which Law(s) Apply to Personal Data in Clouds?' in C. Millard (ed.), *Cloud Computing Law* (Oxford: Oxford University Press 2013)
Hoofnagle C., *Federal Trade Commission Privacy Law and Policy* (Cambridge: Cambridge University Press 2016)
Kelman S., 'Federal Contracting in Context: What Drives It, How to Improve It' in J. Freeman and M. Minow (eds.), *Government by Contract: Outsourcing and American Democracy* (Cambridge, MA: Harvard University Press 2009)
Kimball G., *Outsourcing Agreements: A Practical Guide* (Oxford: Oxford University Press 2010)
Klass G., *Contract Law in the United States* (2nd ed., Alphen aan den Rijn: Kluwer Law International 2012)
Koops B.-J. and others, 'Should Self-Regulation be the Starting Point?' in B.-J. Koops and others (eds.), *Starting Points for ICT Regulation: Deconstructing Prevalent Policy One-liners* (Den Haag, Netherlands: T.M.C. Asser 2006)

Kosta E. and K. Stuurman, 'Technical Standards and the Draft General Data Protection Regulation' in P. Delimatsis (ed.), *The Law, Economics and Politics of International Standardisation* (Cambridge: Cambridge University Press 2015)

Kuner C., 'Applicable Law, Extraterritoriality, and Transborder Data Flows' in *Transborder Data Flows and Data Privacy Law* (Oxford: Oxford University Press 2013)

Lee N., 'Social Networks and Privacy' in N. Lee (ed.), *Facebook Nation* (New York: Springer-Verlag 2013)

Lessig L., *Code: Version 2.0* (New York: Basic Books 2006)

Lord R. A., *Williston on Contracts* (4th ed., London: Sweet & Maxwell 1993)

Lynskey O., *The Foundations of EU Data Protection Law* (Oxford: Oxford University Press 2015)

Marsden C. T., *Internet Co-Regulation: European Law, Regulatory Governance and Legitimacy in Cyberspace* (Cambridge: Cambridge University Press 2011)

Mendelson N., 'Six Simple Steps to Increase Contractor Accountability' in J. Freeman and M. Minow (eds.), *Government by Contract: Outsourcing and American Democracy* (Cambridge, MA: Harvard University Press 2009)

Merry S., 'Firming Up Soft Law' in T. C. Halliday and G. Shaffer (eds.), *Transnational Legal Orders* (Cambridge: Cambridge University Press 2015)

Metheny M., *Federal Cloud Computing: The Definitive Guide for Cloud Service Providers* (Cambridge, MA: Elsevier Science 2012)

Millard C. and Kamarinou D., 'Article 28. Processor' in C. Kuner, L. Bygrave, C. Docksey, and L. Drechsler (eds.), *The EU General Data Protection Regulation (GDPR): A Commentary* (Oxford: Oxford University Press, 2020)

Miller L., *The Emergence of EU Contract Law: Exploring Europeanization* (Oxford: Oxford University Press 2011)

Miller L., 'The Notion of Europeanization and the Significance of Transnational Private Lawmaking' in L. Miller (ed.), *The Emergence of EU Contract Law: Exploring Europeanization* (Oxford: Oxford University Press 2011)

Mills A., 'Public International Law and Private International Law' in J. Basedow and others (eds.), *Encyclopedia of Private International Law* (Cheltenham: Edward Elgar 2017)

Moerel L., *Binding Corporate Rules: Corporate Self-Regulation of Global Data Transfers* (Oxford: Oxford University Press 2012)

Morgan R. and K. Burden, *Morgan and Burden on Computer Contracts* (8th ed., London: Sweet & Maxwell Thomson Reuters 2009)

Negroponte N., *Being Digital* (London: Hodder and Stoughton 1996)

Ojanen T., 'Rights-Based Review of Electronic Surveillance after Digital Rights Ireland and Schrems in the European Union' in D. Cole, F. Fabbrini, and S. Schulhofer (eds.), *Surveillance, Privacy and Trans-Atlantic Relations*, vol. 1 (Oxford: Hart 2017)

Pannetrat A. and J. Luna, 'Standards for Accountability in the Cloud' in M. Felici and C. Fernández-Gago (eds.), *Accountability and Security in the Cloud: First Summer School, Cloud Accountability Project, A4Cloud, Malaga, Spain, June 2–6, 2014, Revised Selected Papers and Lectures* (Cham: Springer International 2015)

Peel E., 'The Common Law Tradition: Application of Boilerplate Clauses under English Law' in G. Cordero-Moss (ed.), *Boilerplate Clauses, International Commercial Contracts and the Applicable Law* (Cambridge: Cambridge University Press 2011)

Polčák R. and D. J. B. Svantesson, *Information Sovereignty: Data Privacy, Sovereign Powers and the Rule of Law* (Cheltenham: Edward Elgar 2017)

Reed C., 'Cloud Governance: The Way Forward' in C. Millard (ed.), *Cloud Computing Law* (Oxford: Oxford University Press 2013)

Reed C., *Making Laws for Cyberspace* (Oxford: Oxford University Press 2012)
Reich N., 'The Public/Private Divide in European Law' in H.-W. Micklitz and Fo Cafaggi (eds.), *European Private Law after the Common Frame of Reference* (Cheltenham: Edward Elgar 2010)
Rotenberg M., 'In re EPIC and the Role of NGOs and Experts in Surveillance Cases' in D. Cole, F. Fabbrini, and S. Schulhofer (eds.), *Surveillance, Privacy and Trans-Atlantic Relations* (Oxford: Hart 2017)
Rubinstein I., G. T. Nojeim, and R. D. Lee, 'Systematic Government Access to Private-Sector Data' in F. H. Cate and J. X. Dempsey (eds.), *Bulk Collection: Systematic Government Access to Private-Sector Data* (Oxford: Oxford University Press 2017)
Ruiz J. and others, 'A Lifecycle for Data Sharing Agreements: How it Works Out' in S. Schiffner and others (eds.), *Privacy Technologies and Policy. APF 2016. Lecture Notes in Computer Science*, vol. 9857 (Cham: Springer 2016)
Ruparelia N., *Cloud Computing* (Cambridge, MA: MIT Press 2016)
Ryngaert C., *Jurisdiction in International Law* (Oxford: Oxford University Press 2008)
Sanz-Requena R. and others, 'A Cloud-Based Radiological Portal for the Patients: IT Contributing to Position the Patient as the Central Axis of the 21st Century Healthcare Cycles' in *2015 IEEE/ACM 1st International Workshop on TEchnical and LEgal aspects of data pRivacy and SEcurity* (IEEE Press 2015)
Soloway S. and A. Chvotkin, 'Federal Contracting in Context: What Drives It, How to Improve It' in J. Freeman and M. Minow (eds.), *Government by Contract: Outsourcing and American Democracy* (Cambridge, MA: Harvard University Press 2009)
Spagnoli F., F. Bellini, and A. Ghi, 'A Methodology for the Impact Assessment of a G-Cloud Strategy for the Italian Ministry of the Economic Development' in C Rossignoli, M Gatti, and R Agrifoglio (eds), *Organizational Innovation and Change: Managing Information and Technology* (Cham: Springer International 2016)
Statsky W., *West's Legal Thesaurus/Dictionary* (Special deluxe ed., Eagan, MN: Thomson West 1986)
Svantesson D., *Extraterritoriality in Data Privacy Law* (Copenhagen: Ex Tuto 2013)
Svantesson D., *Solving the Internet Jurisdiction Puzzle* (Oxford: Oxford University Press 2017)
Swire P., 'US Surveillance Law, Safe Harbour and Reforms Since 2013' in D. Kloza and D. Svantesson (eds.) *Trans-Atlantic Data Privacy Relations as a Challenge for Democracy*, vol. 4 (Cambridge: Intersentia 2017)
Taylor L., *FISMA Compliance Handbook: Second Edition* (Burlington, MA: Elsevier Science 2013)
Tollen D., *The Tech Contracts Handbook: Cloud Computing Agreements, Software Licenses, and Other IT Contracts for Lawyers and Businesspeople* (Chicago, IL: American Bar Association 2016)
Treitel G. H., *The Law of Contract* (8th ed., London: Sweet & Maxwell 1991)
Tzanou M., *The Fundamental Right to Data Protection: Normative Value in the Context of Counter-terrorism Surveillance* (Portland: Hart 2017)
Tønseth M. and others, *Personvernhåndboken* (Oslo: Gyldendal juridisk 2016)
Ustaran E., 'The Scope of Application of EU Data Protection Law and Its Extraterritorial Reach' in I. Noriswadi, Y. Cieh, and E. Lee (eds.), *Beyond Data Protection: Strategic Case Studies and Practical Guidance* (Heidelberg: Springer 2013)
Velasco C., J. Hörnle, and A.-M. Osula, 'Global Views on Internet Jurisdiction and Trans-border Access' in S. Gutwirth, R. Leenes, and P. De Hert (eds.), *Data Protection on the Move: Current Developments in ICT and Privacy/Data Protection* (Dordrecht: Springer 2016)

Vermeulen G., 'The Paper Shield: On the Degree of Protection of the EU-US Privacy Shield against Unnecessary or Disproportionate Data Collection by the US Intelligence and Law Enforcement Services' in D. Kloza and D. Svantesson (eds.), *Trans-Atlantic Data Privacy Relations as a Challenge for Democracy*, vol. 4 (Cambridge: Intersentia 2017)

Vettese M., 'Multinational Companies and National Contracts' in G. Cordero-Moss (ed.), *Boilerplate Clauses, International Commercial Contracts and the Applicable Law* (Cambridge: Cambridge University Press 2011)

Voigt P. and A. von dem Bussche, *The EU General Data Protection Regulation (GDPR)* (Cham: Springer 2017)

Wagle S., 'Cloud Computing Contracts' in A. Lehmann and others (eds.), *Privacy and Identity Management Facing up to Next Steps: 11th IFIP WG 9.2, 9.5, 9.6/11.7, 11.4, 11.6/SIG 9.2.2 International Summer School, Karlstad, Sweden, August 21–26, 2016, Revised Selected Papers* (Cham: Springer International 2016)

Walden I., 'Telecommunications Law and Regulation: An Introduction' in I. Walden (ed.), *Telecommunications Law and Regulation* (Oxford: Oxford University Press 2009)

Walden I. and L. Da Correggio Luciano, 'Facilitating Competition in the Clouds' in C. Millard (ed.), *Cloud Computing Law* (Oxford: Oxford University Press 2013)

Wang F., *Internet Jurisdiction and Choice of Law: Legal Practices in the EU, US and China* (Cambridge: Cambridge University Press 2010)

Weber R. H. and D. Staiger, *Transatlantic Data Protection in Practice* (Cham: Springer 2017)

Weinrib E., *The Idea of Private Law* (Oxford: Oxford University Press 2013)

Weinstein S. and C. Wild, 'Developing the Right Formula for Successful Legal Risk Management, Governance and Compliance' in S. Weinstein and C. Wild (eds.), *Legal Risk Management, Governance and Compliance: A Guide to Best Practice From Leading Experts* (London: Globe Law and Business 2013)

Weitzenböck E., *A Legal Framework for Emerging Business Models: Dynamic Networks as Collaborative Contracts* (Cheltenham: Edward Elgar 2012)

Wilderspin M., 'Contractual Obligations' in J. Basedow and others (eds.), *Encyclopedia of Private International Law* (Cheltenham: Edward Elgar 2017)

Wilderspin M., 'Overriding Mandatory Provisions' in J. Basedow and others (eds.), *Encyclopedia of Private International Law* (Cheltenham: Edward Elgar 2017)

Yoo C., 'Cloud Computing, Contractibility, and Network Architecture' in C. S. Yoo and J.-F. Blanchette (eds.), *Regulating the Cloud: Policy for Computing Infrastructure* (Cambridge, MA: MIT Press 2015)

Yoo C. and J.-F. Blanchette, *Regulating the Cloud: Policy for Computing Infrastructure* (Cambridge, MA: MIT Press 2015)

JOURNAL ARTICLES

Aitchison S., 'Privacy in the Cloud: The Fourth Amendment Fog' (2018) 93 *Washington Law Review* 1019

Alonso J., M. Escalante, and L. Orue-Echevarria, 'Transformational Cloud Government (TCG): Transforming Public Administrations with a Cloud of Public Services' (2016) 97 *Procedia Computer Science* 43

Alsenoy B., 'Liability under EU Data Protection Law: From Directive 95/46 to the General Data Protection Regulation' (2017) 7 *Journal of Intellectual Property, Information Technology and e-Commerce Law* 271

Aman A. and J. C. Dugan, 'The Human Side of Public-Private Partnerships: From New Deal Regulation to Administrative Law Management' (2017) 102 *Iowa Law Review* 883

Amoore L., 'Cloud Geographies: Computing, Data, Sovereignty' (2018) 42 *Progress in Human Geography* 4

Andrews D. C. and J. M. Newman, 'Personal Jurisdiction and Choice of Law in the Cloud' (2013) 73 *Maryland Law Review* 58

Arsham B., 'Monetizing Infringement: A New Legal Regime for Hosts of User-Generated Content' (2013) 101 *Georgetown Law Journal* 28

Auty M. and others, 'Inadequacies of Current Risk Controls for the Cloud' (2010) 2nd IEEE International Conference on Cloud Computing Technology and Science, Indianapolis, IN, 659

Bamberger K. and D. K. Mulligan, 'Privacy on the Books and on the Ground' (2011) 63 *Stanford Law Review* 247

Bender D., 'Having Mishandled Safe Harbor, Will the CJEU Do Better with Privacy Shield? A US Perspective' (2016) 6 *International Data Privacy Law* 117

Bender S., 'Privacy in the Cloud Frontier: Abandoning the "Take It or Leave It" Approach' (2011) 4 *Drexel Law Review* 27

Bilgic S., 'Something Old, Something New, and Something Moot: The Privacy Crisis under the Cloud Act' (2018) 32 *Harvard Journal of Law & Technology* 321

Black J., 'Constructing and Contesting Legitimacy and Accountability in Polycentric Regulatory Regimes' (2008) 2 *Regulation & Governance* 137

Black J., '"Says Who?" Liquid Authority and Interpretive Control in Transnational Regulatory Regimes' (2017) 9 *International Theory* 286

Blackman J. and others, 'Cloud Act Establishes Framework to Access Overseas Stored Electronic Communications' (2018) 30 *Intellectual Property & Technology Law Journal* 10

Blair M. and others, 'Outsourcing, Modularity, and the Theory of the Firm' (2011) 2011 *Brigham Young University Law Review* 263

Blume P., 'Controller and Processor: Is There a Risk of Confusion?' (2013) 3 *International Data Privacy Law* 140

Bolin R., 'Risky Mail: Concerns in Confidential Attorney-Client Email' (2012) 81 *University of Cincinnati Law Review* 601

Bolognini L. and C. Bistolfi, 'Pseudonymization and Impacts of Big (Personal/Anonymous) Data Processing in the Transition from the Directive 95/46/EC to the New EU General Data Protection Regulation' (2017) 33 *Computer Law & Security Review* 171

Bougiakiotis E., 'The Enforcement of the Google Spain Ruling' (2016) 24 *International Journal of Law and Information Technology* 311

Boyne S., 'Data Protection in the United States' (2018) 66 *American Journal of Comparative Law* 299

Brookman J., 'Protecting Privacy in an Era of Weakening Regulation. The Consumer Always Has Rights: Envisioning a Progressive Free Market' (2015) 9 *Harvard Law & Policy Review* 355

Brown K., 'Outsourcing, Data Insourcing, and the Irrelevant Constitution' (2015) 49 *Georgia Law Review* 607

Bygrave L., 'Data Protection by Design and by Default: Deciphering the EU's Legislative Requirements' (2017) 2 *Oslo Law Review* 105

Cafaggi F., 'New Foundations of Transnational Private Regulation' (2011) 38 *Journal of Law and Society* 20

Cafaggi F., 'Transnational Private Regulation and the Production of Global Public Goods and Private "Bads"' (2012) 23 *European Journal of International Law* 695

Calloway T., 'Cloud Computing, Clickwrap Agreements, and Limitation on Liability Clauses: A Perfect Storm' (2012) 11 *Duke Law & Technology Review* 163

Canuel E., 'Comparative Commercial Law: Methodologies, Black Letter Law and Law-in-Action' (2012) 2012 *Nordic Journal of Commercial Law* 1

Carmeli D., 'Keep an I on the Sky: E-discovery Risks Forecasted for Apple's iCloud' (2013) *Boston College Intellectual Property and Technology Forum* 34

Carpenter R. Jr., 'Walking from Cloud to Cloud: The Portability Issue in Cloud Computing' (2010) 6 *Washington Journal of Law, Technology & Arts* 9

Cate F. and V. Mayer-Schönberger, 'Notice and Consent in a World of Big Data' (2013) 3 *International Data Privacy Law* 67

Cate F. and others, 'Systematic Government Access to Private-sector Data' (2012) 2 *International Data Privacy Law* 195

Celestine C., 'Cloudy Skies, Bright Futures? In Defense of a Private Regulatory Scheme for Policing Cloud Computing' (2013) 2013 *University of Illinois Journal of Law Technology and Policy* 141

Chesterman S., '"We Can't Spy . . . If We Can't Buy!": The Privatization of Intelligence and the Limits of Outsourcing "Inherently Governmental Functions"' (2008) 19 *European Journal of International Law* 1055

Citron D., 'The Privacy Policymaking of State Attorneys General' (2016) 92 *Notre Dame Law Review* 747–816

Clarke R., 'Data Risks in the Cloud' (2013) 8 *Journal of Theoretical and Applied Electronic Commerce Research (JTAER)* 60–74 www.rogerclarke.com/II/DRC.html

Clopton Z., 'Territoriality, Technology, and National Security' (2016) 83 *University of Chicago Law Review* 45

Colangelo A., 'What Is Extraterritorial Jurisdiction' (2014) 99 *Cornell Law Review* 1303

Colarusso D., 'Heads in the Cloud, A Coming Storm: The Interplay of Cloud, Encryption, and the Fifth Amendment's Protection against Self-Incrimination' (2011) 17 *Boston University Journal of Science & Technology Law* 69

Cook C., 'Cross-Border Data Access and Active Cyber Defense: Assessing Legislative Options for a New International Cybersecurity Rulebook' (2018) 29 *Stanford Law & Policy Review* 205

Cordero-Moss G., 'International Contracts between Common Law and Civil Law: Is Non-State Law to Be Preferred? The Difficulty of Interpreting Legal Standards Such as Good Faith' (2007) 7 *Global Jurist* 3

Cordero-Moss G., 'Limits to Party Autonomy in International Commercial Arbitration' (2014) 1 *Oslo Law Review* 47

Custers B. and H. Uršič, 'Big Data and Data Reuse: A Taxonomy of Data Reuse for Balancing Big Data Benefits and Personal Data Protection' (2016) 6 *International Data Privacy Law* 4

Daley M., S. C. Bennett, and N. Gerlach, 'Storm Clouds Gathering for Cross-Border Discovery and Data Privacy: Cloud Computing Meets the U.S.A. Patriot Act' (2012) 13 *Sedona Conference Journal* 20

Danaher B. and M. D. Smith, 'Gone in 60 Seconds: The Impact of the Megaupload Shutdown on Movie Sales' (2014) 33 *International Journal of Industrial Organization* 1

Daskal J., 'Microsoft Ireland, the CLOUD Act, and International Lawmaking 2.0' (2018) 71 *Stanford Law Review Online* 9

Daskal J., 'The Un-Territoriality of Data' (2015) 125 *Yale Law Journal* 326

Datesh A., 'Storms Brewing in the Cloud: Why Copyright Law Will Have to Adapt to the Future of Web 2.0' (2012) 40 *American Intellectual Property Law Association Quarterly Journal* 30

De Filippi P. and S. McCarthy, 'Cloud Computing: Centralization and Data Sovereignty' (2012) 3 *European Journal of Law and Technology* 1

Deeks A., 'An International Legal Framework for Surveillance' (2015) 55 *Virginia Journal of International Law* 291

Delic E., 'Cloudy Jurisdiction: Foggy Skies in Traditional Jurisdiction Create Unclear Legal Standards for Cloud Computing and Technology' (2017) 50 *Suffolk University Law Review* 32

Dietz T., 'Contract Law, Relational Contracts, and Reputational Networks in International Trade: An Empirical Investigation into Cross-Border Contracts in the Software Industry' (2011) 37 *Law and Social Inquiry* 25

Diorio S., 'Data Protection Laws: Quilts Versus Blankets' (2015) 42 *Syracuse Journal of International Law and Commerce* 485

Easterbrook F. H., 'Cyberspace and the Law of the Horse' (1996) 1996 *University of Chicago Legal Forum* 207

Edwards C., 'Freedom of Contract and Fundamental Fairness for Individual Parties: The Tug of War Continues' (2009) 77 *University of Missouri-Kansas City Law Review* 647

El Emam K. and C. Álvarez, 'A Critical Appraisal of the Article 29 Working Party Opinion 05/2014 on Data Anonymization Techniques' (2015) 5 *International Data Privacy Law* 73

El-Gazzar R., E. Hustad, and D. H. Olsen, 'Understanding Cloud Computing Adoption Issues: A Delphi Study Approach' (2016) 118 *Journal of Systems and Software* 64

Elvy S., 'Hybrid Transactions and the Internet of Things: Goods, Services, or Software?' (2017) 74 *Washington and Lee Law Review* 77

Emmanuel J. and E. A. Caral, 'Lessons from ICANN: Is Self-Regulation of the Internet Fundamentally Flawed?' (2004) 12 *International Journal of Law and Information Technology* 1

Epstein D. and others, 'An "App" for Third Party Beneficiaries' (2016) 91 *Washington Law Review* 1663

Epstein W., 'Contract Theory and the Failures of Public-Private Contracting' (2013) 34 *Cardozo Law Review* 2211

Esayas S., 'A Walk into the Cloud and Cloudy it Remains: The Challenges and Prospects of "Processing" and "Transferring" Personal Data' (2012) 28 *Computer Law & Security Review* 662

Esayas S., 'The Idea of "Emergent Properties" in Data Privacy: Towards a Holistic Approach' (2017) 25 *International Journal of Law and Information Technology* 139

Esayas S., 'The Role of Anonymisation and Pseudonymisation under the EU Data Privacy Rules: Beyond the "All or Nothing" Approach' (2015) 6(2) *European Journal of Law and Technology* 5

Faulkenberry R., 'Reviewing and Negotiating Cloud Computing Vendor Contracts' (2013) 6 *Journal of Health & Life Sciences Law* 21

Foster N., 'Navigating through the Fog of Cloud Computing Contracts' (2013) 30 *Journal of Information Technology & Privacy Law* 13

Freiwald S. and S. Smith, 'The Carpenter Chronicle: A Near-Perfect Surveillance' (2018) 132 *Harvard Law Review* 205

Friendler E., 'Protecting the Innocent - the Need to Adapt Federal Asset Forfeiture Laws to Protect the Interest of Third Parties in Digital Asset Seizures' (2013) 32 *Cardozo Arts and Entertainment Law Journal* 283

Froomkin A., 'Lessons Learned Too Well: Anonymity in a Time of Surveillance' (2017) 59 *Arizona Law Review* 66

Geis G., 'Business Outsourcing and the Agency Cost Problem' (2007) 82 *Notre Dame Law Review* 955
Gervais D. and D. Hyndman, 'Cloud Control: Copyright, Global Memes and Privacy' (2011) 10 *Journal on Telecommunications and High Technology Law* 53
Gleeson N. and I. Walden, '"It's a Jungle Out There"?: Cloud Computing, Standards and the Law' (2014) 5 *European Journal of Law and Technology* 683
Gleeson N. and I. Walden, 'Placing the State in the Cloud: Issues of Data Governance and Public Procurement' (2016) 32 *Computer Law & Security Review* 683
Gottschalk P. and H. Solli-Sæther, 'Critical Success Factors from IT Outsourcing Theories: An Empirical Study' (2005) 105 *Industrial Management & Data Systems* 685
Gray A., 'Conflict of Laws and the Cloud' (2013) 29 *Computer Law & Security Review* 58
Gstrein O. and G. Ritsema van Eck, 'Mobile Devices as Stigmatizing Security Sensors: The GDPR and a Future of Crowdsourced "Broken Windows"' (2018) 8 *International Data Privacy Law* 69
Hall H., 'Restoring Dignity and Harmony to United States-European Union Data Protection Regulation' (2018) 23 *Communication Law and Policy* 125
Harris D., '*Riley v. California* and the Beginning of the End for the Third-Party Search Doctrine' (2016) 18 *University of Pennsylvania Journal of Constitutional Law* 895
Harshbarger J., 'Cloud Computing Providers and Data Security Law: Building Trust with United States Companies' (2011) 16 *Journal of Technology Law & Policy* 20
Hartzog W., 'The Inadequate, Invaluable Fair Information Practices' (2017) 76 *Maryland Law Review* 33
Hartzog W. and D. Solove, 'The Scope and Potential of FTC Data Protection' (2015) 83 *George Washington Law Review* 2230
Hayes C., J. P. Kesan, and M. N. Bashir, 'Cloud Services, Contract Terms, and Legal Rights' (2013) 17 *Journal of Internet Law* 18
Henry L., 'Information Privacy and Data Security' (2015) 2015 *Cardozo Law Review De Novo* 107
de Hert P. and M. Czerniawski, 'Expanding the European Data Protection Scope Beyond Territory: Article 3 of the General Data Protection Regulation in its Wider Context' (2016) 6 *International Data Privacy Law* 230
de Hert P., V. Papakonstantinou, and I. Kamara, 'The Cloud Computing Standard ISO/IEC 27018 through the Lens of the EU Legislation on Data Protection' (2016) 32 *Computer Law and Security Review* 16
Hill J. W. and others, 'A Proposed National Health Information Network Architecture and Complementary Federal Preemption of State Health Information Privacy Laws' (2011) 48 *American Business Law Journal* 503
Hojnik J., 'Technology Neutral EU Law: Digital Goods Within the Traditional Goods/Services Distinction' (2016) 25 *International Journal of Law and Information Technology* 63
Hon W. K., C. Millard, and I. Walden, 'Negotiating Cloud Contracts: Looking at Clouds from Both Sides Now' (2012) 16 *Stanford Technology Law Review* 79
Hon W. K. and others, 'Policy, Legal and Regulatory Implications of a Europe-Only Cloud' (2016) 24 *International Journal of Law and Information Technology* 25
Hon W. K. and others, 'Cloud Accountability: The Likely Impact of the Proposed EU Data Protection Regulation' (2014) Queen Mary School of Law Legal Studies Research Paper No. 172/2014; Tilburg Law School Research Paper No. 07/2014 http://dx.doi.org/10.2139/ssrn.2405971
Hoofnagle C. and J. Whittington, 'Free: Accounting for the Costs of the Internet's Most Popular Price' (2014) 61 *University of California Los Angeles Law Review* 606

Hutchinson T. and N. Duncan, 'Defining and Describing What We Do: Doctrinal Legal Research' (2012) 17 *Deakin Law Review* 83

Irion K., 'Government Cloud Computing and National Data Sovereignty' (2012) 4 *Policy & Internet* 40

Irion K., 'Your Digital Home is No Longer Your Castle: How Cloud Computing Transforms the (Legal) Relationship between Individuals and Their Personal Records' (2015) 23 *International Journal of Law and Information Technology* 348

Ismail U. and others, 'A Framework for Security Transparency in Cloud Computing' (2016) 8 *Future Internet* 5

Johnson E., 'Lost in the Cloud: Cloud Storage, Privacy, and Suggestions for Protecting Users' Data' (2017) 69 *Stanford Law Review* 867

Joint A. and E. Baker, 'Knowing the Past to Understand the Present – Issues in the Contracting for Cloud Based Services' (2011) 27 *Computer Law & Security Review* 407

Kalinich D. and others, 'Data Sovereignty and the Cloud: A Board and Executive Officer's Guide' (2013) 1 *Cyberspace Law and Policy Centre, UNSW Faculty of Law* 1 www.cyberlawcentre.org/data_sovereignty/CLOUD_DataSovReport_Full.pdf

Kamarinou D., C. Millard, and W. K. Hon, 'Cloud Privacy: An Empirical Study of 20 Cloud Providers' Terms and Privacy Policies – Part I' (2016) 6 *International Data Privacy Law* 79

Kamarinou D., C. Millard, and W. K. Hon, 'Cloud Privacy: An Empirical Study of 20 Cloud Providers' Terms and Privacy Policies – Part II' (2016) 6 *International Data Privacy Law* 170

Kamarinou D., C. Millard, and I. Oldani, 'Compliance as a Service' (2018) Queen Mary School of Law Legal Studies Research Paper No. 287/2018

Kerr O., 'A User's Guide to the Stored Communications Act and a Legislator's Guide to Amending It' (2003) 72 *George Washington Law Review* 1208

Kerr O., 'Searches and Seizures in a Digital World' (2005) 119 *Harvard Law Review* 531

Kerr O., 'The Next Generation Communications Privacy Act' (2014) 162 *University of Pennsylvania Law Review* 373

Kesan J., C. M. Hayes, and M. N. Bashir, 'Information Privacy and Data Control in Cloud Computing: Consumers, Privacy Preferences, and Market Efficiency' (2013) 70 *Washington and Lee Law Review* 341

King V. and V. T. Raja, 'Protecting the Privacy and Security of Sensitive Customer Data in the Cloud' (2012) 28 *Computer Law & Security Review* 11

Kirschenbaum A., 'Beyond Microsoft: A Legislative Solution to the SCA's Extraterritoriality Problem' (2018) 86 *Fordham Law Review* 1923

Kokott J. and C. Sobotta, 'The Distinction between Privacy and Data Protection in the Jurisprudence of the CJEU and the ECtHR' (2013) 3 *International Data Privacy Law* 222

Krebs D., 'Regulating the Cloud: A Comparative Analysis of the Current and Proposed Privacy Frameworks in Canada and the European Union' (2012) 10 *Canadian Journal of Law and Technology* 1

Kuner C., 'Data Protection Law and International Jurisdiction on the Internet (Part I)' (2010) 18 *International Journal of Law and Information Technology* 176

Kuner C., 'Extraterritoriality and Regulation of International Data Transfers in EU Data Protection Law' (2015) 5 *International Data Privacy Law* 235

Kuner C., 'Regulation of Transborder Data Flows under Data Protection and Privacy Law: Past, Present, and Future' (2010) TILT Law & Technology Working Paper 15 http://dx.doi.org/10.1787/5kg0s2fk315f-en

Lachaud E., 'Why the Certification Process Defined in the General Data Protection Regulation Cannot be Successful' (2016) 32 *Computer Law & Security Review* 814

Lametti D., 'The Cloud: Boundless Digital Potential or Enclosure 3.0?' (2012) 17 *Virginia Journal of Law & Technology* 192

Langvardt A. and others, 'A Proposed National Health Information Network, Architecture and Complementary Federal Preemption of State Health Information Privacy Laws' (2011) 48 *American Business Law Journal* 548

LeSieur F., 'Regulating Cross-Border Data Flows and Privacy in the Networked Digital Environment and Global Knowledge Economy' (2012) 2 *International Data Privacy Law* 93

Lessig L., 'The Law of the Horse: What Cyberlaw Might Teach' (1999) 113 *Harvard Law Review* 501

Lindqvist J., 'New Challenges to Personal Data Processing Agreements: Is the GDPR Fit to Deal with Contract, Accountability and Liability in a World of the Internet of Things?' (2017) 26 *International Journal of Law and Information Technology* 45

Lusch S., 'State Taxation of Cloud Computing' (2013) 29 *Santa Clara Computer & High Tech Law Journal* 369

Macioce D. Jr, 'PII in Context: Video Privacy and a Factor-Based Test for Assessing Personal Information (Personally Identifiable Information)' (2017) 45 *Pepperdine Law Review* 331

Marinho C. and others, 'Digital Content and Cloud-Based Contracts in Brazil and the European Union' (2016) 24 *International Journal of Law and Information Technology* 99

Martin B. and J. Newhall, 'Criminal Copyright Enforcement against Filesharing Services' (2013) 15 *North Carolina Journal of Law & Technology* 35

Martin M., 'HIPAA Compliant Clouds: A Reality That Should Not Become a Missed Opportunity by Health Care Providers' (2014) 83 *University of Missouri Kansas City Law Review* 25

Matwyshyn A., 'Privacy the Hacker Way' (2013) 87 *Southern California Law Review* 1

Matwyshyn A., 'The Law of the Zebra' (2013) 28 *Berkeley Technology Law Journal* 155

Matzner T., 'Why Privacy is Not Enough Privacy in the Context of "Ubiquitous Computing" and "Big Data"' (2014) 12 *Journal of Information, Communication and Ethics in Society* 93

Mazur O., 'Taxing the Cloud' (2015) 103 *California Law Review* 1

McGillivray K., 'A Right too Far? Requiring Cloud Service Providers to Deliver Adequate Data Security to Consumers' (2016) 25 *International Journal of Law and Information Technology* 25

McGillivray K., 'Conflicts in the Cloud: Contracts and Compliance with Data Protection Law in the EU' (2014) 17 *Tulane Journal of Technology and Intellectual Property* 36

McGillivray K., 'FedRAMP, Contracts, and the US Federal Government's Move to Cloud Computing: If an 800-pound Gorilla Can't Tame the Cloud, Who Can?' (2016) 17 *The Columbia Science and Technology Law Review* 336

McGillivray K., 'Give It Away Now? Renewal of the IANA Functions Contract and Its Role in Internet Governance' (2014) 22 *International Journal of Law and Information Technology* 3

Medeiros F., 'Is ".com" International? The .com gTLD: An Analysis of its Global Nature through the Prism of Jurisdiction' (2013) 21 *International Journal of Law and Information Technology* 269

Millard C., 'Forced Localization of Cloud Services: Is Privacy the Real Driver?' (2015) 2 *Cloud Computing, IEEE* 10

Mizrahi S., 'The Dangers of Sharing Cloud Storage: The Privacy Violations Suffered by Innocent Cloud Users During the Course of Criminal Investigations in Canada and the United States' (2017) 25 *Tulane Journal of International and Comparative Law* 303

Moskowitz Y., 'MLATS and the Trusted Nation Club: The Proper Cost of Membership' (2016) 41 *Yale Journal of International Law Online* 15

Mowbray M., 'The Fog Over the Grimpen Mire: Cloud Computing and the Law' (2009) 6 *SCRIPTed* 14

Nagel T. and E. M. Kelley, 'The Impact of Globalization on Structuring, Implementing, and Advising on Sourcing Arrangements' (2007) 38 *Georgetown Journal of International Law* 619

Narayanan V., 'Harnessing the Cloud: International Law Implications of Cloud-Computing' (2012) 12 *Chicago Journal of International Law* 783

Nepple M. and M. Sableman, 'Will the Zippo Sliding Scale for Internet Jurisdiction Slide into Oblivion?' (2016) 20 *Journal of Internet Law* 6

Nichols M. and others, 'Chasing the Clouds without Getting Drenched: A Call for Fair Practices in Cloud Computing Services' (2011) 16 *Journal of Technology Law & Policy* 163

Nicholson J., 'Plus Ultra: Third-Party Preservation in a Cloud Computing Paradigm' (2012) 8 *Hastings Business Law Journal* 191

O'Hara O'Connor E., M. M. Blair, and G. Kirchhoefer, 'Outsourcing, Modularity, and the Theory of the Firm' (2011) 2 *Brigham Young University Law Review* 263

Osula A., 'Transborder Access and Territorial Sovereignty' (2015) 31 *Computer Law and Security Review* 719

Padova Y., 'The Safe Harbour is Invalid: What Tools Remain for Data Transfers and What Comes Next?' (2016) 6 *International Data Privacy Law* 139

Padova Y., 'What the European Draft Regulation on Personal Data is Going to Change for Companies' (2014) 4 *International Data Privacy Law* 39

Palmer V., 'From Lerotholi to Lando: Some Examples of Comparative Law Methodology' (2004) 4 *Global Jurist Frontiers* 1

Paquette S., P. T. Jaeger, and S. C. Wilson, 'Identifying the Security Risks Associated with Governmental Use of Cloud Computing' (2010) 27 *Government Information Quarterly* 245

Parker J., 'Lost in the Cloud: Protecting End-User Privacy in Federal Cloud Computing Contracts' (2012) 41 *Public Contract Law Journal* 385

Perritt H. Jr., J. Taylor, and J. Morgan, 'Achieving Legal and Business Order in Cyberspace: A Report on Global Jurisdiction Issues Created by the Internet' (2000) 55 *Business Lawyer* 1801

Pham C., 'E-Discovery in the Cloud Era: What's a Litigant to Do?' (2013) 5 *Hastings Science & Technology Law Journal* 41

Pierce J., 'Shifting Data Breach Liability: A Congressional Approach' (2016) 57 *William and Mary Law Review* 975

Purtova N., 'Between the GDPR and the Police Directive: Navigating through the Maze of Information Sharing in Public–Private Partnerships' (2018) 8 *International Data Privacy Law* 52

Purtova N., 'Private Law Solutions in European Data Protection: Relationship to Privacy, and Waiver of Data Protection Rights' (2010) 28 *Netherlands Quarterly of Human Rights* 179

Rachovitsa A., 'Engineering and Lawyering Privacy by Design: Understanding Online Privacy both as a Technical and an International Human Rights Issue' (2016) 24 *International Journal of Law and Information Technology* 374

Raymond A., 'Heavyweight Bots in the Clouds: The Wrong Incentives and Poorly Crafted Balances That Lead to the Blocking of Information Online' (2013) 11 *Northwestern Journal of Technology & Intellectual Property* 26

Revolidis I., 'Judicial Jurisdiction Over Internet Privacy Violations and the GDPR: A Case of "Privacy Tourism"?' (2017) 11 *Masaryk University Journal of Law and Technology* 7

Robison W. J., 'Free at What Cost?: Cloud Computing Privacy under the Stored Communications Act' (2010) 98 *The Georgetown Law Journal* 1195

Rustad M. and M. V. Onufrio, 'Reconceptualizing Consumer Terms of Use for a Globalized Knowledge Economy' (2012) 14 *University of Pennsylvania Journal of Business Law* 1085

Sako M., 'Outsourcing and Offshoring: Implications for Productivity of Business Services' (2006) 22 *Oxford Review of Economic Policy* 499

Saw C. L. and W. B. Chik, 'Whither the Future of Internet Streaming and Time-shifting? Revisiting the Rights of Reproduction and Communication to the Public in Copyright Law after Aereo' (2015) 23 *International Journal of Law and Information Technology* 53

Schartum D., 'Making Privacy by Design Operative' (2016) 24 *International Journal of Law and Information Technology* 151

Schoorl J., 'Clicking the Export Button: Cloud Data Storage and US Dual-Use Export Controls' (2012) 80 *George Washington Law Review* 632

Schrop K., 'Your Cooperation is Greatly Appreciated: The Fourth Amendment, National Security Letters, and Public-Private Data Sharing' (2018) 122 *Penn State Law Review* 849

Schwartz P., 'Information Privacy in the Cloud' (2013) 161 *University of Pennsylvania Law Review* 31

Schwartz P., 'Legal Access to the Global Cloud' (2018) 118 *Columbia Law Review* 1681

Schwartz P. and D. J. Solove, 'Reconciling Personal Information in the United States and European Union' (2014) 102 *California Law Review* 887

Seddon J. and W. L. Currie, 'Cloud Computing and Trans-border Health Data: Unpacking US and EU Healthcare Regulation and Compliance' (2013) 2 *Health Policy and Technology* 229

Segall S., 'Jurisdictional Challenges in the United States Government's Move to Cloud Computing Technology' (2013) 23 *Fordham Intellectual Property, Media and Entertainment Law Journal* 1105

Selby J., 'Data Localization Laws: Trade Barriers or Legitimate Responses to Cybersecurity Risks, or Both?' (2017) 25 *International Journal of Law and Information Technology* 213

Sloan P., 'The Reasonable Information Security Program' (2014) 21 *Richmond Journal of Law & Technology* 2

Sluijs J. P. J. B., P. Larouche, and W. Sauter, 'Cloud Computing in the EU Policy Sphere Interoperability, Vertical Integration and the Internal Market' (2012) 3(1) *Journal of Intellectual Property, Information Technology and e-Commerce Law: JIPITEC* 12–32

Snukal A., J. I. Rosenbaum, and L. A. Bernstein, 'Cloud Computing – Transcending the Cloud: A Legal Guide to the Risks and Rewards of Cloud Computing, Part One' (2011) 65 *Consumer Finance Law Quarterly Report* 11

Solove D. and W. Hartzog, 'The FTC and the New Common Law of Privacy' (2014) 114 *Columbia Law Review* 583

Solove D. and W. Hartzog, 'The FTC and Privacy and Security Duties for the Cloud' (2014) 13 *BNA Privacy & Security Law Report* 577

Solum L. and M. Chung, 'The Layers Principle: Internet Architecture and the Law' (2004) 79 *Notre Dame Law Review* 815

Spivey G., 'Computer Software Sales and Licenses as Subject to Article 2 of Uniform Commercial Code' (2017) 26 *American Law Reports* § 1

Stegmaier G. and W. Bartnick, 'Psychics, Russian Roulette, and Data Security: The FTC's Hidden Data-Security Requirements' (2013) 20 *George Mason Law Review* 673

Stoolman M., 'The Cause of Action for Breach of Data?: The Problem with Relying on Courts when Managing the Risks of Cloud Services' (2018) 70 *Rutgers University Law Review* 717

Story J., 'Cloud Computing and the NSA: The Carbon Footprint of the Secret Servers' (2014) 9 *Pittsburgh Journal of Environmental and Public Health Law* 33

Summers D., 'Third Party Beneficiaries and the Restatement (Second) of Contracts' (1982) 67 *Cornell Law Review* 880

Surden H., 'Computable Contracts' (2012) 46 *University of California Davis Law Review* 643

Svantesson D., 'Against "Against Data Exceptionalism"' (2016) 10(2) *Masaryk University Journal of Law and Technology* 200

Svantesson D., 'A Legal Method for Solving Issues of Internet Regulation' (2011) 19 *International Journal of Law and Information Technology* 243

Svantesson D., 'A New Jurisprudential Framework for Jurisdiction: Beyond the Harvard Draft' (2015) 109 *AJIL Unbound* 69

Svantesson D., 'Article 4 (1)(a)"Establishment of the Controller" in EU Data Privacy Law – Time to Rein in This Expanding Concept?' (2016) 6 *International Data Privacy Law* 210

Svantesson D., 'Data Protection in Cloud Computing – The Swedish Perspective' (2012) 28 *Computer Law & Security Review* 476

Svantesson D., 'Extraterritoriality and Targeting in EU Data Privacy Law: The Weak Spot Undermining the Regulation' (2015) 5 *International Data Privacy Law* 226

Svantesson D., 'Jurisdictional Issues and the Internet – A Brief Overview 2.0' (2018) 34 *Computer Law and Security Review* 715

Svantesson D., 'The Hypocritical Hype about 'Hypothesis': Why Legal Research Needs to Shed This Relic' (2014) 39 *Alternative Law Journal* 259

Svantesson D. and F. Gerry, 'Access to Extraterritorial Evidence: The Microsoft Cloud Case and Beyond' (2015) 31 *Computer Law & Security Review* 478

Svantesson D. and L. van Zwieten, 'Law Enforcement Access to Evidence via Direct Contact with Cloud Providers – Identifying the Contours of a Solution' (2016) 32 *Computer Law & Security Review* 671

Tene O., 'Privacy Law's Midlife Crisis: A Critical Assessment of the Second Wave of Global Privacy Laws. The Second Wave of Global Privacy Protection' (2013) 74 *Ohio State Law Journal* 1217

Terry N., 'Regulatory Disruption and Arbitrage in Health-Care Data Protection' (2017) 17 *Yale Journal of Health Policy, Law, and Ethics* 207

Thomas R. III, 'A Primer for Negotiating Subcontracts for High-Tech Small Businesses' (2005) 52 *Federal Lawyer* 22

Vanberg A. and M. B. Ünver, 'The Right to Data Portability in the GDPR and EU Competition Law: Odd Couple or Dynamic Duo?' (2017) 8 *European Journal of Law and Technology* 1

Veale M., R. Binns, and J. Ausloos, 'When Data Protection by Design and Data Subject Rights Clash' (2018) 8 *International Data Privacy Law* 105

Ward B. and J. C. Sipior, 'The Internet Jurisdiction Risk of Cloud Computing' (2010) 27 *Information Systems Management* 334

Warren S. and L. D. Brandeis, 'The Right to Privacy' (1890) 4 *Harvard Law Review* 193

Wauters E., E. Lievens, and P. Valcke, 'Towards a Better Protection of Social Media Users: A Legal Perspective on the Terms of Use of Social Networking Sites' (2014) 22 *International Journal of Law and Information Technology* 254

Weber R. H. and D. Staiger, 'Cloud Computing: A Cluster of Complex Liability Issues' (2014) 20 *European Journal of Current Legal Issues* 1

Werbach K., 'The Network Utility' (2011) 60 *Duke Law Journal* 1761

Westmoreland K. and G. Kent, 'International Law Enforcement Access to User Data: A Survival Guide and Call for Action' (2015) 13 *Canadian Journal of Law and Technology* 225

Wolters P. T. J., 'The Security of Personal Data under the GDPR: A Harmonized Duty or a Shared Responsibility?' (2017) 7 *International Data Privacy Law* 165

Woods A., 'Against Data Exceptionalism' (2016) 68 *Stanford Law Review* 729

Yoo C. S., 'The Changing Patterns of Internet Usage' (2010) 63 *Federal Communications Law Journal* 67, 83

Zanfir G., 'The Right to Data Portability in the Context of the EU Data Protection Reform' (2012) 2(3) *International Data Privacy Law* 149

Zons J., 'The Minefield of Back-to-Back Subcontracts' (2010) 11 *Construction Law International* 1

Zuckerman M., 'The Offshoring of American Government' (2008) 94 *Cornell Law Review* 165

REPORTS AND GUIDELINES

Abramatic J. F. and others, 'Privacy Bridges: EU and US Privacy Experts in Search of Transatlantic Privacy Solutions' (2015) https://privacybridges.mit.edu/sites/default/files/documents/PrivacyBridges-FINAL.pdf

Armbrust M. and others, 'Above the Clouds: A Berkeley View of Cloud Computing' Technical Report No UCB/EECS-2009-28 (2009) 16 www.eecs.berkeley.edu/Pubs/TechRpts/2009/EECS-2009-28.html

Badger L. and others, 'Cloud Computing Synopsis and Recommendations' National Institute of Standards and Technology (2012) https://csrc.nist.gov/publications/detail/sp/800-146/final

Badger L. and others, 'US Government Cloud Computing Technology Roadmap Volume II Release 1.0 (Draft)' (NIST Technology 2011) www.nist.gov/sites/default/files/documents/itl/cloud/SP_500_293_volumeII.pdf

Badger L. and others, 'US Government Cloud Computing Technology Roadmap' Volume I & II: High-Priority Requirements to Further USG Agency Cloud Computing Adoption, vol. II (2014) https://nvlpubs.nist.gov/nistpubs/SpecialPublications/NIST.SP.500-293.pdf

Bignami F., 'The US Legal System on Data Protection in the Field of Law Enforcement. Safeguards, Rights and Remedies for EU Citizens' Study for the LIBE Committee (2015)

Brito M., 'Cloud Computing, Multi-Sourcing Create New Challenges in Outsourcing' West Law number 1600655 Aspatore (2014) 1

Burns P. and M. Karlyn, 'What Companies Need to Know About Outsourcing Contracts' WL 1600656 Aspatore (2014) 1

Butterworth G. and others, 'Outsourcing in Europe: An In-Depth Review of Drivers, Risks and Trends in the European Outsourcing Market' Report/Publication Ernst & Young (2013) 1. www.ey.com/Publication/vwLUAssets/Outsourcing_in_Europe_2013/$FILE/EY-outsourcing-survey.pdf

Cafaggi F., A. Renda, and R. Schmidt, 'Transnational Private Regulation' in International Regulatory Co-operation: Case Studies, Vol 3 Transnational Private Regulation and Water Management (OECD 2013) http://dx.doi.org/10.1787/9789264200524-3-en

Catteddu D., 'Security & Resilience in Governmental Clouds - Making an Informed Decision' ENISA (2011)

Cavoukian A., 'Privacy by Design: The 7 Foundational Principles' Information & Privacy Commissioner, Ontario, Canada (2011) https://iab.org/wp-content/IAB-uploads/2011/03/fred_carter.pdf

Chief Information Officers and others, 'Creating Effective Cloud Computing Contracts for the Federal Government Best Practices for Acquiring IT as a Service' US Federal Cloud

Compliance Committee (2012) https://s3.amazonaws.com/sitesusa/wp-content/uploads/sites/1151/2016/10/cloudbestpractices.pdf

CoE, Cybercrime Convention Committee (T-CY), 'Criminal Justice Access to Electronic Evidence in the Cloud: Recommendations for Consideration by the T-CY' Final Report of the T-CY Cloud Evidence Group (2016) www.coe.int/en/web/cybercrime/ceg

Commission, 'Comparative Study on Cloud Computing Contracts' Directorate-General for Justice and Consumers (European Commission) (2015) https://publications.europa.eu/en/publication-detail/-/publication/40148ba1-1784-4d1a-bb64-334ac3df22c7

Conrad I. and others, 'Cloud Computing Contracts – Discussion Paper on Subcontracting' EU Expert Group on Cloud Computing Contracts (2014) https://ec.europa.eu/info/business-economy-euro/doing-business-eu/contract-rules/cloud-computing/expert-group-cloud-computing-contracts_en

Consumer Financial Protection Bureau, Office of the Inspector General, 'Audit of the CFPB's Acquisition and Contract Management of Select Cloud Computing Services' Audit Report 2014-IT-C-016 (2014) https://oig.federalreserve.gov/reports/cfpb-cloud-computing-services-sep2014.pdf

Council of the Inspectors General on Integrity and Efficiency (CIGIE), 'The Council of the Inspectors General on Integrity and Efficiency's Cloud Computing Initiative' (2014)

Danish Agency for Digitization and Kammeradvokaten, 'Cloud Computing and the Legal Framework – Guidance on Legislative Requirement and the Contractual Environment Related to Cloud Computing' (2012)

Davies R., 'Cloud Computing: An Overview of Economic and Policy Issues' European Parliamentary Research Service (2016) www.europarl.europa.eu/thinktank/en/document.html?reference=EPRS_IDA(2016)583786

Defense Information Systems Agency, 'Department of Defense (DoD) Cloud Computing Security Requirements Guide Version 1 Release 1' Report DoD Cloud Computing SRG v1r1 (2015) https://info.publicintelligence.net/DoD-CloudSecurity.pdf

Dekker M. and D. Liveri, 'Cloud Security Guide for SMEs: Cloud Computing Security Risks and Opportunities for SMEs' (2015) www.enisa.europa.eu/activities/Resilience-and-CIIP/cloud-computing/security-for-smes/cloud-security-guide-for-smes

Department of Defense, Inspector General, 'DoD Cloud Computing Strategy Needs Implementation Plan and Detailed Waiver Process' Report No DODIG-2015-045 (2014) 23 www.dtic.mil/dtic/tr/fulltext/u2/a613689.pdf

De Silva S., 'Liability Discussion Paper' EC Expert Group on Cloud Computing Contracts (9 April 2014) https://ec.europa.eu/info/business-economy-euro/doing-business-eu/contract-rules/cloud-computing/expert-group-cloud-computing-contracts_en

Directorate-General for Communications Networks European Commission, Content and Technology, 'Analysis of Cloud Best Practices and Pilots for the Public Sector - Final Report SMART: 2012/0069' (2013) https://ec.europa.eu/digital-single-market/en/news/analysis-cloud-best-practices-and-pilots-public-sector

Environmental Protection Agency, Office of the Inspector General, 'Cloud Oversight Resulted in Unsubstantiated and Missed Opportunities for Savings, Unused and Undelivered Services, and Incomplete Policies' Report No 14-P-0332 (2014) www.epa.gov/sites/production/files/2015-09/documents/20140815-14-p-0332.pdf

Environmental Protection Agency, Office of Inspector General, 'EPA Is Not Fully Aware of the Extent of Its Use of Cloud Computing Technologies' Report No 14-P0323 (2014) www.epa.gov/office-inspector-general/report-epa-not-fully-aware-extent-its-use-cloud-computing-technologies

Environmental Protection Agency, Office of Inspector General, 'EPA Needs to Improve the Recognition and Administration of Cloud Services for the Office of Water's Permit Management Oversight System' Report No 15-P-0295 (24 September 2015) www.epa.gov/sites/production/files/2015-09/documents/20150924-15-p-0295.pdf

European Banking Authority, 'Recommendations on Outsourcing to Cloud Service Providers' EBA/REC/2017/03 (2017) https://eba.europa.eu/regulation-and-policy/internal-governance/recommendations-on-outsourcing-to-cloud-service-providers

European Commission, 'A Digital Single Market Strategy for Europe' COM (2015) 192 final

European Commission, '"Analysis of Cloud Best Practices and Pilots for the Public Sector" and "Annex to the Final Report: Country Files"' A study prepared for the European Commission DG Communications Networks, Content & Technology (13 November 2013) https://ec.europa.eu/digital-single-market/en/news/analysis-cloud-best-practices-and-pilots-public-sector

European Commission, 'Certification Schemes for Cloud Computing' Final Report – Study (2014) https://publications.europa.eu/en/publication-detail/-/publication/a30d111d-df3f-4aa0-b816-9f515c2f6f85

European Commission, 'Communication from the Commission to the European Parliament, the Council, the European Economic and Social Committee and the Committee of the Regions. Unleashing the Potential of Cloud Computing in Europe' (2012) https://eur-lex.europa.eu/legal-content/EN/TXT/?uri=CELEX%3A52012DC0529

European Commission, 'Communication from the Commission to the European Parliament, the Council, the European Economic and Social Committee and the Committee of the Regions European Cloud Initiative – Building a competitive data and knowledge economy in Europe' COM (2016) 178 final https://ec.europa.eu/digital-single-market/en/news/communication-european-cloud-initiative-building-competitive-data-and-knowledge-economy-europe

European Commission, 'Communication from the Commission to the European Parliament, the Council and the European Economic and Social Committee: Digital Contracts for Europe - Unleashing the Potential of E-commerce' COM (2015) 633

European Commission, 'Comparative Study on Cloud Computing Contracts' (2015) https://publications.europa.eu/en/publication-detail/-/publication/40148ba1-1784-4d1a-bb64-334ac3df22c7/language-en

European Commission, 'Comparative Study on Cloud Computing Contracts' Annex 1: Country Report Overview Work Package 1' (2015) https://publications.europa.eu/en/publication-detail/-/publication/c854e3e9-8f7a-4a38-b811-46e799747858/language-en

European Commission, 'Comparative Study on Cloud Computing Contracts' Final Report - Annex 2: Methodology and Sample Country Selection Work Package 2' (2015) https://publications.europa.eu/en/publication-detail/-/publication/40148ba1-1784-4d1a-bb64-334ac3df22c7

European Commission, 'Comparative Study on Cloud Computing Contracts' Final Report - Annex 3: Template Questionnaire with Information Note Used to Gather Input for Work Package 3' (2015) https://publications.europa.eu/en/publication-detail/-/publication/40148ba1-1784-4d1a-bb64-334ac3df22c7

European Commission, 'Comparative Study on Cloud Computing Contracts' Annex 4: Comparative Study on Cloud Computing Contracts: Final Report - Annex 4: Country Report Overview Work Package 3' (2015) https://publications.europa.eu/en/publication-detail/-/publication/13f8fb54-f159-4ff1-ba72-a8478a33a072/language-en

European Commission, 'Content and Technology Unit E2 – Software and Services, Cloud Computing Service Level Agreements: Exploitation of Research Results' (2013) https://ec

.europa.eu/digital-agenda/en/news/cloud-computing-service-level-agreements-exploitation-research-results

European Commission, 'Facilitating Cross-Border Data Flow in the Digital Single Market: Study on Data Location Restrictions' SMART 2015/0054 (2017)

European Commission, 'Measuring the Economic Impact of Cloud Computing in Europe: Study Report' (10 January 2016) https://ec.europa.eu/digital-single-market/en/news/measuring-economic-impact-cloud-computing-europe

European Commission, 'Report from the Commission to the European Parliament and the Council on the First Annual Review of the Functioning of the EU–U.S. Privacy Shield' COM (2017) 611 final

European Commission, 'Standards Terms and Performance Criteria in Service Level Agreements for Cloud Computing Services' SMART 2013/0039 Final Report (2015)

European Commission, 'What is VAT?' Taxation and Customs Unit http://ec.europa.eu/taxation_customs/business/vat/what-is-vat_en

European Commission Directorate-General for Communications Networks European Commission, Content and Technology, 'Analysis of Cloud Best Practices and Pilots for the Public Sector – Final Report' (2012) https://ec.europa.eu/digital-single-market/en/news/analysis-cloud-best-practices-and-pilots-public-sector

European Parliament, 'Fighting Cyber Crime and Protecting Privacy in the Cloud' Committee on Civil Liberties, Justice and Home Affairs (2012) www.europarl.europa.eu/thinktank/en/document.html?reference=IPOL-LIBE_ET%282012%29462509

European Telecommunications Standards Institute, 'Cloud Standards Coordination Final Report' (November 2013) www.etsi.org/images/files/Events/2013/2013_CSC_Delivery_WS/CSC-Final_report-013-CSC_Final_report_v1_0_PDF_format-.PDF

European Union Agency for Network and Information Security, 'Critical Cloud Computing: A CIIP Perspective on Cloud Computing Services Version 1.0' (2012) www.enisa.europa.eu/publications/critical-cloud-computing

European Union Agency for Network and Information Security, 'Good Practice Guide for Securely Deploying Governmental Clouds' (2013) www.enisa.europa.eu/publications/good-practice-guide-for-securely-deploying-governmental-clouds

European Union Agency for Network and Information Security, 'Procure Secure: A Guide to Monitoring of Security Service Levels in Cloud Contracts' (2 April 2012) www.enisa.europa.eu/publications/procure-secure-a-guide-to-monitoring-of-security-service-levels-in-cloud-contracts

European Union Agency for Network and Information Security, 'Security & Resilience in Governmental Clouds – Making an Informed Decision' (2016) www.enisa.europa.eu/publications/security-and-resilience-in-governmental-clouds

European Union Agency for Network and Information Security, 'Survey and Analysis of Security Parameters in Cloud SLAs Across the European Public Sector' Final Report (2011) www.enisa.europa.eu/publications/survey-and-analysis-of-security-parameters-in-cloud-slas-across-the-european-public-sector

Federal Trade Commission, 'A Brief Overview of the Federal Trade Commission's Investigative and Law Enforcement Authority' (2008) Appendix A www.ftc.gov/about-ftc/what-we-do/enforcement-authority

FedRAMP PMO, 'Tips and Cues' Report (January 2018) www.fedramp.gov/assets/resources/documents/FedRAMP_Tips_and_Cues.pdf

Ficsor M., 'The WIPO "Internet Treaties" and Copyright in the "Cloud"' ALAI Congress (2012) 1 www.alai.jp/ALAI2012/program/paper/The%20WIPO%20Internet%20Treaties%

20and%20copyright%20in%20the%20Cloud%20%EF%BC%88Dr.%20Mih%C3%A1ly%20J.%20Ficsor%EF%BC%89.pdf

Figliola P. and E. A. Fischer, 'Overview and Issues for Implementation of the Federal Cloud Computing Initiative: Implications for Federal Information Technology Reform Management' (20 January 2015) www.fas.org/sgp/crs/misc/R42887.pdf

Forgó N., I. Nwankwo, and J. Pfeiffenbring, 'Cloud Legal Guidelines: Final Report' Optimis EU FP7 Project (2013)

Friedman G., 'Department of Energy (DoE) Office of Inspector General, Office of Audits and Inspections, Audit Report: The Department of Energy's Management of Cloud Computing Activities' (2014)

Føyen Torkildsen AS, 'Utredning av Juridiske Forhold ved Bruk av Nettsky i Kommunal Sektor – En Mulighetsstudie' [Report on the Legal Aspects of Cloud Computing in the Municipal Sector: A Feasibility Study] Norwegian Association of Local and Regional Authorities R&D Project No 144008 (2015) www.ks.no/globalassets/endelig-rapport-om-bruk-av-skytjenester-i-kommunal-sektor.pdf

Gasser U., 'Cloud Innovation and the Law: Issues, Approaches, and Interplay' Berkman Center Research Publication (No. 2014-7) (2014) https://dash.harvard.edu/handle/1/16460372

Government Accountability Office, 'Cloud Computing: Additional Opportunities and Savings Need to Be Pursued' GAO-14-753 (2014) www.gao.gov/products/GAO-14-753

Government Accountability Office, 'Cloud Computing: Agencies Need to Incorporate Key Practices to Ensure Effective Performance' GAO-16-325 (2016) www.gao.gov/products/GAO-16-325

Government Accountability Office, 'Information Technology Reform: Progress Made but Future Cloud Computing Efforts Should Be Better Planned' GAO-12-756 (2012) www.gao.gov/assets/600/592249.pdf

Hustinx P., 'Opinion of the European Data Protection Supervisor on the Commission's Communication on "Unleashing the Potential of Cloud Computing in Europe"' (2012) https://edps.europa.eu/sites/edp/files/publication/12-11-16_cloud_computing_en.pdf

Jansen W. and T. Grance, 'Guidelines on Security and Privacy in Public Cloud Computing' SP 800-144 (2011) https://nvlpubs.nist.gov/nistpubs/Legacy/SP/nistspecialpublication800-144.pdf

Kemp R., 'Seeding the Global Public Sector Cloud: Part II – The UK's Approach as Pathfinder for Other Countries' (2015) www.kempitlaw.com/seeding-the-global-public-sector-cloud-data-classification-security-frameworks-and-international-standards/

Kundra V., 'Office of E-Government and Information Technology, Federal Cloud Computing Strategy' (2011) https://obamawhitehouse.archives.gov/sites/default/files/omb/assets/egov_docs/federal-cloud-computing-strategy.pdf

Liu F. and others, 'NIST Cloud Computing Reference Architecture' NIST Special Publication 500-292 (2011) www.nist.gov/publications/nist-cloud-computing-reference-architecture

Liu F. and others, 'NIST Cloud Computing Standards Roadmap' NIST Special Publication 500-291 (2011)

Liveri D. and M. A. C. Dekker, 'Security Framework for Governmental Clouds: All Steps from Design to Deployment' ENISA (2015) 3 www.enisa.europa.eu/publications/security-framework-for-governmental-clouds

Maconick E., 'Climate Change: Cloud Sourcing as the New Normal for IT Outsourcing Transactions' WL 1600650 Aspatore (2014) 8: 2

Maxwell W. and C. Wolf, 'A Global Reality: Governmental Access to Data in the Cloud: A Comparative Analysis of Ten International Jurisdictions' White Paper (2012) www.hldataprotection.com/uploads/file/Revised%20Government%20Access%20to%20Cloud%20Data%20Paper%20(18%20July%2012).pdf

McCallister E., T. Grance, and K. A. Scarfone, 'Guide to Protecting the Confidentiality of Personally Identifiable Information (PII)' NIST Special Publication 800-122 (2010)

Mell P. and T. Grance, 'The NIST Definition of Cloud Computing' NIST Special Publication 800-145 (2011) https://csrc.nist.gov/publications/detail/sp/800-145/final

Nagel T., 'Structuring Multi-Supplier IT Environments' WL 1600651 Aspatore (2014) 1

NASA Office of Inspector General, 'NASA's Progress in Adopting Cloud-Computing Technologies' (29 July 2013) https://oig.nasa.gov/docs/IG-13-021.pdf

NIST Joint Task Force Transformation Initiative, 'Security and Privacy Controls for Federal Information Systems and Organizations' NIST Special Publication 800-53 (2011)

Norwegian Ministry of Local Government and Modernisation, 'Cloud Computing Strategy for Norway' Publication Number H-2365 E (2016) www.regjeringen.no/en/dokumenter/cloud-computing-strategy-for-norway/id2484403/

NTT Communications Report, 'NSA After-Shocks: How Snowden Has Changed ICT Decision-Makers' Approach to the Cloud' (2013) http://nsaaftershocks.com/wp-content/themes/nsa/images/NTTC_Report_WEB.pdf

OECD, 'Cloud Computing: The Concept, Impacts and the Role of Government Policy' (OECD 2014) http://dx.doi.org/10.1787/5jxzf4lcc7f5-en

Office of Inspector General USDA, 'Audit Report 50501-0005-12: USDA's Implementation of Cloud Computing Services' (2014) www.usda.gov/oig/webdocs/50501-0005-12.pdf

Petroleumstilsynet [Petroleum Safety Authority], 'Uriktige påstander om IKT-tilsyn i NRK' [Incorrect Claims on ICT Supervision at NRK] (2016) www.ptil.no/nyheter/uriktige-pastander-om-ikt-tilsyn-i-nrk-article12392-702.html

PICSE, 'Procurement Innovation for Cloud Services in Europe: D3.1 Procurement Barriers Report' N:644014 (2015) www.picse.eu/publications/deliverables/d31-procurement-barriers-report

PICSE, 'Procuring Cloud Services Today: Experiences and Lessons Learned from the Public Sector' (2016) www.picse.eu/sites/default/files/Procuring%20cloud%20services%20today_22072015.pdf

Powner D. and United States Government Accountability Office, 'Information Technology: Federal Agencies Need to Address Aging Legacy Systems' Report GAO-16-696T (25 May 2016) www.gao.gov/assets/680/677454.pdf

PricewaterhouseCoopers, 'Pulse Survey: US Companies Ramping up General Data Protection Regulation (GDPR) Budgets' (2017) www.pwc.com/us/en/services/consulting/library/general-data-protection-regulation-gdpr-budgets.html

Procurement Innovation for Cloud Services in Europe (PICSE), 'PICSE – Procurement Innovation for Cloud Services in Europe: D3.2 Procurement Best Practices Report' EU Project H2020-ICT-2014-1 (2016) www.picse.eu/publications/deliverables/d32-procurement-best-practices-report

Rauhofer J. and C. Bowden, 'Protecting Their Own: Fundamental Rights Implications for EU Data Sovereignty in the Cloud' Edinburgh School of Law Research Paper No 2013/28 (2013) www.research.ed.ac.uk/portal/files/13528951/Rauhofer_Protecting_their_own.pdf

Reuters Staff, 'Statoil Moves Key IT Tasks from India Back to Norway' Reuters (30 June 2017) www.reuters.com/article/statoil-norway-cyber-idUSL8N1JR41E

References

Sanner J. 'Cloud Computing Strategy for Norway' Norwegian Ministry of Local Government and Modernisation, Publication Number: H-2365 E (2016). www.regjeringen.no/en/dokumenter/cloud-computing-strategy-for-norway/id2484403/

SLALOM, 'Final Legal Terms for Adoption D2.2' SLALOM Legal Model Terms (2016) EU Project http://slalom-project.eu/node/176

SLALOM, 'Report on Jurisprudence and Case Law D2.3' (13 June 2016) http://slalom-project.eu/sites/default/files/slalom/public/content-files/article/SLALOM_D2.3_%20FINAL13June%20_v1.315Sep2016_1.3.pdf

Trans Lex, 'No. IV.1.2 - Sanctity of Contracts' www.trans-lex.org/919000

UK Crown Commercial Service, 'G-Cloud 9 Framework: Overview and Buyers Guide' (2017) www.gov.uk/guidance/g-cloud-buyers-guide

UK Crown Commercial Service, 'Procurement Policy Note – Changes to Data Protection Legislation & General Data Protection Regulation' Action Note PPN 03/17 (2017) www.gov.uk/government/publications/procurement-policy-note-0218-changes-to-data-protection-legislation-general-data-protection-regulation

UK Crown Commercial Service, 'The Total Value of Sales through the G-Cloud Framework' (2017) www.gov.uk/government/statistical-data-sets/g-cloud-framework-sales-up-to-31-july-2017

UK Government Digital Service, 'Government Cloud First Policy' (3 February 2017) www.gov.uk/guidance/government-cloud-first-policy#consider-cloud-solutions-before-alternatives

UK Government Digital Service, 'Guidance: Make Privacy Integral' (6 November 2017) www.gov.uk/guidance/make-privacy-integral

UK Government Digital Service, 'Guidance: Terms and Conditions of Digital Marketplace Frameworks' (18 April 2016) www.gov.uk/guidance/terms-and-conditions-of-digital-marketplace-frameworks

United States Department of Agriculture, Office of Inspector General, 'USDA's Implementation of Cloud Computing Services' Audit Report 50501-0005-12 (2014) www.usda.gov/oig/webdocs/50501-0005-12.pdf

United States Department of State, '7 Foreign Affairs Manual' (2013) https://fam.state.gov/fam/07fam/07fam0960.html

United States Postal Service, 'Cloud Security' (2015) https://about.usps.com/handbooks/as805h/welcome.htm

VanRoekel S., 'Security Authorization of Information Systems in Cloud Computing Environments' Office of Management and Budget (8 December 2011)

Venturini J. and others, 'Terms of Service and Human Rights: An Analysis of Online Platform Contracts' Study/Report (Editora Revan 2016) http://bibliotecadigital.fgv.br/dspace/handle/10438/18231

Vincent M., 'Cloud Computing Contracts White Paper: A Survey of Terms and Conditions' White Paper (2011) www.ficpi.org.au/articles/White_Paper_June2011.pdf

Wyld D., 'Moving to the Cloud: An Introduction to Cloud Computing in Government' 33 IBM Center for the Business of Government (2009) www.businessofgovernment.org/sites/default/files/CloudComputingReport.pdf

Zevin S., 'Standards for Security Categorization of Federal Information and Information Systems' US Department of Commerce, FIPS Publication 199 (2004) https://citadel-information.com/wp-content/uploads/2012/08/FIPS-PUB-199-final.pdf

NEWSPAPER AND BLOG ARTICLES

Aitoro J., 'The Mysterious Bankruptcy Case of Global Computer Enterprises' *Washington Business Journal* (12 September 2014) www.bizjournals.com/washington/blog/fedbiz_daily/2014/09/the-mysterious-bankruptcy-case-of-government.html

Boal E., 'Fun with Processor Clauses' *Society for Computers and Law (SCL)* (2018) www.scl.org/articles/10117-fun-with-processor-clauses

Brodkin J., 'Google Apps Not Cutting It for LA's Finest' *Wired Online* (20 October 2011) www.wired.com/2011/10/google-apps-los-angeles-police/

Drape J., 'Cloud Computing Takes the Preakness, Ending Always Dreaming's Crown Hopes' *New York Times Online* (20 May 2017) www.nytimes.com/2017/05/20/sports/horse-racing/Cloud-computing-wins-preakness-stakes-always-dreaming.html

Gibbs S., 'Typo Blamed for Amazon's Internet-Crippling Outage' *The Guardian* (3 March 2017) www.theguardian.com/technology/2017/mar/03/typo-blamed-amazon-web-services-internet-outage

Henley J., 'Sweden Scrambles to Tighten Data Security as Scandal Claims Two Ministers' *The Guardian* (1 August 2017) www.theguardian.com/technology/2017/aug/01/sweden-scrambles-to-tighten-data-security-as-scandal-claims-two-ministers

Hersher R., 'Amazon and the $150 Million Typo' *National Public Radio Online* www.npr.org/sections/thetwo-way/2017/03/03/518322734/amazon-and-the-150-million-typo

Hills H., 'Key Error in India Halted Production at Mongstad' *Norway Today Online* (28 October 2016) http://norwaytoday.info/finance/key-error-india-halted-production-mongstad/

Jørgenrud M., 'Her er brevet som forbyr Google Apps' [Here is the Letter Prohibiting Google Apps] (24 January 2012) www.digi.no/887985/her-er-brevet-som-forbyr-google-apps

Konkel F., 'The Details about the CIA's Deal with Amazon $600 Million Computing Cloud Built by an Outside Company is a "Radical Departure" for the Risk-Averse Intelligence Community' *The Atlantic* (17 July 2014) www.theatlantic.com/technology/archive/2014/07/the-details-about-the-cias-deal-with-amazon/374632/

Lauchlan S., 'G-Cloud's "Biggest Single Barrier" – Two Year Contracts in a World of 13 Year Outsourcing Deals' *Diginomica* (26 April 2016) https://government.diginomica.com/2016/04/26/g-clouds-biggest-single-barrier-two-year-contracts-in-a-world-of-13-year-outsourcing-deals/

Mazmanian A., 'Cloud Contractor to Pay US $9M to Settle False Claims Charges' *Washington Tech* (8 May 2015) http://washingtontechnology.com/articles/2015/05/08/gce-false-claims.aspx

Metz C., 'The Epic Story of Dropbox's Exodus from the Amazon Cloud Empire' *Wired Business Online* (14 March 2016) www.wired.com/2016/03/epic

Miller J., 'Inside the Reporter's Notebook: Labor Pinched by Poor Cloud Contracting; Financial Shared Services Progresses' *Fed News Radio* (9 December 2013) www.federalnewsradio.com/?nid=533&sid=3521104

Pepper D., 'Ignoring That Harmless Looking "Force Majeure" Clause in Your Cloud Services Provider Agreement?' *CLOUDAVE* (15 April 2013) www.cloudave.com/27723/ignoring-that-harmless-looking-force-majeure-clause-in-your-cloud-services-provider-agreement/

Perkins B., 'Lessons to be Learned from a Project Nightmare' *Computerworld* (11 March 2015) www.computerworld.com/article/2895066/lessons-to-be-learned-from-a-project-nightmare.html

Remen A. and L. Tomter, 'Tastefeilen Som Stoppet Statoil' [The Typo That Stopped Statoil] *NRK* (28 October 2016) www.nrk.no/norge/xl/tastefeilen-som-stoppet-statoil-1.13174013

Richards T., 'The G-Cloud Security Approach' *Accreditation* (9 June 2014) https://digitalmar ketplace.blog.gov.uk/2014/06/09/the-G-Cloud-security-approach/
Shah S., 'Director Who Outsourced Swedish Government Database to the Cloud, Where Critical Data Was Compromised, Fined Just £6,500' *Computing* (24 July 2017) www .computing.co.uk/ctg/news/3014334/director-who-outsourced-swedish-government-database-to-the-cloud-where-critical-data-was-compromised-fined-just-gbp6-500
Shein E., 'CASB Market Poised for Channel Growth' *Tech Target Blog* (July 2016) https://searchitchannel.techtarget.com/feature/CASB-market-poised-for-channel-growth
Tomter L. and A. C. Remen, 'Datatilsynet Fant Lovbrudd: Millionbøter Etter outsourcing av Sykehus-IT' [The Norwegian Data Protection Authority Found a Violation of the Law: Million NOK Fine for the Outsourcing of Hospital IT] *NRK* (27 October 2017) www.nrk.no /norge/millionboter-etter-outsourcing-av-sykehus-it-1.13751516
Tomter L. and A. C. Remen, 'Globalisering på norsk: Vipps-indere på overtid og en tastefeil på Mongstad: Metode-rapport til SKUP 2017 fra NRK Nyheter' [Globalisation in Norwegian: Vipps Indian employees working overtime and a typo at Mongstad: Methodology Report for Scoop prise 2917] (2017) http://skup-norge.no/wp-content /uploads/2017/03/metoderapport-globalisering-pn-norsk.pdf
Vijayan J., 'Plans to Migrate LAPD to Google's Cloud Apps Dropped: Service is Incompatible with FBI's Security Requirements, City Says' *Computerworld* (22 December 2011) www .computerworld.com/article/2500649/cloud-computing/plans-to-migrate-lapd-to-google -s-cloud-apps-dropped.html
Walsh B., 'Your Data is Dirty: The Carbon Price of Cloud Computing' *Time Online* (2 April 2014) http://time.com/46777/your-data-is-dirty-the-carbon-price-of-cloud-computing/

SELECTED CONTRACTS

Battelle Energy Alliance, LLC, and DoE, 'General Provisions for Commercial Items/ Services' Applicable to Contract No 00109064 (29 August 2011)
Battelle Energy Alliance (BEA) and Unisys Corporation, 'Contract for Unisys Corporation to Furnish Messaging Replacement SOW' Contract No 00109064 (US Gov't No DE-AC07 -05ID14517) (2 September 2011)
British Library and Bravo Solutions UK Ltd, Ref # FIN 8895 (10 February 2014)
Difi, 'Driftsavtalen (SSA-D)' [Operational Services Contract] (2018) www.anskaffelser.no /verktoy/kontrakter-og-avtaler/kjopsavtalen-ssa-k
Difi, 'Avtale om løpende tjenestekjøp (SSA-L)' [Agreement Concerning Ongoing Purchases of Services via the Internet] (2018) www.anskaffelser.no/verktoy/avtale-om-lopende-tjenestekjop-ssa-l
Direktoratet for forvaltning og ikt (Difi) [The Norwegian Agency for Public Management and eGovernment], '*Kjøpsavtalen* (SSA-K)' [IT Sales and Purchase Agreement] (2018) www .anskaffelser.no/verktoy/kontrakter-og-avtaler/kjopsavtalen-ssa-k
EPA and AVANTI Corporation, Contract #EP-BPA-12-C-0010 (24 January 2012) Task 4
FAA and Computer Sciences Corp., Contract DTFACT-15-D-0003 1-81 (26 August 2015)
FAA Cloud Services DTFACT-15-D-00003, Attachment J-1 Cloud Computing Services Description 1-40 (21 August 2015)
FedRAMP Standard Contract Language (27 June 2012) www.fedramp.gov/files/2015/03/ FedRAMP_Standard_Contractual_Clauses_062712_0.pdf

Financial Conduct Authority (FCA), 'FG16/5: Guidance for Firms Outsourcing to the "Cloud" and Other Third Party IT Services' (2016) www.fca.org.uk/publications/finalised-guidance/fg16-5-guidance-firms-outsourcing-cloud-and-other-third-party-it

General Services Administration (GSA), 'FedRAMP Control Specific Contract Clauses: Version 2.0' (6 June 2014)

Google Inc and Battelle Energy Alliance, 'Google Apps for Government and Postini via Reseller Agreement, "BEA-DOE Contract" US Gov't No DE-AC07-05ID14517' (25 August 2011)

Idaho National Laboratory, 'Infrastructure as a Service Statement of Work (SOW)' Document ID: SOW-10558, 1–13 (26 October 2012)

Idaho National Laboratory, 'Messaging Replacement Statement of Work (SOW)' Document ID: SOW-9406, 1–28 (26 March 2015)

Joint Enterprise Defense Infrastructure (JEDI) for Use by the US Military, 'JEDI Cloud Request for Proposal (RFP)' Solicitation Number: HQ003418R0077_JEDI_CLOUD_RFP (2018) www.fbo.gov/index?s=opportunity&mode=form&tab=core&id=38bd3e33414337cdc805c21004d85477&_cview=0

NASA and eTouch Systems Corp., Contract Number NNH05CC35D, 2.2.4 (2005)

Norwegian Agency for Public Management and eGovernment (Difi), 'Avtale om løpende tjenestekjøp (SSA-L)' [Agreement Concerning Ongoing Purchase of Services via the Internet (SSA-L)] (2018) www.anskaffelser.no/verktoy/avtale-om-lopende-tjenestekjop-ssa-l

Police and Crime Commissioner for Avon & Somerset and Iken Business Limited, 'Relating to the Provision of G-Cloud Services' (Call-Off Terms, 17 March 2014)

Sprint II Model Contract (Framework Agreement) Thames Valley Police Authority and Specialist Computing Services, 'Contract Relating to the Provision of IT Products and Services VISAV Ltd (Model Contract v 1.00)' (2012)

UK G-Cloud Framework 9, 'Framework Contract' (8 May 2017)

UK G-Cloud Framework 9, 'Call-Off Contract' (8 May 2017)

UK G-Cloud Framework 12, 'Framework Agreement' RM1557.12 (19 October 2020)

UK G-Cloud Framework 12, 'Call-Off Contract' RM1557.12 (19 October 2020)

US Department of the Treasury on Behalf of the Consumer Financial Protection Bureau (CFPB) and Deloitte Consulting LLP, Contract No TDP-CFP-12-C-0008 (23 May 2012)

USPS and Autonomy Inc, Contract No 1BITSV-11-B-1007 (30 June 2011)

USPS and Autonomy Inc, Statement of Work (SOW) for Contract No 1BITSV-11-B-1007 (21 September 2010)

USPS and THISMOMENT Inc, Contract #2BTCON-13-B-0075 (30 September 2013)

SELECTED CLOUD CERTIFICATION SCHEMES

CISPE's Self-Declaration EU GDPR Code of Conduct: https://cispe.cloud/code-of-conduct/

Cloud Certification Schemes List: https://resilience.enisa.europa.eu/cloud-computing-certification

Cloud Industry Forum Self-Certification: www.cloudindustryforum.org/content/code-practice-cloud-service-providers

Cloud Security Alliance: https://blog.cloudsecurityalliance.org/about-cloud-security-alliance/

Cloud Security Alliance's Security, Trust and Assurance Registry: https://cloudsecurityalliance.org/star/#_overview

Cloud Select Industry Group (C-SIG), 'Cloud Certification Schemes': https://ec.europa.eu/digital-single-market/en/cloud-select-industry-group-certification-schemes
Cloud Select Industry Group (C-SIG), 'Code of Conduct': https://ec.europa.eu/digital-single-market/en/cloud-select-industry-group-code-conduct
Cloud Select Industry Group (C-SIG), 'Data Protection Compliance': https://ec.europa.eu/digital-single-market/en/news/data-protection-code-conduct-cloud-service-providers
Cloud Select Industry Group (C-SIG), 'Standardization of SLAs': https://ec.europa.eu/digital-single-market/en/news/cloud-service-level-agreement-standardisation-guidelines
EuroCloud Star Audit Certification: www.eurocloud.org
Google, 'Service Organization Controls (SOC) 3 Report on the Google Cloud Platform System Relevant to Security, Availability, Processing Integrity, and Confidentiality for the Period 1 May 2016 to 30 April 2017': https://cloud.google.com/files/GCP_SOC3_2017.pdf
ISO Standards Catalogue for Cloud Computing: www.iso.org/ics/35.210/x/; www.ssae-16.com/
New Zealand Cloud Computing Code of Practice: https://cloudcode.nz/About
SLA Ready Project: www.sla-ready.eu/

WEBSITES

Amazon Web Services, 'Compliance Programs' https://aws.amazon.com/compliance/programs/
FedRAMP, 'Branding Guidance' (2020) www.fedramp.gov/assets/resources/documents/FedRAMP_Branding_Guidance.pdf
FedRAMP, 'Program Overview' www.fedramp.gov/aboutus/about/
G-Cloud, 'Cloud Security Principles' (2014) www.gov.uk/government/publications/cloud-service-security-principles/cloud-service-security-principles
GoGrid, 'GoGrid Legal Documents' www.datapipe.com/gogrid/legal/servepath-sla
National Information Standards Organization, 'Understanding Metadata' (2004) www.niso.org/publications/press/UnderstandingMetadata.pdf
UK Cabinet Office, 'Government Security Classifications Version 1.1' (May 2018) https://assets.publishing.service.gov.uk/government/uploads/system/uploads/attachment_data/file/709003/May-2018_Government-Security-Classifications.pdf

THESES

Marinho Martins de Castro C., 'On the Regulation of Cloud Computing Contracts' (Unpublished PhD thesis, Universidade Federal De Pernambuco Centro De Informática 2014) https://repositorio.ufpe.br/bitstream/123456789/12060/1/TESE%20Clarice%20Marinho%20de%20Castro.pdf
Tapanelli P., 'Cloud Computing Contracts' (PhD thesis 2014). Unpublished PhD on file with author.

Index

access, to data
　in government cloud computing, 45–46
　for Government Cloud system, limitations on, 24
　by intelligence agencies, 84–89
　　under Executive Order 123333, 85–86
　　under Foreign Intelligence Surveillance Act, 85–86
　　limitations for, 88–89
　　PRISM program, 86–88
　　remedies for, 88–89
　　UPSTREAM program, 87–88
　law enforcement agencies and, 3–4
　security services on, 3–4
accountability
　in government cloud computing, 44–45, 57–58
　Health Insurance Portability and Accountability Act of 1996, 148
accountability principle, data protection and, 110
agreements. *See* framework agreements; master services agreement; service level agreement; *specific agreements*
AstraZeneca v International Business Machines Corporation, 225–26
audits
　for data processors, obligations of, 119–20
　in standardization of cloud computing contracts, 243–44
　transparency in, 43

B2B agreements. *See* Business-to-Business agreements
B2C agreements. *See* Business-to-Consumer agreements
B2G agreements. *See* Business-to-Government agreements
back-to-back contracts, 187–88
binding corporate rules (BCRs), 134

blockchain contracts, 248
breach, of cloud computing contracts, 209–11
Brexit, 7, 100
Business-to-Business agreements (B2B agreements), 14–15, 205
Business-to-Consumer agreements (B2C agreements), 14–15
Business-to-Government agreements (B2G agreements), 14–15

CaaS. *See* Communications as a Service
call-off contracts, 171–77
carbon footprint, of cloud computing, xi–xii
Carpenter v. US, 146–48
Charter of Fundamental Rights of the European Union, 92
CIA. *See* Confidentiality, Integrity, and Availability of data
Clarifying Lawful Overseas Use of Data Act (CLOUD Act), US (2018)
　for cloud service providers, 80–84, 90
　in *Microsoft* warrant case, 76–77
　mutual legal assistance treaties and, 81, 83
cloud barriers, to government cloud computing, 47–50
cloud clients
　Business-to-Consumer agreements, 14–15
　definition, 11
　government as, 42–46
　　accessibility and, 45–46
　　accountability in, 44–45, 57–58
　　availability and, 45–46
　　legitimacy and, 45, 57–58
　　loss of competence and, 46
　　transparency for, 43–44, 57–58
cloud computing. *See also* cloud computing contracts; cloud service providers; data controllers; data processors; government cloud

286

computing; United Kingdom; United States
carbon footprint of, xi–xii
concepts for, 9–14
copyright laws and, 4
during COVID-19 pandemic, xii
critiques of, 8
definitions in, 9–14
  for services, 19–20
deployment models, 23–25
  community clouds, 24
  hybrid clouds, 25
  private clouds, 24
  public clouds, 24–25
environmental impact of, xi–xii
historical development of, 3–4
in information and communications technology, 3
outsourcing of, 4
law of the parties applicable to, 159
legal requirements for, 7–8
  in contracts, 14–15
  identification of, 15
  limitations of, 15
  theoretical approach to, 14–15
long-term impact of, 8–9
public debate over, xi–xii
security issues for, 25–28
  Confidentiality, Integrity, and Availability of data, 25–26
  logical protections, 27
  transparency in, 27
subcontracting and, 120–22
subprocessing and, 120–22
cloud computing contracts, 159–60. See also service level agreements; standardization, of cloud computing contracts
  applicable law for, 220–22
  breach of, 209–11
  call-off contracts, 171–77
  characteristics of, 170–77
  Cloud Legal Project, 159–60
  compliance mechanisms, 233–37
  confidentiality in, 196–203
    discovery requirements and, 200–1
    in Government Cloud system, 197–98
    law enforcement access and, limitations on, 202–3
    non-disclosure agreements, 196–98
    in US, 198
  contract damages, 209–11
    consequential, 210–11
    direct, 210, 213
    limitations in sum, 217
    liquidated, 214
    UK approach to, 211–13, 214–17
    US approach to, 213–17
  data portability, 226–32
    data hostage clauses, 227
    under General Data Protection Regulation, 228–30
    in US states, variability between, 230–32
  Data Protection by Design and by Default obligations in, 176
  disclosure in, 196–203
    discovery requirements and, 200–1
    under Freedom of Information Acts, 198–200
    LEA access and, limitations on, 202–3
    non-disclosure agreements, 196–98
  elements of, 167–70
  European Commission guidelines on, 166
  European Data Protection Supervisor guidelines on, 176
  Force Majeure clauses, 207–9
    definition of, 208–9
  framework agreements, 171–77
    definition of, 172
    for Government Cloud system, 174
    for outsourcing, of information technology, 169
    public contract requirements, 174–75
  functions of, 165–66
  jurisdiction of, 220–22
    in EU, 221–22
  liability in, 203–7
    exclusions from, 204–7
    indemnity clauses, 206–7
    limitations of, 204–7
    warranties against, 204–6
  limits of, 165–66
  location of, 220–22
  master services agreement, 170–71
    for outsourcing of information technology, 169
  metrics and measurements in, 177–86
  organization of, 170–77
    for outsourcing, of information technology, 168–70
    in framework agreements, 169
    in master service agreements, 169
    multi-sourcing model, 169–70
    in service level agreements, 169
    single-sourcing model, 168–69
    in statements of work, 169
  overview of, 195, 246–47
  partners in, 186–95
  privacy harms, 210
  public procurement structure for, in EU, 172–73

cloud computing contracts (cont.)
    Restatement (Second) of Contracts, 193–94, 214
    standard terms
        unilateral amendment of, 217–20
        variation of, 217–20
    statements of work, 177–78
        for outsourcing of information technology, 169
    subcontractors and, 186–95
        back-to-back contracts, 187–88
        in EU, 188–89
        privity of contract doctrine, 191–95
        in UK, with Government Cloud system, 189–90
        in US, with Environmental Protection Agency, 190–91
    termination of services, 222–26
    in UK
        case studies for, 232–37
        compliance mechanisms, 233–37
        contract damages in, 211–13, 214–17
        under Freedom of Information Act, 234–37
        Government Cloud system and, 189–90, 214–20, 233–37
        subcontractors and, with Government Cloud system, 189–90
    in US
        case studies for, 232–37
        compliance mechanisms, 233–37
        confidentiality in, 198
        contract damages in, 213–17
        data portability in, state-to-state variability in, 230–32
        Federal Risk and Authorization Management Program and, 214–20, 233–37
        under Freedom of Information Act, 234–37
        subcontractors and, with Environmental Protection Agency, 190–91
    warranties and, 217
        against liability, 204–6
cloud consumers. See cloud clients
cloud first strategy, in US, 56–57
Cloud Legal Project (CLP), 159–60
cloud service providers (CSPs). See also data controllers; data processors; data transfers; government cloud computing; specific topics
    Computer Science Corporation and, 22
    contract terms for, 6–7
    data location with, 60–61
        in EU, 62
        in United States, 62
    definition of, 11
    Government as a Service, 23
    government cloud computing and, 4–5, 6–7, 16–17
    Infrastructure as a Service, 22–23
    infrastructure of, 4–5
    jurisdiction of, 42
        under CLOUD Act, 80–84, 90
    law enforcement access and, 75
    liability for, 42
    location of, 60–64
    models for, 22–23
    types of, 22–23
    parties in, 20–22
        cloud auditors, 20–21
        cloud brokers/integrators, 21–22
    Platform as a Service, 22–23
    for small and medium-sized enterprises, 6–7
    Software as a Service, 22–23
    virtual machines and, 18–19
    warranties for, 42
cloudification, 52
CLP. See Cloud Legal Project
Coco Cloud. See Confidential and Compliant Clouds project
Communications as a Service (CaaS), 23
community clouds, 24
compliance
    in cloud computing contracts, 233–37
    Microsoft warrant case and, 77–80
    in standardization of cloud computing contracts, 241–42
    in US data privacy mechanisms, 152
Computer Science Corporation (CSC), 22
Confidential and Compliant Clouds project (Coco Cloud), xii
confidentiality
    in cloud computing contracts, 196–203
    discovery requirements and, 200–1
    in Government Cloud system, 197–98
    law enforcement access and, limitations on, 202–3
    non-disclosure agreements, 196–98
    in US, 198
    in data protection, in EU, 109
    in US data privacy approach, 154
Confidentiality, Integrity, and Availability of data (CIA), 25–26
conflict of laws, 60
consent, subcontracts and, 121–22
consequential damages, 210–11
contracts. See also cloud computing contracts
    back-to-back, 187–88
    blockchain, 248
    Business-to-Business agreements, 14–15, 205
    Business-to-Consumer agreements, 14–15

Index

Business-to-Government agreements, 14–15
for data controllers, 113–17
  designations for, 113–14
  under Freedom of Information Act, 113–14
  under General Data Protection Regulation, 114–17
  obligations for, 114–17
  subcontracts for, 120–22
for government cloud computing, in US, 56
legal frameworks for, 164–166
principle of freedom for, 164
privity of contract doctrine, 191–95
smart, 248
standard terms
  for cloud service providers, 6–7
  procurement requirements for, with outsourcing template, 48–49
  transparency as element of, 43
subcontracts, for data controllers and processors, 120–22
in UK
  under Freedom of Information Act, 163
  Government Cloud system, 162
US government, under Freedom of Information Act, 160–164, 162
control, of data, 59. *See also* data sovereignty
copyright laws, cloud computing and, 4
Council of Europe's Convention, on data protection, 142–43
Court of Justice of the European Union. *See also* *Schrems II*
  cross-border data transfers and, 128–41
  data controllers/processors and, in legal cases, 112–13
  General Data Protection Regulation cases, 96, 97, 99
  Schrems I, 131–33
COVID-19 pandemic, cloud computing during, xii
cross-border data transfers. *See* data transfers
CSC. *See* Computer Science Corporation
CSPs. *See* cloud service providers

DaaS. *See* Data as a Service
damages, cloud computing contracts and, 209–11
  consequential damages, 210–11
  direct damages, 210, 213
  limitations in sum, 217
  liquidated damages, 214
data access. *See* access
Data as a Service (DaaS), 23
data breaches, 3–4, 25–26, 42, 94, 117–19
  determination of causation, 209
  non-disclosure agreements and, 197

notification requirements, 148
data controllers, data protection and, 110–27
  contracts for, 113–17
  designations for, 113–14
  under Freedom of Information Act, 113–14
  under General Data Protection Regulation, 114–17
  obligations for, 114–17
  controller-to-controller clauses, in standard contractual clauses, 133
  in Court of Justice of the European Union cases, 112–13
  Data Protection by Design and by Default, 122–24
  qualifications for, 111–12
  subcontracting and, 120–22
    consent in, 121–22
    timing factors in, 122
  subprocessing and, 120–22
    timing factors in, 122
data hostage clauses, 227
data location
  with cloud service providers, 60–61
  in EU, 62
  in United Kingdom, 61
  in United States, 62
  of external data storage, 60–61
  security of, 60–61
data portability, 226–32
  data hostage clauses, 227
  under General Data Protection Regulation, 228–30
  in US states, variability between, 230–32
data privacy
  data protection compared to, 12–13, 93
  definition of, 12–13
  in EU, 92–104
  lack of control over, 3–4
  theoretical approach to, 249–50
  US approach to, 141–55
    Carpenter v. US, 146–48
    compliance mechanisms in, 152
    confidentiality aspects in, 154
    constitutional privacy protections, 144–48
    fair information principles in, 142–43
    Federal Acquisition Regulation and, 153–54
    in federal statutory law, 148–50
    Federal Trade Commission and, 150–52
    FedRAMP and, 152–54
    in financial sector, 148
    under Health Insurance Portability and Accountability Act of 1996, 148
    under HITECH Act, 148
    as individualistic, 142

data privacy (cont.)
  overview of, 154–55
  under Privacy Act of 1974, 148–49
  providing principles in, 148
  Riley v. California, 146
  security aspects in, 154
  state regulations in, variability in, 143
  in Supreme Court cases, 146–48
  under Videotape Privacy Protection Act, 149–50
data processors, data protection and, 110–27
  contracts and
    under General Data Protection Regulation, 114–17
    requirements for, 127
  in Court of Justice of the European Union cases, 112–13
  Data Protection by Design and by Default, 122–24
  liability for, 117–19
    under General Data Protection Regulation, 118–19
    requirements for, 127
  obligations for, 117–19, 126–27
    for audits, 119–20
    in EU, 120
    in UK, 119–20
  qualifications for, 111–12
  subcontracting and, 120–22
    consent in, 121–22
    timing factors in, 122
  subprocessing and, 120–22
    timing factors in, 122
data protection, in EU, 92–104. *See also* data controllers; data processors; General Data Protection Regulation
  accountability principle and, 110
  accuracy in, 108
  authorities for, 10
  under Charter of Fundamental Rights of the European Union, 92
  confidentiality in, 109
  Council of Europe's Convention on, 142–43
  data minimization and, 108
  data privacy compared to, 12–13, 93
  data quality and, 105–10
    processing requirements, 106
    purpose limitation principle and, 106–8
  EU Data Protection Board, 9–10, 83–84, 94, 103–4
  under EU Data Protection Directive, 9–10
  European Commission guidelines on, 91
  under European Convention on Human Rights, 92

under European Data Protection Board, 9–10
fairness in, 106
under General Data Protection Regulation, 155–56
of personal data, 104–5
pseudonymization and, 109
storage limitations, 108–9
in territories outside EU, 102–4
theoretical approach to, 249–50
transparency in, 106
Data Protection as a Service (DPaaS), 23
data protection authorities (DPAs), 10
Data Protection by Design and by Default (DPbD), 122–24, 176
Data Protection v Facebook. See Schrems II
data residency, 35
data security, 12. *See also* data protection
  data privacy law and, 124–26
  General Data Protection Regulation and, 124–26
data sovereignty
  data residency compared to, 35
  definition of, 12, 36
  in government cloud computing, 42, 58
    barriers to cloud and, 35–36
  state sovereignty and, 63–64
data storage
  data protection and, storage limitations, 108–9
  data shard in, 78
  external, 60–61
  in US government cloud computing, 55
data transfers, cross-border, 127–41
  adequacy determinations for, 129–32, 136–37
  binding corporate rules for, 134
  in Court of Justice of the European Union cases, 128–41
  definition of, 128–29
  derogations, 140–41
  encryption in, 139
  EU Data Protection Board guidance on, 139–40
  European Commission and, 129–32, 133–34
  European Data Protection Supervisor and, 128–29
  means of, 129–32
  Privacy Shield Framework, 132–33, 136–37
  Safe Harbour Framework for, 131
    Privacy Shield Framework and, 132–33
    Schrems II and, 140
  Schrems I, 131–33
  Schrems II, 134–40
    legal legacy of, 141
    Safe Harbour Framework and, 140
    standard contractual clauses after, 135–40
  standard contractual clauses and, 133–34
    controller-to-controller clauses, 133

Index

after *Schrems II*, 135–40
standard processes for, 127–28
in US, 130–31
derogations, cross-border data transfers and, 140–41
direct damages, 210, 213
disclosure, in cloud computing contracts, 196–203
  discovery requirements and, 200–1
  under Freedom of Information Acts, 198–200
  LEA access and, limitations on, 202–3
  non-disclosure agreements, 196–98
DPaaS. *See* Data Protection as a Service
DPAs. *See* data protection authorities
DPbD. *See* Data Protection by Design and by Default

EBA. *See* European Banking Authority
EC. *See* European Commission
EDPB. *See* EU Data Protection Board
EDPS. *See* European Data Protection Supervisor
effects principle, 104
EIOPA. *See* European Insurance and Occupational Pensions Authority
encryption, in cross-border data transfers, 139
enforcement jurisdiction, 70
environmental issues. *See also* green computing
  carbon footprints, of cloud computing, xi–xii
  cloud computing's impact on, xi–xii
Environmental Protection Agency (EPA), 181–82, 190–91
Equinor, in Norway, 39–40
EU. *See* European Union
EU Data Protection Board (EDPB), 9–10, 83–84, 94, 103–4, 116–17
  on cross-border data transfers, 139–40
EU Data Protection Directive, Article 29 (WP29), 9–10
European Banking Authority (EBA), 120
European Commission (EC)
  on cross-border data transfers, 129–32, 133–34
  data protection guidelines, 91
European Convention on Human Rights, 92
European Data Protection Supervisor (EDPS), 83–84, 128–29
European Insurance and Occupational Pensions Authority (EIOPA), 120
European Union (EU). *See also* data protection; European Commission; General Data Protection Regulation; United Kingdom
  Charter of Fundamental Rights of the European Union, 92
  cloud computing contracts in, jurisdiction of, 221–22
  Confidential and Compliant Clouds project, xii
  data location in, for cloud service providers, 62
  data privacy in, 92–104
  data processor obligations in, 120
  EU Data Protection Board, 9–10, 83–84, 94, 103–4, 116–17
    on cross-border data transfers, 139–40
  EU Data Protection Directive, Article 29, 9–10
  European Data Protection Supervisor, 83–84, 128–29
  Free Software Foundation Europe, 16
  government cloud computing in, 50–53
    adoption strategies for, 51
    marketplace and procurement model, 51–52
    procurement requirements, 47–48
    resource pooling model, 52–53
    standalone applications for, 53
  Human Brain Project, xii
  service level agreements in, regulation mechanisms for, 185–186
  Treaty on the Functioning of the European Union, 33
Everything as a Service (XaaS), 23
Executive Order 123333, data access under, 85–86
extraterritorial application, of jurisdiction, 71–73

FAA. *See* Federal Aviation Administration
fair information principles (FIPs), 142–43
FAR. *See* Federal Acquisition Regulation
FCA. *See* Financial Conduct Authority
FDA. *See* Food and Drug Administration
Federal Acquisition Regulation (FAR), US, 153–54
Federal Aviation Administration (FAA), 183–185, 184
Federal Risk and Authorization Management Program (FedRAMP), 7–8, 34–35, 56–57, 152–54, 190–91
  cloud computing contracts and, 214–20, 233–37
  standardization of, 238–39
Federal Trade Commission (FTC), 150–52
FedRAMP. *See* Federal Risk and Authorization Management Program
Financial Conduct Authority (FCA), 119–20
FIPs. *See* fair information principles
FISA. *See* Foreign Intelligence Surveillance Act
flexibility, in standardization of cloud computing contracts, 243
FOI. *See* Freedom of Information
FOIA. *See* Freedom of Information Act; UK Freedom of Information Act
Food and Drug Administration (FDA), 182
Force Majeure clauses, 207–9
  definition of, 208–9
Foreign Intelligence Surveillance Act, US (1978) (FISA), 85–86

framework agreements, 171–77
  in cloud computing contracts, 169
  definition of, 172
  for Government Cloud system, 174
  for outsourcing, of information technology, 169
  Privacy Shield Framework, 132–33, 136–37
  public contract requirements, 174–75
  Safe Harbour Framework, 131
    Privacy Shield Framework and, 132–33
    Schrems II and, 140
Free Software Foundation Europe, 16
Freedom of Information (FOI)
  under Government Cloud system, 162
  in UK, 163
Freedom of Information Act, US (FOIA)
  agreements under, xii, 7–8
  data controller contracts under, 113–14
  disclosure requirements under, 198–200
  disclosure under, 198–200
  service level agreements under, 182–83
FTC. *See* Federal Trade Commission

GaaS. *See* Government as a Service
G-Cloud system. *See* Government Cloud system
General Data Protection Regulation (GDPR), EU, 9–10, 83, 91–92, 93–94
  application of, 95–104
  in Court of Justice of the European Union cases, 96, 97, 99
  data controller contracts and, 114–17
  data portability under, 228–30
  data processor liability under, 118–19
  data protection under, 155–56
  effects principle, 104
  jurisdiction of, 100
  material scope of, 95–104
  principle of territoriality, 102–4
  pseudonymization, 99
GovCloud, 24
Government as a Service (GaaS), 23
government cloud computing, 4–7. *See also* United Kingdom; United States
  adoption of, 16–17, 33–34
  assumptions about, 16–17
  budget requests for, 4
  cloud barriers to, 47–50
  as cloud client, 42–46
    accessibility and, 45–46
    accountability in, 44–45, 57–58
    availability and, 45–46
    legitimacy and, 45, 57–58
    loss of competence and, 46
    transparency for, 43–44, 57–58
  cloud service providers and, 4–5, 6–7, 16–17

cloudification, 52
community clouds, 24
  Government Cloud system, 24
  data sovereignty in, 42, 58
  barriers to cloud and, 35–36
  in EU, 50–53
    adoption strategies for, 51
    marketplace and procurement model, 51–52
    procurement requirements, 47–48
    resource pooling model, 52–53
    standalone applications for, 53
  Free Software Foundation Europe campaign for, 16
  Freedom of Information Act requirements in, 33–34
  under Treaty on the Functioning of the European Union, 33
  information and communications technology outsourcing, 4
  Intelligence Community Information Enterprise, 31–32
  long-term issues with, 16–17
  markets for, government influences on, 9
  outsourcing for, 33, 37–42
    information and communications technology and, 4
    in Norway, 37–40
    State of Indiana v. IBM, 40–42
    in Sweden, 38
  in private markets, 42–46
  procurement requirements, 47–50
    data location barriers, 49–50
    in EU, 47–48
    price comparisons, 47–48
    standard contracts, with outsourcing template, 48–49
  risk factors for, 5–6
  state clouds, 37–42
  theoretical approach to, 31–35
  in UK, 53–55
    for public sector organizations, 54
  in US, 55–57
    cloud first strategy, 56–57
    contract terms for, negotiation of, 56
    data storage systems and, 55
    legacy systems for, 55–56
Government Cloud system (G-Cloud system), in UK, 7–8, 34–35, 54–55
  access to data for, limitations on, 24
  in cloud computing contracts, 189–90, 214–20, 233–37
  cloud computing contracts and, confidentiality in, 197–98
  community clouds, 24

framework agreements and, 174
Freedom of Information under, 162
governments. *See also* Norway; Sweden; United Kingdom; United States
   definition of, 13
   sovereignty of, data sovereignty and, 63–64
green computing, xi

Hammond, Philip, 72–73
HBP. *See* Human Brain Project
Health Insurance Portability and Accountability Act of 1996 (HIPAA), US, 148
Health South-East, in Norway, 37–38
HIPAA. *See* Health Insurance Portability and Accountability Act of 1996
HITECH Act, US, 148
Human Brain Project (HBP), xii
hybrid clouds, 25

IaaS. *See* Infrastructure as a Service
ICITE. *See* Intelligence Community Information Enterprise
indemnity clauses, 206–7
India, government cloud computing outsourced to, 39–40
information and communications technology (ITC)
   government uses of
      budget requests for, 4
      outsourcing and, 3
      outsourcing for, 3
      by governments, 4
information security, 12
Infrastructure as a Service (IaaS), 22–23, 193
Intelligence Community Information Enterprise (ICITE), 31–32
international law. *See* private international law; public international law
Internet, jurisdiction on, 64–71
investigative jurisdiction, 70–71
ITC. *See* information and communications technology

Joint Enterprise Defense Infrastructure contract (JEDI contract), 252
judicial jurisdiction, 69–70
jurisdiction. *See also Microsoft* warrant case
   assertion of, on Internet, 64–71
   under CLOUD Act
      for cloud service providers, 80–84, 90
      in *Microsoft* warrant case, 76–77
      mutual legal assistance treaties and, 81, 83
   of cloud computing contracts, 220–22
   of cloud service providers, 42

   under CLOUD Act, 80–84, 90
   conflict of laws and, 60
   definition of, 60, 64–65
   enforcement, 70
   extraterritorial application of, 71–73
   of General Data Protection Regulation, 100
   investigative, 70–71
   judicial, 69–70
   law enforcement access and, 74–75
      cloud service providers and, 75
      mutual legal assistance treaties, 74–75
   mutual legal assistance treaties
      under CLOUD Act, 81, 83
      law enforcement access and, 74–75
      in *Microsoft* warrant case, 76
   personal, 60
   personality principle and, 67
   prescriptive, 60, 68–69
   in private international law, 67–68
   protective principle and, 67
   in public international law, 67–68
   state sovereignty and, 64–65
   territoriality principle and, 66, 71–73

law enforcement, data access and, 3–4
law enforcement access (LEA), 74–75
   under cloud computing contracts, limitations on, 202–3
   cloud service providers and, 75
   mutual legal assistance treaties, 74–75
legitimacy, of government cloud computing, 45, 57–58
liability
   in cloud computing contracts, 203–7
   exclusions from, 204–7
   indemnity clauses, 206–7
   limitations of, 204–7
   warranties against, 204–6
   for cloud service providers, 42
liquidated damages, 214
location. *See also* data location; jurisdiction
   cloud computing contracts and, 220–22
   of cloud service providers, 60–64
Lynch, Gerard E., 79

MaaS. *See* Monitoring as a Service
marketplace and procurement model, for government cloud computing, 51–52
master services agreement (MSA), 41, 169, 170–71
McNealy, Scott, 250
Microsoft warrant case, 75–80
   appeals for, 76–77
   under CLOUD Act, 76–77
   compliance issues in, 77–80

Microsoft warrant case (cont.)
    Microsoft services in, 77–80
    mutual legal assistance treaties and, 76
    under Stored Communications Act, 76–77
minimization of data, 108
MLATs. *See* mutual legal assistance treaties
Monitoring as a Service (MaaS), 23
MSA. *See* master services agreement
mutual legal assistance treaties (MLATs)
    under CLOUD Act, 81, 83
    law enforcement access and, 74–75
    in *Microsoft* warrant case, 76

NaaS. *See* Network as a Service
NDAs. *See* non-disclosure agreement; non-disclosure agreements
Network as a Service (NaaS), 23
non-disclosure agreements (NDAs), 196–98
    data breaches and, 197
Norway, government cloud computing in, outsourcing for, 37–40
    for critical infrastructure, 39–40
    Equinor, 39–40
    Health South-East, 37–38
    to India, 39–40

offshoring, definition of, 13–14
outsourcing
    in cloud computing contracts, 168–70
        in framework agreements, 169
        in master services agreement, 169
        multi-sourcing model, 169–70
        in service level agreements, 169
        single-sourcing model, 168–69
        in statements of work, 169
    definition of, 13–14
    for government cloud computing, 33, 37–42
        information and communications technology and, 4
        in Norway, 37–40
        State of Indiana v. IBM, 40–42
        in Sweden, 38
    for information and communications technology, 3
    by governments, 4

PaaS. *See* Platform as a Service
personal jurisdiction, 60
personality principle, 67
Platform as a Service (PaaS), 22–23
prescriptive jurisdiction, 60, 68–69
principle of freedom, in contracts, 164
PRISM program, 86–88
privacy. *See also* data privacy
    in cloud computing contracts, 210
    in Data Protection by Design and by Default, 122–24
Privacy Act of 1974, US, 148–49
Privacy Shield Framework, 132–33, 136–37
private clouds, 24
private international law, jurisdiction of, 67–68
private sector
    government cloud computing in, 42–46
    public embrace of, 18
privity of contract doctrine, 191–95
procurement
    in cloud computing contracts, structure for, in EU, 172–73
    marketplace and procurement model, 51–52
    in standard contract terms, 48–49
    theoretical approach to, 251
protection. *See* data protection
protective principle, 67
providing principles, in data privacy, 148
pseudonymization, 99, 109
public clouds, 24–25
    in UK, 54
public international law, jurisdiction of, 67–68
public sector
    public embrace of, 18
    in United Kingdom, government cloud computing in, 54
purpose limitation principle, 106–8

Re Warrant to Search a Certain Email Account Controlled & Maintained by Microsoft Corporation, 59–60
resource pooling model, for government cloud computing, 52–53
Restatement (Second) of Contracts, 193–94, 214
Riley v. California, 146

SaaS. *See* Software as a Service
Safe Harbour Framework, 131
    Privacy Shield Framework and, 132–33
    Schrems II and, 140
SCCs. *See* standard contractual clauses
Schrems, Maximillian, 131–33, 134–40
Schrems I, 131–33
Schrems II (Data Protection v Facebook), 134–40
    legal legacy of, 141
    Safe Harbour Framework and, 140
    standard contractual clauses after, 135–40
SECaaS. *See* Security as a Service
security. *See also* data security; information security
    for cloud computing, 25–28

Confidentiality, Integrity, and Availability of data, 25–26
  logical protections, 27
  transparency in, 27
 data location and, 60–61
 transparency and, 43
Security as a Service (SECaaS), 23
security services, data access and, 3–4
service level agreements (SLAs), 178–86
 in cloud computing contracts, 169
 components of, 178–79
 definition of, 178
 in EU, regulation mechanisms for, 185–186
 exception from uptime guarantees, 180–81
 exclusions in, 179
 functions of, 179–80
 importance of, in cloud computing, 179–185
 for outsourcing of information technology, 169
 transparency of, 43
 in UK, 186
 in US government contracts, 181–185
  with Environmental Protection Agency, 181–82
  for Federal Aviation Administration, 183–185, 184
  for Food and Drug Administration, 182
  under Freedom of Information Act, 182–83
SGSA. *See* Supply of Goods and Services Act
SLA. *See* service level agreement
small and medium-sized enterprises (SMEs), cloud service providers for, 6–7
smart contracts, 248
SMEs. *See* small and medium-sized enterprises
Snowden, Edward, 72
Software as a Service (SaaS), 22–23, 48, 178, 193
sovereignty. *See also* data sovereignty
 jurisdiction and, 64–65
SOWs. *See* statements of work
standard contract terms
 in cloud computing contracts
  unilateral amendment of, 217–20
  variation of, 217–20
 for cloud service providers, 6–7
 for government cloud computing, with outsourcing template, 48–49
 for legal requirements, incorporation of, 239–40
 transparency as element of, 43
standard contractual clauses (SCCs), 133–34
 controller-to-controller clauses, 133
 after *Schrems II*, 135–40
standardization, of cloud computing contracts, 237–45
 audits, 243–44
 compliance requirements for, 241–42
 core requirements for, 240–41
 flexibility in, 243
 inventories, 243–44
 of legal requirements, 237–39
  incorporation of, through standard terms, 239–40
 monitoring mechanisms, 243–44
 policy objectives as contract element in, 244–45
state clouds, 37–42
State of Indiana v. IBM, 40–42, 207–8
statements of work (SOWs), 169, 177–78
states, definition of, 13. *See also* governments
Stored Communications Act, US, 76–77
subcontractors, in cloud computing contracts, 186–95
 back-to-back contracts, 187–88
 in EU, 188–89
 privity of contract doctrine, 191–95
 in UK, with Government Cloud system, 189–90
 in US, with Environmental Protection Agency, 190–91
subcontracts, for data controllers and processors, 120–22
 consent in, 121–22
 timing factors in, 122
subprocessing, for data controllers and processors, 120–22
 timing factors in, 122
Supply of Goods and Services Act (SGSA), UK, 186
Sweden, government cloud computing in, 38

termination of services, in cloud computing contracts, 222–26
territoriality principle
 in General Data Protection Regulation, 102–4
 jurisdiction and, 66, 71–73
transparency
 in audits, 43
 in cloud computing security, 27
 in data protection, 106
 in government cloud computing, 43–44, 57–58
 security and, 43
 of service level agreements, 43
 in standard contracts, 43
Treaty on the Functioning of the European Union, 33

UK. *See* United Kingdom
UK Freedom of Information Act (UK FOIA), 7–8
 disclosure requirements under, 198–200
 government cloud computing requirements under, 33–34

UK Freedom of Information Act (cont.)
  under Treaty on the Functioning of the
    European Union, 33
United Kingdom (UK). *See also* cloud computing
    contracts; Government Cloud system
  Business-to-Business agreements in, 14–15, 205
  data location in, 61
  data processor obligations in, 119–20
  Financial Conduct Authority, 119–20
  Freedom of Information Act, 7–8
    disclosure requirements under, 198–200
    disclosure under, 198–200
    government cloud computing requirements
      under, 33–34
    under Treaty on the Functioning of the
      European Union, 33
  government cloud computing in, 7–8, 53–55
    for public sector organizations, 54
  service level agreements in, 186
  Supply of Goods and Services Act, 186
United States (US). *See also* cloud computing
    contracts; data privacy
  CLOUD Act
    for cloud service providers, 80–84, 90
    in *Microsoft* warrant case, 76–77
    mutual legal assistance treaties and, 81, 83
  cross-border data transfers in, 130–31
  data location in, with cloud service providers, 62
  data protection in, data protection authorities, 10
  Environmental Protection Agency, 181–82,
    190–91
  Executive Order 123333, data access under,
    85–86
  Federal Acquisition Regulation in, 153–54
  Federal Risk and Authorization Management
    Program, 7–8, 34–35, 56–57, 152–54, 190–91
    cloud computing contracts and, 214–20,
    233–37
  Federal Trade Commission, 150–52
  Foreign Intelligence Surveillance Act, 85–86
  Freedom of Information Act, xii, 7–8
    data controller contracts under, 113–14

disclosure requirements under, 198–200
service level agreements under, 182–83
GovCloud access limitations, 24
government cloud computing in, 7–8, 55–57
  cloud first strategy, 56–57
  contract terms for, negotiation of, 56
  data storage systems and, 55
  legacy systems for, 55–56
Health Insurance Portability and Accountability
  Act of 1996, 148
HITECH Act, 148
Privacy Act of 1974, 148–49
*Re Warrant to Search a Certain Email Account
  Controlled & Maintained by Microsoft
  Corporation*, 59–60
service level agreements, in government con-
  tracts, 181–185
  with Environmental Protection Agency,
    181–82
  for Federal Aviation Administration,
    183–185, 184
  for Food and Drug Administration, 182
  under Freedom of Information Act, 182–83
Stored Communications Act, 76–77
Videotape Privacy Protection Act, 149–50
UPSTREAM program, 87–88
US. *See* United States

Videotape Privacy Protection Act (VPPA),
  US (1988), 149–50
virtual machines (VMs), cloud service providers
  and, 18–19
VPPA. *See* Videotape Privacy Protection Act

warranties
  in cloud computing contracts, against liability,
    204–6
  for cloud service providers, 42
warrants. *See Microsoft* warrant case
WP29. *See* EU Data Protection Directive

XaaS. *See* Everything as a Service